Marking the Mind

Memory is one of the few psychological concepts with a truly ancient lineage. Presenting a history of the interrelated changes in memory tasks, memory technology and ideas about memory from antiquity to the late twentieth century, this book confronts psychology's 'short present' with its 'long past'. Kurt Danziger, one of the most influential historians of psychology of recent times, traces long-term continuities from ancient mnemonics and tools of inscription to modern memory experiments and computer storage. He explores historical discontinuities, showing how different kinds of memory became prominent at different times, and examines these changes in the context of specific themes, including the question of truth in memory, distinctions between kinds of memory, the project of memory experimentation and the physical localization and conceptual location of memory. Danziger's unique approach provides a historical perspective for understanding varieties of reproduction, narratives of the self and short-term memory.

KURT DANZIGER is Professor Emeritus, York University, Canada and Honorary Professor, the University of Cape Town, South Africa.

Marking the Mind

A History of Memory

KURT DANZIGER

CAMBRIDGE
UNIVERSITY PRESS

KH

CAMBRIDGE UNIVERSITY PRESS
Cambridge, New York, Melbourne, Madrid, Cape Town, Singapore, São Paulo, Delhi

Cambridge University Press
The Edinburgh Building, Cambridge CB2 8RU, UK

Published in the United States of America by Cambridge University Press, New York

www.cambridge.org
Information on this title: www.cambridge.org/9780521726412

First published 2008

Printed in the United Kingdom at the University Press, Cambridge

A catalogue record for this publication is available from the British Library

Library of Congress Cataloguing in Publication data
Danziger, Kurt, 1926–
   Marking the mind : a history of memory / Kurt Danziger.
      p.   cm.
   Includes bibliographical references and index.
   ISBN 978-0-521-89815-7 (hardback) – ISBN 978-0-521-72641-2 (pbk.)
   1. Memory–History.   I. Title.
   BF371.D36 2008
   153.1'209–dc22   2008020515

ISBN 978-0-521-89815-7 hardback
ISBN 978-0-521-72641-2 paperback

11/2/09

Contents

Acknowledgements

When I embarked on the studies that form the basis for this book I regarded them simply as extensions of previous interests that would provide some amusement in old age. Gradually, this solitary pursuit turned into a book, a process that could not have come to fruition without the help of others. It is pleasant and appropriate to recall the stimulation provided by my Berlin friends, Lorraine Daston and Gerd Gigerenzer, who opened up important vistas for me. Subsequent conversation with David Murray showed me how much I did not know about the psychology of memory.

In the later stages, Alan Collins, Gerry Cupchik and John Mills made many suggestions for which I am grateful, especially those pertaining to arguments that seemed perfectly clear to me but, apparently, to no one else. At very early and very late stages of this project my former students Adrian Brock, Jennifer MacDonald and Jim Parker made specific contributions that are much appreciated.

I would like to thank Andrew Peart for his crucial role in keeping the publication of this book on track. Judy Manners's indispensable assistance with the manuscript proved that even a typographically challenged writer like me can be transformed into a publishable author. My son, Peter, went far beyond the call of twenty-first-century filial duty in providing technical advice whenever it was needed.

This is also the place to acknowledge permission from Princeton University Press to quote passages from Plato's *Collected Dialogues*, edited by Edith Hamilton and Huntington Cairns.

1   Does memory have a history?

All human societies remember their ancestors but they do so in very different ways. Where there is no writing, memory of one's forebears is evoked by shared reminiscences, mementos or ceremonies, but never by rereading their letters or obituaries. In some places, ancestors are recalled by donning masks, by imitating their gestures and by going into a trance.[1] We remember our dear departed when we pay a visit to the cemetery. But cemetery visits, as we know them, are essentially a nineteenth-century innovation.[2] Memorial practices change through the ages. The role played by monuments and processions, for example, has varied historically, not only in commemorating one's immediate ancestors, but also in the way the collective memory of societies is mobilized.[3]

Historical change in social practices of recall is not limited to ancestral memory. Among non-literate people, rules and regulations cannot be recalled by consulting written documents, though consultation of elders is common. There may also be specialists in memory whose services may be required even after the introduction of writing. Ancient Greece had the institution of the *mnemon*, a person whose job it was to remember religious or legal matters relevant to decision-making and jurisprudence.[4] Roman politicians and lawyers were known to own *graeculi*, 'little Greeks', who were intellectually trained slaves that were also required to memorize social and technical information so that they could prompt their masters during court sessions and political or social events.[5] With the accumulation of written documents the essential function of these slaves would be passed on to archivists and librarians. But this took many centuries, and in the Middle Ages oral testimony in court would still enjoy greater trust than documentary evidence.[6]

Individual memory as a historical problem

That the practices and institutions of social memory are historically embedded is not a matter open to doubt. Whether this has serious implications for the understanding of individual memory is, however, a far trickier question. The literature of modern psychology strongly implies that history has no relevance for the study of individual memory processes. Within that body of work the lack of any relationship between the history and the psychology of memory appears to be taken for granted, for there are virtually no psychological studies that so much as raise the question. The neurophysiological basis of memory processes is frequently addressed, their social basis rarely.

Yet recognizing the neurophysiological, and hence biological, basis of human memory processes should lead one to the conclusion that these processes must indeed have undergone a certain historical development. The biological evolution of human brain physiology simply cannot account for the kinds of memory skill that the modern individual employs every day: 'Human memory is clearly not an adaptation for remembering telephone numbers, though it performs this function fairly well, nor is it an adaptation for learning to drive a car, though it handles this rather different problem effectively too.'[7]

Any activity that involves reading must rely on memory processes that could not have existed *in that form* before the invention of writing, a comparatively recent development in human history. Certainly, the *possibility* of such a development may be considered to have been latent in the biological equipment of the species *homo sapiens*, but that still leaves open the question of how this equipment became adapted to serve the memory tasks that are routinely accomplished by literate individuals. There can be no question of biological adaptation here because the time-scale is far too short. One is dealing with developments that take place in social-historical time, counting perhaps in centuries rather than the millions of years of biological time. We cannot expect to explain how we ended up with the cognitive abilities we have by short-circuiting human cultural and social development.[8]

Such short-circuiting has sometimes taken the form of treating historical change as a mere continuation of biological evolution, explained by the same principles. For example, in the course of biological evolution, a trait originally selected for one kind of adaptation may eventually come to serve quite a different function. Feathers may have served the function of thermoregulation long before they were used to fly. Darwin's term was 'preadaptation', whose teleological connotations are hopefully avoided by the more recent neologism, 'exaptation'.[9] Applying this principle to the social evolution of human memory, however, at best provides a statement of the problem, while drawing attention away from the direction in which a solution must be sought. The increasing complexity of human society and vast technological progress have greatly multiplied the functions that human memory has to serve. It follows that whatever memory facilities were selected in the course of human evolution must have come to serve a host of new functions in the course of human history. But this is merely to state the obvious. The question that should be on our agenda now concerns the course of this functional change, a course that takes place within socio-historical time, not biological time. For an understanding of this process we have to turn to concepts and categories that are adequate to socio-historical change, which 'preadaptation' and its variants are not.

Theoretical speculations about the evolution of human cognitive abilities have thrown little or no light on the development of human memory in historical time. This is because they have been preoccupied with the evolution of proto-humans into humans and with human functioning during the hunter-gatherer stage. Very little psychological attention has been directed at the huge cognitive changes, particularly in human memory, that took place after the advent of permanent settlement and literacy.

The work of Merlin Donald remains a notable exception.[10] Although the bulk of his work is concerned with the development of proto-human and human cognitive skills before the advent of literacy, he identifies the fundamental link between the earlier and the later periods and recognizes that human cognitive change did not stop with the early cave paintings of *homo sapiens*. It may be true that our brains have not changed over the last few millennia, but what sort of brain are we talking about? First of all, it is not the brain of an isolated creature. In its natural environment this organ functions within a network of social interaction linking the activity of several brains. Second, this organ specializes in plasticity, so that its functioning can be profoundly affected by the networks it is part of. Human brains are specifically adapted for life within human culture. That includes highly developed capacities for representation, the ability to use one cognitive content to signify another.

For the history of human memory the crucial development involves the use of materials outside an individual's body for purposes of representation. If those materials possess some permanence, such as marks on a rock surface or a tree bark, they come to function as an external memory. Acts of remembering may now be evoked, not only by the immediate presence of other individuals, or by some kind of bodily activity, but also by previously constructed symbols preserved by means of an external medium. From then on the further development of human memory is inextricably bound up with the historical development of external memory, a link that becomes particularly close once external memory takes the form of writing.

External memory is based on the purposeful modification of a physical medium by means of specifically designed tools and skills. In short, external memory constitutes a kind of technology, and like all technology it exhibits historical change and improvement that depend on the social conditions of its employment but also affect those conditions in turn. The technology of external memory is a part of human history. But it can only function as part of a system that includes the biologically constrained equipment of human individuals. A tool is a tool only for those who know how to use it. Developing various external memory systems was not just a matter of material invention but also of acquiring the specific skills needed to get the most out of those inventions. This means that the functioning of individual memory, too, would be subject to historical change. The relatively brief time-scale of human history may preclude significant phylogenetic change, but this does not mean that human memory functions exactly the same way now as it did 5,000 years ago.

For technologies of inscription to be of any use people had to acquire the art of reading, something that was not hard-wired in their brains. But for inscriptions to function as a useful external memory, people had to develop memory skills that were just as novel as reading once was. They had to discover ways of linking their own memories to the memory that was potentially available outside. Without pointlessly reproducing everything that was in external memory, they had to find ways of making the content of external memory accessible. In other words, they faced special retrieval tasks that were different from any retrieval tasks they would have faced in the absence of external memory. Old mnemonic aids lost their value and new ones had to be invented. As the archive of external memory became more extensive, complex phonological and situational cues became much less useful for recovering its content. Instead, people had to learn to organize this content so that it became accessible through the use of new kinds of address systems and logical arrangements. Externally archived material is useful only to the extent that its organization is reflected in individual memory. If the archive's organization changes, as it certainly has in the course of history, individual memory eventually has to adapt its own organization.

But perhaps the organization of external memory is simply a reflection of features that were already built into individual memory before there was any external memory at all. This can be true only in the tautologous sense that humans would not have been able to develop ways of linking external and internal memory that were beyond the physiological limits of their biological equipment. However, as those limits allow considerable latitude in the forms of actual memory organization, these forms cannot be derived from them. It certainly does not look as though the organization of external memory required only the projection of an organization already established in the human brain. If that had been the case, one would have expected far more rapid advances in the organization of external memory than are observed in human history. The slow rate of progress suggests rather a co-evolution of external memory and the corresponding cognitive functions.

With the benefit of numerous inventions, accumulated over many centuries, it is easy for us to assume that forms of memory organization which we were taught in childhood are direct pointers to the way 'natural' memory operates. We are thoroughly accustomed to accomplishing the retrieval of verbal information by using indexes, titles, hierarchical arrangement and so on. Yet all these devices had to be gradually developed in the course of many centuries during which people were slowly learning how to make the most of their new forms of external memory. Nor were the advantages of each new invention immediately obvious: there were false starts, setbacks and long delays before mnemonic aids that seem to us so natural became widely adopted.[11] Thus, even after the adoption of alphabetic script, the use of single-word units for representing and remembering written information was far from natural to human external memory users. For those using the non-Semitic scripts of the West, the very concept of 'word', as we understand it, appears as a *consequence* of extended use of written information.[12]

Such observations raise questions about what exactly is being investigated in modern memory research. Is it the constitution of a species-wide and generic 'human memory' that is being studied in twenty-first-century laboratories, or is it a socially embedded way of functioning that is the result of a long period of adaptation to a gradually developing culture of literacy? To decide this question the use of historical evidence is indispensable.

Individual memory is not only closely linked to historically changing forms of external memory, it also does its work in the service of tasks whose parameters are set by changing social demands and conventions. Consider some of the culturally embedded memory tasks that have provoked thought and wonder about the nature of human memory at various times. There is, for example, the task faced by the designated storyteller, bard or keeper of traditional lore in a non-literate society. Some of these individuals appear to accomplish prodigious memory feats when they reproduce verbal narratives that extend over many hours. Their reproduction is of something heard, not read; they cannot go back to check the script in the middle of their narration, yet they do not falter. How do they manage this feat? More to the point in the present context, do they employ the same memory skills as a lawyer in classical Rome mustering legal arguments without a prepared text in front of him? Do either of them have anything in common with the medieval preacher exhorting his flock by piling up biblical analogies and quotations that he has not only 'learned by heart' but also 'taken to heart'? If so, what? Without looking at the historical evidence we cannot know. Nor can we know whether the findings of modern memory research represent anything more than a documentation of how human memory functions when confronted with memory tasks that are as historically culture-bound as the tasks faced by an illiterate storyteller, a Roman lawyer or a medieval preacher.

Because human memory functions in a social context, engaged in tasks that bear the stamp of specific social demands, it has a history, a history that did not stop when the first psychological memory experiment was set up. Social demands give *direction* to the activity of remembering. In some social contexts exact reproduction of certain words is important, for example, in liturgical renderings of sacred texts or in many classical memory experiments. In other situations the exact words need not be remembered as long as their emotional impact is faithfully reproduced, for example, in the retelling of an ancient legend. Sometimes there is a premium on remembering the logical structure of an argument; at other times it is vital to remember the layout of a building. But such memory tasks do not vary at random between cultures and historical periods. At certain times and in certain places, accurate memory for sacred texts is terribly important, but under different circumstances this sort of memory may actually be discouraged. The same can be said of all the other examples mentioned above and of most instances of remembering one might care to think of. The point is that the social context of memory is marked by what one might call *mnemonic values* that give direction to the process of remembering.

Many of the historical changes in memory are due to changes in these mnemonic values. They affect not only *what* is to be remembered, but also *how* it is to be remembered. For example, medieval texts devoted to the memory practices of monastic culture emphasize that biblical narratives must be remembered with full emotional engagement.[13] The kind of memory that is sought after here is very different from the depersonalized storage of discrete facts that has been so highly valued in more recent educational contexts (and in many memory experiments). The memory the monks were trying to develop did not express itself in the regurgitation of 'information' but in a kind of reliving, body and soul, of sacred narratives and parables.[14] In another historical period, the Renaissance, a more embodied, emotionally involving kind of memory would be compared to falling in love or being lovesick.[15] People have not always remembered in the same way, and their most valued ways of remembering have not always been the same.

A conceptual history

The array of experiences, functions and capabilities to which the term 'memory' was applied changed in the course of human history. The details of this process are complex and include many different aspects that await specific elucidation. Some aspects are more easily investigated, because they have left records in the form of monuments, images or linguistic inscriptions. Other aspects we know about because they are mentioned in surviving documents, for example, the use of mnemonic techniques in what used to be called the 'art of memory'. Yet other aspects, mainly pertaining to memory in oral speech situations, can still be observed in contemporary forms that may point to cultural survivals.

Describing and analyzing the social context for different ways of remembering is a task best left to professional historians. In this book I draw heavily on their work in order to supply the necessary background for my main topic, the conceptualization of memory in the texts of different historical periods. In these texts memory has become an identified object of reflection. No doubt acts of remembering had sometimes occasioned comment, discussion and speculation before the advent of literacy, but the exploration of that kind of evidence requires the methods of the anthropologist and the oral historian. That dimension is not covered in this book because it would inordinately expand a topic that is already too large. There are many aspects to the history of memory, and the aspect that provides the focus here emerges in the writings of philosophers, physicians, psychologists and others who ensured the dissemination of beliefs about memory that these writings had probably helped to crystallize in the first place. With the advent of this textual material *concepts* of memory became part of the historical archive and therefore an identifiable part of intellectual history.[16]

In these writings memory is posited as a distinguishable feature or category about which things can be said. It forms the objective pole in a subject–object relationship. As an object, memory is marked by a certain degree of resistance or even recalcitrance. It does not automatically do what one would like or expect it to. It plays tricks on one, refuses its help when one needs it, distorts and decays. But perhaps it can be tamed? In one way or another, all the historical moves discussed here constitute attempts at doing just that, domesticating memory.

Concepts of memory have never constituted an isolated domain of ideas – they were always deeply connected to social practices and cultural artefacts. Some of these social practices, such as ancient mnemonic techniques or modern experimental techniques, have been directly targeted at memory itself; other practices, such as those of literacy, have had an indirect, though pervasive, effect on the conceptualization of memory. Cultural artefacts whose history is intertwined with that of memory include written and printed texts, more modern recording devices and digital computers. Although the examination of concepts of memory forms the thread that runs through this book, these concepts are placed in the relevant context of changing practices and artefacts whenever the available historical evidence permits.

During the period covered by this book, remembering ceases to be something that people just do without being conscious of what they are doing. They have come to separate remembering from their many other activities and to reify it in the form of an object called memory. They begin to reflect on this object, invent models for its working, intervene in its processes, supply it with ever more sophisticated aids, and generally seek to overcome its unreliability and recalcitrance. All this is happening in the context of vast changes in their societies and their technologies, changes that make new demands on human memory but also offer new possibilities for its effective employment. Unreflective acts of remembering were supplemented by deliberate attempts to modify the way memory operated and to enlist it in specific human projects. Beliefs about memory, efforts to improve memory and the social tasks for which memory was mobilized, affected each other in a complex, historically changing interrelationship.

If one observed the manifestations of memory at any particular time one would be getting a snapshot of a particular moment or phase in the long history of this interrelationship. If one then forgot about the historical dimension one might be tempted to imagine that people's beliefs and theories about memory are quite separate from the object itself. In that case, ideas relating to memory would be on a par with theories in physics: the theories might change but that would not affect their objects. One function of a historical perspective is to remind us of the limitations of this analogy.

Perhaps a better analogy would be one that compared the way memory works to the way a physical world transformed by technoscience works. Such a world owes its existence to human insights and practices applied to the physical world, though the laws of physics are still the same. Analogously, the way memory operates in its social context – and there is always a social context – depends in part on the way memory tasks and techniques have been modified by beliefs, values and presuppositions applied to memory. This does not imply any changes in the principles of neurophysiology, because there is a fundamental difference between the socially embedded achievements and failures of memory and the physiological resources that provide the possibility of such achievements and failures. Achievements and failures are always socially defined and therefore historically variable.

Ways of remembering are affected by changing *mnemonic values*: culturally grounded assumptions about what is most worth remembering, what ought not to be or need not be remembered, how the shards of memory should fit together, what kinds of tasks memory should be expected to serve. Such mnemonic values always imply certain conceptions of the nature of memory and sometimes these conceptions are made explicit in texts that address the topic. Historically, changes in memory practice were associated with changes in discourse about memory, reflecting a change of mnemonic values.

For example, the *precise* reproduction of material from external memory began to be highly valued in the period of the European Enlightenment and became a common feature of everyday experience during the Industrial Revolution. The emphasis on accurate factual memory affected educational practice as well as business and industrial institutions. Some of the technological advances of this time led to the development of new visual and auditory recording devices (camera and phonograph) that provided a ready source for theoretical models of memory as a machine for the copying, storage and exact reproduction of sensory input.[17]

The very concept of memory had changed. In previous times, as we will see later, the copying function of memory had been recognized but subordinated to other functions, such as moral improvement or imaginative production. In modern times, the conception of memory as essentially a copying machine meshed smoothly with the kind of memory work that was increasingly being demanded in rapidly expanding commercial and indus-trial institutions. When widely shared, this conception helped to focus the deliberate exercise of memory in a particular direction and encouraged the development of certain kinds of memory skills. Memory concepts, technology, mnemonic values, institutional practices and memory perform-ance were linked in a network of reciprocal influence.

Precisely because they have never existed in isolation, but have always been part of a network of interrelated phenomena, conceptions of memory have been implicated in the social manifestations of memory. Their history therefore has to be examined in relation to memory technology and the social practices linked to memory. There has never been any doubt that theories about memory have changed historically. But one only needs to look at the mnemonically relevant context of these changes to recognize that historicity is a feature, not only of the theoretical component, but of many other important aspects of human memory as well.

The history of memory and the discipline of psychology

For the discipline of psychology, historical change in human memory is a non-topic. There are two broad sets of reasons for this, one related to psychology's understanding of its subject-matter, the other to its place among the disciplines. Let us consider these in turn.

Traditionally, the subject-matter of psychology was defined in terms of what went on within individual minds. The behaviourist interlude changed that by introducing environmental adaptation, but the concept of 'environment' con-sidered appropriate for a psychological level of analysis was totally abstract. As long as one was doing psychology, the kind of environmental richness encountered in historical studies would be irrelevant because all environmental features were reducible to generic 'stimuli' whose effects were governed by behavioural 'laws' that did not vary across species, let alone across historical periods. When behaviourism lost its attractiveness the traditional definition of psychology's subject-matter reasserted itself in a form that excluded any psychological relevance for history as effectively as ever.

With the exception of some marginalized clinical studies, the psychological study of memory now came to share the assumptions and precepts of what became known as cognitive science. According to a widely cited and sym-pathetic overview of cognitive science of the mid-1980s, the principles that guided its approach included: (1) a commitment to a level of analysis 'wholly separate' from the sociological or cultural; (2) 'faith that central to any understanding of the human mind is the electronic computer'; (3) a 'deliberate decision to de-emphasize ... the contribution of historical and cultural factors'; and (4) a list of relevant disciplines that significantly excluded history.[18]

Within this framework what was called 'memory' consisted essentially of a linear three-part process that encoded, stored and then retrieved informational input from the environment. The entire sequence was understood as taking place inside an individual mind/brain. What happened before encoding and after retrieval was not considered part of the psychology of memory. Guided by an inappropriate analogy with digital computers, this model constructed a 'memory' whose link with the outside world took the form of 'inputs' and 'outputs'. Inputs took the form of presented information and outputs were fed into an entirely separate sensori-motor system that was not part of the psychology of memory. The system was iterative only with respect to *cognitive* output in the form of symbols, which generated more symbols. What was outside the scope of the model was the kind of feedback that occurs when system-produced motor action in a material environment affects the system's own perceptual input. The limitation to pre-packaged presented information cut the intrinsic link between memory and perception and reduced memory to one functionally independent cognitive 'module' among others. Processing of information in such modules was supposed to occur via symbols that were defined purely syntactically, i.e. in terms of their relation to other symbols, rather than in terms of anything they represented.

It was of course recognized that this kind of model could not deal with real-world action in a socio-cultural context. But it was felt that such features could be added later, once the basic architecture of human cognition had been worked out. This strategy of cognitive science reflected an essentially Cartesian metaphysics that prioritized the thinking individual's mind excerpted from any social and cultural entanglements.[19] The 'memory' of such a mind would be outside human history: it dwelt only in the walled interior of the universalized individual. Within such a framework, a history of memory would not merely be irrelevant but would actually make no sense.

Towards the end of the twentieth century the limitations of this framework became more and more apparent. Although it still underlies a great deal of research in cognitive science, some fundamental rethinking has been occurring in various quarters.[20] Most relevant in the present context is a growing realization that the rigid boundary between what is inside and outside the individual mind should be abandoned, and that cognitive functions like memory should not be isolated from perception and from action in the world. Cognition is said to be 'situated' in a world that includes other individuals and material artefacts. From this point of view 'memory may not be something really located within the individual'.[21] That kind of shift creates a conceptual space within which a historical psychology of memory could play a relevant role. Potentially, the historical interlinking of memory culture, memory technology and memory theory becomes significant for an understanding of the psychology of memory. Bridging the gap between human cognition and human history becomes not only possible but also desirable.

However, such an enterprise is likely to face formidable obstacles, some grounded in genuine difficulties, others deriving from traditional prejudices against any collaboration between psychology and history that long antedate the more recent 'cognitive revolution'. These prejudices have their origin in psychology's long-standing concern about its position among the disciplines and more particularly about its status as a natural science.

In the psychological literature on memory, the contrast between frequent neurophysiological references and the virtual absence of historical references is striking. One might argue that people trained as psychologists are not equipped to handle historical evidence and should stay away from it. There is much to be said for this argument, but it does not provide a valid reason for psychologists' ignoring of historical information. Psychologists usually leave the technical conduct of neurophysiological investigations to physiologists, but no one would conclude from this that they should therefore ignore neurophysiological information. This unequal treatment of history and physiology suggests that there is more involved than merely the principle of maintaining a strict segregation between disciplines. It is as though we were still operating in terms of an essentially nineteenth-century model of a causal hierarchy of disciplines that obliges psychology to look to biology for its explanations but not to history, because biology represents a lower, more fundamental, level in this hierarchy than psychology. On this model, history should look to psychology for its explanations rather than the other way around.

Where this model is not fully adopted, the contrast between the positive affinity of psychology to physiology and its negative affinity to history at least carries the implication that psychology belongs with the natural rather than the social sciences or the humanities. That is connected to the way it defines its subject-matter. A natural science investigates natural objects, that is, objects regarded as part of the natural order, objects whose characteristics conform to universal regularities and whose properties are independent of human beliefs and practices. In so far as psychology is defined as a natural science, the assumption is that its subject-matter is essentially of this type and that means it is unaffected by human history.

In practice, however, this has not been treated as an assumption but as something that is self-evident and beyond question.[22] To a very large extent, psychology has investigated its subject-matter as though it belonged to an ahistorical human nature. This may have produced results but the assumption of ahistorical validity remains only an assumption until it is tested against relevant evidence. The relevant evidence in this case would have to be historical, and that leads one straight to the history of psychological categories such as memory. In other words, the scientific grounding of the belief that historical evidence is redundant would itself require evidence from history. In the case of memory, the more recent work of historians has actually yielded quite extensive evidence that is relevant to this question.

But historians cannot be expected to concern themselves too much with the psychological implications of their work. It seems, therefore, that psychologists themselves will have to look more closely at the historical material if its psychological implications are not to be lost.

In the past, historians of psychology have shown little interest in memory. I think this is because they shared the belief of their scientific colleagues that memory was essentially a biological category and therefore had only a phylogenetic, not a social, history. If that is so, then historical inquiries into memory would be concerned only with theories *about* memory, not the historical constitution of the concept of memory itself.[23] In a style that has long been derided by historians, such inquiries tend to look for anticipations of modern conceptualizations, such as information processing, in ancient texts.[24] More generally, the traditional history of psychology has tended to assume that 'the subject of psychology is universal',[25] that there existed a distinct part of objective reality that was 'psychological' and that did not change through history; what changed was valid knowledge about it. History then becomes the story of the discovery of truths about matters that were at least as old as the human species and sometimes older. This view of the relationship between psychology and history converged beautifully with the self-understanding of a discipline that considered itself part of the natural sciences.

Is there any way of escaping this type of narrative? That depends on how one interprets the relationship of the past to the present. One way is to take the present as representing the truth, so that the past becomes the story of how this truth triumphed and error was defeated. However, there is another way of using the present as a starting-point. Instead of equating the present with the truth, one can trace back its certainties so as to demonstrate their historical contingency. One can turn to the past in order to interrogate the present about the stuff out of which it was constructed.[26]

What are contemporary researchers doing when they investigate memory? There are two stories to be told here. In one story, the one researchers like to tell themselves, they are engaged in a process of *discovery*, a tale of an unknown continent that is slowly being opened up. History here is an account of these discoveries, of experimental 'findings' and the theories to which they give rise, or, occasionally, of inspired guesses that antedate these achievements. But if one replaces this narrow historical framework by the broader framework of human cultural history there is another story to be told. From this perspective, what modern scientists do when they investigate memory is to reconstitute memory as an object of human knowledge and human practice in accordance with the exigencies and requirements of their time.

But in constituting, representing and investigating their subject-matter, modern investigators are obliged to start with the technical and discursive resources they inherited. They may have built on these resources but they were never free to start from scratch and invent their own scientific language and their own technology in a vacuum. In the case of psychology, part of their inheritance was an everyday psychological language and a more specialized philosophical language that already posited psychological reality in a certain way. Psychologists were users of this everyday language and generally took for granted the kind of psychological reality that was presupposed by this use. In the course of time, scientific psychology did develop its own language by dropping large parts of everyday psychological language as well as much of the philosophical language (e.g. 'soul', 'will' and 'character'), modifying the meaning of other parts and inventing new terms with new meanings. This kind of transformation did not take place without profound change in the denotation of psychological terms. The 'behaviour' that is an object of study for scientific psychology has almost nothing in common with the 'behaviour' that is an object of ethical judgment. The 'personality' that is investigated by the methods of psychological science has hardly even a family resemblance to the 'personality' of great men and women as explored by their biographers. Other psychological categories, including 'intelligence', 'attitude' and 'motive', underwent transformations that were no less profound.[27]

The history of these transformations is a relatively recent one, virtually co-extensive with the history of modern psychology itself. It is a history that is closely tied up with the history of psychology as a scientific discipline. Changes in the meaning of psychological categories were contingent on changes in psychology's investigative practice, psychologists' professional project, external social pressures on the discipline, cultural currents and so on. This raises the suspicion that the content of modern psychology, its way of defining, dividing up and understanding psychological phenomena, is entirely a matter of 'social construction'. That much of this content is socially constructed is hardly open to doubt; the interesting question now is whether we can glimpse a remainder of 'natural kinds' beyond layers of construction.[28]

Can historical studies contribute anything to answering this question? They might do so, particularly if they were able to shed light on continuities between the discursive practices of modern psychology and those of the pre-scientific period. Although there is a pervasive discontinuity to be taken into account, it is not certain that this excludes any continuity at all.[29] There is, for example, a modern psychology of thinking pursued by scientific means. Is this the same 'thinking' that was the subject of ordinary and philosophical discourse centuries before the advent of modern psychology? Even if the answer turns out to be 'in some respects but not in others', as seems likely, one would have made some progress in identifying the aspects that show historical continuity across long periods of time. Having identified these aspects, one could then ask further questions about the reasons for their historical survival. Did they survive because they referred to universal features of the human mind that were unaffected by socio-historical contingencies, or did they survive because of certain continuities in discursive practices that bridged the transition to the practices of modern psychology? If so, what was the nature of these continuities?

Did any categories of modern psychology exhibit sufficient continuity of meaning over long periods to make them candidates for the kind of historical study contemplated here? I have already mentioned 'thinking', but this has too often been a marginalized category in modern psychology. Similar considerations would apply to 'imagination'. Other promising candidates, such as 'perception', raise issues of terminological change that would needlessly complicate the inquiry. Yet others, such as 'consciousness', have a history that is altogether too short. Skipping a tedious discussion of the pros and cons of a potentially vast list of candidates, let us proceed at once to the psychological category whose history forms the subject-matter of this book – memory.

Unlike most of the terms in the modern psychologist's vocabulary, memory has a truly ancient lineage. It has been called one of 'the great primordial concepts of psychology'[30] and provides evidence for the antiquity of psychology that is about as good as such evidence gets. There is probably no other psychological object that can be traced so far back without even a change in its name. Plato and Aristotle engaged in speculations about memory that have attracted comment and discussion right up to the present. Ancient Roman writers addressed the subject of memory as part of their discourse on rhetoric, a topic they took very seriously. Monastic authorities of the Middle Ages added their own interpretation of the nature and uses of memory. During the Renaissance there was an outburst of writings devoted to memory, and over the centuries there was also speculation about a physical basis for memory. Eventually, in the nineteenth century, memory emerges as an object of investigation for modern science, especially psychological and medical science. There is obviously much discontinuity here, but also, it seems, a thread of continuity, though it is not easy to say what that consists in, other than a mere name.

About this book

Any history that concentrates on conceptual change faces peculiar problems of chronology. A comprehensive general history of a particular period may simply recount what happened and what happened next in a relatively unproblematic chronological order. But a history of conceptual change has to face up to the arbitrariness of its selection of relevant material and hence the dubious nature of any chronology it constructs. Such chronologies owe their existence to the perspectives afforded by subsequent, more contemporary, categorizations, boundaries, beliefs, etc. The fact that we are now able to construct such a chronology, going forward from earlier to later periods, does not mean that there was anything pre-ordained or necessary about this historical sequence.[31] At each point, a change in the historical contingencies might have led to a different out-come. Although later periods were never totally unaffected by what had gone before, there was at least as much deliberate rejection of the past as, an often unnoticed, continuing influence of age-old concepts. In any case, the take-up of the past was always selective; some old things proved more durable than others.

Though an element of chronology, a rough succession of before and after, may be unavoidable in a purportedly historical exposition, the history of 'memory' does not constitute a linear progression, and it would be seriously misleading to present it as such. The main reason for this is that historical references to memory occur in a wide variety of theoretical and practical contexts, and, depending on the context, quite different aspects of memory are addressed in each case. There is no *single* object of reference on which all discussions converge. The topic of this book is provided by a loose assembly of problems, practices and assumptions, each of which can be said to have its own history. These will not be historians' histories aiming at a full contextualization of events, but they will retain two of the great values of the historical approach: the explication of the 'otherness' of the past and the demonstration of the impermanence of human constructions.

In the structure of this book, topics take precedence over chronology. The chapters are organized by topic, but within each chapter there is usually a vaguely chronological arrangement such that the order in which topics are discussed follows the sequence of their historical prominence. (The excep-tion is the last chapter, in which chronological arrangement appears only within each sub-section.) That arrangement reflects the reality of different topics enjoying prominence at different times as well as the historical suc-cession of their authors. Chapters 2 and 3 are largely devoted to historically earlier material, chapter 4 is a transitional chapter, while chapters 5, 7 and 8 deal largely with twentieth-century developments. The remaining chapters (6 and 9) span diverse periods.

In a sense, each chapter of this book is concerned with a different history, and these histories do not form any kind of narrative sequence. Each chapter has a time line of its own, depending on the historical trajectory of the topic under discussion. For example, metaphors of memory, discussed in the next chapter, have a history that stretches over millennia, whereas the experi-mental psychology of memory, addressed in chapter 5, hardly extends back more than one century. Yet metaphors are still relevant during this late period. So the reader must be prepared for a great deal of chronological backtracking and crossing.

When a topic is related to an active area of contemporary research it remains open-ended and an arbitrary limit has to be imposed on its discussion in a historical context. Where exactly does the past end and the present begin? The question has only to be formulated to reveal its silliness. Past and present are distinctions imposed on a continuous process for the sake of discursive convenience. However, distinctions between periods relatively close to the present moment and more distant periods do have a real basis, and an account that is concerned with the bearing of the one on the other needs a decision about when to stop. The closer one gets to the immediate present the harder it becomes to maintain the kind of perspective that an essentially historical account demands. In this book I have used two stopping rules, where appropriate. The first rule is completely arbitrary: it is given by the end of the twentieth century. But this does not mean that the end comes precisely in the year 2000. It means that I am prepared to consider anything written up to the last decade of the century as part of the subject-matter for this book. Whether it is in fact included depends on my second stopping rule, which prescribes increasing selectivity in the choice of material as the historical account comes closer to the present day. This is not only a matter of practical necessity in the face of an impossibly large accumulation of potentially relevant material, it is also required by the need to maintain the focus of this book on *conceptual* change.

I emphasize this focus because I want to avoid any false expectations. As I have already indicated, by conceptual change I mean change in the pre-suppositions, hidden metaphors, values, unreflected practices, implicit beliefs that determine the form of explicit theoretical models and the interpretation of empirical observations. In the case of memory, the history of this kind of change extends much further back than the history of empirical research in the modern manner. Empirical issues do have a history, but it is a relatively shallow history that rarely goes back more than a few decades. One encounters this kind of history in scientific literature reviews devoted to the evaluation of specific hypotheses in the light of new empirical data. They serve a very useful purpose that is quite different from the goals of the present study.[32] Much of the empirical literature has little bearing on the topic of conceptual change, because it is concerned with projects carried out within an *implicit* conceptual framework. That remains the most effective way of pushing ahead with day-to-day research. However, empirical data and specific hypotheses advanced to explain them will enter the present account only in so far as they reflect on the plausibility of some underlying conceptualization.

My task would have been considerably easier if I had adopted a more remote cut-off date for this study. Had I ended a century or even half a century earlier I would have been able to present a strictly historical account that stayed well clear of contemporary psychological issues. But that would have preserved the traditional gap between the past and the present, embodied in the segregated accounts of two mutually estranged disciplines, history and psychology. There are good reasons for the existence of this segregation, but the space between should not be left forever empty; bridging it has potential benefits, as I have suggested. There are also problems. In particular, bringing the recent past into a historical account leads to problems of distancing. It is obviously difficult to escape a myopic perspective on developments that are still taking shape in front of one's eyes, even when one has no direct involvement in these developments.

My primary interest, however, lies in the links, the continuities and discontinuities, between the near-present and the past. This entails a somewhat different view of the recent past from that of many practitioners in the memory sciences, who are justifiably proud of real technical improvements and interesting empirical findings. Because this book focuses on another set of issues there will be little reporting on these matters and greater concern with forgotten contributions, false starts, dissonant voices, hidden assumptions that were once explicit and broader social implications that are often problematic. There are aspects of the past that are of purely antiquarian interest, but there are other aspects that continue to be relevant, perhaps because they offer certain parallels to the present, perhaps because they simply show that currently popular ways of conceptualizing memory are not the only conceivable ones, or, most commonly, because they are still active under the surface.

A clear example of the last case is provided by the deployment of metaphor to explain the nature of memory. In particular, a set of metaphors depicting memory as a kind of storage *container*, and memories as stored experience, continues to be alive today, though its origins go back well over two millennia. These origins are explored in chapter 2, where Plato's famous wax tablet model of memory becomes the fulcrum for a discussion of the relationship between durable memory metaphors and the inscriptive practices that are an essential part of literacy. This leads to a more general exploration of how activities employed in the service of external memory often become the favoured source of models for explaining the workings of internal memory.

Theoretical discourse on the nature of memory forms only half of the relevant historical legacy of the pre-modern period. The other, perhaps more important, half consists of the practice-orientated discourse of the 'art of memory' explored in chapter 3. From the first recorded texts addressing the subject of memory, the interests of the authors were not purely theoretical, but were also concerned with practices that might make memory work better. Inevitably, there was a link between practical and theoretical concerns, and during both the Roman and the medieval period this link was a very close one. This reflects the links between advances in the technology of external memory and adaptations of internal memory that can be so clearly observed during this period. The flourishing and eventual decline of the mnemonic system of 'local memory' is of special interest here.

Profound historical changes separate the classical and medieval interest in the topic of memory from the active pursuit of memory studies in the twentieth century. Chapter 4 is devoted to the most salient aspects of this transformation. It begins with the topic of imagery, which lost much of its ancient importance during this period, and then considers some historical markers of the increasing 'privatization' of memory. The later sections of the chapter deal with the increasing role of science and medicine in nineteenth-century conceptualizations of memory and also some of the consequences of that development. Throughout the period covered by this chapter, there is a tendency to make memory the object of special forms of knowledge that were quite incompatible with one another. Changes in concepts of memory largely depended on the emergence, elaboration and historical displacement of these divergent ways of knowing memory.

Since antiquity, the experience of conscious recall had been part of the core meaning of the term 'memory'. However, in the late nineteenth century the drawing of analogies between biological and psychological phenomena became a popular intellectual pastime that transformed the meaning of quite a few psychological concepts, including 'intelligence', 'learning' and 'memory'. The term 'memory' was stretched to cover virtually any change in physiological function as a result of exercise, without any necessary link to conscious recall. Memory in the traditional, psychological, sense became simply a special manifestation of a more fundamental biological process.

Chapter 5 is concerned with a topic that takes us well into the twentieth century, namely the emergence and subsequent history of memory as an object of investigation for experimental psychology. Compared to traditional mnemonic practices, this involved a change in the methods of intervention from those dedicated to the improvement of memory to those dedicated to the improvement of knowledge about memory. However, the elaboration of appropriate experimental techniques required much theoretical work on the concept of memory, and the chapter traces this work through some of its historically more interesting stages. Two interrelated questions run through this chapter: how to balance the reproductive and the reconstructive aspects of memory, and what investigative tools would be most appropriate for an empirical science of memory?

The range of what was to be covered by the term 'memory' has fluctuated historically, as has its core meaning. At times it was regarded as an essentially intellectual process, at other times as something more automatic or as something more affective. From the beginning of recorded discourse on the matter there was a recognition that memory phenomena were not unitary, that different forms of memory had to be recognized. These attempts at distinguishing between different kinds of memory are discussed in chapter 6. Plato had noted a profound difference between remembering and reminding, as well as giving special importance to a form of memory he referred to as *anamnesis*. Aristotle distinguished between memory and recollection, and the Scholastics developed a whole architecture of memory faculties. In more recent times, philosophers, beginning with Henri Bergson, turned their attention to memory kinds, and psychologists followed suit, distinguishing, for example, between short-term and long-term memory, or episodic and semantic memory. Neither the empirical grounding nor the conceptual foundation of these distinctions can, however, be regarded as secure, and this raises the more general issue of whether any of these distinctions can claim to be anything other than an artificial construction.

In the seventh chapter I consider the controversial relationship of memory and truth, an issue that acquired new political connotations in recent times. A historical perspective on this relationship requires some understanding of the background for the sharp distinction between memory and imagination that characterized some twentieth-century positions. Another aspect concerns the genesis of the modern version of 'hidden truth', and this is addressed in a section devoted to psychoanalysis. I then take up the historical thread that links the late nineteenth-century notion of 'traumatic memory', first discussed in chapter 4, to its politicization in the late twentieth century.

Implicitly or explicitly, memory has always been assigned a place in the scheme of things. One way of doing this is to localize memory in the physical world. That forms the subject-matter of chapter 8. Even in pre-modern times there was speculation about what was sometimes called the 'seat' of memory, whether that seat be in the heart, the brain, the nerves or specific parts of the brain. In due course, this discourse of localization became entwined with the discourse on memory kinds discussed in chapter 6. Various forms of phrenology were the result. Beginning in the nineteenth century, technological developments produced a succession of new twists in the persistent attempt to pin down aspects of memory in specific locations. However, certain conceptual problems inherent in the project of spatial localization resisted solution by technological progress. In this chapter the problems of writing a history that extends virtually to the present become particularly acute. I have therefore limited myself to issues for which the continuity of past and present is evident and left aside other developments where any attempt at a historical assessment would be premature.

Quite apart from localizing memory in a physical sense, there is the question of placing it in relation to other concepts referring to powers or functions of the psyche. Conceptions of memory have always depended on the place assigned to memory in a network of other more or less psychological and biological concepts. In chapter 9 some of the historically more important of these networks are described, beginning with the Aristotelian notion of an inner sense of which memory was a part. A section on faculty psychology is followed by a discussion of some nineteenth- and twentieth-century conceptions of the relationship between memory and more modern psychological categories, especially those of perception and personality. One historical constant has been the fuzziness of the boundaries separating various psychological categories, a phenomenon that is nicely illustrated by ancient controversies about whether medical diagnosis depended on 'memory' or on 'reason'.

Finally, there is the question of whether memory should be thought of as something essentially *within* the individual or whether it is as much outside as inside. Early on, feats of memory were attributed to an influence that was definitely outside the human individual, the goddess Mnemosyne. Placing memory unambiguously inside the individual constituted a major change. Then there is the question of whether memory must be located in physical space or whether its place is somewhere else, perhaps in a moral or symbolic order. More recently, alternatives to the physical and the intra-individual location of memory have multiplied side by side with the flourishing research programme of neural localization. These matters are discussed in the final section of chapter 9.

The issues addressed in these chapters clearly constitute a selection of the many topics that might be considered relevant for a history of memory. The field, if one can even describe it as such, straddles several disciplines and would require a library of books to do it justice. One author who has looked into the topic describes it as 'the quintessential interdisciplinary interest'.[33] A cultural historian would have approached the topic in a different way, a historian of science in yet another way, and one can easily imagine other possible perspectives, such as that of psychiatric history, cultural anthropology, the history of philosophy and so on. There is no definitive list of topics that deserve inclusion in any assembly relevant to the history of memory concepts. Nor would a single lifetime suffice for doing justice to such an undertaking. So there can be no question of writing *the* history of memory discourse, though it is possible to construct histories of particular issues.

The selection of issues for this book was guided by the goal, already referred to, of interrogating the conceptual basis of contemporary psychological approaches in the light of historical discourse regarding memory. My goal entailed a focus on questions of memory in individuals, not questions of collective memory. Such a distinction is not an unproblematic one, as is made clear in the last section of the book, but it is not simply based on current disciplinary borders. There is an extensive history of speculation about memory as an individual attribute, and this forms an archive with reasonably distinct boundaries.

Not being a professional historian, I have not sought to add to this archive but merely to employ some portions of it as a resource in exploring continuities and discontinuities in various conceptualizations of memory, including recent ones. Disciplinary specialization and isolation has resulted in a situation where information relevant to the historical conceptualization of memory is scattered across the literature of several disciplines and sub-disciplines. My aim here is to assemble at least some of this information in a coherent form so as to allow connections to emerge that would otherwise be lost.

None of us can escape the influence of his or her time. This influence is pervasive, so that the past that forms one's framework is only the past as currently interpreted. Nevertheless, the opening of windows onto the past is likely to bring advantages when compared to a life behind shutters, even if the view outside is somewhat limited and distorted. I certainly have biases, and they will become apparent in the course of my exposition. I am sceptical of claims that such biases can be avoided. The dangerous biases are the unconscious ones, and I can only hope that these do not prove overwhelming.

Among the limitations of which I am aware, the most serious one pertains to the Eurocentric or 'Western' nature of the domain covered in this book. My own experience of working for many years in Asia and Africa makes me very conscious of this disturbing fact. Unfortunately, I do not have the resources to do anything meaningful about it. Rather than pepper my work with the odd reference to information from non-Western sources in a pretence at cross-cultural generality, I have decided to draw a sharp boundary here and leave the crossing of that boundary to those who are far better qualified to do so than I am. I fully expect that if and when that happens, major revisions to many of my hypotheses and interpretations will be necessary. The topic of memory has been important for many different cultural traditions, so the possibility of comparative studies exists. But this will require collaborative scholarship that is both international and transdisciplinary. In the meantime, it seems preferable to avoid 'token gestures of incorporation'.[34]

Notes

1. P. Connerton, *How societies remember* (New York: Cambridge University Press, 1989), p. 68.
2. P. Ariès, *The hour of our death* (New York: Alfred A. Knopf, 1981).
3. E. Hobsbawm and T. Ranger, *The invention of tradition* (Cambridge: Cambridge University Press, 1983).
4. J. Le Goff, *History and memory* (New York: Columbia University Press, 1992).
5. W. Schönpflug and K. B. Esser, 'Memory and *graeculi*: Metamemory and control in extended memory systems', in C. A. Weaver, S. Mannes and C. R. Fletcher (eds.), *Discourse comprehension: Essays in honor of Walter Kintsch* (Hillsdale, NJ: Erlbaum, 1995), pp. 245–55.
6. M. T. Clanchy, *From memory to written record: England, 1066–1307* (Cambridge, MA: Harvard University Press, 1979).
7. D. F. Sherry, and D. L. Schacter, 'The evolution of multiple memory systems', *Psychological Review* 94 (1987), 439–54.
8. M. Tomasello, *The cultural origins of human cognition* (Cambridge, MA: Harvard University Press, 1999).
9. S. J. Gould, 'Not necessarily a wing', in *Bully for Brontosaurus: Reflections in natural history* (New York: W. W. Norton, 1992), pp. 139–51.
10. M. Donald, *Origins of the modern mind: Three stages in the evolution of culture and cognition* (Cambridge MA: Harvard University Press, 1991; also *A mind so rare: The*

evolution of human consciousness (New York: W. W. Norton, 2001); and 'The mind considered from a historical perspective: Human cognitive phylogenesis and the possibility of continuing cognitive evolution', in D. M. Johnson and C. E. Erneling (eds.), *The future of the cognitive revolution* (New York: Oxford University Press, 1997), pp. 355–65.

11. J. P. Small, *Wax tablets of the mind: Cognitive studies of memory and literacy in classical antiquity* (London: Routledge, 1997).

12. D. R. Olson, *The world on paper: The conceptual and cognitive implications of writing and reading* (New York: Cambridge University Press, 1994).

13. I. Illich, *In the vineyard of the text: A commentary on Hugh's* Didascalion (Chicago: Chicago University Press, 1993).

14. M. Carruthers, *The book of memory: A study of memory in medieval culture* (New York: Cambridge University Press, 1990).

15. L. Bolzoni, *The gallery of memory: Literary and iconographic models in the age of the printing press*, trans. J. Parzen (Toronto: University of Toronto Press, 2001).

16. I prefer to use the term 'concept' to 'theory' in this context. Theories are usually distinguished from observations and imply an explicit formulation with explanatory intent. Concepts are sometimes expressed in this form but are often implicit. Their role is to interpret, to provide meanings, to unify, to categorize experiences that would otherwise be chaotic. Theories require concepts, but not the other way around. This distinction is more common in the continental than in the Anglo-Saxon literature. It is found, for example, in studies in the history of science indebted to the work of Georges Canguilhem and in German *Begriffsgeschichte*. For a brief English-language introduction to the relevant aspects of Canguilhem's approach, see G. Gutting, 'Continental philosophy and the history of science', in R. C. Olby, G. N. Cantor, J. R. R. Christie and M. J. S. Hodge (eds.), *Companion to the history of modern science* (London: Routledge, 1990), pp. 127–47; for *Begriffsgeschichte*, see M. Richter, '*Begriffsgeschichte* and the history of ideas', *Journal of the History of Ideas* 48 (1987), 247–63.

17. D. Draaisma, *Metaphors of memory: A history of ideas about the mind* (Cambridge: Cambridge University Press, 2000).

18. H. Gardner, *The mind's new science: A history of the cognitive revolution* (New York: Basic Books, 1985), p. 6.

19. R. A. Wilson, *Cartesian psychology and physical minds: Individualism and the sciences of the mind* (Cambridge: Cambridge University Press, 1995).

20. The following conclusion represents one result of this rethinking: 'We must be wary of any definition that treats memory and belief as if they could be simple primitives existing only inside the brain.' C. Westbury and D. C. Dennett, 'Mining the past to construct the future: Memory and belief as forms of knowledge', in D. L. Schacter and E. Scarry (eds.), *Memory, brain and belief* (Cambridge, MA: Harvard University Press, 2000), pp. 11–32 (p. 29).

21. R. Pfeifer and C. Scheier, *Understanding intelligence* (Cambridge, MA: MIT Press, 1999), p. 514.

22. During the twentieth century, this was somewhat less true of the continental European literature, where one can find attempts at linking history and psychology, though rarely by psychologists. See, for example, J.-P. Vernant, 'History and psychology', in F. I. Zeitlin (ed.), *Mortals and immortals: Collected essays* (Princeton, NJ: Princeton University Press, 1991), pp. 261–8.

23. D. J. Hermann and R. Chaffin (eds.), *Memory in historical perspective: The literature before Ebbinghaus* (New York: Springer-Verlag, 1988).

24. S. Kemp and G. J. O. Fletcher, 'The medieval theory of the inner senses', *American Journal of Psychology* 106 (1993), 559–76.

25. For a historian's reaction to this assumption, see R. Smith, 'Does the history of psychology have a subject?', *History of the Human Sciences* 1 (1988), 147–77. For a

philosopher's radical alternative, see D. M. Johnson, *How history made the mind: The cultural origins of objective thinking* (Chicago: Open Court, 2003).

26. N. Rose, *Inventing our selves* (Cambridge: Cambridge University Press, 1996); H. J. Stam, 'Retrieving the past for the future: Boundary maintenance in historical and theoretical psychology', in D. B. Hill and M. J. Kral (eds.), *About psychology: Essays at the crossroads of history, theory, and philosophy* (Albany, NY: State University of New York Press, 2003), pp. 147–63.
27. K. Danziger, *Naming the mind: How psychology found its language* (London: Sage, 1997).
28. I. Hacking, *The social construction of what?* (Cambridge, MA: Harvard University Press, 1999).
29. K. Danziger, 'How old is psychology, particularly concepts of memory?', *History & Philosophy of Psychology* 4 (2002), 1–12.
30. W. W. Rozeboom, 'The concept of "memory"', *Psychological Record* 15 (1965), 329–68.
31. M. Foucault, 'Nietzsche, genealogy, history', in D. F. Bouchard (ed.), *Language, counter-memory, practice: selected essays and interviews by Michel Foucault* (Ithaca, NY: Cornell University Press, 1977), pp. 139–64.
32. Seminal ideas on the historical aspect of scientific literature reviews are presented in G. Markus, 'Why is there no hermeneutics of natural sciences? Some preliminary theses', *Science in Context* 1 (1987), 5–51.
33. P. H. Hutton, *History as an art of memory* (Hanover, VT: University Press of New England, 1993), p. xiii.
34. R. Smith, 'The big picture: Writing psychology into the history of the human sciences', *Journal of the History of the Behavioral Sciences* 34 (1998), 1–13. See also, L. E. Sullivan, 'Memory distortion and anamnesis: A view from the human sciences', in D. L. Schacter (ed.), *Memory distortion: How minds, brains and societies reconstruct the past* (Cambridge, MA: Harvard University Press, 1995), pp. 386–400.

2   The rule of metaphor

CHAPTER OUTLINE

The persistence of metaphor

Throughout its history, memory discourse has provided a rich field for the play of metaphors. This continued to be the case even after memory became a topic for scientific psychology. In fact, this area of psychology is unusual in the frankness with which the role of metaphor has been widely recognized. Little more than a decade ago a discussion of metaphors in memory research in the journal *Behavioral and Brain Sciences* drew in some twenty-five contributors, the great majority of them experimental psychologists.[1] Yet well over two thousand years ago metaphor already played a major role in the first sustained discussion of memory in Europe, that of Plato. Nor is it difficult to find numerous examples of memory metaphors during the intervening centuries.[2] What accounts for this amazing persistence? Any answer to that question requires a closer look at the nature of memory metaphors.

First of all, it is necessary to remind ourselves that, when one speaks of 'metaphors' in this context, one is not referring to isolated figures of speech used as a literary device. It is rather a question of interconnected 'metaphoric networks',[3] whose members are linked by ties of analogy and resemblance. There is often a convergence of meaning on a so-called 'root metaphor'[4] that is felt to define something essential about the field to which it is applied. Such formations encourage the production of new metaphorical variants and extensions that exploit the implications of the core metaphor. Used in this way, metaphors become discursively 'generative';[5] they lead to previously unexplored questions and the projection of the metaphor onto new areas of experience and practice.

In terms of their historical fate, memory metaphors fall into two groups: those that persist over long periods of time and those that are relatively ephemeral. In the title of the recent discussion already referred to (see note 1) we find one of each group: the storehouse metaphor, which is far older than modern psychology, and the so-called correspondence metaphor, which is new and unlikely to have a long life. The persistence of metaphor clearly depends on the first and not the second group. Furthermore, it turns out that the members of the durable group tend to have a family resemblance to each other, to be members of one recognizable metaphoric network. Thus, the storage metaphor, which invites one to think of memory as a container holding 'traces' of some kind, recurs in many recognizably similar guises over the centuries.

In the late twentieth century, the metaphor of memory storage received a powerful reinforcement in the shape of the digital computer. But this was by no means a one-way street, because psychology had supplied some of the basic items for the emerging language of computer science in the first place. The use of 'memory', when referring to computer storage, is of course the most obvious example of such borrowing; 'retrieval' is another. For the psychology of memory the proliferation of digital computers provided a more differentiated language, 'computer-speak', that made possible the development of a whole family of derivative metaphors from an ancient root metaphor.[6] Computers also sealed the victory of one of two variants in which the storage metaphor had appeared for many centuries.

One variant represents memory storage in terms of very concrete analogies: either the storage container or the items stored, and often both, are depicted in terms of palpable material objects. Architectural analogies for the container were long a favourite. 'We make search in our memory for a forgotten idea, just as we rummage our house for a lost object ... We turn over the things under which, or within which, or alongside of which, it may possibly be', wrote William James at the dawn of modern psychology.[7] And a few years later, Freud too suggests a house as an admittedly crude analogy for the container of memories: 'The unconscious system may therefore be compared to a large ante-room ... adjoining this is a second smaller apartment, a sort of reception room, in which consciousness resides.'[8]

This kind of analogy recurs throughout the history of discourse about memory and it seems to have little to do with the philosophical commitments of the authors. At the end of the seventeenth century, John Locke, often regarded as the father of modern empiricism, referred to memory as 'the storehouse of our ideas'.[9] Well over a thousand years earlier, the storehouse metaphor had been celebrated by St Augustine, who wrote about 'the fields and vast palaces of memory' and 'memory's huge cavern, with its mysterious secret and indescribable nooks and crannies'.[10] Describing memory as a 'vast hall' and as 'wonderful storerooms', his text played a significant role in propagating the storehouse metaphor over a very long period during which memory discourse was governed by Christian authority.

Some medieval variants of the storage metaphor employed concrete images of containers that went beyond common architectural specimens such as houses, rooms, palaces and halls. Boxes and chests used for storing valuables were often referred to, and some writers liked purses or money-bags that could be used to convey the idea of memory as a compartmentalized store.[11] In twentieth-century psychology, the image of the purse is not unknown, and is joined by that of a bottle, a junk box and a garbage can.[12]

But the most venerable of these very concrete memory containers is probably the birdcage, whose ubiquitous metaphorical role is attested to by the verb 'to pigeon-hole', meaning to store away to be forgotten or perhaps recalled at some future date. Famously, the birdcage metaphor for memory already occurs in Plato:

> now let us suppose that every mind contains a kind of aviary stocked with birds of every sort ... When we are babies we must suppose this receptacle empty, and take the birds to stand for pieces of knowledge. Whenever a person acquires any piece of knowledge and shuts it up in his enclosure, we must say he has learned or discovered the thing of which this is the knowledge and that is what 'knowing' means.[13]

The choice of birds is interesting. In later versions of the storage metaphor, the stored elements are often imagined as inert bits of treasure, but Plato would clearly have us think of them as very active and difficult to catch hold of. His introduction of the birdcage metaphor leads to the recognition that, if memory involves storage, the *retrieval* of memories becomes a problem. The birds of his metaphor provide an image that very effectively draws our attention to the issue of memory recovery:

> Well, our illustration from hunting pigeons and getting possession of them will enable us to explain that the hunting occurs in two ways – first before you possess your pigeon in order to have possession of it; secondly, after getting possession of it, in order to catch and hold in your hand what you have already possessed for some time. In the same way, if you have long possessed pieces of knowledge about things you have learned and know, it is still possible to get to know the same things again, by the process of recovering the knowledge of some particular thing and getting hold of it.[14]

For Plato, the storage aspect of memory was not nearly as interesting or important as the recovery aspect, which played a fundamental role in his philosophy and to which he returned in several of his *Dialogues*. For him, the question of memory was much less one of acquisition than of using what was potentially at one's disposal; hence his distinction between *possessing* knowledge – possessing a well-stocked aviary – and actually *having* it – holding one of one's birds in one's hand.

The process of memory recovery leads to the introduction of an additional metaphor, that of *hunting*, which conveys the active, searching nature of recovering knowledge from memory storage. This metaphor was taken up by Plato's successor, Aristotle, who treated recollection as a separate topic distinguished from the storing of memory images. Recollection involved 'searching for an image', going from one to another as 'we hunt up the series'.[15] In the centuries that followed, the development of metaphors of retrieval depended much less on images of hunting and searching than on analogies that grew out of a more promising variant of the storage metaphor.

How the gift of mnemosyne changed

All the examples considered so far have involved storage in a very concrete, material sense: objects deposited in buildings, chests, purses, cages and so on. But there is another kind of storage that is linked to human memory in a much more intimate way, namely, the kind of storage that occurs when people avail themselves of the possibilities of external memory, when they deliberately make traces on some medium such as stone, wood, wax, parchment, paper, film or magnetic tape. This process of inscription provides a far more powerful source of memory metaphors than any other. There are several reasons for this.

First of all, inscription had a technological aspect which was capable of enormous historical development in terms of the medium employed and the gradual exploitation of the possibilities offered by these media. With each significant step in the development of inscriptive technologies, new memory metaphors became available. Thus, before the most recent period of computer memory, the phonograph and the photographic plate had already been proposed as metaphors for memory,[16] and, long before that, books and libraries had filled that role. As a source of memory metaphors, inscriptive technologies proved to have far greater potential than activities of collecting and storing material objects in physical containers. This was not only due to technological developments associated with the proliferation of media of inscription; to an even greater extent it depended on developments in the symbolic functions of inscriptions. Unlike the objects – coins or birds, for instance – put away in the cruder versions of the storage metaphor, what was stored in metaphors of inscription were symbols, and symbols were capable of infinite development in terms of their nature and organization. They might be concrete images of animals and humans, or geometric designs, or letters, numbers, texts or auditory and visual recordings. Moreover, there were endless possibilities for the arrangement and organization of these symbols. No wonder the infinite variants of inscription have eclipsed mere physical storage as a source for memory metaphors in historical time.

But there is another reason for the dominant role of metaphors of inscription. The point is that inscription is literally, and not just metaphorically, implicated in human memory. The memory of *homo sapiens* appears always to have relied on some form of inscription on an external medium. We know about ancient cave paintings because special conditions allowed them to survive for very long periods, but less durable media, such as wood and bark, probably have an equally long history. As far as we know, humans always used external marks and images produced by inscription to remind them of matters they wished to be reminded of. In certain contexts these marks were therefore part of the process of remembering.

Of course, there were other contexts in which remembering proceeded without the help of inscriptions, orally related narratives, for example. However, it was inscription that provided the key metaphor for conceptualizing memory as such. The model for this development is found in Plato's analogy of the wax tablet, probably the most influential image in the entire history of discourse about memory:

> Imagine, then, for the sake of argument, that our minds contain a block of wax, which in this or that individual may be larger or smaller, and composed of wax that is comparatively pure or muddy, and harder in some, softer in others, and sometimes of just the right consistency ...
>
> Let us call it the gift of the Muses' mother, Memory, and say that whenever we wish to remember something we see or hear or conceive in our own minds, we hold this wax under the perceptions or ideas and imprint them on it as we might stamp the impression of a seal ring. Whatever is so imprinted we remember and know so long as the image remains; whatever is rubbed out or has not succeeded in leaving an impression we have forgotten and do not know.[17]

Plato's reference to 'the gift of the Muses' mother, Memory' may be obscure to many modern readers; to his contemporaries it would probably have been surprising rather than obscure. From the legends with which they were familiar, they would have known about Mnemosyne, the mother of nine daughters, the muses, whose father was Zeus. Among these daughters were Klio, the celebrator and later muse of history; Thalia, to become muse of comedy; Melpomene, player of songs; Terpsichore, who delights with dance; Polyhymnia, muse of sacred music; and Kalliope, muse of beautiful speech. Mnemosyne's daughters were all public performers whose arts were on display at civic and religious festivals, where they gave life to traditional cultural forms. To do this effectively, they all had to rely on something that came to them from their mother, this was 'the gift of mnemosyne', a gift that could be bestowed in turn on mortal performers on special occasions and under special conditions.

Those who received these gifts experienced them not as welling up from some inner talent, but as an inspiration from an external source. The poet Hesiod (c. 700 BCE) describes this:

> These are the muses who once taught Hesiod beautiful song as he was pasturing his flock in the foothills of holy Mount Helikon. This is the speech with which I was first addressed by these goddesses ...
>
> Thus did they speak, these eloquent daughters of almighty Zeus and they gave me a rod, the shoot of a flowering laurel, which they had plucked, a marvellous thing, and breathed a divine voice into me to sing of what will be and what was before.[18]

The muses enabled the poet to sing of what was before, to recount legends he had no doubt heard in the past. In our terms, this performance required prodigious feats of memory, for cultural transmission at this point was still almost entirely oral – Hesiod is unlikely to have *read* the myths he recounts, he could only have heard them.[19] Writing was just beginning to come into use among the Greeks, so Hesiod and other performers of his time had no 'script' to refer back to. Under these conditions, remembered versions can be compared only to other remembered versions, not to an unalterable original fixed in some material medium like parchment or paper. This means that strict accuracy of reproduction is much more difficult to establish and hardly enforceable as a general standard. What now counts as an acceptable reproduction of a song, an epic, a traditional tale, etc. is likely to allow more scope for individual variation than when definitive texts provide a readily available standard of comparison.

Recordings of traditional performances learned by oral transmission reveal that there can be significant variations from one rendering to another.[20] Not only are some parts left out – which could be the result of simple forgetting – but other parts are altered and sometimes new parts are inserted. In our terms, such performances are not only a function of repro-ductive memory, but involve some elements of composition as well. How-ever, no distinction between reproduction and composition can be detected in the earliest Greek literature that refers to mnemosyne. Strictly speaking, the meaning of mnemosyne is not 'memory' but rather 'remembrance', the exercise of memory as an activity.[21] The conceptualization of 'the gift of mnemosyne' as pure memory occurs only after the introduction of written records which bring definitive versions of verbal texts into existence. Early on, remembering means listening to a voice, later it means looking some-thing up in an inscribed record.

But how did oral performers represent this kind of remembering to themselves? Not by postulating a quasi-psychological faculty they possessed individually, but by invoking specific mythical figures on which, according to tradition, their performance depended. In this respect, the representation of memory was no different from the representation of any other function later to be characterized as 'psychological'. Where a modern writer would provide internal, psychological, reasons for a character's conduct, the Homeric epics, whose written form is not far removed in time from Hesiod's poetry, will often appeal to the influence of divine and mythical beings.[22]

It is now possible to appreciate the full extent of the change that Plato's introduction of the wax metaphor wrought. First of all, memory has changed its location: it has taken up its abode in the minds of individuals. The secrets of memory are locked up within the person. In the days of Hesiod, on the other hand, memory in the form of Mnemosyne and her daughters dwelt in the public space of song, dance, poetry and ritual performance. In this sense, images of collective memory can be said to be prior to the objectification of individual memory. Of course, such an observation can be made only from a point of view for which the distinction between public and private memory already exists. At the time of Hesiod and his cohorts, that distinction had not yet appeared on the horizon.[23]

Another feature of the earlier version of mnemosyne was that the goddess's gift did not represent memory in general but only memory as manifested in certain culturally defined situations of public performance. A good performance undoubtedly required much effort and practice and could not be taken for granted. This was not an everyday event, but a special occasion, when the exercise of memory became problematic and aroused attention. But there is nothing to indicate that the notion of memory in general existed at this point. A common feature among a particular set of social events had been objectified in a mythical figure, but this was not seen as a universal feature of all human remembering.

For Plato, however, memory has become abstract. He can discuss memory as such without reference to its specific manifestations. The process of imprinting on wax is meant to convey something essential about memory in general, irrespective of particular occasions for its use. There is a hidden metaphor within the obvious one offered by Plato. To say that memory is somehow like an imprint on a block of wax is also to say that memory is like an object that can be detached from its surroundings and held up for an examination of its own nature.

Plato's wax metaphor also helps to demystify, to naturalize, memory. When metaphor replaces myth as the preferred way of objectifying memory, the images through which memory is reflected change. They are no longer based on figures supplied by ancient myth, but are now taken from relatively mundane objects and practices of urban life. What makes memory intelligible now are not legends but the metaphors that liken it to mundane devices and activities. With this move memory becomes much less mysterious and takes its place among natural objects open to inspection and analysis. The wax metaphor opens up a whole network of analogies that act like a new prism through which the phenomena of memory may be interpreted naturalistically:

> When a man has in his mind a good thick slab of wax, smooth and kneaded to the right consistency, and the impressions that come through the senses are stamped on these tables of the 'heart' ... then the imprints are clear and deep enough to last a long time. Such people are quick to learn and also have good memories, and besides they do not interchange the imprints of their perceptions but think truly ... or when the block is muddy or made of impure wax, or oversoft or hard, the people with soft wax are quick to learn, but forgetful, those with hard wax the reverse. Where it is shaggy or rough, a gritty kind of stuff containing a lot of earth or dirt, the impressions obtained are indistinct; so are they too when the stuff is hard, for they have no depth. Impressions in soft wax also are indistinct, because they melt together and soon become blurred. And if, besides this, they overlap through being

crowded together into some wretched little narrow mind, they are still more indistinct. All these types, then, are likely to judge falsely.[24]

Here, and in some of his other dialogues, Plato indicates that memory belongs to the category of phenomena about which general questions of truth and falsehood can and should be raised. A good memory allows one to 'think truly', a poor memory makes one 'likely to judge falsely'. Memory has become an aspect of cognition, of true or false knowledge. Ever since Plato, there have been powerful precedents for regarding memory as an essentially cognitive phenomenon. Even in twentieth-century experimental psychology memory was investigated first and foremost as a kind of cognition, the kind about which it is appropriate to raise questions of truth and error. It does not have to be so. For example, one could regard memory as essentially an affective experience, or as a matter of collective commemorative practice or as a property of the living body. Some of these alternatives are explored in later chapters.

Inscription: writing as memory

Plato's extended metaphor of impressions on wax was meant to explain some commonly observed variations in human memory. His mouthpiece, Socrates, functions as a teacher who uses a familiar practice as a way of conveying some understanding of things that had previously been unexplained. That was no more than sensible pedagogic practice, relying on his audience's presumed familiarity with blocks of wax, or, more particularly, wax as a material for receiving imprints. But how did educated Athenians of the fourth century BC gain this familiarity? There can be little doubt that the primary source would have been the technology of writing as practised at the time. Indeed Plato says as much:

> It appears to me that the conjunction of memory with sensations, together with the feelings consequent upon memory and sensation, may be said as it were to write words in our souls. And when this experience writes what is true, the result is that true opinions and true assertions spring up in us, while when the internal scribe that I have suggested writes what is false we get the opposite sort of opinions and assertions.[25]

Wooden tablets covered with wax were among the earliest writing surfaces known to the Greeks, and anyone who had received some schooling in Plato's time is likely to have become familiar with them. They were used for school notes and exercises, as well as sketches of compositions.[26] People would certainly have known impressions on wax as prime examples of the process of leaving a record. It did not require a huge leap of imagination to take this practice as a model for what might be happening when individuals remember without such external aids.[27]

In introducing writing as a metaphor for memory, Plato stands at the beginning of a long line of writers who draw on the same root metaphor.

What is first made explicit in his writings recurs again and again in later discourse on memory.[28] Writing becomes part of the taken-for-granted way of representing memory. Thus Cicero, an authoritative Roman source, says of one reputed memory expert that 'as he wrote with letters on wax, so he wrote with symbols as it were, whatever he wished to remember on those places which he had conceived in imagination'.[29] He, as well as other Latin authors on the art of memory, also applied the wax tablet metaphor to systems of memory improvement.[30] Later, the metaphor is adjusted to the replacement of wax tablets by parchment and paper, and memory is likened to a book.[31] More recently, there has even been a massive revival of explicit writing metaphors, first by Sigmund Freud in the form of his analogical use of the 'mystic writing-pad' that actually returns to the use of wax, and then in the form of computer analogies that are full of references to various kinds of 'writing' and 'reading'. 'The metaphor of writing shows the stubbornness of a palimpsest: apparently completely scratched out, but on closer inspection still vaguely legible among the words written later.'[32]

In the ancient world the pervasive recourse to writing as a metaphor for memory had less to do with Plato's authority as a philosopher than with the gradual spread of literacy. Writing was becoming deeply implicated in many aspects of life.[33] It was used to keep a record of economic transactions, such as contracts, sales and offers of sale, receipts, changes of ownership, etc. In the political sphere treaties, edicts, laws, as well as civil and military proceedings, were recorded.[34] In their private lives people used this technology to make notes to themselves, and to record their wishes in letters, instructions and wills. It became a regular part of formal education. And of course it was used to transmit works of literature, religion, science and philosophy, as well as information on a wide range of other subjects. Most people could not read, but we do not know whether they had any notions regarding the nature of memory. The only information we have on this topic comes from people who were steeped in literate culture. When such people began to speculate about human memory they appear to have taken the external memory system, which was so much part of their daily lives, as the model for an internal memory that was assumed to run its course within each person.

In comparing the operations of individual memory to writing and reading, the philosophers of antiquity were not simply engaged in a semantic exercise. They were giving life to a new discursive object modelled on a new area of human activity and a new set of artefacts. On this level the direction of metaphorical transfer, from external to internal memory, is quite clear in the relevant texts. Plato does not try to explain the nature of writing on wax tablets by appealing to well-known facts about individual memory, but rather the other way around.[35]

Making memory an object of intellectual inquiry depended on the proliferation of the external memory system, for it was the artefacts of this system which displayed memory as an object that could be appropriated, used, inspected and ultimately studied. This development created a split, a distinction, between remembering subjects and the objects on which their memory was exercised. In an inspired oral performance, or in ordinary dialogue for that matter, memory is expressed in speech action that is inseparable from living human subjects. When speech is written down, however, it becomes separated from its individual author and begins to have an existence as a quasi-permanent object that can be inspected by many subjects and may even outlive its author. A written record may depend on and refer to the memory of a particular writer, but it is quite different from that memory – it belongs to a class of memory products that are neither speech nor individual experience. These products have a material existence – as marks on wax, paper or whatever – that is clearly not that of their human origin. Such visible distinctions gave plausibility to the concept of memory as a distinguishable attribute of individual subjects. In the formulation of this concept the social practice of written record-keeping provided the obvious metaphorical resources.

Plato lived at a time when the benefits of literacy were not yet taken for granted. After all, his revered teacher, Socrates, wrote nothing and relied entirely on oral transmission. Schooling in Plato's time had only recently begun to deviate from the tradition of oral instruction by introducing written exercises.[36] The Platonic dialogues contain much internal evidence that attests to the important role still played by oral recitation and recapitulation at this time.[37] Writing was then still a fairly new technology for the Athenians and new applications for it were still being discovered.[38] The dialogical form of much of Plato's own writing can be seen as expressing a reluctance to give up the advantages of oral discourse.[39] This is a kind of writing, which still appears as a representation of a spoken interchange and has not yet usurped the role of actual dialogue.[40] Plato represents a transitional period in which metaphors based on writing were still fresh and enlightening, though this could be accompanied by a clear sense of their limitations.

For a writer like Plato, who combined great competence in the use of this medium with a significant degree of cultural conservatism, the attraction of writing was tempered by an awareness of what would be lost if it became a substitute for memory. Though inscription provided Plato with an interesting metaphor for the understanding of certain cognitive phenomena, he also left no doubt that the reach of this metaphor was limited to relatively superficial manifestations of memory. For deeper insights one would have to turn elsewhere.[41] He let it be known that he considered writing to be a technology that was likely to diminish memory. In at least two places he relates a legend about the discovery of writing which illustrates this point. According to this story, writing was invented by the Egyptian god Thot or Theuth, patron of scribes and literate officials, who then tried to persuade the king, Ammon, that his invention provided 'a recipe for memory and wisdom'. But the king was not at all convinced. On the contrary, he thought that writing would have an effect exactly the opposite of the one promised by its inventor:

> If men learn this, it will implant forgetfulness in their souls; they will cease to exercise memory because they rely on that which is written, calling things to remembrance no longer from within themselves but by means of external marks. What you have discovered is a recipe not for memory but for reminder.[42]

Plato makes it clear that his sympathies lie with the king, going on to say that anyone who believes that 'writing will provide something reliable and permanent must be exceedingly simple-minded; he must really be ignorant of Ammon's utterance if he believes that written words can do anything more than remind one who knows that which the writing is concerned with'.[43] So the proper role of writing lies in the recording, not in the acquisition, of knowledge. Implicitly, this involves a serious limitation of the inscription model of memory, and Plato traces this limitation directly to the socially decontextualized nature of writing. Writing cannot be interrogated, it cannot answer back and, as a medium for learning, it is therefore decidedly inferior to the oral dialogue:

> It is the same with written words; they seem to talk to you as though they were intelligent, but if you ask them anything about what they say, from a desire to be instructed, they go on telling you just the same thing forever.[44]

There is something unsatisfactory about the use of writing, 'to sow words that can't either speak in their own defence or present the truth adequately'. Such 'dead discourse' is to be contrasted with 'the living speech' which 'goes together with knowledge and is written in the soul of the learner'.[45]

Here, Plato's ambivalence about writing emerges particularly clearly. Virtually in the same breath, he condemns writing as the source of 'dead discourse' and yet opts for the metaphor of writing to indicate how 'living speech' gets into the soul of the listener. However, different aspects of writing are involved. There is writing as inscription, which supplies a useful metaphor for memory acquisition, but there is also the product of writing – text – which constitutes a sort of freezing of living memory.[46] So, while the laying down of memories may be analogous to writing, the recall of memories is not like the reading of a text. Remembering, Plato insists, must be distinguished from reminding. A text can remind, but only a person can remember.[47]

Placed in a transitional situation, in which writing had not yet become a taken-for-granted, transparent medium, Plato was able to discern complexities in the relation of literacy and memory that became increasingly invisible to subsequent generations.[48] That development is already apparent in the approach taken by Plato's successor, Aristotle.

First sketch of a literary model: Aristotle

Most of Plato's texts were written in dialogue form and therefore preserved a certain link with living speech. Aristotle's texts, on the other hand, have the form of rather dry and not infrequently abstruse prose pieces. They were notes and outlines, made by and perhaps for students, based on expository lectures that communicated a content that was already in textual form, quite different from the dialogical form of Socratic speech situations which Plato tried to capture. Where Plato employed living metaphors that vividly illustrated different aspects of memory, Aristotle was much less explicit about his metaphors and often left them hidden behind the surface of his sometimes quite technical prose.

In the area of memory there is one notable exception to this. Aristotle quite clearly takes over the metaphor of inscription and in doing so helps to perpetuate it. Memory, he says, is 'like a sort of picture', the mark formed by 'a sort of imprint, as it were, of the sense-image, as people do who seal things with signet rings'.[49] The metaphorical reference to signet rings is still there, but Aristotle ends up with a pretty literal interpretation of memorial imprinting by relating it to crude features of a person's body. Dwarf-like individuals, including children, have relatively poor memories, he says, 'because they have a great weight resting on the perceptive part'.[50] The same effect is claimed to occur in those 'whose upper parts are especially large'. In the Aristotelian texts there is a more literal, somatic conception of what it means to have a memory. Inscription, or imprinting, no longer has the freshness as a metaphor that it had in Plato's time; it is beginning to become a dead metaphor and in due course its metaphorical status will no longer be recognized.

At the same time, certain features which had remained implicit in Plato's metaphors became much more explicit. The wax model had focused on one very concrete aspect of inscriptive practices, the making of relatively permanent marks on a physical medium. But there was more than that to those practices. In particular, there was the fact that traces inscribed on wax, clay or stone had to be laid out in physical space, and therefore the deciphering of such traces involved reading the meaning of spatial patterns. This spatialization of inscriptions could be metaphorically transferred to those interior inscriptions that were held to constitute an individual's memory. This is what we find in the work of Aristotle.

Plato's metaphor of the birdcage had also implied a spatialization of memory: The holding of memories was pictured as taking place in a confined but extended space, the cage, and at any one time each memory, or bird, was in a particular location within that space, where it would have to be found and recovered. Aristotle did not use such an obvious metaphor. Instead, he developed a model that was meant to be taken literally but that resembled Plato's aviary in its spatialization of memory.

Aristotle's account of what is actually supposed to be happening when remembering occurs begins by positing a kind of inscription process when a memory trace is laid down. But what is the nature of the inscription? It is, says Aristotle, an image (*phantasma*), 'a sort of picture, the having of which we say is the memory', and it is located 'in the soul and in that part of the body which contains the soul'.[51] This image is a copy or likeness (*eikon*) of what was originally perceived. Calling up such an image is like looking at a picture – Aristotle's illustration is that of contemplating a drawing. Images have spatial dimensions, even if the original did not: 'And similarly someone who is thinking, even if he is not thinking of something with a size, places something with a size before his eyes but thinks of it not as having a size.'[52] One can *think* of things that have no spatial extension, but memory, according to Aristotle, does not belong to the thinking but to the imaginative part of the soul, and images are spatial. The spatially extended nature of images leads to a natural affinity between the imagist theory of memory and the metaphor of storage. It is easy to think of spatially extended things as being stored somewhere.[53]

Remembering, as distinct from thinking, is conceived as a kind of internal seeing. The paradigmatic examples of remembering are all visual – the examination of an interior figure seen as having some kind of spatial extension and location. Is remembering then a kind of internal visual perception? It is, but in a very specific sense. Aristotle takes care to point out that there are two kinds of seeing. In one case, we simply take in a figure as it presents itself; in the other case we regard it as a copy, a representation of something else. In ordinary perception one usually sees in the first way, but a memory image is always seen as a copy, a reminder of something else that is not actually present now but was once present. This is what makes it a memory and not a perceptual image.

In other words, a memory image is not just seen, it is *read*. Regarding a memory image is very much like the special kind of perception that takes place in the act of reading, where the visual patterns of letters, drawings or diagrams are seen, not simply as spatial configurations, but as configurations that refer to or stand for something that is not directly perceived at that time. Remembering means 'reading' the memory image, the 'copy', left behind by a previous perception.

Aristotle did not inherit Plato's ambivalence about writing and had no qualms about extending the analogy of inscriptive practice to the whole of memory. For Plato, writing could only *remind* and was therefore limited to one aspect of memory. But in Aristotle's model there is no place for the distinction between reminding and remembering, because it is entirely based on inscriptive practices.[54] In this model the skills employed in using an external memory system were provided with hypothetical internal analogues that could explain individual memory in situations where no external memory was involved.

The culture of literacy and its standard model of memory

Historically, the topics of literacy and memory are closely inter-twined. Due regard for the history of literacy is indispensable for a historian of memory. However, literacy is itself a tricky concept that can as easily mislead as illuminate inquiries on related topics. Care must therefore be taken to avoid the traps associated with some earlier conceptions of literacy that have not stood up to criticism.[55] In the first place, literacy is not a 'mentality' to be contrasted with its opposite, the 'oral' mentality. Literacy is first of all a cultural, not a psychological, phenomenon. Like all cultural phenomena it may of course have psychological aspects and consequences. For one thing, previously non-existent skills must be developed. Mental operations that depend on particular forms of external memory must have features that were absent before this dependence developed. But this does not constitute a different way of being human.

Second, literacy is not simply a matter of possessing a particular tech-nology, but of how that technology is used.[56] In other words, it is a matter of social practice. Third, literate and non-literate practices co-exist over long periods, and the relative importance of literate practices, as well as their relationship to non-literate practices, varies, not only historically, but also across cultures.[57] In the present context our principal concern is limited to the relationship between literate practices and conceptions of memory in one part of the world.

Life in a 'culture of literacy'[58] requires the frequent use of the devices and practices of external memory, and this provided the conceptual resources for imagining how an internal memory, a memory inscribed on a person's body, might be constituted. That did not happen all at once. Externally inscribed memory extended its hold over different aspects of life quite gradually, and as it did so, its different aspects were seized upon, one by one, to amplify the models of internal memory that its increasing familiarity suggested. The visible, material aspects of external inscription, the wax tablets, were noticed first. Later, the human skills that are a necessary part of any functioning external memory system provided a template on which a more detailed model of internal memory could be constructed. In people's lives, external and internal memory did not work independently but formed an interacting whole. This entailed the use of memory skills that were adapted to the form of representation employed in written inscriptions.[59] When philosophers like Aristotle attempted to account for memory as such, it was this area of their experience that provided them with a plausible paradigm.

The assembly of material artefacts, skills of literacy, social applications, symbolic products and habits of mind that constituted the culture of literacy was, however, far from static. For a considerable period, after the time of

Plato and Aristotle, it spread outward, affecting more people and more aspects of their lives. There followed a period of decline that lasted for several centuries, but by the High Middle Ages the culture of literacy was once again on the march. After the invention of printing it was set to take over the world. That illustrates the important role of technological developments in creating new *possibilities* for expanding the influence of literacy on life, though the exploitation of these possibilities depended on prevailing social and cultural realities. Technologies impinge on existing social interests and styles of life. They may be actively promoted by groups to whom they are useful or opposed by those who see them as a threat. Sometimes, people will also be mistaken about these things. The actual deployment of technologies of external memory will always depend on the life of the communities that use them. Because the availability of these technologies as a source of metaphors for human memory depends on how they are actually deployed, not on how they might be deployed, the use of these metaphors varies widely between peoples and between historical periods.

Long before printing there had been useful developments in the technology of literacy that led to the gradual improvement of the means for making inscriptions, of the methods for storing inscribed surfaces and of the organization (and therefore the retrieval) of written content. Parchment, skins and paper replaced stone, clay and wax as writing surfaces. Tablets became scrolls and then pages in a book. People learned more effective ways of displaying written text so that it could be read and remembered more easily.[60] Written manuscripts began to accumulate in certain places that became archives or libraries. Techniques of organizing such collections were gradually developed.

These and other developments provided a potential source for a network of analogies that would link the expanding visible world of external memory with its supposed internal counterpart. Although analogies helped to identify and define the aspects of human activity that were mobilized by technologies of external memory, they tended to reify the causes of these activities and locate them within individual human agents. A new domain of discourse developed, taking memory as its object and treating it as a distinct human power whose mode of operation required explanation. This discourse was explicitly *about* memory, constituting a kind of metamemory. Now, actual human remembering would be accompanied or shadowed by beliefs generated within the discourse of metamemory.[61] In the last analysis, the historical durability of concepts of memory depended on the durability and the expansion of inscriptive practices. Metaphor was the medium by means of which technologies of inscription were transplanted into the individual human subject. Memory as an object of psychological science owes many of its features to this deep historical background.[62]

The Aristotelian account had provided a first sketch of a model of internal memory that was entirely based on practices connected with external memory. As these practices developed and expanded, new features could be added to this model, and different aspects emphasized. Many implications of these practices that had at first been obscure became articles of faith in the course of time. Gradually, over many centuries, there developed an assembly of beliefs about individual memory with their roots in analogies derived from external memory. This assembly of beliefs can be regarded as offering the conceptual resources for what would be a standard account of memory as a reflection of inscriptive practices. Historically, no one writer gave explicit expression to these beliefs, but their explicit and implicit presence pervades large parts of Western discourse and practice regarding memory.

The popularity of this account tended to wax and wane with the spread or constriction of literacy. It thrived in Roman times, and then suffered eclipse, only to be revived at the height of the Middle Ages, when it benefited from the spread of a bookish monastic culture and any theory of memory based on the practices of literacy was assured of a bright future. In fact, some elements of an essentially Aristotelian account survived into the twentieth century.[63] What I have referred to as the standard account is still with us. It is therefore worth listing its more important analogically based components:

> First, there is the splitting of memory into three distinct operations: One, akin to writing, which records perceptions, a second which stores these records, and a third, akin to reading, which later retrieves something like the original perception from the stored records. These operations are linked in a unidirectional temporal sequence, constituting memory as a three-stage process. In late twentieth century psychology this model was generally taken for granted by experimentalists who frequently used it to organize their research as targeting 'encoding', storage, or retrieval, as the case might be. There were theories about what went on at each of these stages but the distinctions among the stages remained at the level of what was occasionally recognized as 'a pretheoretical orientation'.[64]

The analogy between remembering and inscriptive practices also leads to certain assumptions about the nature of what is stored in memory. As already noted, written inscriptions preserving the memory of something past represent a particular version of the past. Inscribing an account of an event, a piece of knowledge or a human action preserves them in a specific form. It is only in that form that they will be available for later inspection. Inscription provides a 'definitive version' of what is memorable, except for the relatively unusual case where more than one version of the same content was inscribed at the same time. This contrasts with oral speech situations, where there will typically be many remembered versions, often as many as there were participants or observers. If individual memory is interpreted as storing traces that are analogous to written inscriptions, those traces will be assumed to exist in a definitive form, usually as a copy of the original experience. The reproduction of a publicly available definitive version then becomes the paradigm case of human remembering. Many everyday instances of remembering patently do not fit the textual model, yet inscription of definitive texts as the central metaphor for memory has proved remarkably tenacious.[65]

As has already been noted, inscription spatializes representations. It transforms the flow of speech, for example, into symbols with spatial properties. Moreover, the manner of spatial representation is discontinuous. The inscriptions that become intertwined with conceptions of memory do not represent the world analogically but make use of separate elements, ideograms, letters, numbers, etc. These inscriptions leave a bounded spatial trace, a letter, a word, a drawing, that is distinct from other traces of their kind. When the theoretical imagination analogically transfers such inscriptions to the minds of individuals, storage in individual memory is also assumed to be in the form of separate units. If that is how memories are preserved in internal memory, remembering becomes a matter of dredging up specific items of inscribed experience. In antiquity this aspect of the inscription model proved useful in the development of mnemonic techniques that relied on a dissection of experience into specific components and the deliberate formation of imaginary links between them.[66] The spread of printing with individually handled movable type seems to have given new life to images of memory storage in terms of separate and distinct items. By the seventeenth century there was speculation about the number of 'ideas' that could be stored in one learning session, or over an individual's lifetime.[67] In more recent times, the experimental techniques of classical memory research investigated retention by counting the number of distinct 'items' remembered under different conditions.[68]

At this point it is important to note that the practice of writing, especially alphabetic writing, constitutes *one* form of inscriptive practice. Although writing is potentially by far the most important inscriptive practice, it took a long time for that potential to be realized. Because of its obvious importance writing is often used metonymically to stand for the whole range of inscriptive practices, but it does have its own special features.

Consider the fact that the inscriptions which constitute writing typically do not preserve the social features of speech – gestures, tone of voice, facial expressions, as well as other aspects of paracommunication that often convey participants' feelings, intentions, doubts, degree of seriousness and so on – all matters that indicate how their verbal communication is to be taken. What written inscriptions tend to preserve is some cognitive content that has been separated from the persons of speakers or listeners, writers or readers.[69] Although developments in the technique of written composition gradually found ways to describe features of interpersonal communication, their representation of these features necessarily substituted explicit verbal description for communications that were inherently fuzzy, ambiguous and analogical. Similarly, knowledge which remained implicit in human skills, shared projects, unarticulated beliefs, affective reactions, etc., could not be represented in verbal inscriptions unless it was reformulated in explicit terms. Thus, what could be conveyed through the medium of written texts remained essentially decontextualized knowledge. In principle, the meaning of a written inscription was preserved for anyone with the appropriate skills and did not depend on the social or human context of its production. (This potentially infinite mobility was of course one of the great advantages of written texts.) However, theories based on hidden analogies with written text were bound to fail in the face of memory for content that was deeply con-textualized or defied explicit verbal representation that was adequate to it.

As a source of analogies for memory, writing also privileges the semantic component. Where unadorned written text becomes the reigning paradigm, verbal memory becomes the model for the whole of memory. This is not yet the case in the Aristotelian account. Aristotelian memory images are not verbal; on the contrary, the emphasis seems to be on figurative images. This is an account based on the general features of inscriptive practice, not on its specifically linguistic form. One of these general features is the representative nature of what is stored in memory. Memory is a repository of signs, not of experiences. Signs are read, experiences are lived. But there is no insistence, no expectation even, that the signs would be verbal. Indeed, the admixture of verbal text and figurative representation continues in the artefacts of external memory for many centuries after Aristotle. Illuminated medieval manuscripts provide the best-known and most aesthetically pleasing examples. It is only from the period of the European Enlightenment onwards that the pure written text provides the essential and often the sole source of inscriptive metaphors for individual memory. Some aspects of this development will be discussed in subsequent chapters (especially chapters 3, 5 and 9).

Physical analogies

Plato had drawn analogies between variation in the properties of a block of wax and variations in the memory capacity of human individuals, but this remained strictly a metaphor. However, as we saw earlier, Aristotle already suggested that memorial imprinting involved the human body in ways that were subject to observable causal effects. Properties like hardness and fluidity were attributed to parts of the body and accounted for differences in memory capacity. In the old, for example:

> the receiving surface being frayed, as happens to old walls, or owing to the hardness of the receiving surface, the requisite impression is not implanted at all. Hence both very young and very old persons are defective in memory; they are in a state of flux, the former because of their growth, and the latter owing to their decay. Similarly, both those who are too quick and those who are too slow have bad memories. The former are too moist, the latter too hard, so that in the case of the former the image does not remain in the soul, while on the latter it is not imprinted at all.[70]

It hardly needs saying that modern, post-Cartesian, conceptions of mind–body relationships should on no account be read into these ancient texts. Of course, Aristotle and his contemporaries had no inkling of the Cartesian distinction between a *res extensa* and a *res cogitans*. So when he speaks of physical processes in living bodies these are not to be understood in terms of directionless mechanisms. Conversely, the Aristotelian soul, *psyche*, was by no means equivalent to pure mind or consciousness but was essentially a biological principle, distinguishing the living from the inanimate part of nature. Therefore, implicating the body in the formation of memory traces did not in any way exclude the soul. The question of whether memory traces are physical or mental would have been meaningless for Aristotle because the categories that divided up his world did not coincide with those of post-Cartesian dualism.[71]

Nevertheless, the change of medium from a metaphorical block of wax to the human body facilitated the assimilation of Aristotelian conceptions by classical Galenic medicine and its numerous derivatives. Within these medical systems there grew up a vast lore regarding physical remedies for problems of memory. Many of these remedies were *ad hoc*, and if they ever had a physical rationale, it was lost with the passing of centuries. In other cases, however, the link to ancient analogies was explicit. In the Middle Ages and beyond the seat of memory was commonly located at the back of the head (see chapter 8), and ointments applied to this part of the anatomy were recommended in the treatment of memory problems.[72] They were supposed to work because they generated heat and warmed the seat of memory, causing it to become more active. Direct heat was also sometimes recommended for the same reason. However, by the sixteenth century at the latest, there were also warnings about the dangers inherent in such measures. Giambattista della Porta, best known for his work on physiognomy, advises that the brain should be not too hot nor too cold, for 'from cold comes absent-mindedness, and from extreme cold comes lethargy, from much heat come fevers and madness'.[73] Hence he and others warned that the practice of warming the head, or at least its back, in order to cure problems of memory could be dangerous and cause madness and agitation.

After the early seventeenth century it is impossible not to notice a crucial change in the prominence, the nature and the function of physical analogies for memory. First of all, proposals for such analogies multiply and are discussed more seriously than before. Second, the analogies become *mechanical*, whereas previously they had been limited to ancient phenomenal qualities like dryness, heat, hardness, size and so on. In contrast to these readily perceptible qualities the physical analogies of this later period invoked a hypothetical world of invisible *machinery*, usually located in the brain and nerves, that was no mere analogy but was considered likely to have a real existence. Therefore, third, the appeal to this invisible machinery is not meant to further an analogical understanding of the qualities of memory by invoking 'similitudes',[74] but to provide a *causal* explanation of how memory might operate as a mechanical system. I will briefly describe three examples that illustrate this post-medieval change in the use of physical analogies, one each from the first and second half of the seventeenth century and one from the first half of the eighteenth.

The first and best-known example is provided by René Descartes (1596–1650), the philosopher and quasi-scientist whose work played a seminal role in establishing the contours of post-Renaissance thought. Descartes famously divided the world into pure thought (*res cogitans*) and matter (*res extensa*). Both parts were endowed with memory, but the 'intellectual memory' of pure thought was neither elaborated upon by Descartes nor is it relevant in the present context. Material memory, on the other hand, he described in some detail with the help of a series of physical models which he regarded not as metaphors but as representations of real processes. The earliest of these models surprisingly repeats the ancient image of impressions on wax. However, the explicit insistence on a real brain change is new: 'Nor must we think that a mere analogy is in question here: we must think of the external shape of the sentient body[75] as being really changed by the object in exactly the same way as the surface of the shape of the wax is altered by the seal'.[76]

Descartes also has other metaphors, but there is no indication that he considered them incompatible with the ancient wax version. One alternative was to think in terms of folding paper instead of making an impression on wax. The principle was the same: an impression is retained by a yielding surface that happens also to be a common material for recording written inscriptions.[77] However, as in the case of impressions on wax, Descartes rejects mere metaphor and claims that there really are folds in the brain (and in nerves and muscles) that retain memory impressions.

On other occasions Descartes seems to imply a certain resemblance of brain tissue to woven cloth. He imagines a structure consisting of fibres or filaments with spaces or holes between them. This may well be a more powerful model than wax or paper, because the combination of fibres and gaps is not a homogeneous surface but is *patterned*. When impressions are made on this cloth-like surface these patterns are changed, and that influences the receptiveness of the surface to future impressions. Folds in paper have a similar effect because of a tendency for the paper to fold again along the already existing creases. However, a weave of fibres offers more complex possibilities. In this case Descartes imagines the impressions consisting of changes in the size and shape of the 'pores' between the fibres and consequent rearrangements in the position of the fibres.[78] This model can accommodate subtle changes in the patterned structure of fibres and the spaces between them. The impressions themselves, according to Descartes, were made by 'animal spirits' travelling inside nerves and blood vessels, whose flow could also be influenced by movements of the pineal gland at the behest of the immaterial soul.[79] The more frequently these spirits flowed through certain 'pores' between fibres the easier their passage became. So once they started flowing into the pores of some previously established pattern of fibres and pores they would, taking the path of least resistance, flow into the rest of the pattern as well. This provided a mechanical basis for the successive recollection of previously associated impressions.

Descartes's model of animal spirits, conceived as invisible bits of highly mobile matter, flowing through nerves and through the tiny spaces between brain fibres, provided a kind of template for many later neural models of memory, even after the animal spirits were replaced by electrical impulses. This was a version of the inscription model that allowed for the possibility of inscription without human agency. Physical patterns and structures in the brain could be altered simply through the effect of material impulses that might originate, not in some human agency, but in a sense organ. Descartes himself seems to have thought that this accounted fully for memory in animals. However, in humans the soul intervened in this mechanism via the pineal gland. Subsequent versions of mechanism often made room for a similar kind of dualism even though the details of Descartes's story were generally rejected. Where dualism did not explicitly define the boundaries of mechanistic models a secret homunculus could usually be found lurking in some dark corner.

The next example of early modern forays into the physical explanation of memory is taken from a lecture given in 1682 by the Curator of Experiments to the Royal Society, Robert Hooke. Its title is revealing: *A Hypothetical Explication of Memory; how the Organs made use of by the Mind in its Operation may be mechanically understood.*[80] Hooke (1635–1702) was a prominent representative of the new approach to the investigation of natural phenomena which had become institutionalized in the Royal Society. Although he conducted no experiments on memory, he did draw on experimental observations in formulating his attempt at explaining memory, an explanation that was based on mechanical analogies from the material world. He did not question the ubiquitous equation between human memory and a storehouse, by now a dead metaphor, but he suggested new analogies for understanding how storage might come about. The source of these analogies was not the world of human activities, keeping coins in purses, treasures in boxes, inscriptions on wax or paper, but the material world of nature. His prize exhibit was the phenomenon of phosphorescence, exhibited by substances which did not reflect light but became luminescent after exposure to light. They seemed to store light! What if there was some such substance in the human brain? It might well store visual perceptions and 'emit' them later in the form of memories. Hooke also referred to bells and vases that did not reflect but re-emitted a changed sound, but phosphorescence remained the main source for his analogies.

A century earlier such analogies might well have occurred within an alchemical framework that endowed natural substances with spiritual qualities and whose natural analogies were therefore not strictly material at all. But Hooke's analogies were intended to refer to natural processes conceived as unambiguously material, in fact 'mechanically understood', as he says in his title. This was the novelty of his metaphor. Memory was no longer to be conceived as an essentially human, mindful activity, but as determined by material processes similar to those found in the inanimate world. No wonder Hooke had to be careful to avoid the very serious charge of materialism.[81] But in fact Hooke was a thoroughly modern dualist who had no wish to deny the soul its rightful place; he just insisted it did not belong in the mechanical world of matter. His universe was a post-Cartesian one, and this included a soul that had a seat somewhere in the brain and made use of the mechanical organ of memory.

Hooke's hypothetical model of this organ provided a glimpse of the wonders that mechanical metaphors held in store. Memory was to be regarded as sharing fundamental properties characteristic of physical systems. In particular, the contents of memory must be thought of as occupying space. However, this was not the everyday perceptual space of Aristotelian images but the mathematized space of a Cartesian *res extensa* that was uniform in all its parts. Memory contents were naturally composed of idea units, 'in themselves distinct ... and separate from another'.[82] In their arrangement these units displayed linearity, that is, they followed each other one by one without superimposition, fusion or other messiness. As time passed, new memory units were added to the line, so that the line itself constituted a spatial representation of a person's lifetime experience. With this network of metaphors in place Hooke could proceed to a topic that seemed particularly important to him, the introduction of 'Mensuration' into the field of memory. One could think of different individuals forming ideas in memory at different rates, and one could even ask questions about the number of memories the average person might have stored in his or her brain. Hooke thought the most reasonable guess for a man of fifty might be of the order of two million.[83]

Whereas the concept of memory storage might be given a physical and geometricized interpretation with some degree of plausibility, the phenomenon of remembering is far trickier. Whereas ideas are not conscious while stored, and could therefore have a purely physical existence, remembering those ideas seems to be a conscious phenomenon and must therefore involve the soul. Hooke took on this challenge by mobilizing yet another metaphor from the science of the time. Descartes' optical theory suggested to him that one could think of the soul as a kind of radiating sun whose rays strike all the stored ideas and provide it with a reflected image of everything that is in its somatic storehouse. The soul can then make use of this information as it wishes, retrieving this or that idea from storage, for example. Turning the soul into a radiating sun, however, provides but scant cover for the fact that it functions as a homunculus, a little man in the brain that is actually responsible for doing the remembering. But explaining the remembering performed by an actual person in terms of the work done by a little person in the head does not seem like much of an explanation at all. The phantom of the homunculus would return to haunt more modern memory theories based on mechanical metaphors even though they were much more sophisticated than Hooke in hiding the homunculus.

In any case, Hooke would not have been concerned to hide the homunculus. He was a religious man whose dualism served to preserve a place for the soul in an otherwise material universe. His immediate successors, however, found other ways of rescuing religion from any scepticism induced by the new science of nature. They realized that science could be placed in the service of religion if one supposed that the laws of the physical world were in fact God's laws which He had designed to produce outcomes that incorporated His purpose in creating the world. This opened up the possibility of using physical analogues of human attributes in order to demonstrate Divine Providence. Such was the goal of David Hartley (1705–57), a student of medicine, mathematics and theology, who applied Newtonian principles to human physiology in order to show that humans were so constituted as to enact a divinely preordained moral order.[84]

In pursuit of this project Hartley proposed that sensory impressions produced physical vibrations in the nerves and ultimately in the brain. These vibrations continued after the cessation of their sensory origin in the form of little vibrations, or 'vibratiuncles', which constituted the physical basis of memory traces. What was most significant about these nervous vibrations, however, was their interaction. Vibrations produced in close temporal proximity became linked, and the more frequent this linkage the stronger it became. Now, when one of these vibrations occurred on its own, it would automatically 'excite' others with which it had become linked. The psychological result is that, when two sensations have frequently occurred together in the past, the occurrence of just one of them will automatically call the other to mind. Hartley had provided a physical analogue for what was then becoming known as mental association. The association of sensations was the simplest case, but associations could also be formed among and between ideas and movements.

As a physical model for memory processes Hartley's version repeated the unitising and the linearity of memory content that had already been present in Hooke's version. But, as a naturalistic explanation of remembering, it was superior to the latter because the intervention of the soul was no longer required. Whereas in Hooke's model, ideas had to 'excite' the soul in order to be recovered from the repository of memory, in Hartley's model the physical traces of ideas merely have to excite each other in order for one to lead to the memory of the other. The soul has become dispensable. It so happened that Hartley's Newtonian physiology proved to be a dead end. Nerves were not solid conductors of vibrations and 'vibratiuncles' were not plausible representations of what happened in the brain. Nevertheless, the idea of providing memory with a physical basis by positing the formation of excitable links among nervous units was to be revived in the nineteenth century and to survive in the twentieth.

As for Hartley's machinery of vibrating nerves, even his own supporters soon discarded it as so much unnecessary baggage.[85] All that one really needed for a naturalistic model of memory was the supposition that there was an analogy between the principles of Newtonian physics and the principles on which the human mind operated. The material instantiation of these principles was not important. David Hume (1711–76), a philosophically more competent contemporary of Hartley's, fully recognized this when he elaborated an alternative version of an associationistic mental philosophy. Like Hartley, Hume was highly impressed by Newtonian natural philosophy and regarded it as a model to be followed in explaining the coming and going of mental events. However, with greater insight than Hartley, he did not see the potential psychological relevance of Newtonianism in the relatively low level theory of vibrations, but in the overall approach that sought the explanation of phenomena in the forces that operated between corpuscular bodies. After Newton, this was thought to be the way the physical world operated, and the emergent theory of association among mental contents seemed to provide the mental analogue to that understanding of the physical world. If mental contents could be regarded as corpuscular in character – distinct ideas and impressions, for example – then the mental associations between them could be regarded as analogues of the forces (gravity, for example) that held the physical world together. That is exactly what Hume proposed. In reference to the principles of mental association he wrote:

> These are therefore the principles of union or cohesion among our simple ideas, and in the imagination supply the place of that inseparable connexion, by which they are united in our memory. Here is a kind of *attraction*, which in the mental world will be found to have as extraordinary effects as in the natural, and to show itself in as many and as varied forms. Its effects are everywhere conspicuous; but as to its causes, they are mostly unknown.[86]

With this model in place the recall of mental contents from memory can be explained in terms of the operation of the natural laws of association conceived as analogues of the natural laws of physics. The phenomena of recollection depend as little on the intervention of a spiritual agency or soul as the rotation of the earth around the sun depends on the intervention of God. Deists like Newton and Hartley could believe that natural laws had a divine origin; the sceptical Hume was quite content to believe that this origin, like so many other things, was simply unknown. In the course of time, this form of 'mental mechanism'[87] proved highly attractive to the embryonic science of psychology because it provided a framework within which a mechanistic psychology could flourish without being dependent on the advancement of physiological knowledge. This mechanistic psychology benefited from a certain historical amnesia for its original analogical relationship to Newtonian mechanics.

Computer memory

Two nineteenth-century inventions, photography and the phonograph, marked a return to memory metaphors based on specific physical models. Both were followed by attempts to draw analogies between their functioning and the operation of human memory.[88] Unlike the source models employed by Hartley and Hooke, however, photographic plates and phonographs were human creations, artefacts of a civilization that had become industrial. They were early examples of a new generation of recording devices that became part of everyday life from the beginning of the twentieth century. Familiarity with such devices was likely to enhance the plausibility of accounts that constructed memory in the image of such devices. The appeal to modern inventions could also convey an illusion of conceptual progress, a feeling that explanations based on recent technological advances must be better than older variants.

But in fact the modernity in this case was quite superficial. When transferred to the level of human memory the model of the recording device strongly resembled ideas that had been part of the empiricist philosophy of mind for some time. In both cases memory has a passive registering function that converts sensory input into a sensory trace that can be reactivated so as to reproduce the original input. The equation of memory and reproduction had been proposed by empiricist philosophers long before the advent of modern recording devices. But at a deeper level the appeal to these devices can also be regarded as a modern form of the master metaphor of inscription. Wax tablets may have been replaced by photographic plates and magnetic tapes, but memory is once again likened to an inscription on a medium that permits relatively permanent storage of a likeness that can later be recovered. However, the notion that such an inscription has the symbolic character of writing is not preserved in these latter-day variants of the metaphor.

The advent of the digital computer changed that. Computers were not primarily recording devices but machines for solving logical/computational problems. Logic machines combined the modern passion for physical instantiation with the much more ancient interest in symbolic representation. The content of their 'processing' could be given a consistent symbolic interpretation by the human user who typed input or read the output of these machines, yet at the same time, they *were* physical devices whose operations depended entirely on an application of the appropriate technology. As metaphors for human cognitive processes logic machines had a peculiar status. There was always a strong temptation to regard their operations as providing not simply an analogy, but a *simulation* of human cognition. They were 'machines that think'.

In order to perform their computational tasks computers had to have some capacity for storing instructions in the form of electronic information. At first, such storage was not referred to as 'memory', and in some languages that is still not common practice.[89] However, in 1945 the *emigré* mathematician von Neumann developed a highly speculative analogy between digital computers and brains in the course of which he endowed computers with what he called a 'memory', a storage component that enabled them to 'remember'.[90] His use of 'memory' with reference to computers was strictly metaphorical, for he had no hard evidence to support the analogy between computer storage and biological memory, but he clearly meant the analogy to be taken seriously as a working hypothesis guiding future research. He believed that computer storage and biological memory *really* were profoundly similar. Unlike Plato's wax tablet or Descartes's woven cloth, the concept of computer 'memory' was not meant to be taken *merely* metaphorically; it also implied that the same kind of machinery really was at work in the computer and in the brain.

One reason von Neumann's terminology caught on was that it fitted in with a new approach to human–machine relationships that had begun during World War II and became firmly established during the subsequent transition to the Cold War. The progressive mechanization of military tasks, especially in the US forces, led to a thorough interlocking of human and machine functions and the formation of so-called man–machine systems. The development and technical improvement of such systems required that similar terms be used in reference to the functions of humans and machines.[91] As digital computers became a vital part of man–machine systems and took over some of the previously human functions the analogy between the capabilities of humans and computers became more and more compelling. Memory, in the sense of the retention of 'information', was an obvious example of these shared capabilities.

Subsuming computer storage and human memory under the same category of 'memory' always had the potential to suggest the use of computers as models for human memory. American psychologists at major centres of academic influence were particularly susceptible to the charms of the new analogy because of lingering doubts about their discipline's scientific status. Emulation of the 'hard' sciences had become an accepted part of building a truly scientific psychology in the 1930s, and that had led to engineering models of the mind, such as the telephone exchange.[92] For a psychologist whose professional outlook had been formed in this atmosphere, the digital computer could appear as the perfect model for the human mind. One of the key figures in this development exclaimed at the end of the century: 'The generation before me felt that you couldn't use a term without having a physical instantiation of it, we now have physical instantiations, by means of computers, of fabulous things.'[93]

However, before those research psychologists who had not worked closely with communication engineers were ready to take up the computer model, they had to become familiar with the use of these devices. It is only with the gradual incorporation of computers into psychological research practice that memory models based on the computer metaphor began to have a profound and widespread appeal among psychologists.[94] The first group of psychologists who became familiar with the use of computers were those who had actually been involved in the relevant military research. But their use of the metaphor was limited to so-called short-term memory, the kind of memory that is actually found in man–machine systems.[95] It is a huge step from this context to the kinds of phenomena that would ordinarily be regarded as examples of human memory, and the first widely adopted model of 'long-term' memory based on the computer metaphor was not published until 1968.[96] By that time a sufficient number of psychologists were becoming familiar with the operation of computers to make the following decade the period when this kind of model achieved dominance in the field of memory research. In the following years, theorizing inspired by computers continued to exert a profound effect.[97]

Of course, the advent of digital computers did represent a revolution in the technology of human external memory. The widespread replacement of printed records by electronic records certainly evokes analogies with the much earlier replacement of pictorial records by writing. One analogy is suggested by the reluctance with which theoretical discourse adapts to the new reality. Plato, as we have seen, was ambivalent about the implications of what was for him a fairly new-fangled technology. He seized on it as a source for his wax tablet model of memorial inscription, but he also expressed his suspicions of the new techniques in his important distinction between remembering and reminding. Aristotle was more complacent about the inscription metaphor, and, crucially, insisted on the symbolic, representational quality of what memory retained. But he still gave pride of place to analogical representations in the form of imagery. The shift to writing (and the bookish products of writing) as the essential prototype for the inscriptions of memory was slow and not quite completed until the beginning of the modern age.

One would expect the influence of the computer metaphor to make itself felt much more rapidly than that, and indeed it has. Yet it already seems clear that during the first few decades of its reception the main effect of the new technology was to reinforce existing presuppositions about the operations of memory. The storage function built into digital computers was regarded as yet another inscription device that need not disturb the ancient three-stage model of writing, storage and reading. What had changed was the nature of the symbolic medium. The long-completed change from pictorial images to written text was now followed by a switch to logical symbolism. Computers are logic machines. They process and store information, not in the form of analogical pictorial representations or alphabetic writing, but in the form of digital symbols with logical interrelationships. Therefore the generic processes of writing and reading now take the form of translating from ordinary text or image into computer language and back again. What is fed into the computer is first re-inscribed by being *encoded* and then retrieved by being *decoded*.

Inscription had always involved a kind of translation, from perceptual to graphic image, from a direct experience to a textual representation, for example. The interpolation of computer language added a further step to the process of translation but did not call for a revision of the generic metaphor of inscription. However, familiarity with computers certainly helped to draw attention to the topic of translation. The computer analogy encouraged the assumption that memory traces must be stored in some kind of representational code, with the result that questions about human memory tended to become questions about the relationship between the encoding and subsequent decoding of these coded mnemonic traces.[98]

The conservative aspect of the computer as memory model also made itself felt in conceptions regarding the nature of the code for inscribing memory traces. That this code has the properties of written text is an ancient idea, although there was always the alternative of analogical, pictorial representation. Two major implications of the analogy with written text were powerfully reinforced by the example of the digital computer. First, the memory code was assumed to be written in discrete finite symbols (just like the letters of the alphabet) that produced complex patterns by syntactic combination. Second, this was a code that excluded representation of the contextual features of human gestural and speech interaction that had also been excluded by alphabetic writing. In fact, computer language preserved this aspect of literary inscription in an exaggerated form, being limited to logical connections among its discrete symbols. With these features, computer analogies would inevitably strengthen purely cognitive conceptions of human memory that ignored the embeddedness of cognitive operations in affectively toned motivated action.

In so far as computer memory became the paradigm for human memory there was a confirmation of the traditional literate conception of memory as a kind of record-keeping. What is stored in memory exists in the form of an explicitly formulated definitive version, an unambiguous description, of some state of affairs. Remembering then involves a search for the stored item that best corresponds to the requested information, rather like an actual computer search of a defined data base. But in this kind of task computers functioned much better than humans. Was human memory essentially an inferior version of computer memory, or was it quite different? Perhaps the most important long-term result of the earlier enthusiasm for computer analogies was the gradual recognition that computer memory represents a sort of counter-example demonstrating what human memory is not.

Dazzled by an ever-accelerating technological bonanza, early advocates of the computer analogy were inclined to overestimate its revolutionary implications and to overlook its hidden conservative features. One of these features had become an article of faith for Western conceptions of memory centuries before the digital computer was thought of. I am referring to the deeply ingrained notion that memory must be something entirely within the individual, more specifically within the head. From the wax tablets of Plato to the woven cloth of Descartes, the metaphorical imagery of memory had been assigned a definite location, and that location was inside the skin. The possibility that memory might be an intrinsic feature of an individual's relationship to an outside world was effectively excluded by all the standard analogies.[99]

The first generation of computer analogies was entirely in thrall to this ancient tradition. It was machinery enclosed by the cranium that was likened to a digital computer. Although this machinery is part of an ongoing system of organism–environment interactions, the computer analogy perpetuated the idea that only what went on inside the brain–computer was relevant to an understanding of memory, the relationship to the environment being something extraneous that could be added on *ad hoc*. Computers have no contact with any world outside the symbols fed into them. They are logic machines, and, in their most common employment, the utilization of their output for action in and on the real world was left to human operators. The metaphor of the isolated computer therefore perpetuates and even exaggerates the traditional divorce between individuals' private equipment and the world they must live in. That life provides them with a history in the world that computers lack. It is this history that forms the basis of memory. Designers of computers make up for the absence of history by installing programs.[100] When this became the model for the operation of human memory in real-life settings, human action was interpreted as script-following, the script-in-the-head functioning like a linear computer program.[101] For such a model to work, the (social) environment had to remain essentially unchanged. That might be exactly the case in laboratory investigations, but an account of the role of memory in adapting to a constantly changing world would require a different basis.[102]

In any case, the major impact of the computer metaphor was not to be found in specific attempts at computer simulation of human memory, but on the level of conceptualization and language. What had become firmly established after half a century of usage was a language that referred to the accomplishments of humans and 'thinking machines' in exactly the same terms. This was the language of 'information processing', the product of a multiple metaphorical transfer of terms from psychology to computer engineering and vice versa. The early use of the psychological term 'memory' to characterize computer storage was only the most far-reaching of many similar borrowings. The term 'information' to refer to the stuff on which memory operated came a close second. It made it possible to speak of human memory and the electronic storage of logical formalizations as though the profound differences between them did not matter. But because the technical and the everyday meaning of 'information' persisted, the term merely became thoroughly corrupted, its ambiguity frequently serving as the basis for false claims of scientific precision on the one hand and applications to everyday life on the other. Other terms that wandered across the boundary between psychology and computer engineering in both directions, carrying their metaphorical baggage with them, were 'search', 'input', 'output', 'address', 'matching', 'retrieval' and 'encoding', though these were not the only ones.

It must be emphasized that these borrowings were not just a matter of terminological convenience. These terms were not isolated symbols. Together, they formed a conceptual framework that could be fleshed out by means of specific theories, but only certain kinds of theories fitted this framework. This could easily lead to the creation of a closed conceptual world in which anything that was not expressible in the language of information processing remained unseen, unrecognized and unexplored. However, this language did prove very useful in allowing communication between otherwise diverse disciplinary communities. Having started as a way of describing the behaviour of human–machine systems, the metaphorical language of information processing blossomed into a medium for scientific talk across disciplinary fences.[103]

Notes

1. A. Koriat and M. Goldsmith, 'Memory metaphors and the real-life/laboratory controversy: Correspondence versus storehouse conceptions of memory', *Behavioral and Brain Sciences* 19 (1996), 167–228.
2. Draaisma, *Metaphors of memory*.
3. P. Ricoeur, *The rule of metaphor*, trans. R. Czerny (Toronto: University of Toronto Press, 1977).
4. S.C. Pepper, *World hypotheses* (Berkeley: University of California Press, 1942).
5. K. Danziger, 'Generative metaphor and the history of psychological discourse', in D.E. Leary (ed.), *Metaphors in the history of psychology* (New York: Cambridge University Press, 1990), pp. 331–56.
6. See, for example, E.F. Loftus, *Memory: Surprising new insights into how we remember and why we forget* (Reading, MA: Addison-Wesley, 1980).
7. W. James, *Principles of psychology* (New York: Holt, 1890), vol. I, p. 654.
8. S. Freud, *A general introduction to psychoanalysis* (New York: Washington Square Press, 1924/1952), p. 305.
9. J. Locke, *An essay concerning human understanding* (New York: Dover, 1690/1959), p. 193.
10. St Augustine, *Confessions* (Oxford: Oxford University Press, 1991).
11. Carruthers, *Book of memory*, pp. 33–45.
12. H.L. Roediger III, 'Memory metaphors in cognitive psychology', *Memory & Cognition* 8 (1980), 231–46.
13. Plato, *Thaetetus*, 197e, in E. Hamilton and H. Cairns (eds.), *The collected dialogues of Plato* (Princeton, NJ: Princeton University Press, 1963).
14. Plato, *Thaetetus*, 198d.

15. Aristotle, *On memory*, in J. Barnes (ed.), *The complete works of Aristotle* (Princeton, NJ: Princeton University Press, 1984), vol. I, pp. 714–20.
16. Draaisma, *Metaphors of memory*.
17. Plato, *Thaetetus*, 191c–d.
18. Hesiod, *Theogeny*, 24: 22–32, in R. M. Frazer (trans.), *The poems of Hesiod* (Norman: University of Oklahoma Press, 1983).
19. R. Lamberton, 'Introduction', in S. Lombardo (trans.), *Hesiod:* Works and days *and* Theogeny (Indianapolis: Hackett, 1993).
20. A. B. Lord, *The singer of tales* (Cambridge, MA: Harvard University Press, 1964). See also D. C. Rubin, *Memory in oral traditions: The cognitive psychology of epic, ballads, and counting-out rhymes* (Oxford: Oxford University Press, 1995).
21. E. A. Havelock, *The muse learns to write: Reflections on orality and literacy from antiquity to the present* (New Haven: Yale University Press, 1986), p. 79.
22. However, this does not mean that these poets had no sense of human intentionality, as some modern writers have concluded. For a critique of this interpretation of the ancient texts, see I. Leudar and P. Thomas, *Voices of reason, voices of insanity: Studies of verbal hallucinations* (London: Routledge, 2000), chapter 2.
23. Metaphors of oral narration are often based on the activity of *spinning*, using images of yarn, spindle and loom. See I. Illich and B. Sanders, *The alphabetization of the popular mind* (San Francisco: North Point Press, 1988), p. 30. Even today it is still possible to 'spin a yarn'. But as a metaphor for the operations of memory, spinning never achieved great importance. Did its gendered associations have anything to do with this? Remarkably, all the figures associated with oral remembrance in Greek myth were female. This is a dimension that invites further study.
24. Plato, *Thaetetus*, 194c, d, e; 195a.
25. Plato, *Philebus*, 39a, in E. Hamilton and H. Cairns (eds.), *The collected dialogues of Plato* (Princeton, NJ: Princeton University Press, 1963).
26. Carruthers, *Book of memory*, pp. 21–2.
27. The historian who knows the relevant literature better than anyone writes: 'It has been remarkable to me ... that none of the texts I have encountered makes the slightest distinction in kind between writing on the memory and writing on some other surface.' Carruthers, *Book of memory*, p. 30.
28. Plato's metaphor achieved the status of a prototype, so that a contemporary scholar was able to use it quite appropriately in the title of her monograph on memory in classical antiquity: Small, *Wax tablets of the mind*.
29. M. T. Cicero, *De oratore*, in J. S. Watson (ed.), *Cicero on oratory and orators* (Carbondale, IL: Southern Illinois University Press, 1970), p. 189.
30. See chapter 3.
31. Carruthers, *Book of memory*.
32. Draaisma, *Metaphors of memory*, pp. 45–6.
33. W. V. Harris, *Ancient literacy* (Cambridge, MA: Harvard University Press, 1989).
34. Aristotle already mentions the usefulness of writing and reading 'in money-making, in the management of a household, in the acquisition of knowledge, and in political life' (*Politics*, 1338a, pp. 15–17), but it was the Romans who greatly extended the administrative applications of writing.
35. On the other hand, it does not seem that the polysemous nature of the Greek and Latin words for reading has any unambiguous implications for the direction of metaphorical transfer from internal to external memory or the reverse, because these are not explicitly and exclusively memory words. Here I differ from Carruthers, *Book of memory*, p. 30.
36. Harris, *Ancient literacy*.
37. T. M. Lentz, *Orality and literacy in Hellenic Greece* (Carbondale, IL: Southern Illinois University Press, 1989).

38. The adoption of writing by the Greeks was quite a gradual process. Initially, it was used more as an adjunct to oral communication, but by the time of Plato it had achieved considerable autonomy and was accorded greater respect. See R. Thomas, *Literacy and orality in Ancient Greece* (Cambridge: Cambridge University Press, 1992).

39. There is a certain analogy between adopting the new inscriptive technology of writing and the initial adoption of personal computers: 'The computer revolution resembles the Greek Revolution in that it too has as one of its major elements the intertwined issues of memory and literacy.' Small, *Wax tablets*, p. 243.

40. S. Burke, ' "Who speaks? Who writes?" Dialogue and authorship in the *Phaedrus*', *History of the Human Sciences* 10 (1997), 40–55.

41. It is perhaps significant that Plato turned to wax tablets for his metaphor and not to a surface that might have been more suitable for a permanent inscription. Wax tablets were more likely to be used for exercises, notes, memos and other relatively short-term purposes, because the inscriptions could be easily wiped out and the surface reused (see note 37). Making the link to contemporary categories, one could say that Plato's wax tablet model had more in common with notions of short-term than long-term memory. Plato's views on memory's more profound aspect, *anamnesis*, are discussed in chapter 4.

42. Plato, *Phaedrus*, 275a, in E. Hamilton and H. Cairns (eds.), *The collected dialogues of Plato* (Princeton, NJ: Princeton University Press, 1963).

43. Plato, *Phaedrus*, 275d. The belief that reliance on writing weakens the memory was not uncommon in antiquity (and beyond). For example, Julius Caesar comments on the Druids' prohibition against writing down their sacred lore by suggesting that they did not wish 'to see their pupils neglect their memory by relying on writing, for it almost always happens that making use of texts has as its result decreased zeal for learning by heart and a diminution of memory'. (Cited in Le Goff, *History and memory*, p. 57.)

44. Plato, *Phaedrus*, 275d.

45. Plato, *Phaedrus*, 276a.

46. J. Fentress and C. Wickham, *Social memory* (Oxford: Blackwell, 1992), p. 9.

47. John Shotter has criticized contemporary cognitive psychology for having paid no attention to Plato's 'distinction between … an embodied remembering which is, so to speak, continuous with one's existence as the person one is, and a remembering which is dependent upon "traces", "representations" or other "external signs" of some kind'. J. Shotter, 'The social construction of remembering and forgetting', in D. Middleton and D. Edwards (eds.), *Collective remembering* (London: Sage, 1990), pp. 120–38 (p. 136).

48. However, in their practical approach to the reading of texts, later generations did attempt to make texts answer back by developing techniques of textual interpretation. Eventually, this led to theories of hermeneutics and an understanding of the relationship between text and reader that took its cue from Plato's Socratic *method* of questioning rather than his prejudice against texts. See H.-G. Gadamer, *Truth and method* (London: Sheed and Ward, 1979), pp. 325–41; also U. Eco, *The open work*, trans. A Cangogni (Cambridge, MA: Harvard University Press, 1989).

49. Aristotle, *On memory*, 450a, 29–31.

50. Aristotle, *On memory*, 453a, 33.

51. Aristotle, *On memory*, 450a, 29.

52. Aristotle, *On memory*, 449b, 35.

53. M. Warnock, *Memory* (London: Faber & Faber, 1987), p. 16. Although silent reading did not become common until much later, and hearing was still implicated in reading in Aristotle's time, experience with a spatially extended recording medium now becomes crucial for developing models of internal memory.

54. It is in Aristotle that one first finds extensive discussion of philosophical positions in terms of the relevant texts. Thomas, *Literacy and orality*.

55. Earlier claims regarding the conceptual consequences of literacy, especially in its alphabetical form, as in Havelock, *The muse learns to write*, have been largely discredited: See, for example, D. H. Green, 'Orality and reading: The state of research in medieval studies', *Speculum* 65 (1990), 267–80. However, there may have been a temptation to throw out the baby with the bathwater: A. B. Lord, *The singer resumes the tale* (Ithaca, NY: Cornell University Press, 1995). There are 'transitional texts' (Lord) that show an influence of literacy without losing features more characteristic of oral transmission.

56. The classical demonstration of this is to be found in S. Scribner and M. Cole, *The psychology of literacy* (Cambridge, MA: Harvard University Press, 1981). On the broader issues of substituting the technology for the social practice, see N. Ueno, 'The reification of artifacts in ideological practice', *Mind, Culture, and Activity* 2 (1995), 230–9.

57. For examples from some non-European cultures, see R. Finnegan, *Literacy and orality: Studies in the technology of communication* (Oxford: Blackwell, 1988); R. Narsimhan, 'Literacy: Its characterization and implications', in D. R. Olson and N. Torrance (eds.), *Literacy and orality* (Cambridge: Cambridge University Press, 1991), pp. 177–97.

58. J. Brockmeier, 'Literacy as symbolic space', in J. W. Astington (ed.), *Minds in the making* (Oxford: Blackwell, 2000). Also, D. R. Olson, 'Literate mentalities', in D. R. Olson and N. Torrance (eds.), *Modes of thought: Explorations in culture and cognition* (Cambridge: Cambridge University Press, 1996), pp. 141–51.

59. 'A book is a cognitive tool only for those who know how to read.' D. A. Norman, *Things that make us smart: Defending human attributes in the age of the machine* (Reading, MA: Addison-Wesley, 1993), p. 47.

60. This is discussed in the next chapter.

61. The analogy between the emergence of 'language' and 'memory' as epistemic objects has been noted in J. Brockmeier, *Literales Bewusstsein: Schriftlichkeit und das Verhältnis von Sprache und Kultur* (Munich: Fink, 1997), pp. 228–32.

62. Danziger, 'How old is psychology'.

63. The ghost of Aristotle haunted the 'imageless thought' controversy in early twentieth-century psychology as well as empiricist theories of memory from Hume to Bertrand Russell. See G. Humphrey, *Thinking* (London: Methuen, 1950); and N. Malcolm, *Memory and mind* (Ithaca, NY: Cornell University Press, 1977).

64. M. J. Watkins, 'Mediationism and the obfuscation of memory', *American Psychologist* 45 (1990), 328–35.

65. D. Edwards and J. Potter, *Discursive psychology* (London: Sage, 1992), See also chapter 9.

66. These techniques are discussed in chapter 3.

67. J. Willis, *The art of memory as it dependeth upon places and ideas* (London: Jones, 1621).

68. See chapter 5.

69. Olson, *The world on paper*.

70. Aristotle, *On memory*, 450b, 4–11.

71. Modern authors have often found it difficult to come to terms with this fact. See C. D. Green, 'The thoroughly modern Aristotle: Was he really a functionalist?', *History of Psychology* 1 (1998), 8–20.

72. The last of a long line of medically influenced memory treatises includes this prescription: 'Divers Plaisters, when we find a Decay in Memory, may be useful for the helping the brain: As a Plaister made of Mustard-seed, and clapt to the hinder part of the Head, or the Oil of Mustard-seed when applied to that Part. Or if you please to be at greater Expense, take Florentine, Lilies, the Herbs *Hermodactyle* and

Pyrethrum, Leaves of the wild Vine, Pigeon-dung, Mustard-seed, of each an Ounce; mix them with *Moschata* Nuts, Spice, Cloves, Cinnamon, and Pepper, and make a Plaister, which you may likewise apply to the hinder part of the Head, and you will find it will increase and help the Memory.' M. D'Assigny, *The art of memory: A treatise useful for such as are to speak in publick* (London: Andrew Bell, 1697), p. 55. This volume, closely modelled on one by Gulielmus Gratarolus published in 1553, was more characteristic of a period that was about to close than of new developments then in the offing. (See also A. B. Laver, 'D'Assigny and the art of memory', *Journal of the History of the Behavioral Sciences* 9 (1973), 240–50.)

73. Cited in Bolzoni, *Gallery of memory*, pp. 145–6.

74. M. Foucault, *The order of things* (London: Tavistock, 1970).

75. Descartes is referring to the brain.

76. R. Descartes, in J. Cottingham, R. Stoothoff and D. Murdoch (trans.), *Descartes: The philosophical writings* (Cambridge: Cambridge University Press, 1985), vol. I, p. 40.

77. Cottingham, *Descartes*, vol. III, p. 143.

78. Cottingham, *Descartes*, vol. I, pp. 107, 344.

79. The notion of 'animal spirits' had a very messy ancestry which is of only tangential interest here; see G. S. Rousseau, 'Discourses of the nerve', in F. Amrine (ed.), *Literature and science as modes of expression* (Dordrecht: Kluwer, 1989), pp. 29–60; D. P. Walker, *Music, spirit, and language in the Renaissance* (London: Variorum Reprints, 1985). Unlike earlier writers, Descartes seems to have thought of animal spirits in essentially materialist terms; this is discussed further in chapter 8.

80. In R. Waller (ed.), *The posthumous works of Robert Hooke* (London: Smith & Walford, 1705).

81. For a concise appreciation of Hooke's views, see G. Richards, *Mental machinery: The origins and consequences of psychological ideas from 1600 to 1850* (London: Athlone Press, 1992), pp. 67–9.

82. B. R. Singer, 'Robert Hooke on memory, association and time perception', *Notes and Records of the Royal Society of London* 31 (1976), 115–31 (p. 120).

83. For a more detailed account of Hooke's speculations, see Draaisma, *Metaphors*, chapter 3.

84. D. Hartley, *Observations on man, his frame, his duty, and his expectations*, (London: 1749; reprinted by Scholars' Facsimiles & Reprints, Gainsville, FL, 1966; and by Georg Olms Verlagsbuchhandlung, Hildesheim, 1967).

85. Joseph Priestley, a great admirer of Hartley, republished the latter's major work without the hypothetical physiology in 1775. It was this version that became widely known and appreciated among nineteenth-century associationists such as James Mill.

86. D. Hume, *A treatise of human nature*, 2nd edn, ed. L. A. Selby-Bigge (Oxford: Clarendon Press, 1978; first published 1739), pp. 12–13.

87. For an introduction to 'mental mechanism' and its Newtonian roots, see R. Lowry, *The evolution of psychological theory: 1650 to the present* (Chicago: Aldine, 1971). For a more general introduction to 'the culture of Newtonianism', see B. J. T. Dobbs and M. C. Jacob, *Newton and the culture of Newtonianism* (Atlantic Highlands, NJ: Humanities Press, 1995).

88. These attempts are described in some detail in Draaisma, *Metaphors*.

89. In German, for example, a computer's 'memory' has always been just a *Speicher*, a store.

90. J. Shurkin, *Engines of the mind: A history of the computer* (New York: Norton, 1984).

91. P. N. Edwards, *The closed world: Computers and the politics of discourse in Cold War America* (Cambridge, MA: MIT Press, 1996). This development is discussed further in the last section of chapter 6.

92. This was particularly noticeable in the work of Clark Hull, for a time the most admired of the 'neo-behaviourists', who was in fact trained as an engineer.

93. From an interview with G. A. Miller in B. J. Baars, *The cognitive revolution in psychology* (New York: Guilford Press, 1986). The background for these sentiments is explored in H. Crowther-Heyck, 'George A. Miller, language, and the computer metaphor', *History of Psychology* 2 (1999), 37–64.

94. This is an example of Gerd Gigerenzer's 'tools to theories' process in which the properties of research tools become the source for theoretical models in psychology. See G. Gigerenzer and G. Goldstein, 'Mind as computer: Birth of a metaphor', *Creativity Research Journal* 9 (1996), 131–44; G. Gigerenzer, 'Discovery in cognitive psychology: New tools inspire new theories', *Science in Context* 5 (1992), 329–50; G. Gigerenzer, 'From tools to theories: A heuristic of discovery in cognitive psychology', *Psychological Review* 98 (1991), 254–67.

95. This is discussed in chapter 6.

96. R. L. Atkinson and R. M. Shiffrin, 'Human memory: A proposed system and its control processes', in K. W. Spence and J. T. Spence (eds.), *The psychology of learning and motivation: Advances in research and theory* (New York: Academic Press, 1968), vol. II, pp. 90–197.

97. For an extensive exposition, see P. N. Johnson-Laird, *The computer and the mind* (Cambridge, MA: Harvard University Press, 1988).

98. Quite often, the term *retrieval* is used instead of decoding. But this term does not have a fixed meaning. For some, it is little more than a synonym for decoding, but for others it conveys a wider reference to contextual factors.

99. As we have already seen, Plato understood that inscription was not the perfect model for memory. He also recognized that the memory within required a 'midwife' outside to become manifest. This thread is taken up again in the last section of this book.

100. C. Carello, M. T. Turvey, P. N. Kugler and R. E. Shaw, 'Inadequacies of the computer metaphor', in M. S. Gazzaniga (ed.), *Handbook of cognitive neuroscience* (New York: Plenum, 1984), pp. 229–48. The problem of history also arises on the level of 'hardware'. In the digital computer, both hardware and software are installed in a finished form and do not affect each other subsequently. In the human organism, the construction of the 'hardware' (brain circuits) occurs over a period of time and depends on the individual's interaction with an environment. There is an interesting discussion of this aspect in J.-P. Changeux and A. Connes, *Conversations on mind, matter and mathematics* (Princeton, NJ: Princeton University Press, 1995), pp. 168–71.

101. The classical example was the extremely influential script model of Atkinson and Shiffrin, referred to in note 96. For some of the reverberations of this 'modal model', see Gardner, *Mind's new science*, 122–4.

102. Note that it is the metaphorical role of the *isolated* computer that is at issue here, because that is the way the computer metaphor was generally applied in late twentieth-century memory psychology. Computer networks working in parallel and computers as a component in robotics are not subject to some of the critical considerations summarized here. See chapter 9 for some further discussion of these alternatives.

103. The background for the emergence of the language of information processing is further discussed in the last sections of chapters 5 and 6. See also Draaisma, *Metaphors*, for a useful account of this metaphorical language.

3   The cultivation of memory

From the singer of tales to the art of memory

Recitations of oral poetry, oral history, legends, epics and religious incantations always made heavy demands on memory. In ancient Greece, poets and bards would appeal for divine inspiration to help them with their performance. But they did not leave it at that: they also had other means of helping their memory along. The poet Hesiod, as we saw in the last chapter, may have appealed to the goddess of remembrance, but there is no mention of her by Homer, who is not likely to have lived all that long before Hesiod (where 'Homer' stands for the person or persons who collected the texts we know as the Homeric epics). Perhaps 'he' found the other memory aids at his disposal quite adequate without additional divine help. These aids consisted first of the rhythmic strumming of a musical instrument together with regular variations in intonation, and second of a plethora of mnemonic devices built into the text, such as metre, alliteration, rhyming, repetitive phrasing, formulaic word patterns and so on. However, there is no indication that these aids were ever thought of collectively and explicitly as a mnemonic art. They were *ad hoc* practical devices that were automatically acquired as part of the training of a bard.

Whereas we have to infer the operation of these mnemonic devices from the practice of oral recitation, explicit didactic texts on mnemonics become available after the advent of literacy. The oldest surviving complete texts are Roman and date from the first century BC, but according to one of them, the topic was by then 'well known and familiar', and they all refer to Greek predecessors whose work is lost to us except for the odd fragment.[1] However, these texts do not address the mnemonic problems of traditional bards but of people who were living under conditions in which literary practices had acquired a significant role. The advice collected in these texts pertained to what became known as 'the art of memory', a set of practices explicitly devoted to the cultivation of memory improvement.

This new art focused directly on memory as an object of deliberate intervention. Prayers for divine inspiration have been left behind and replaced by quite mundane forms of training potentially accessible to anyone. In this literature memory is accepted as a universal but variable individual attribute that can be improved like any other human skill. The effect of the art of memory on memory as an object of discourse converged with the efforts of the philosophers, who had attempted to describe the operation of individual memory through the medium of metaphorical projection. By picking out individual memory as the target of specific interventions mnemonic practices confirmed its existence and helped to characterize its properties. These practices made their contribution by implying the attributes of a real-world object, individual memory, that made the practices intelligible.

The circumstances which called for the cultivation of memory in the age of the art of memory were very different from the circumstances under which the ancient bards had accomplished their feats of memory. Although literate practices had only become accessible to a minority of the population, and although their role remained limited to certain contexts, there is no doubt that the art of memory flourished in a culture of literacy. There were certain settings in which special feats of memory were required, but unlike the settings in which the bards performed, these newer settings all required the use of written documents. However, the situations in which the art of memory flourished were not those in which written documents simply functioned as a substitute for internal memory – that was still rare – but situations in which the advent of written notes and records actually imposed new and difficult demands on individual memory. In public life such situations were most likely to arise in the courts, in political contests and in philosophical disputations.

Legal, political and philosophical proceedings remained largely oral but were increasingly informed by an expanding corpus of written documents. Those involved in trials had to marshal recorded laws, contracts and depositions whose relevance had to be established and whose relationship to each other had to be proved. This required memory work of a high order. In the political domain, oral persuasion was crucial but now had to manipulate information from written sources as well as still powerful oral traditions. Textually presented arguments transformed all these situations, but none more so than that of philosophical presentations, which now deviated much more strongly from normal dialogue and accommodated themselves increasingly to the textual form of written arguments. This meant that the unnoticed acts of remembering which are part of everyday social interaction would no longer suffice but had to be supplemented by new kinds of memory work that required special training.

People who found themselves in these new situations, and who were faced by tricky demands on their memorial skills, had a use for a new kind of technology. As the sheer volume of potentially relevant written material increased, a massive problem developed: how to summon up this material when it was needed? Nowadays we are accustomed to using a multiplicity of highly sophisticated finding aids, from catalogues and indexes to internet searches. In other words, we make the content of external memory available and accessible by exploiting the resources of external memory itself. But in doing so we are benefiting from techniques of literary retrieval that took many centuries to discover and develop. In classical antiquity these techniques – which now seem so obvious – had not yet been thought of at all or were still in their infancy. Finding ways of turning external memory on itself turned out to be a painfully slow and difficult process.[2]

In the meantime, an alternative route promised some relief. Instead of focusing on the objects and practices of external memory, why not concentrate on improving the act of remembering itself? The result was a different kind of technology, one that disciplined internal memory so that it would become much better at deploying whatever external memory resources were at its disposal. Such a technology has become known under the appropriate modern title of 'mnemotechnics' or simply 'mnemonics'. It comprises publicly advocated and systematically described methods for improving the efficiency of one's memory, not through the use of inscribed records, but through the use of special practices of remembering that require no external aids but rely on a kind of mental gymnastics.

What form did classical mnemotechnics take? Critical remarks in later works suggest that lost earlier versions advocated the rote learning of verbal material. But, by the first century BC, such methods were regarded as suitable mainly for children, or perhaps for the learning of poetry for purposes of recitation. Adults might practise rote learning as a sort of mental exercise. For more serious tasks an elaborate system of mnemonics based on visual imagery had been devised.

In the method of so-called 'local memory' the practitioner has to mentally construct an imagined system of 'places' or 'backgrounds' (loci) which might consist of a building sub-divided into rooms, a room filled with various pieces of furniture, a row of columns or arches with spaces between or under them or some other imagined spatial construction. These 'places' should be imagined as well-lighted but not glaring, they should be of appropriate size, clearly distinguishable from each other and at an optimum distance from each other (sometimes specified as 30 feet). The topics to be remembered would each be represented by a concrete image in sharply outlined visual form. Striking and novel images were to be preferred, but their choice was up to the individual. The ancient memory treatises provide only sparse and disappointing examples: an anchor to depict navigation or a spear to depict military affairs, for instance. Each image would then be assigned to a particular place in the mentally constructed system of places, the sword at the entrance to one's imagined house perhaps, the anchor in the middle of the first room, and so on.

In order to retrieve information stored in this way, one was to imagine oneself entering the location containing one's memory images at a certain point and then making one's way from image to image. As one reached each image the appropriate memory content would become available. Entering one's imagined building, one would perhaps encounter the imaginary sword that had been placed there and this would remind one to address the topic of warfare. Proceeding into the first room, one would notice the imaginary anchor and be reminded that the topic was to be naval warfare in particular. Further elaboration of the topic would follow as one mentally progressed from one 'place' to the next, each with its own previously stored image. With practice, the recall of the place would automatically lead to the recall of its assigned visual image and thus of the topic or sub-topic represented by that image. One would then be able to call up a sequence of subjects in the proper order by taking a mental walk through one's imagined building, room, row of columns or some other structure of *loci*.

In its classical Roman form local memory was taught as part of the subject of rhetoric. The task for which it was mobilized involved the utilization of information cast in a literary mould for purposes of oral delivery. Typically, this delivery took the form neither of a conversation nor a recitation but of a speech, a sermon or a lecture. These forms were dedicated to the trans-mission to an audience of content whose gist was preserved as written text, legal, philosophical or religious. As a recent historical study puts it, 'much of the speaking was directed toward a goal of impressing written words on the speakers and listeners'.[3]

This was the essential memory task that faced the rhetor in the formal speech situations of legal argument, political oratory and philosophical debate, and it involved much more than simply the accurate reproduction of written texts. Classical textbooks of rhetoric also recognized this latter memory task and recommended a different set of mnemonic practices to be applied to it. For purposes of simple verbal reproduction of text, the material should first be divided into manageable sections. Frequent practice was essential: reading the material aloud and testing oneself from time to time for recall of different sections. Interspersing a night's rest between learning and recollection was considered highly beneficial.[4]

A rhetor's memory task, however, was more complex and presumably more difficult. It was not a matter of regurgitating chunks of text but of marshalling previously acquired knowledge for the purpose of constructing a persuasive argument. The system of local memory was meant to facilitate this task. In recommending its use the classical texts on rhetoric made no bones about the artificiality of the system, sometimes expressing doubts about its usefulness. It was recognized that people would not spontaneously make use of such an elaborate combination of mnemonic devices but had to be explicitly taught by experienced teachers and recognized textbooks. A general distinction was made between two kinds of memory: *natural* and *artificial*. Natural memory operates spontaneously, without deliberate effort or reflection; artificial memory relies on explicit procedures that generally need to be acquired from a source and then intentionally practised and applied. At the core of this distinction, is the feature of being a voluntary, and therefore conscious and deliberate, act that characterizes some forms of remembering but not others. When that feature is paired with a second feature, namely the use of explicit and systematized learned techniques, the result is artificial memory.

While the distinction between natural and artificial memory was maintained in both practice and theory, it was generally recognized that artificial memory had to rely on the individual's endowment with natural memory, that it could only improve on what was already there. Artificial memory had to respect the natural characteristics of human memory if it was to be effective. The most extensive of the classical texts on artificial memory expressed this clearly:

> Let art, then, imitate nature, find what she desires, and follow as she directs. For an invention nature is never last, education never first; rather the beginnings of things arise from natural talent, and the ends are reached from discipline.[5]

In conceptualizing how artificial memory worked, the classical Latin sources made heavy use of the metaphor of inscription. When Cicero outlines the system of local memory, his description is framed by this metaphor: 'We should use the places as waxen tablets, and the symbols as letters,' he says, and then comments on the benefits of a 'power of retention, that they seem not to have poured their discourse into your ears, but to have engraven it on your mental tablet'. To a noted Greek expert on mnemonics, Metrodorus of Scepsis, he attributes the declaration that 'as he wrote with letters on wax, so he wrote with symbols as it were, whatever he wished to remember on those places which he had conceived in imagination'.[6] Another of the classical texts uses the same metaphorical framework: 'For the backgrounds are very much like wax tablets or papyrus, the images like the letters, the arrangement and disposition of the images like the script, and the delivery is like the reading.'[7]

The idea that memory was a kind of inner writing and reading seems to have been commonly accepted among the ancient authorities on mnemonics. Written text is of course a striking example of linear order. Words are presented in sequence, with the temporal order of speech being replaced by a spatial order of text. What classical mnemotechnics seems to have attempted was an emulation of the linear order of text by substituting ideational content for words. In writing, human speech is divided up into individual words which are then placed in serial order along a line inscribed on some material medium.

An earlier, and not much recommended, form of mnemotechnics apparently attempted an elaborate mental duplication of words or phrases by allowing each of their parts to suggest a mental image that evoked the meaning of this part. Thus, the image of Achilles might evoke the word 'courage', that of the god Vulcan 'metal-working'.[8] But this was a ridiculously cumbersome procedure, which was later recommended more as a mental exercise than as a practically useful technique. In fact, it remains a puzzle how a procedure that seems to make the task of memorizing more complicated and difficult could ever have been thought of as a mnemonic aid. Could it have been the product of irrational enthusiasm generated by the success of the technology of writing as an aid to external memory? Representing strings of individual words and syllables by a succession of mental images was more likely the product of a hopeful search for some internal memory analogue to the role of writing in external memory than a practically proven mnemonic technique.

Development of a viable mnemonic technique depended on changing the units represented by memory images from words and their parts to the subjects that those words stood for. In that case a whole situation, argument or complex of ideas could be represented by a single image rather than an immense collection of images.[9] By the time the Roman memory treatises appeared, the benefits of taking this step seem to have been generally recognized. Accordingly, a distinction is made between two kinds of mnemonic techniques, and two kinds of memory, referred to as *memoria verborum* and *memoria rerum*. The first is memory for words, the second, usually translated somewhat inadequately as 'memory for things', is memory for the content that words refer to, a scene, a situation, concepts, subject-matter, etc. Classical mnemotechnics was more concerned with this second kind of memory than with memory for words, which was often assigned to a preliminary stage of memory training.

Where the transmission of texts is entirely oral, there may be a distinction between sacred texts that must be reproduced verbatim and other texts where no difference between verbatim recall and recall of the gist is recognized. However, this is not conceptualized as a difference in memory but a difference in the authority of the text: the words of the divine have an intrinsic efficacy and therefore must not be tampered with. Though respect for sacred words survives beyond the period of oral transmission, the development of literate skills leads to an altogether different distinction which is eventually applied even to sacred texts.

As long as the socially defined memory task could be satisfied by the recitation of poetic or sacred words in an appropriate manner, memory for words might be quite an important matter. But this kind of memory performance was already well served by techniques relying more on auditory than on visual imagery. A different mnemonics was required when the social task changed to the marshalling of appropriate information in the setting of a trial, a political speech or a philosophical debate. This new mnemonics would be based on written texts, not only because much of the information that had to be remembered now existed in written form, but also because the written form provided the template for the presentation of information in the new institutionalized settings. Memory recall now became a form of mental reading that was obliged to rely mostly on visual imagery. But this entailed the decline of any mnemonics dedicated to the recall of actual forms of words. Not only is the recall of verbal strings of any length by means of visual imagery very difficult, a point on which all the ancient memory treatises agree, it is also seldom asked for.[10] Even on those occasions when the marshalling of a particular form of words was important, as in the text of a law or a learned book, reliance on individual memory was no longer crucial, because the words of the sources were now firmly fixed as a written record that could be consulted. But while words could increasingly be left to the devices of external memory, the extraction of meaning from those words still required individual mental work and therefore individual memory.

Twentieth-century field studies of the recital of traditional epics by rural bards suggest that these men made no distinction between words and 'things', that is, between the exact words they used in their performance and the meaning behind those words.[11] Although tape recordings of their rendering of a particular epic on different occasions showed that the verbal text of those renderings differed considerably from one occasion to another, the performers were convinced that what they presented was exactly the same every time. This conviction seemed to persist even in the face of contrary evidence from the tape recordings. In other words, what counted for these performers was not the exact form of words but the gist, the overall meaning, of the narrative. The distinction between the underlying meaning and a particular verbal expression of that meaning, closely related to the classical distinction between 'words' and 'things', did not strike a chord with these performers. They seemed unwilling or unable to grant the significance of such a distinction. The idea that words by themselves could be an object of regard, irrespective of their reference, was not one with which they were familiar.[12]

One consequence of writing and literacy was the emergence of language as an autonomous object for practices that were distinct from other practices associated with the content that language referred to.[13] Relatively permanent textual records in material form could now be created, altered, forged, memorized and reproduced as forms of words quite independently of their relationship to the world of 'things' outside language. Writing transformed words into objects with a material presence that could be seen, copied, preserved and exchanged among individuals. Written language, the 'words' of the law and of human or divine authorities, could now become an object of discourse that was separate from other objects, including those objects the words referred to. What the words were was one thing, what they meant was another. Memory for words was not equivalent to memory for 'things'.

Writing allowed the emergence of 'language' as a distinct object of discourse because it constituted language as the specific target of a set of deliberate actions that were directed at a form of language and at nothing else. In an analogous fashion, the deliberate practice of explicit mnemonic procedures, regarded as a kind of inner writing, established 'memory' as the specific object targeted by those procedures. What had been constituted only metaphorically by Plato's analogy of outer and inner writing was now firmly anchored in the real world through the behaviour of individuals who targeted their own remembering activity as the object of a distinct set of practices. Because the activity of remembering was regarded as a manifestation of a basic human attribute, memory, practices which focused attention on the activity of remembering also helped to objectify, and ultimately to reify, the 'memory' that lay behind remembering.

The order of places and the order of things

Because they recognized that mnemonic techniques exploited certain features of natural memory, those who taught the art of artificial memory sometimes commented on these features. However, this was at best a secondary interest. The main reason for devising and teaching the procedures of artificial memory was to satisfy purely pragmatic interests. Nevertheless, the Roman teachers of rhetoric did draw attention to a few characteristics of memory in general.

First of all, the frequent use of the metaphor of writing served to underline the importance of serial order for arranging items in memory. Beyond this, there was also a recognition that the artificial system of 'local memory' depended on the natural effectiveness of spatial location in assisting recall: 'For when we return to a place after considerable absence, we not merely recognise the place itself, but remember things we did there, and recall the persons whom we met and even the unuttered thoughts which passed through our minds when we were there before.'[14] In both natural and artificial memory spatial locations do not exist in isolation from one another but are linked in some kind of order. The difference is that in the one case the order is simply given, whereas in the other case it is the result of deliberate construction.

Legend attributed the invention of mnemonics to Simonides of Ceos (an actual person about whom very little is known), who left a building shortly before it collapsed and was afterwards able to help identify the remains of those who had been killed by remembering exactly where each had sat. 'Admonished by this occurrence, he is reported to have discovered that it is chiefly order that gives distinctness to memory; and that by those, therefore, who would improve this part of the understanding, certain places must be fixed upon, and that of the things which they desire to keep in memory, symbols must be conceived in the mind, and ranged, as it were, in those places.' Cicero lauds Simonides for having 'discovered that it is chiefly order that gives distinctness to memory ... thus the order of places would preserve the order of things'.[15]

The imposition of a spatial order on any subject-matter potentially freed reproduction from the constraints of a fixed narrative form and facilitated its logical ordering. Unlike a story, one could enter a mental structure of images anywhere and then pursue any one of a number of previously established links. The advantages of such a cognitive structure were certainly appreciated by the more advanced practitioners of the mnemonic art:

> For example, if we should see a great number of our acquaintances standing in a certain order, it would not make any difference to us whether we should tell their names beginning with the person standing at the head of the line or at the foot or in the middle. So with respect to the backgrounds. If these have been arranged in order, the result will be that, reminded by the images, we can repeat orally what we have committed to the backgrounds, proceeding in either direction from any background we please ... That is why it also seems best to arrange the backgrounds in a series.[16]

One author whose interest in memory was not as closely tied to practical considerations as that of his Latin successors was Aristotle. That is not to say that 'artificial memory' was not a significant influence on his work in this area. Although this work precedes that of the Latin authors by a couple of centuries we know from these authors that they had Greek predecessors to whom they attributed earlier forms of the practices they described. The work of these earlier Greek advocates of the art of memory is essentially lost to us, but it was certainly known to Aristotle. He refers to mnemonic practices on several occasions. For instance, in his book on the soul, *De anima*, the example he chooses to illustrate what he means by the act of imagining is this: 'we can call up a picture, as in the practice of mnemonics by the use of mental images'.[17] In discussing dreams he observes that people who try to remember dreams 'according to the mnemonic rule' will 'frequently find themselves to be mentally putting into its place some other image apart from the dream'.[18] In his rather brief text on memory he mentions that 'persons are supposed to recollect sometimes by starting from "places"'.[19]

Aristotle distinguishes between the topics of 'memory' and 'recollection' (*anamnesis*), and it is in his discussion of recollection that the influence of mnemonic practices becomes apparent. Aristotle's conception of 'recollection' has much in common with later notions of 'artificial memory'. A distinctly practical bent pervades the treatment of both. He sees recollecting in terms of going serially from one image to another, just as people were advised to do when they practised mnemonics.

Like the mnemonicists, Aristotle offered some suggestions on how we find the successor to a particular image. Though brief, his remarks on this topic are interesting because they had a strange sequel much closer to our own time. When 'we hunt up the series', Aristotle says, we start in our thoughts 'from the present or some other, and from something either similar, or contrary, to what we seek, or else from that which is contiguous with it'.[20]

These rather casual remarks provided a basis for enrolling Aristotle as the first associationist once the doctrine of the association of ideas had achieved the status of a fact of nature.[21] Read in this light, Aristotle's words seemed to indicate that he had glimpsed a truth about the mind that was to be fully established by modern associationism many centuries later.

However, similarity, opposition and contiguity are mentioned by Aristotle only in the very specific context of recollection, not in connection with the formation of memory traces. Although he recognizes the role of 'habit' (*ethos*) in the order of memory images there is no suggestion that this is governed by any 'principles', let alone 'laws', of association. For the modern empiricists, on the other hand, the principles of association were equivalent to natural laws that governed the stamping in of memory traces. Remembering was essentially a mechanical process which a person underwent. For Aristotle, recollection was 'a sort of investigation', 'as it were a mode of inference', an intentional activity which, unlike memory, only humans are capable of.[22] His metaphors for recollection – a search or hunt – have a strongly agentic quality quite at variance with an associationism that traced all memory phenomena to the operation of the same set of natural laws and lacked the Aristotelian distinction between passive memory and active recollection.[23]

What does emerge in Aristotle's texts are not the 'laws' of association but an interesting variant of the mnemonic concept of 'places'. In the Roman, rhetorical, version of mnemonic procedure recollection of successive members of a series was facilitated by forming an image of their location in physical space. In the Aristotelian version the reference to physical space is replaced by logical relationships among the contents to be recalled. In 'hunting for the successor', he suggests, look for something that is linked to the starting-point by relationships of similarity, opposition or contiguity. He is clearly concerned with a different kind of memory task from the one that Simonides is supposed to have solved. For recalling a set of individuals that all had a physical presence, forming a spatialized visual image might well be a good recipe. Such images might also have their uses for an orator thinking on his feet and seeking to sway an audience by vivid rhetorical appeals. But these were not Aristotle's primary concerns. What he usually had in mind in connection with problems of recall was dialectical argument. That provided the social setting within which the active side of human memory became problematized.

Dialectical debate, both as a form of training in clear thinking and as a way of arriving at true insights about the world, had become a recognized institution in Athens and probably elsewhere, and there were teachers who offered to help contestants improve their performance. Aristotle was among these. One of his major works, *Topics*, was devoted to instruction in the art of dialectical argument, and it clearly presupposes institutionalized contests based on recognized rules.

The title of this book is rather curious. It is a rendering of the Greek *topoi*, which actually means 'places'. Why would a book devoted to the methodology of logical argument be called 'places'? A spatial metaphor appears to be at work here, as it is in such English forms as 'commonplace' and 'in the first place', which probably have their ultimate source in Aristotle.

It had been common for instructors on dialectical debate to stress the importance of a good memory. But it seems that what they advocated was the memorizing of specific arguments, the learning by rote of effective verbal formulations. In this kind of practice oral transmission and auditory memory were still prominent. By the time that Aristotle lectured on these matters, however, dialectical debates were unlikely to be won by reeling off memorized points. What he advocated was a good memory for the *general patterns* of logical argument.[24] 'It is better to commit to memory a proposition of general application', he says.[25] The description and enumeration of these general patterns form the content of *Topoi*. For instance, Aristotle describes three 'ways we talk of sameness', ten categories of predication which 'are the subjects on which arguments take place', 'four possible ways of preventing a man from working his argument to a conclusion', 'five kinds of criticism', and so on.[26] Large parts of the text are devoted to instruction in the rules of dialectical argument, neatly presented in sequential order. For instance, there is a list of all the ways in which an opponent's argument can be destroyed, each item on the list preceded by 'next'. This is surely a form of presentation that is meant to facilitate memorization by students.

Even when it is a matter of remembering general rules and propositions, rather than concrete images or lively episodes, the link between spatialization and recall is not entirely lost. The general points enumerated are still called 'places', and near the end of the exposition the connection becomes explicit: 'For just as in a person with a trained memory, a memory of things themselves is immediately caused by the mere mention of their "places", so these habits too will make a man readier in reasoning, because he has his premises classified before his mind's eye, each under its number.'[27] The title's allusion to the 'places' of classical mnemonics is therefore explained by an analogy between them and the mnemonic devices useful in the recall of abstract content, namely, classification and enumeration. Common to both is the organization of the material in terms of distinct items arranged in serial order, so that recall becomes a matter of methodically proceeding from one to the next. In this sense, even abstract items each have their 'place'.

In order for recollection to do its work efficiently the material to be recalled must already be organized in a particular manner. It must be divided into distinct items arranged in series; each item must be marked or represented by a symbol, either numerical or iconic; and links, either spatial or logical, must have been established between items and between series. Emerging out of the mnemonic practices of oratory and dialectical debate, the Aristotelian concept of recollection and the Roman concept of artificial memory both recognized the need for cognitive organization prior to the act of recollection itself. Certain fundamental features of this organization were common to both – itemization, serial order, symbolic representation and interconnections. However, the manner of realizing these features differed because of the different circumstances under which recollection occurred. Rhetorical goals were better served by individualized visual images ordered by means of a spatialized representational framework, whereas the philosophical goal of arriving at general, timeless truths was better served by abstract markers and logical interconnections.[28]

Nevertheless, the mnemonic context always presupposed some prior effort at cognitive organization, although the agents of this effort were not the same in the rhetorical and the dialectical context. In the rhetorical context, the organization of the material was undertaken by the orator himself, with some rather sketchy advice on mnemonic schemes from teachers and textbooks. These sources emphasized that, in order to be really useful, mnemonic schemes had to be personalized. In the system of 'local memory' one had to provide one's own order of places and make up one's own concrete images to represent the subject-matter of one's exposition. An orator not only had to use a scheme that suited his personal inclinations, he also had to adapt the scheme to the requirements of different audiences and different situations. To a large extent, he had to rely on his own resources in constructing a cognitive organization that would serve his mnemonic purposes.

The situation of the dialectician, at least as postulated by the Aristotelian texts, was different. Although in the *Topics* Aristotle does insert some advice on how to vary one's line of argument depending on the kind of opponent one is facing, the overwhelming thrust of his exposition implies the universal validity of the rules he sets out and the abstract truth of the logical relationships he describes. So his text functions simultaneously as a mnemonic aid, as indeed its title suggests, and also as an account of quite impersonal rules of method designed not only to win dialectical debates, but also to arrive at universally valid truths. The fact that Aristotle happens to be the author of these rules has no relevance for their validity, and in employing the rules the student is not free to adapt them to the requirements of the moment. Doing so would lead to sophistry, the misuse of logic and argument for ulterior purposes. In other words, Aristotle presents the cognitive organization of his text as corresponding to the organization of the world, at least in certain relevant respects. Its usefulness does not primarily derive from its possible mnemonic function but from its function as a means for uncovering truths to which everyone would have to assent. The mnemonic function, the fact that contents are neatly laid out in sequential numbered bits that are logically interrelated, is a consequence of the textual representation of an ordered world. True knowledge has mnemonic properties because it is logical and orderly.

Monastic memory

After the demise of the Greek institution of dialectical debate the Aristotelian linking of memory and logic was not widely appreciated. In a rhetorical context the distinction between dialectics and sophistry was likely to be overlooked, and in the early Christian period that followed the heyday of rhetoric the entire Aristotelian approach would have seemed beside the point, even if it had been available.[29] Not only did the destruction of literate culture in the wake of the Roman empire's collapse result in the loss of all the relevant resources, but the few remaining centres of literacy in the West had altogether different mnemonic interests. They were monasteries whose inhabitants devoted themselves to the service of God.

This service demanded the intense study of sacred texts that relayed the word of God directly or commented on it authoritatively. Some texts related the exemplary character of the lives and deeds of saints. One studied such texts in order to become a better person, not in order to extract some item of useful information or a clever debating point. 'The pious reader desires to be possessed by the word, not to manipulate it.'[30] Texts that had the quality of sanctity were not read in the same way one would consult an encyclopaedia or journal article. One read them in an effort to make their message part of oneself; what they imparted were not bits of information one hoped to *possess* but some intimation of the kind of person one hoped to become.

In part, memory became an object of cultivation in the monastic period because of a long tradition that assigned memory an important role in the formation of moral virtues. For Aristotle an ethical character depended on memory of past virtuous actions. Many classical authors followed Cicero in regarding memory as part of the virtue of prudence. In communities devoted to moral excellence the ethical implications of a good memory were likely to become central. In this context, a 'good' memory would be an ethically effective memory, not one excelling at the accumulation of morally neutral 'facts'. Such a memory was acquired by close involvement with sacred or inspirational texts. This involvement was 'reading' of a special kind, reading in the service of moral excellence, devotional reading as a form of religious meditation.[31]

For the devout, the sacred text was not a repository of items of 'information' to be extracted and possessed while the source always remained an object separate from the appropriating reader. What medieval advice on reading and remembering stressed was rather the goal of making the text part of oneself. In the words of Gregory the Great: 'We ought to transform what we read into our very selves, so that when our mind is stirred by what it hears, our life may concur by practicing what has been heard.'[32] Metaphors of digestion, such as chewing the cud, ruminating or 'the stomach of memory', are commonly used at this time to convey the idea that remembering a text is like transforming external nourishment into one's own substance. That perspective may be contrasted with the common twentieth-century separation between 'remembering what' and 'remembering how'. What much of the medieval literature on memory addressed was a process in which the 'what' of the text was transformed into the 'how' of the reader's life. Significantly, that 'how' was not modelled on technical and motor skills, as it would be later, but on the moral bearing of an ethical personality. Images of good conduct, remembered as a result of inspirational reading, played a crucial role in individuals' identification with exemplary characters at times of decision.

All accounts of memory entail an explicit or implicit conception of what memory is for. In the rhetorical context, memory was necessary for the effectiveness of persuasive argument. In a dialectical context, mnemonic order reflected logical order. In many modern interpretations memory is there to preserve factual information. Clearly, monastic memory was different from all of these in that its primary domain was the fostering of the virtuous life. This it accomplished when the individual became immersed in textual depictions of virtue to the point that they took over his or her life. In order to reach this point one was encouraged to imagine oneself wandering through the text as though one were surrounded by beautiful countryside.[33] One was led on by the unfolding narrative, biblical or hagiographic. In later, more systematic advice, the temporal organization of actions and events ranked as a significant memory aid.

The text, the book, the manuscript were intimately tied up with medieval memory discourse. The medieval notion of *memoria* referred not to a psychological attribute of individuals, but to a cultural complex that necessarily included texts and the way in which individuals were supposed to relate to them. Monastic reading surmounted what Plato had seen as the great deficiency of written texts, their muteness. Its methods transformed ordinary reading into a dialogue between two memories, one shared and public, the other individual. 'Texts are the primary medium of the public memory, the archival *scrinia* available to all', as Carruthers puts it, 'from which ... an individual stores, *ad res* or *ad verba*, the chest of his or her own memory.'[34] When medieval authors use the verb 'remember' in describing hell or heaven they are referring to images that they have experienced, not on actual visits to these places, but in the course of their meditative reading of appropriate texts.

In the world of classical antiquity a deep metaphorical link had been established between writing and memory. But in the medieval period that link took a far more concrete form. Memory became inescapably connected to the products of writing – books and manuscripts – which were regarded as its essential field of operation. The mnemonic practices of this period were therefore marked by a massive turn to the written page as the primary vehicle for innovations in the 'art of memory'. Older versions of the art, local memory in particular, were eventually rediscovered and cultivated, but the most significant contributions of the medieval period were based on the exploitation of the mnemonic potential of the inscribed page and of assembled text.

Medieval manuscripts as mnemonic devices

Before printing, all books were rare and valuable objects that might exist only in the form of a single exemplar or, with the exception of the Bible, in just a few copies. If one wanted to make use of a text, one could not count on a readily available copy of the corresponding book at a convenient library. There was therefore much more memorizing of books or folios, in whole or in part, than would be necessary after the spread of printing.[35] Anything that facilitated this task would be welcome.

One way in which memory for text could be facilitated was through the *display* of text on the page. Putting text in a frame and presenting script symbols in the form of clearly distinct lines were early achievements but the separation of alphabetic symbols into separate word units had a long history that throws some light on the link between memory and its external aids. In Roman manuscripts there were no spaces between words, just a continuous line of letters called *scriptura continua*. How could this possibly aid memory? A major clue to the answer lies in the fact that people at that time generally read aloud, not silently as we do. They also attached great value to forms of memory performance that are relatively less important today: public declamations, prepared speeches delivered without notes, recitations of texts learned by heart. Texts were remembered auditorily, as speech, and reading was taught on the basis of phonic recognition, combining letters into syllables and words. Remembering inflection, cadence, stress, rhythm and so on, was crucial when texts were meant to be remembered auditorily. A piece of writing represented a pattern of sound that the reader could chunk according to the demands of oral delivery.

Centuries later, when different mnemonic values came to the fore, various ways of separating written words appeared, a separation that made writing less similar to speech.[36] Increasingly, reading relied on visual cues and phonic memory became much less important. Copying manuscripts was less often accomplished by dictation, as it had been in the past, and became a matter of visual reproduction. In the Middle Ages, written texts lost their close link to speech but were increasingly compared and related to each other in the course of theological and legal disputes carried on between a network of dispersed localities. A clear change of mnemonic values can be observed. Rhythmical elegance in the delivery of prepared speech is no longer important, so that aural memory is no longer a significant target for cultivation. There is a more analytical attitude to text and a growing emphasis on the logical interrelationship among its parts.

Books still functioned as mnemonic artefacts, but they did so in the context of changed social tasks. Demands now placed on memory had little to do with oral reproduction and much more to do with thematic content. The task of chunking text largely shifted from the reader to the writer. Increasingly, texts were prepared so as to facilitate their use as mnemonic aids in the retention of idea content. The slowly spreading use of spacing to separate, not only words, but whole chunks of text in the form of a paragraph or section served this purpose, as did the use of punctuation marks.

Several other developments that affected the presentation of text on the page also enhanced the mnemonic function of books.[37] A kind of colour coding was introduced when headings, summaries and first letters of paragraphs were coloured, often in red, a practice still hinted at in the etymology of the word 'rubric', which harks back to the Latin word for red. For purposes of comparison, texts were often set out in parallel columns or in tables. Key words were extracted from the text and placed in the margins. Finally, there was a slow spread of the practice of providing chapters with titles and summaries.[38] The primary function of these devices was to make texts presented in books easier to absorb. As indicated in the previous section, the absorption of text, making it one's own, was the major purpose of monastic reading. Advances in textual display served this function. They facilitated the mental imprinting of text so that it might be reproduced at any time, even in the absence of the written page.

Techniques for displaying text in books have changed relatively little for several centuries. We take them for granted. But the same cannot be said for a second category of memory aids, namely pictorial illustrations. These have changed a great deal, partly of course because of major technological advances. Photographic illustrations only emerged in the nineteenth century and computer-generated images much more recently. In the Middle Ages illustrations in manuscripts had to be drawn by hand, but were none the less quite plentiful. In many instances they were not really illustrations of the text's contents but purely mnemonic in their function. For example, a finger would be drawn in the margin, pointing to a part of the text that it was considered particularly important to remember, rather like the 'NB' we still use in pencilled marginal annotations. This finger, like the words *'nota bene'*, does not *illustrate* anything in the text; it is simply a memory aid.

In many cases, of course, a picture might function both as illustration and as memory aid, but in medieval manuscripts pictures that have only a mnemonic function are common. For instance, in the thirteenth century so-called marginal drolleries become common. These are drawings of grotesque creatures engaged in activities that mimic human behaviour, leading to images that are weird, striking and suggestive; in a word, memorable. By this time the basic texts of classical mnemonics had been recovered and their advice had been taken up by prominent medieval authorities like Albertus Magnus and Thomas Aquinas. Classical mnemonics, it will be recalled, assigned great importance to the formation of vivid mental images that would facilitate the recall of previously learned material. It is not difficult to see the marginal drolleries of later medieval manuscripts as an attempt to transfer such mnemonic images to the pages of written texts. The unusual and grotesque nature of these images would make them easier to recall, and this would, it was hoped, facilitate the recall of the text to which they had been juxtaposed on the manuscript page. The deliberate evocation of vivid and unusual images had been a favourite procedure of classical 'artificial memory'. But the mental procedures addressed by the classical memory treatises represented only one aspect of artificial memory, the apparatus of external memory in written records represented another. The same basic principles could be applied to both aspects.

Some marginal decorations in medieval manuscripts even evoked a sort of metamemory. These were drawings that referred to memory and retrieval through images drawn from the pervasive metaphors of storage and hunting or fishing. What was depicted were vessels or containers, such as pouches, chests, bins or bird coops, and also valued objects that were commonly laid away, collected or preserved, such as jewels, coins, flowers and birds. Other drawings, for instance of footprints or fish hooks, were drawn from the metaphorical repertoire for memory recall or retrieval. In many cases no meaningful connection between these marginal decorations and the adjacent text can be made out – their reference is not to the specific material to be remembered but to the need to engage one's memory as one is reading. They served as reminders to store away, to preserve in one's memory, the textual treasures that were being presented and to use appropriate mnemonic devices to facilitate later recall.

Pictorial illustrations of textual content were of course used as well. These were often distributed over the page in accordance with some schema that represented conceptual links and served mnemonic functions as well. In fact, the localization of figural images at certain places on the page has much in common with classical prescriptions for mnemotechnology. In both cases concrete images are assigned to fixed places in some stable background framework, though in the classical art of memory this is done mentally and three-dimensionally, whereas in book illustration an external representation is produced two-dimensionally. In the classical art of memory, the stable framework was usually provided by imagined architectural schemes, houses, streets and so on. In book illustration, the stable framework was first of all provided by the borders of the page, sometimes accentuated by a drawn border. Within these borders diagrammatic frameworks were used to place concrete images appropriately. Trees and ladders provided popular models for the diagrammatic arrangement of interrelated images, but more abstract schemes, such as concentric circles or tables of rows and columns were also used.[39] Pictures that illustrated such content as biblical stories or lists of virtues and sins could then be located at their appropriate 'places' within the diagrammatic framework; just as in the classical mnemonic scheme visual images were assigned places in the rooms of a house or along a street. The mnemonic benefits conferred by the diagrammatic placing of pictorial images were clearly recognized by medieval authorities.

Among these authorities, a twelfth-century figure, Hugh of St Victor, deserves special mention because he discussed the topic of memory facilitation through the use of mnemonic devices in several manuscripts, one of which, the *Didascalion*, became rather well known.[40] In a relatively brief summary that forms part of the preface to a larger work, Hugh enumerates three ways in which material could be organized so as to facilitate its retention. One way was by means of spatial location:

> Therefore it is a great value for fixing a memory-image that when we read books, we study to impress on our memory ... not only the number and order of verses or ideas, but at the same time the colour, shape, position, and placement of the letters where we have seen this or that written, in what part, in what location (at the top, the middle, or the bottom) we saw it positioned.[41]

Writing towards the middle of the twelfth century, he clearly appreciated the mnemonic functions of textual layout and the organization of material on the written page.

As Hugh's reference to 'the number and order of verses or ideas' indicates, he considered the serial numbering of textual sub-sections to be another useful mnemonic device. This involved breaking up longer texts and assigning numbers to the parts. Then the number series functioned as a stable grid onto which textual material could be placed. For mnemonic purposes, numbers might be attached not to a lengthy section of text, but to the opening words of such a section or perhaps to a previously constructed verbal summary of the section to be remembered.

Number grids were not the only form of fixed schemes for organizing textual material. Alphabetical arrangement had had a limited use in antiquity and later gained in popularity. Other schemes, such as the signs of the zodiac, were sometimes used but none had the universal appeal and longevity of numbers and letters.

Apart from number and location, Hugh also advocated the use of a third schematic component, which he called 'occasion', to facilitate memorization of textual material. 'Occasion' referred to temporal organization: 'What was done earlier and what later, how much earlier and how much later, by how many years, months, days this preceded that and that was followed by this other.'[42] Temporal arrangement of actions and events applied particularly to memory for 'historical' material, that is to say, narrative accounts of the actions of persons in particular situations. Although manuscript pages are not extended in time, attempts to use them for depicting temporal sequences are not lacking. One way would be through the temporal organization of narrative accounts, where the story line progresses in an orderly way from the beginning to the end of an action sequence. A more graphic illustration of temporal organization is provided by those medieval manuscripts which show an interconnected sequence of drawings that depict a story in the manner of a comic strip.

The juxtaposition of medieval manuscripts and medieval advice on the improvement of memory shows that analogous mnemonic schemes were being applied to the materials of external memory and to the mental operations of internal memory. Chunking, or itemization of text to facilitate memory, could be performed mentally by a person, but it could also be incorporated into the written text by using spacing of words and paragraphs on the page. Similarly, the itemized parts could be serially arranged in a numbered sequence on the page and also organized in that way by a person trying to remember them. Spatial and temporal organization could be employed in the presentation of material in books or it could be imposed mentally for purposes of later recall. The important point here is that there was a convergence of the technology of external memory and the procedures characteristic of 'artificial' internal memory, that is to say, the deliberate manipulation of mental content for purposes of mnemonic efficiency. The technology of external memory, the arrangement and presentation of recorded text, became progressively better at preparing material for internal memory. It anticipated the requirements of the latter and took over much of the work that would have had to be performed by an internal memory trying to cope with poorly presented text. One might think of it in terms of a metaphor of food that is tenderized and divided into little pieces for a child or an invalid. But in predigesting what is to be remembered external memory also imposes its own version of mnemonic procedures on internal memory. The techniques of external memory, its numbering and lettering schemes, its diagrams and patterns of illustration, its way of chunking text and so on, quickly gave rise to mnemonic conventions that individual memorizers were obliged to adhere to if they wished to avoid much extra work and probable confusion. Textual records and individual memories became part of one system in which the parts were appropriately attuned to another.

Unfortunately, the existence of such interrelationships sometimes leads to rather sterile arguments of the chicken-and-egg type. Which came first, the technology or the natural features of human memory? Well, of course, the development of both technology and deliberate intervention in internal memory processes depend on human potentials. Dogs and cats develop neither. But the manner and rate of their development will depend on particular historical conditions which might favour one or the other. The fact that mnemonic schemes for sub-dividing biblical text existed for centuries before they were incorporated into books entails no general conclusion about the priority of mental schemes, because the Bible had a unique status as a sacred object. On the other hand, there are examples of the priority of technology that are hard to ignore. To mention only one, the use of writing entailed the possibility of checking the accuracy of reproduction of verbal material without relying on individual informants. This led to a distinction between two kinds of accuracy in remembering: purely verbal, and pertaining to the content of what was reproduced. Different mnemonic procedures could then be developed for each. But this is not to say that the entire historical development of mnemonics was simply technology driven. 'Artificial' internal and external memory developed in interaction with one another.[43] What is false is the view that all the parameters of human memory were fixed for all time at the moment the species *homo sapiens* appeared. These parameters underwent significant changes in the course of human history, and knowledge of these changes is crucial for the identification of relatively constant features.

At a more profound level, the chicken-and-egg question about the priority of technology depends on an unrealistic separation of two components that generally work together in the functioning of human memory. With the possible exception of dreamlike states, memory does not operate in an environmental or psychological vacuum. It operates while individuals are exposed to input from the environment and in the context of ongoing wishes, interests and fears. In Donald Norman's well-chosen words, 'the world remembers things for us, just by being there', because 'the intellect is tightly coupled to the world'.[44] Memorial technology is one instance of this pervasive coupling, though a rather important one for the historical development of memory processes. Its effects are obvious, but they are the effects of changes in one part of a system on the system as a whole, not the effects of an independent factor impinging on memory from the outside.

Working with texts

By the late Middle Ages it is possible to detect a change in the role that texts played in various human situations. It had long been a function of texts to serve as *reminders* of important actions and relationships: heroic deeds, authoritative orders and pronouncements, social obligations, lines of descent, property possessed and owed, etc. Texts had been an auxiliary device in the service of personal memories that were part of life itself. But gradually, and with many local exceptions, written texts achieved considerable autonomy and an authority that could even replace that of unaided human memory. In legal practice, for example, the ritualized swearing of oaths and the word of a witness long took precedence over mere documentary evidence. But eventually written records came to be increasingly trusted as the repository of the truth.[45] Instead of serving as mere reminders of what had happened, their *representation* of what had happened came to define the truth of the matter. Written texts could now function as a substitute for lived experience. In many important social situations one had to turn to them for an authoritative guide to the past.

Prior to the thirteenth century, medieval mnemonics had been primarily concerned with providing assistance to the *reader* of texts, facilitating the process of absorption. But in a decisive shift, help for the *user* of texts now became the major function of mnemonic devices. A user of texts might be a priest delivering a sermon, a scholar engaged in a disputation or a lawyer arguing a case. For such users the memory problem was essentially one of *retrieval*. They operated in an environment of multiple texts that provided the resources for meeting the demands of particular social tasks. But to be useful the resources appropriate to each task had to be mnemonically available when needed. That required procedures to facilitate textual retrieval. The need for such procedures affected the presentation of written text, but it also kindled a new interest in the devices of classical artificial memory.

As long as literacy had been largely confined to a contemplative monastic culture the memorizing of texts had served essentially meditational purposes. Retrieval, in the sense of locating a particular item among a large assembly of items, was hardly an issue then. There was a well-known and limited corpus of sacred writings, and the important task was to make them an ingrained part of one's being, not to 'retrieve' this or that item for clever use in the pulpit, the law court or the schoolroom. However, by the thirteenth century, new memory tasks required mnemonic practices that could be put to just such uses. There were three social contexts in which problems of retrieval were becoming particularly significant: the preparation of sermons, the advent of universities as centres of learning and changed legal practices. In all three cases it was not personal transformation through the absorption of texts that was called for but the retrieval of knowledge for pragmatic purposes.

The preparation of sermons became mnemonically more demanding as audiences changed and the goals of sermonizing became more ambitious. Some preachers had to face an increasingly learned audience at new centres of academic life; others, notably the mendicant friars, attempted to achieve a deeper religious involvement on the part of the laity. Both situations required a more effective use of the resources potentially available in sacred and scholarly texts. Such texts were a source of authority. In conveying their message the preacher had to be careful to remain true to them while yet varying his delivery in accordance with the demands of specific occasions and specific audiences. Compared to earlier times, many more texts were now available, and some of them were of considerable complexity. That offered much scope for varying one's delivery by judicious selection and arrangement of relevant excerpts. However, the source texts could not be extensively consulted during the act of preaching. In the case of travelling preachers they would not even have been available in the intervals between sermons, though the gradual introduction of portable books helped a little.

Delivering a sermon appropriate to a particular audience and occasion posed memory problems of no mean order. Preachers, schoolmen and legal advocates had to be able to recall relevant parts of authoritative texts when they needed them, without being able to consult the originals then and there. They were in a situation analogous to that of the classical orator in so far as they had to make use of previously acquired knowledge for a formal presentation before an audience. The presentation had to exhibit sustained coherence in the service of a particular communicative goal. Public speakers in both situations could not simply rely on 'natural memory' to take its course, as they could in ordinary conversation; they had to call upon some sort of 'artificial memory', the deliberate employment of technical memory aids, to enable them to perform in these formal situations.

There were two kinds of problem to be faced. One was the problem of delivery: making sure that previously acquired knowledge was reorganized in a manner that would ensure smooth and effective production of an oration or sermon. Classical architectonic mnemonics was designed to handle this problem. But it was not much help with the second problem, the selection of pertinent material to be included in the delivery. Suggestions for choosing vivid and affectively potent memory images implicitly recognized the problem but did not go very far. Perhaps there was little need for help in selecting pertinent material, because the topics addressed by the orator were often closely circumscribed by a particular situation, a specific court case or specific political issue. Textual material was certainly used but tended to be subordinate to the requirements of the concrete case being addressed. By contrast, the sermon style of the later Middle Ages was much more text-bound. The Romans lacked anything approaching the Christian Bible in terms of absolute textual authority. Respected authors were treated as stylistic guides, but their texts were not sacred as texts. For the preacher, however, reference back to the appropriate textual authority was part of every sermon. This must have created a more urgent need for mnemonic finding aids than classical orators had experienced.

In any case, the technology of textual retrieval hardly existed in antiquity. The concept of a table of contents or an index did not exist, if only because there was no way of referring to the exact place where a particular textual item could be found. Hand-produced manuscript rolls were hardly compatible with a system of page numbering that could be relied on for all copies of a work.[46] Although writing was quite widely employed in antiquity, its full potential had not yet been discovered, and even when discovered was not fully appreciated. One is taken aback to find Quintilian, a generally very sensible writer on the art of oratory, advising against the use of written summaries with headings and sections when preparing a speech. He thinks it would be bad for one's style and would confuse one's memory![47] During this period textual organization remained primitive and therefore of very limited value mnemonically.

In the High Middle Ages the memory tasks faced by preachers, theologians and lawyers led to a new emphasis on various retrieval tools. To assist in composition of sermons, elaborate biblical concordances became available in the thirteenth century and later.[48] For a large number of key words, different biblical meanings were distinguished and each meaning illustrated by biblical excerpts. These excerpts were provided with tags that gave their location in the biblical text and therefore made it possible to look them up. A concordance functioned as a semantically based retrieval tool. Because it was meant to facilitate the recontextualization of textual content its unit of meaning was the word, not an entire theme or episode. This allowed for much greater flexibility in the rearrangement of semantic content. Instead of simply reproducing a particular line of narration or a particular precept in its original context, a preacher could select his material from different contexts and recombine the parts to form a new whole.

In order to find parts of an existing text that might be of use in the construction of a new text, it is necessary to locate these parts in the original text. Some locating system must be superimposed on the original text for this purpose. This is best achieved by sub-dividing the text into sections and items that can each be provided with an identifying tag derived from some familiar system of tags. The obvious candidates for such a system of tags are natural numbers and the alphabet. These had previously been used for the mnemonic purpose of sub-dividing long slabs of texts into shorter sections that were more easily retained for purposes of verbatim reproduction. But a number series could also function as a stable grid onto which textual material could be placed for purposes of decontextualized retrieval. Numbers might be attached to a phrase or to a previously constructed summary that conveyed the gist or argument of the text. Alphabetical tagging could be applied in a similar way and had occasionally been so used since antiquity. The use of numbering, however, really came into its own with the adoption of Arabic rather than cumbersome Roman numerals and may in fact have helped to motivate the switch from the one to the other. More esoteric schemes, such as the signs of the zodiac, were sometimes used, but none had the universal appeal and longevity of numbers and letters. Books could now be used as works of reference, as stores of factual knowledge rather than as direct sources of moral inspiration. The external memory of the book could be entered randomly and its contents extracted, item by item.[49]

For lecturers, students and disputants at the new academic institutions that emerged in the thirteenth century, and also for jurists, effective techniques of textual retrieval were probably even more important than for preachers. All of them faced the problem of recontextualizing textually recorded information, that is, extracting and rearranging parts of previously recorded texts in the light of present requirements. But scholars and jurists were more affected than preachers by a significant growth in manuscript collections that was proceeding apace. Theology and jurisprudence were becoming professionalized fields in which certain standards were expected. To be effective in such a field the practitioners had to cast their net wide, culling and comparing items from many different sources. Access to these sources, both physical and cognitive, was a matter of considerable importance.

Physical access not only implied the existence of manuscripts in sufficient number and variety but also the ability to locate them when one wanted them. Medieval libraries did grow during this period, and valuable texts from antiquity became available, but to make effective use of these riches a convenient method of manuscript retrieval was needed. Fortunately, the same principle of imposing a location grid that was being applied to finding parts of manuscripts could be applied to the problem of finding whole books. The technique of superimposing a numerical or alphabetical location system on text made possible the practice of indexing or cataloguing. Whole manuscripts or an entire collection of manuscripts could thus be covered by a stable and mnemonically accessible grid of locations that permitted the extraction of any item from its original textual embedding and its use in a different context. Subject indexes and catalogues were the external products of this technology.

Early medieval libraries do not seem to have had anything like a catalogue in our sense.[50] There might be lists of manuscripts just as there were lists of other kinds of property, but the memory of the librarian would usually be the best guide to where things were to be found. Alphabetic catalogues made their appearance in the twelfth century, and a century later the physical location of books finally began to be linked to their subject-matter.[51]

But the effective use of the new technology of textual retrieval depended upon the users of this technology making corresponding adaptations in their memory habits. As always, changes in external and internal memory went hand in hand. The use of textual location devices required and encouraged the mnemonic employment of summaries of textual content. To use the new reference tools effectively, one had to be adept at abstracting the gist of a textual item from the words in which it was conveyed. Contrary to Quintilian's advice, formal speech (in sermons and lectures) was now often preceded by the making of summaries. St Thomas Aquinas used lecture notes. (In their preparation he had the benefit of technological advances such as the availability of paper as a comfortable and relatively cheap writing surface and the reinvention of cursive writing, better suited to notes and memos to oneself.) Students also began to be supplied with lecture notes, so that the process of instruction, which previously had been largely oral, became more text-bound.

The new devices of external memory could only be used effectively by a person who knew how to employ the appropriate procedures. Tables of contents, subject indices, alphabetical and numerical location systems, catalogues, etc. could function as aids only for a memory that was itself geared to the retrieval of decontextualized textual information. There had to be a kind of duplication of external memory organization in the memory of individuals making effective use of such an organization. External and internal memory organization had to converge if they were to work together as a functioning system. It is therefore not surprising that memory was sometimes explicitly referred to as a book or a library, and that this analogy was often implicit in the mnemonic schemes of the later Middle Ages. Similar heuristic schemes were taught for organizing one's memory and employed for locating manuscripts in a library.[52] Some medieval scholars developed their own system of indexing to suit their particular preferences and purposes. They had organized their own textual memory for purposes of retrieval with random access.

Before the widespread use of printing there were few copies of any one manuscript, and this meant that citations often had to be made from memory, without checking against the textual source. A memory organized in terms of the retrieval schemes of the time would greatly enhance the availability of an appropriate and relevant citation; what it could not ensure was the verbatim accuracy of the citation. That would have required a check against the actual manuscript. Apart from some exceptional cases, individual memory could generally not be relied on for verbatim accuracy, and this probably explains the frequent inaccuracy of medieval quotations. But it also reminds us that the modern social standard which attaches great importance to precise accuracy of recall depends not only on literacy and textuality as such, but also on the practicality of maintaining accuracy when texts become readily available in multiple identical copies.

Decline of mnemonics and memory discourse

After the high esteem of *memoria* in the Middle Ages, the modern sequel seems like a change from a major to a minor key. The Enlightenment not only changed the balance among the mnemonic arts, it also diminished their role in the life of the literate minority. Stripped of high moral purpose or the promise of profound understanding, these arts were reduced to a mindless drill more suitable to the needs of uninspired schoolmasters or low-brow salesmen than of serious scholars. By the nineteenth century, systems of mnemonics were being marketed, much like medical nostrums and elixirs, by entrepreneurs who hoped to cash in on generally spurious claims of originality and past success.[53]

The ancient arts for the cultivation of memory had begun to suffer a loss of status as early as the sixteenth century. Several factors contributed to this development. There was the tremendous expansion of external memory in the wake of the discovery of printing. Texts became far more accessible and cheaper, and this opened up new possibilities for designing special texts as sources of stored up knowledge that could be conveniently consulted. Individuals began to rely more on this externally available knowledge and less on their own recollections. By the seventeenth century, they were being advised to do so because of a new emphasis on the contrast between the unreliability of individual memory and the reliability of written records. The philosopher Descartes declared: 'We shall leave absolutely nothing to memory but put down on paper what we have to retain.'[54] This was no mere personal preference on his part but an early reflection of a working style that was to be widely advocated and adopted.

Careful record-keeping had proven its value in the ever-expanding world of commercial transactions, and was to be an indispensable part of the standard procedures of the new experimental science. In their personal lives individuals would become assiduous compilers of diaries and 'commonplace' books that recorded things experienced or read in places considered more reliable than their unaided memories. It was as though memory, which had long been esteemed as an internal writing, was now being returned to the external artefacts of record-keeping. Mnemonic advice, which had hitherto been governed by the need to improve memory in the absence of external aids, now included the admonition to make copious use of written notes on everything considered worth remembering. This eighteenth-century example is typical:

> Let us, therefore, often write down, not only the sentiments we learn from books, and teachers, and conversation; but also those that are peculiarly our own, of which a considerable number may arise in the minds of most men every day. And, though many of these might, no doubt, be forgotten without loss, yet some may be found worthy of a lasting remembrance.[55]

The turn from internal to external record-keeping was facilitated by the gradual spread of effective literacy and the vast increase in the information that was circulating in printed form. In the eighteenth century the full impact of printing became pervasive. Dictionaries and encyclopaedias flourished, and impressive arrays of printed books brought together all the collective wisdom that had slowly accumulated over the centuries, as well as the rapidly expanding new knowledge of science and technology, including descriptions of the planet, its history and its forms of life, human and non-human. The machinery of the state became more centralized, bureaucratic and efficient, relying increasingly on archival depositories. Museums and public libraries followed suit.[56] Inevitably, written records were becoming a regular part of the daily lives of more and more people.

But the nature of these records was also changing. The ideal of good representation had come to favour the form of verbal propositions or numerical data rather than elaborate imagery. This reflected partly a puritanical iconoclasm that had begun with a Protestant attack on religious imagery and then generalized to a distrust of all forms of imagery.[57] Truth was to be sought in words, not in visual images. The form of truth was the written statement permanently fixed in texts whose content could be reproduced by individual minds.[58] Images held in the mind distracted from true knowledge, which was propositional, because they distorted true knowledge of reality and replaced it with phantasms. Memory, located within the individual soul, becomes personal and idiosyncratic, whereas knowledge inscribed on paper is better able to represent facts that are independent of the experience of any one individual. The modern split between subjectivity and objectivity emerges, and the classical memory arts have no relevance for either side of this divide.[59]

For individuals working with records of factual information some sort of mnemonic technique might still have its uses under certain circumstances, for instance, when they were being examined on their factual knowledge. But the old mnemonics based on vivid imagery would more likely be distracting in this context. By the beginning of the eighteenth century the ready availability of a relatively efficient external memory system had made the whole subject of mnemonics somewhat redundant, so that there are few publications on this topic.[60]

But pretty soon one encounters a new approach to mnemonics. Instead of using spatial localization and iconic imagery to facilitate memory, reliance was now placed on the manipulation of verbal tokens in written form. Instead of using the layout of the written page as a template for memory grids, the newer systems explored the mnemonic potential of the constituents of written words, that is to say, letters and syllables, to an unprecedented degree. The technology of typesetting, involving the breaking up and reassembling of text, may well have influenced this development.

A new approach was first popularized by Richard Grey, whose *Memoria Technica* came out in some thirty editions over a period of 150 years, from 1730 to 1880.[61] He had numerous imitators in the nineteenth century, who seldom acknowledged their debt to him.[62] Grey was himself a clergyman, but it is not memory for theological arguments that his mnemonics was designed to facilitate. What he offered, and what there was obviously a significant market for, was help in remembering the dates of specific events, the names of historical personages, geographical information regarding cities, islands, rivers and so on, the distances of the planets from the sun, as well as factoids regarding coins, weights, etc. What Grey promises is 'exactness' in memory. He will help you to remember, not the moral or theological significance of biblical events, but their (supposed) dates. He demonstrates the utility of his system by showing how it can be used to remember that the world was created in 4004 BC, that Noah's flood took place in 2348 BC, that the Israelites left Egypt in 1491 BC, and so on.

The new mnemonics was typically applied to precoded information that was presented and had to be reproduced in an already unitized form. It was devised not to help you remember the gist of an argument, but to help you remember bits of information accurately and precisely. A nineteenth-century grammar-school headmaster's recommendation of Grey's mnemonics puts it this way: this technology, it says, is for those who 'prefer accuracy and fidelity to confused recollection and imperfect remembrance'.[63]

This was a major departure from tradition. Classical sources unanimously emphasized that memory for subject-matter or content was much more valuable than mere rote learning. Accordingly, the classical system of local memory was designed to facilitate memory for meaningful content, not verbatim recall. The truly striking aspect of eighteenth- and nineteenth-century mnemonics is that this ancient preference is reversed. A good memory is now an accurate memory, where accuracy is assessed in terms of the exact reproduction of some precisely defined informational input.

Whereas in ancient times mnemonics had formed part of rhetoric, it had in the nineteenth century found a home in an educational system that, among other things, was dedicated to teaching its charges reliable habits of precision and accuracy in transmitting written information. This was achieved by teaching methods that emphasized the accurate reproduction of a kind of textual content that lacked any personal interest or significance for the learner.

The methods of the new mnemonics were also strikingly different from those of its predecessors. Instead of using spatial localization and iconic imagery to facilitate memory, reliance was now placed on the manipulation of digitalized tokens. For example, a core component of the newer systems consisted of so-called number alphabets where numerical digits are represented by letters of the alphabet. Any number could then be represented by artificial words that were supposed to facilitate their recall.

The widespread appeal of this and similar systems suggests that by this time many people felt sufficiently comfortable manipulating the components of written words to use them as a mnemonic crutch to help them remember material they experienced as more difficult. So far from needing the help of imagery and spatial localization to remember verbal material they were now able to use verbal tokens to help them remember numbers and bits of factual knowledge. By the twentieth century, however, most people may have grown sufficiently comfortable with numerical information to have had no use for number alphabets and similar systems.

This change is part of a more general change in *mnemonic values*, that is, the kind of memory performance that is culturally favoured. The classical system of local memory was designed to facilitate the use of memory in the process of composing a new cognitive product based on existing records. One might call this *constructive* memory. For eighteenth- and nineteenth-century mnemonics, however, memory becomes a vehicle for the exact reproduction of some precisely defined informational input. It is *reproductive* memory that is valued.

In a rhetorical context, mnemonics had been employed to facilitate the composition of persuasive speeches and arguments, but in modern pedagogical mnemonics the elements of persuasion and composition disappear. These systems were designed to facilitate the accurate reproduction of a mass of specific learned facts about the world. Gone is the old emphasis on the use of vivid images that synthesize complex ideas. The content to be remembered is assumed to be in the form of discrete items, and the purpose of mnemonics is to make lists of such items memorable.

The history of mnemonics indicates that there have been changes in what is experienced as easy to remember and what is experienced as hard to remember. In other words, there seem to have been significant changes in the *mnemonic affordances* of different types of material. The whole point of mnemonics is to invoke the help of something that is experienced as relatively easy to remember when the task requires remembering something that is experienced as relatively hard to remember. The history of mnemonics shows, however, that what is easy and what is difficult does not necessarily remain the same over the centuries. One should therefore reflect carefully before tracing reductive speculative links between currently observed memory phenomena and their biological basis. Many of these phenomena depend on individuals' familiarity with technologies and mnemonic values that have existed only for a relatively brief period. The specific capacities on which they depend were developed in historical time, not in biological time. Of course, these specific capacities ultimately depend on certain biologically given possibilities, but to equate the two will prevent us from asking the crucial question of how these possibilities were converted into the specific forms of memory performance that can be observed now.

Notes

1. See Cicero, *De oratore*; Quintilian, *Institutio oratoria*, trans. H.E. Butler (Cambridge, MA: Harvard University Press, 1922); *Rhetorica ad Herennium*, in H. Caplan (ed.), *Cicero in twenty-eight volumes* (Cambridge, MA: Harvard University Press, 1954, reprinted 1981), vol. I. (Cicero is not in fact the author of this volume, whose true author remains unknown.)
2. An extensive review of the problems of literary retrieval in classical antiquity leads to the apt conclusion that, as far as the Greeks and Romans were concerned, 'it rarely occurred to them to use written words to find other written words'. Small, *Wax tablets*, p. 71.
3. M. Carruthers and J.M. Ziolkowsi, *The medieval craft of memory* (Philadelphia: University of Pennsylvania Press, 2002), p. 18.
4. Quintilian, *Institutio*, pp. 227–37.
5. *Ad Herennium*, p. 221.
6. Cicero, *De oratore*, pp. 187, 189.

7. *Ad Herennium*, p. 209.
8. A more detailed description of this technique is provided in Small, *Wax tablets*, p. 113.
9. The standard example is given in *Ad Herennium*, p. 215 where a defence attorney in a court of law is shown how to construct a single image that will incorporate all the salient features of the prosecution's case.
10. Small, *Wax tablets*, p. 133, points out that Greek and Latin had no specific word for 'memorize' and that 'verbatim' appears only in the fifteenth century AD. Accurate verbal reproduction was associated only with special contexts and did not become more generally valued until post-medieval times.
11. Lord, *The singer of tales*.
12. In view of the considerable literature that has been devoted to the question of verbatim recall in oral cultural transmission (e.g. Finnegan, *Literacy and orality*) it is perhaps necessary to mention that this is not the issue being addressed here. The fact that great significance may be attached to the verbatim repetition of an orally transmitted sacred text, for example, is entirely consonant with the absence of a distinction between the form of words and some underlying meaning. Indeed, the absence of this distinction may favour the verbatim reproduction of words that have a divine authorship, because tampering with the words is then equivalent to tampering with their meaning and thus challenging the intentions of their author.
13. Brockmeier, *Literales Bewusstsein*; Olson, *The world on paper*.
14. Quintilian, *Institutio*, p. 221.
15. Cicero, *De oratore*, pp. 186–7.
16. *Ad Herennium*, p. 211.
17. Aristotle, *On the soul*, 427b, p. 20.
18. Aristotle, *On dreams*, 458b, p. 22.
19. Aristotle, *On memory*, 452a, p. 13.
20. Aristotle, *On memory*, 451b, pp. 19–20.
21. Ironically, the link between Aristotle and latter-day associationism seems first to have been suggested in the course of an early nineteenth-century attempt (by Coleridge) to discredit Hume by accusing him of having plagiarized Aristotle. This was a direct challenge to Hume's own claim, which was that: 'if anything can entitle the author to so glorious a name as *inventor*, it is the use he makes of the principle of the association of ideas, which enters into most of his philosophy' (D. Hume, *An abstract of a treatise of human nature, 1740*, ed. J. M. Keynes and P. Sraffa (Cambridge: Cambridge University Press, 1938), p. 31; originally published 1740). Coleridge's specific accusation of plagiarism was easily refuted by Hume's supporters, though they followed Coleridge in seeing some similarity between the two authors. This enabled them to turn the tables: it was not Hume who should be condemned for plagiarizing Aristotle, it was the latter who should be praised for having 'anticipated' Hume's marvellous 'discovery'. The image of Aristotle as associationist received its canonical form in G. Grote's 1880 text *Aristotle*, ed. A. Bain and G. C. Robertson (New York: Arno Press, 1973). It was neither the first nor the last example of appealing to Aristotle in order to claim ancient authority for contemporary beliefs. In the latest version Aristotle has become a precursor of late twentieth-century functionalism; Green, 'The thoroughly modern Aristotle'.
22. Aristotle, *Complete works*, 453a, 10, p. 720.
23. Danziger, 'Generative metaphor'. Metaphors of hunting, fishing or tracking down prey became traditional for describing recollection and survived well into the Middle Ages. Carruthers, *Book of memory*, p. 247.
24. R. Sorabji, *Aristotle on memory* (Providence: Brown University Press, 1972).
25. Aristotle, *Complete works*, 163b, 31, p. 276.
26. Aristotle, *Complete works*, pp. 171, 173, 271, 272.
27. Aristotle, *Complete works*, 163b, 27, p. 276.

28. But this explanation can be taken further because rhetorical and dialectical tasks flourished in different cultural contexts, Roman in the one case and Greek in the other. The characteristically Roman appreciation of spatial backgrounds that are physical, and often architectural, does not manifest itself only in connection with the art of memory but contrasts more generally with the relatively abstract Greek style. See Small, *Wax tablets*, pp. 95ff.

29. Before the twelfth century the cultivation of memory is generally discussed in treatises on prayer, meditation and scriptural study. Subsequently, there is a literature that addresses the nature of memory more philosophically.

30. Illich, *Vineyard of the text*, p. 43.

31. Carruthers, *Book of memory*, chapter 5.

32. Carruthers, *Book of memory*, p. 164.

33. Illich, *Vineyard of the text*.

34. Carruthers, *Book of memory*, p. 189.

35. One of the classical sources on the art of memory had already advocated a direct mnemonic employment of written texts: 'There is one thing which will be of assistance to everyone, namely, to learn by heart from the same tablets on which he has committed it to writing. For he will have certain tracks to guide him in his pursuit of memory, and the mind's eye will be fixed not merely on the pages on which the words were written, but on individual lines, and at times he will speak as if he were reading aloud' (Quintilian, *Institutio*, pp. 229–30). Memory recall would become a form of reading in a very literal sense. Written pages would first be inscribed on the mind and then read off like an actual page of text.

36. P. Saenger, *Space between words: The origins of silent reading* (Stanford, CA: Stanford University Press, 1997). In Semitic writings, consisting only of consonants, divisions between words were an earlier necessity.

37. Carruthers, *Book of memory*, especially chapters 3 and 7; Illich and Sanders, *The alphabetization of the popular mind*.

38. Many of the most familiar organizational aids, such as the regular use of paragraphs, variation of fonts and numbering of chapters, did not become common until after the invention of printing. Small, *Wax tablets*, p. 15.

39. It is possible that the expression 'by rote', whose origins are obscure, derives from the Latin 'rota', wheel, via the circular diagrams of medieval texts. Carruthers, *Book of memory*, p. 252.

40. Illich, *Vineyard of the text*; Carruthers, *Book of memory*, appendix A; G. A. Zinn, 'Hugh of St Victor and the art of memory', *Viator* 5 (1974), pp. 211–34.

41. Carruthers, *Book of memory*, p. 264.

42. Ibid.

43. 'I do not believe that the book mimes memory; its relationship to *memoria* is not that of a mirror or copy, any more than letters or parchment mime their contents. The relationship is functional; the book "supports" *memoria* because it serves its requirements, some of which are biological, but many of which, in the memorial cultures of the Middle Ages, were institutional and thus conventional, social, and ethical.' Carruthers, *Book of memory*, p. 194.

44. Norman, *Things that make us smart*, pp. 146–7.

45. Clanchy, *From memory to written record*. Documents were often forged and people lied, but ultimately it proved easier to avoid and detect forgery than to escape the propensity of human memory to lie.

46. Small, *Wax tablets*, pp. 16–17, 70.

47. Quintilian, *Institutio*, p. 151.

48. M. A. Rouse and R. H. Rouse, *Authentic witnesses: Approaches to medieval texts and manuscripts* (Notre Dame, IN: University of Notre Dame Press, 1991).

49. Line and page numbers were not reliable with written texts but came into widespread use after the invention of printing standardized the physical location of any item of text.

50. On the problematic status of catalogues in the libraries of classical antiquity, see Small, *Wax tablets*, pp. 44ff.

51. Rouse and Rouse, *Authentic witnesses*.

52. 'All of these schemes bespeak the assumption that a good memory is a library of texts, and a thoroughly catalogued and indexed one at that.' Carruthers, *Book of memory*, p. 116.

53. The life of an early representative of the world of nineteenth-century mnemonics is discussed in A. B. Laver, 'Gregor Feinagle, mnemonist and educator', *Journal of the History of the Behavioral Sciences* 15 (1979), pp. 18–28.

54. Descartes, *The philosophical writings*, vol. I, p. 67.

55. J. Beattie, *Dissertations moral and critical* (London: 1783; reprinted Bad Cannstatt: Verlag Günter Holzboog, 1970), p. 41.

56. A summary of these developments in the context of the history of memory is to be found in Le Goff, *History and memory*. See also T. McArthur, *Worlds of difference: Lexicography, learning and language from the clay tablet to the computer* (Cambridge: Cambridge University Press, 1986).

57. Much relevant historical detail is to be found in chapter 12 of Frances A. Yates's classic study, *The art of memory* (Chicago: University of Chicago Press, 1966).

58. Fentress and Wickham, *Social memory*, chapter 1.

59. Further aspects of this development are discussed in the first section of the following chapter.

60. The exception was the popular *Art of memory* by Marius D'Assigny, which was first published in 1697 and subsequently republished. This was a pot-boiler, largely copied from older works, with a heavy concentration on quasi-medical nostrums rather than the classical art of memory. See chapter 2, note 72.

61. R. Grey, *Memoria technica or method of artificial memory applied to and exemplified in chronology, history, geography, astronomy, also, Jewish, Grecian, and Roman coins, weights, measures, etc.* (London: C. King, 1730).

62. For evidence of this, see A. E. Middleton, *All about mnemonics* (London: Simpkin, Marshall & Co., 1885). A more elaborate mnemonic system that resembled Grey's in some fundamental respects was developed by Aimé Paris in France in the early nineteenth century. See M. K. Matsuda, *The memory of the modern* (New York: Oxford University Press, 1996), chapter 3.

63. The Rev. Lawson, 'Recommendatory character', in R. Grey, *Memoria technica* (Oxford: J. Vincent, 1841), p. xvii. Accuracy and fidelity here do not mean being faithful to the sense or gist of a complex original but reproducing an already unitized original bit by bit. Grey promises to achieve this by what amounts to a kind of *recoding*, but where the original is not already unitized, mnemonics has a more difficult organizational task. A distinction between coding and organizational mnemonics has been proposed on the basis of experimental studies: F. S. Belleza, 'Mnemonic devices: Classification, characteristics, and criteria', *Review of Educational Research* 51 (1981), pp. 247–75.

4 Privileged knowledge

If one compares a sixteenth-century and a twentieth-century work on memory one soon realizes that they are not really concerned with the same topic. An eighteenth-century text would seem less strange to a twentieth-century reader, yet the differences would still be immense. What accounts for these impressions? Let us leave aside the differences that would exist between *any* texts separated by centuries and focus on differences peculiar to the way the topic of memory is handled. Certainly, the older writings contain unfamiliar terms and concepts relating to memory, but even when each of these has been explained there remains a pervasive strangeness that signals another age. This strangeness, I would suggest, has much to do with the profound changes that occurred in the meaning of *knowledge about* memory.

One thread can be detected in an otherwise very diverse literature between the end of the Middle Ages and the beginning of the modern period. It is formed by an implicit conviction that there is a special kind of knowledge to be obtained about memory if one adopts the right approach. Conceptions of what constitutes the right approach change completely during this period, but the idea that there certainly is such an approach remains. With the exception of the Platonists, to whom I will return presently, earlier memory discourse had had a somewhat pragmatic flavour. It addressed memory largely in terms of its usefulness in various contexts, rhetorical, dialectical or religious. In the post-medieval period, however, there is much more interest in memory as an object of knowledge, though conceptions of the nature of this knowledge change quite fundamentally.

Whereas earlier discussions of memory had mostly stayed quite close to common human experience – which is why these discussions are still meaningful today – the newer interest in memory-knowledge entailed a certain distance from the everyday. There were special attitudes to be adopted, special methods to be learned, to gain access to this knowledge. In that sense it was always a privileged knowledge, not available without some training. The amount and the nature of the training varied enormously, but there was always a distinction between those who were in the know and those who were not.

I will consider three versions of privileged memory-knowledge here. These succeeded each other chronologically, though only the oldest is now a historical curiosity. This was the Renaissance version of Neoplatonism, for which the art of memory was not a few tricks to improve one's public speaking but a means for unlocking the secrets of the universe. Long after this strange endeavour had been abandoned there arose the promise of knowledge about a private inner history that might be discovered if one developed the appropriate sensibility and practised a new technique called 'introspection'. Finally there emerged the hope of a medical–scientific knowledge of memory that would be available to those who knew how to adopt the 'objective' attitude of modern natural science and apply its methods.

Esoteric knowledge

Plato had introduced his foundational metaphor of memory as an inscription on a wax tablet[1] in the context of a discussion about relativity and error in human knowledge. The block of wax metaphor allowed him to blame cases of distorted or false knowledge on the imperfections of a faulty medium – the wax of our memory may be muddy or gritty, too soft or too hard. This manoeuvre helped to rescue the idea of true knowledge from the assaults of relativism.

But what is true knowledge? For Plato there was a difference between what might be called mundane knowledge and a deeper, true knowledge. An example of mundane knowledge is the case of recognizing someone one knows from the past and now sees at a distance. This can be explained in terms of the correspondence between the wax imprint of the appearance of the person in memory and the perception of the person in the present.

Fair enough, but there are other, more profound, mathematical or moral truths whose link with memory is not so clear. Here the metaphor of the wax tablet provides little illumination. Because Plato was chiefly interested in this more elusive knowledge, his famous metaphor constitutes only part, and perhaps the less characteristic part, of his contribution to the history of memory discourse. The part that is typically identified with the set of doctrines known as 'Platonism' has much more to do with the notion that true knowledge is esoteric in the sense that it lies buried in memory and requires special measures to make it explicit. Plato's *Dialogues* are illustrations of how he thought this could be accomplished by means of the form of inter-locution practised by his admired teacher, Socrates.

Young men would turn to Socrates for answers to weighty questions, such as the nature of virtue, but he would not instruct them, would not spell out the answers for them. Instead, by questioning, pointing out inadequacies and contradictions in their answers, drawing attention to neglected aspects of the question and so on, he promoted a deeper understanding of the issues. But Socrates believed that his methods could work only if his partner in dialogue in some sense already had the understanding that he sought. People knew more than they realized, and the purpose of the Socratic method was to bring as much as possible of this hidden knowledge out into the open.

Socrates tells one of his dialogue partners that he is the son of a midwife and adds: 'I practice the same art.'[2] He then explains that his dialogical technique is really a kind of midwifery, though what is delivered is not a bodily child but some kind of knowledge. Metaphorically, the baby can be delivered only if the woman is already pregnant. If she is not, no amount of effort on the midwife's part will produce a child. In other words, if one is not in some sense pregnant with an idea even the dialogical skills of a Socrates will not bring it to the surface.

But if the role of Socrates is that of a midwife, then the learning that goes on when young men discuss their perplexities with him must involve a kind of remembering. Socrates helps only to bring out knowledge that was already there, but hidden and unavailable. His task, as he sees it, is to assist his inter-locutor to remember what he already knows without knowing that he knows.

The best-known illustration of this process at work is provided in Plato's *Meno*, where Socrates' questioning gradually leads an untutored slave-boy to display knowledge of Pythagoras' theorem. Plato (through Socrates) denies that the questioning amounted to instruction and claims that it merely helped the boy to remember something he already knew but was previously unable to articulate. If this is so, then 'what we call learning is recollection'.[3]

The word which Plato uses here (*anamnesis*) is not the same as the word for memory. In translation the distinction is customarily made by rendering *anamnesis* as recollection or reminiscence. Unfortunately, this has the effect of hiding a crucial aspect of the distinction. In English, the verbal forms of recollection and reminiscence are active, but in Greek the verbal form of *anamnesis* is passive.[4] More precisely, then, when Plato speaks of what is translated as recollection he is actually referring to a process of being reminded. In the *Meno* the slave-boy is being reminded of something he no longer knows by Socrates playing the role of midwife.

According to Plato, we are born with knowledge we do not realize we have until something or someone reminds us of it. The slave-boy certainly did not know he had any knowledge of geometry until Socrates coaxed it out of him.[5] What was the nature of this hidden knowledge? Plato thought that it related to eternal verities in such areas as mathematics, aesthetics and morality. Here the role of memory in cognition is reversed. Far from being a source of error it now functions as a repository of fundamental truths. For Plato there is no contradiction, however, because the two forms of memory are identified by separate terms. Fallible mundane memory is *mneme*, whereas memory of unchanging truths is *anamnesis*. Both can exist side by side.

The idea of a pre-existing source of knowledge which did not depend on individual experience had a strong appeal to many later philosophers, and, in the course of time, various interpretations of the content of inborn knowledge gained prominence: knowledge of God or of the principles that order the cosmos, an intuitive understanding of such categories as time and space, inherited biological responses, archetypes of social relationships, to mention only a few. Ever since Plato, the topic of mundane, everyday memory has been shadowed by the intriguing possibility that there might also be a kind of memory that transcends this worldly individual experience in some way.

The history of Platonic memory might well form the subject of one or more specialized monographs. For a general overview of conceptions of individual memory, however, much of this history has little more than tangential significance and will not be touched on here. But one notable exception that cannot be passed over in silence concerns the Neoplatonist revival of Renaissance Europe. One of the characteristic features of this revival was a reinvigoration of the art of memory, so that in the sixteenth century memory books were launched in unprecedented profusion. Certainly, the advent of printing greatly assisted this development, but printing multiplied the number of all books, and it is not clear why memory books should have been specially favoured. It is also true that many of the memory treatises of the sixteenth century owed nothing to Neoplatonism and everything to a post-medieval popular diffusion of knowledge connected to the loss of the Church's monopoly on learning. But one of the consequences of the popularization of the art of memory at this time was trivialization, a decline of a once highly respected art to a compendium of tricks for scoring points in the game of life. Where Renaissance art of memory retained its high intellectual ambitions it did so because of its Neoplatonic inspiration.

Perhaps the strongest affinity to the Platonic spirit was to be found among those Renaissance figures who developed arts of memory designed to reveal a hidden order of the world that existed behind and beyond mundane experience. Platonic, too, was the contrast between the fluctuation of the latter and the permanence of the underlying order. But it is the novel features of Renaissance memory arts that are of greater historical interest.

Whereas the Socratic method had relied on the verbal and essentially auditory form of dialogue, Renaissance art of memory adopted an overwhelmingly visual approach. This took two main forms: the use of space for the representation of conceptual connections and the deployment of elaborate imagery for establishing the relationship between knower and known. Both spatial location and images had of course long been basic devices of the classical art of memory, but in the Renaissance they underwent a florid development that ultimately contributed to the bad repute in which the art was held subsequently.

There is no better illustration of the strange use of spatialization as a mnemonic device than the Renaissance 'theatre of memory'.[6] These theatres existed mostly in the imagination, though one or two actual models seem to have been built. As in a normal theatre, they provided a way of displaying scenes for the benefit of the spectator. However, the spatial relationship between viewer and viewed was the reverse of the one found in the trad-itional Roman amphitheatre, where spectators typically sit in circular tiers from where their views converge on a central stage. In a memory theatre, on the other hand, the viewer occupies the central position and looks out over a display of figures and symbols arranged in an orderly array of rows and sectors analogous to a real amphitheatre.

If held in one's memory, such a display would, it was hoped, provide the ultimate localization mnemonic. Whereas traditional forms of local memory, employed in a rhetorical context, had worked with places and images devised for specific occasions, the people who designed Renaissance theatres of memory had encyclopaedic ambitions. The nature, positioning and interrelationship of the images occupying the theatre were meant to convey a universe of knowledge. If anyone really succeeded in carrying such a theatre around in their head they would be a kind of walking encyclopaedia.

But it would be quite anachronistic to think of such an encyclopaedia as conforming to later models of the genre. Strictly speaking, the Renaissance memory theatre contained no empirical facts, the very conception of a fact being an invention of later centuries. What was valued in such a theatre was its potential for representing insights that would not be readily available if one followed more mundane paths to knowledge. That is why the greatest care and effort was applied to the appropriate choice of images and to their correct placing in the theatre. If this work was successful the theatre would convey esoteric knowledge about the world, knowledge that was ordinarily hidden.[7] Much of this knowledge depended on astrological symbolism and necromancy, earning the disapproval of Renaissance humanists as well as the Church.

Nevertheless, the spatialization of knowledge, for which the theatre of memory provided the ultimate public display, had deep historical roots that extended back to Platonic geometry and Aristotelian 'topics' and had been nourished by the cultivation of 'local memory'. The profound appeal of clothing cognitive content in spatial forms had long been apparent, and the possibilities opened up by the technology of printing surely enhanced that appeal. But the spatialization of knowledge had long been utilized in the service of two rather different cultural goals. There was the broadly Platonic goal of arriving at more profound insights, but there was also a more pragmatic, quasi-pedagogical goal of mobilizing spatialized knowledge to promote the effectiveness of one's arguments and to increase the availability and accessibility of an individual's store of knowledge. In the Renaissance period epistemic and pedagogical goals became quite strongly linked. It was believed that the true representation of reality would enhance its memorability. Finding the most appropriate representation of the structure of the world would at the same time serve mnemonic purposes, because memory had an affinity for the truth, no matter how complex.

Platonic memory theatres therefore had their pedagogical aspects, though they were much too cumbersome to be very convincing learning devices. Their historical failure was no surprise to many contemporaries, though the affinity between truth and memory which these theatres presupposed was based on Neoplatonic doctrines that enjoyed quite wide currency at the time. The key to the relationship between true knowledge and memory was provided by the intimate relationship that was supposed to exist between the structure of the universe, the macrocosm, and the structure of the individual human, the microcosm. For the principal architects of theatres of memory the display they aspired to was as much a representation of external reality as of human interiority. The theatre also functioned as a window through which the structure and content of human subjectivity was made visible.[8] But 'subjectivity' is here used anachronistically, because, for this philosophy, the division between subjectivity and objectivity did not yet exist.

The faculty of imagination played a crucial role in crystallizing and elaborating the union of microcosm and macrocosm, and the link between imagination and memory was extremely close. Imagery, not language, was the primary vehicle of mnemonic representation. Never has the power of imagery been held in greater awe. Its capacity for dominating the life of the individual was likened to the power of eros, and the nostrums for freeing a person from the effects of unwanted imagery were similar to those prescribed for curing love-sickness. The time was ripe for the emergence of the negative counterpart of the art of memory, *ars oblivionalis*, the art of forgetting. So strong was the grip of imagery that there was now a market for advice manuals that taught how to get rid of intrusive and disturbing images. This was to be accomplished by mobilizing countervailing imagery: one was to imagine the unwanted images being smashed, destroyed by fire or killed off. The same degree of care and effort had to be applied to the destruction of images as had been applied to their construction.

Some believed the potential power of images to be great enough to be used for influencing not only the individual microcosm, but also the macrocosm. If one lavished enough concentration on certain images one could exert an influence on the external world. This, of course, was magic, and magical beliefs were indeed a widespread feature of Renaissance Neoplatonism. However, this version of magic had a relatively respectable grounding in the older belief that vision, and by extension visual imagination, involved a transmission from eye to object, not only from object to eye. A magical effect on objects by a projection of visual imagery would therefore form a not altogether implausible counterpart to ordinary perception.

However, the extraordinary emphasis on the power of imagery, accompanied by a blurring of the distinction between memory and imagination, marked the final efflorescence of an art of memory that had its roots in classical schemes of local memory. The extravagance of Renaissance versions of the art served to bring it into disrepute and after the sixteenth century its decline was very rapid. It was in any case out of tune with contemporary developments that pointed to a future very different from the traditions that fed its elaborate constructions. Even while some were still designing theatres of memory based on imagery, others were working on the use of spatial relationships for representing *logical* relationships. This led to the elaboration of diagrams and schematic tables that also served visual memorization but with content that was abstract and analytical. Memory was no longer harnessed to esoteric cognitive goals but to step-by-step procedures of logical dissection and classification that would produce an essentially public knowledge. The chimerical promises of Neoplatonic memory arts were being replaced by the more sober claims of Method.[9]

The fierce iconoclasm that was such a prominent feature of the cultural revolution of Protestantism was bound to take offence at the florid use of imagery characteristic of Renaissance Neoplatonism. Puritan disapproval of religious icons, talismans and the like was not likely to stop at these external manifestations. In the form of an 'inner iconoclasm'[10] it was also directed at the excessive recourse to sensuous imagery in the mental life of the individual.[11] Truth was to be sought in words and other arbitrary symbols, not in analogical images. What appealed to the new sensibility was not the dream of secret visions but the public advancement of knowledge by the systematic employment of Method. The new epistemic goals were not to be achieved by the positioning and manipulation of traditional imagery, but by exploiting the combinatorial possibilities of abstract and arbitrary symbols, such as those of mathematics and partially or wholly artificial languages.[12]

These developments did not come to fruition until the seventeenth and eighteenth centuries, at which time the predominance of a new natural philosophy, later to be identified as 'natural science', or simply 'science', entailed the total eclipse of the traditional art of memory and the rise of a modern form of mnemonics that worked with verbal tokens and digital units, as described in the final section of chapter 3. Not only was a different kind of memory now cultivated, the entire topic of memory lost the central significance it had enjoyed for so many centuries. In part, this was of course due to an enormous and ever-growing expansion in the resources of external memory. But profound cultural changes also played a role. As long as cognitive goals remained closely tied to appeals to tradition, memory was assured of an honoured place. This applied not only to the content but also to the form of cognitive representation. While the favoured form of that representation constantly drew on a huge stock of concrete images derived from a wide range of historical models,[13] efforts of memory remained intimately bound up with the achievement of knowledge. But with the switch to combinatorial rules and a relatively small number of digital symbols, the role of memory in the generation of knowledge was much reduced. Where Method could be relied on to grind out new knowledge with almost mechanical assurance Memory could safely be relegated to lesser tasks, such as rote learning and personal reminiscence.

The privatization of memory

After the florid cultivation of memory during the sixteenth century there was a sharp drop in publications devoted to the memory arts and a devaluation of memory's role in generating knowledge and understanding, a development already noted in the last section of chapter 3. Profound social changes following the collapse of medieval civilization formed the broader historical context for this development. The steady replacement of subsistence agriculture with commodity production for profit, the increasing importance of trade and commerce, the growth of essentially urban lifestyles, the change in the relative power of various social classes, the advance of technology and natural science, the loosening influence of religious institutions, the spread of secular knowledge and secular values, the pervasive social mobility and all the other ferments of germinating modernity, produced a gamut of reactions that ranged from desperate attempts to hold on to the security of a fast vanishing past to an enthusiastic embrace of whatever the new age had to offer. At the very least, there was a recognition that times had changed drastically and required a re-examination of old habits. Sometimes this led to the deliberate re-affirmation of those habits, but more often it made old habits of thought seem threadbare and inadequate. That easily led to the conviction that, in the face of the new realities, new knowledge and new ways of obtaining that knowledge were required. Tradition was seriously devalued, and memory was too closely linked to tradition not to be significantly affected.

In the writings of the first major representative of modern philosophy, René Descartes, the ramifications of this new attitude to memory are quite explicit. Unlike his medieval and Renaissance predecessors Descartes does not elevate memory to a source of moral virtue or profound understanding but reduces it to a source of prejudice and unreliability. The existence of a memory of the soul, so-called intellectual memory, is acknowledged but it seems little can be said about it. What Descartes does elaborate upon is the memory that is imprinted on the body, as we saw towards the end of chapter 2. This memory, however, depends on the contingent history of the individual body and is a better guide to bias and distortion than to truth. To arrive at the latter, we need not memory, but Method. Descartes juxtaposes the old approach to knowledge, which relied on memory, tradition and history, and the new approach that relies on universally valid rules of rational investigation. In fact, memory was an obstacle to the pursuit of genuine insight: 'we must not allow a needless effort of memory to distract a part of our mind from its knowledge of the object before it'.[14] In the post-Cartesian world logic and, later, scientific method replaced memory as the guarantors of true knowledge and therefore as objects of profound interest. For Descartes (and those who shared his orientation), 'memory, then, was to be avoided in favour of a methodic reason that was always primary'.[15]

Development of the new, scientific, path to true knowledge depended on a complete rejection of the close links between microcosm and macrocosm that had been the foundation of Renaissance Neoplatonist philosophy. The macrocosm was transformed into an 'object' and the microcosm into a 'subject', and the relationship between the two was marked by distance rather than closeness. Scientific knowledge, whether rational or empirical, demanded a prior disengagement of the subject from the object. So-called subjective factors were obstacles to true knowledge, a source of bias, distortion and error. Individual memory was undoubtedly to be counted among these subjective factors: it was unreliable as a record of objective events and was valuable only when confirmed by a number of observers.

But, ideally, observations should be recorded as soon as they were made, thus entrusting the preservation of knowledge entirely to external memory and eliminating individual memory altogether. The form of truth was the written statement expressing a proposition describing some state of affairs. Such truths were permanently fixed in texts whose content was capable of more or less accurate reproduction by individual minds.[16]

This entailed a much sharper distinction between memory and knowledge than in the preceding period. Memory becomes personal and unreliable, located within the individual soul, whereas knowledge is inscribed on paper and represents facts that are independent of the experience of any one individual. The modern split between subjectivity and objectivity emerges, and the classical memory arts have no relevance for either side of this divide.

It hardly needs saying that the principle of disengagement between observer-subject and natural object was enormously successful in promoting true knowledge of the natural world. But hardly anyone was prepared to say that the world of nature was all there was. The existence of a moral world, a world of human action and responsibility, was a fact of life, and here the disengagement of subject and object had somewhat different implications. Descartes dealt with the matter in terms of his metaphysical dualism between soul and body. The subject, represented by the soul, was able to observe and, as far as possible, control the body-object.[17] The philosopher had been obliged to address this issue as a result of requests for advice from two aristocratic ladies with moral concerns.[18]

However, such concerns were hardly limited to female members of the aristocracy. In fact, the Reformation and Counter-Reformation had been associated with practices of moral self-examination that depended on subjects becoming objects to themselves. For centuries the Christian practice of institutionalized confession had encouraged an examination, not only of one's actions, but increasingly also of one's secret intentions and feelings. This culminated in the examination of one's moral life *as a whole*, either in the form of a Calvinist questioning of one's elect or damned status or in the form of a regular 'general confession' promoted by the Counter-Reformation.[19] Memory would obviously play no small role in these exercises, though this was the memory of an involved participant, not a disengaged observer. In moral self-examination, subject and object, though distinguishable, were intimately connected and not separated as they were in the observation of nature. For a time, a dispassionate factual memory and a memory infused by moral passion existed side by side.

But this was not to last. A first step in their convergence was represented by the practice of keeping a moral diary. Here the emotionally laden direct re-experience of a sinful life was distilled into a written record where subject and object were more clearly distinct. On subsequent occasions, the subject could rely on the external record of his or her sinful life and did not need to rely entirely on what fallible personal memory revealed.

Self-examination may have originated in a religious context, but many of its practices were readily transferable to a secular context. As the role of religion became less and less significant for the everyday lives of many individuals, the secularization of self-examination proceeded apace. Diaries were kept of day-to-day experiences without any profound concern for their moral significance. Reminiscence was more likely to serve personal than religious ends. The term 'introspection' had been introduced in the seventeenth century to refer to the religiously motivated self-examination that was so characteristic of that time. But subsequently its meaning became secularized, just like the practices to which it referred. It came to describe dispassionate self-observation without any moral overtones, and it is in this guise that 'introspection' became a term of psychology. Observing one's own actions and experiences without any explicit moral intent became a recognized practice among enlightened individuals.

Memory necessarily played a role in such exercises in self-examination, but this was a personalized memory, not the memory for external facts that Enlightenment mnemonics addressed. However, this new privatized memory was utterly different from the personal immersion and re-experiencing that monastic memory had valued and that Plato had contrasted with mere reminding. The clue to the difference is provided by the relationship of personal memory to writing. For Plato, writing had a destructive effect on memory as re-living, and the monastics certainly did not regard saintly conduct as essentially governed by literary form.[20] However, for Montaigne, who offered an early example of modern personal memory, writing was crucial in imposing order and accessibility on an otherwise chaotic and elusive jumble of memories.[21] Outside religious forms, the more determined practitioners of personal memory in the early modern period relied on writing, whether as diarists, like Samuel Pepys, or as essayists, like Montaigne. But writing down one's own experiences implies a certain distance between self and experience that is not present in a direct re-living of the experience. The difference between the disengaged self practising the objective observation of nature and the self that writes down its own experiences is therefore not as great as might appear at first. A distancing of subject and object is a necessary feature of both practices.

A theoretical reflection of this state of affairs is to be found in the discourse of classical philosophical empiricism. In John Locke's foundational *An essay concerning human understanding* the contents of the human mind were depicted as resulting from the action of the senses, receiving impressions from external objects or from the mind's own activity. We perceive the external world through sight, hearing, touch and so on, but we also have an *inner sense* that perceives inner mental events. That would include memories. The concept of inner sense was very old, but Locke uses it in a new way. In the Aristotelian tradition the inner sense was the site of cognitive activities that transformed the experiences mediated by the external senses.[22] For Locke, however, the activity of the inner sense is essentially perceptual. The inner sense *perceives* what is going on in the mind in much the same way as the outer senses perceive the external world.[23]

This analogy between outer and inner perception had profound consequences for the understanding of personal memories. In his conception of external perception Locke accepted the Cartesian divide between a disengaged subject and a morally neutral object. But he radicalized this division by extending it to subjects' perceptions of their own mental life.[24] Whenever we perceive, says Locke, we also perceive ourselves perceiving.[25] This also applies to perceptions recalled from the past, that is, memories, when we perceive ourselves remembering. He called this double perception *consciousness*, a term that was quite new at the time.

Empiricism asserted the sensory origin of all knowledge, not only of the external world, but also of the internal life of the mind. It did so at a time when the objective observation of the external world was beginning to pay massive dividends in the form of what would eventually be called scientific knowledge. Small wonder that the possibility of a science of the mind, based on internal observation, suggested itself within a generation after Locke's death. In Germany this science was called empirical psychology from the beginning.[26] In Britain the term 'psychology' did not come into use until the mid-nineteenth century, though introspective observation of the mind was freely practised by all members of the dominant philosophical school of empiricism.

For empiricist introspectionism the new, disengaged way of knowing the external world became the model for knowledge of inner states of mind. The texts of this school of thought described the objects of inner observation, including one's memories, as though they could be examined and analysed in the same distanced way as the external objects studied by the new natural philosophy. This implied a profound separation between an observing self and the contents of its own mind. On that basis it became possible to describe mental contents analytically in terms of separate units linked by quasi-mechanical bonds of association.[27]

Because empiricism was profoundly committed to the sensory basis of all knowledge, these mental units were regarded as *copies* of primary sensory experiences. Memories were therefore copies of previous sensory impressions that were somewhat fainter than the originals. Because memories were essentially reproductions of some original experience, they differed from each other in the adequacy of that reproduction. A very faint copy would be a poor reproduction; a vivid copy would constitute a good reproduction. In the empiricist world-view memories could be interrogated as to their truth, a truth that depended on the accuracy with which they reflected some prior sensory input.

It is worth noting the convergence between the theoretical discourse of philosophical empiricism and the kind of mnemonics that began to be advocated at virtually the same time. As described in chapter 3, the new practice of mnemonics was dedicated to the improvement of accuracy and quantity in the reproduction of bits of factual knowledge. Was this not the appropriate practical counterpart to a theoretical discourse that reduced memory to the function of copying units of sensory information?

Reduced to a kind of copying machine, memory was unlikely to attract much intellectual interest. But there was a particular extension of Locke's doctrines that restored some importance to memory. In the second edition of his *Essay* Locke had linked the sum total of an individual's conscious memories to the concept of personal identity:

> Wherever a man finds what he calls himself, there, I think, another may say is the same person. It is a forensic term, appropriating actions and their merit; and so belongs only to intelligent agents, capable of a law, and happiness, and misery. This personality extends itself beyond present existence to what is past, only by consciousness, – whereby it becomes concerned and accountable, owns and imputes to itself past actions, just upon the same ground and for the same reason as it does the present.[28]

In other words, I am constituted by my memories, and I am personally accountable for actions I can remember. These were claims that aroused a great deal of controversy, not least because they dispensed with the immortal soul as the foundation of personal identity and responsibility and replaced it with a self as an empirically observed entity.[29] But Locke's account of the sources of personal identity restored to memory an importance it had not had for a century. What individual memory had lost to Method and to the vastly expanded resources of external memory it now seemed to regain in terms of its foundational role in the formation of personal identity and personal accountability.[30]

At a time when it was no longer important in relation to sacred texts or to esoteric knowledge, memory became interesting again because it provided access to an object of ever-greater cultural significance, the individual personality, and especially its inner, private, life. A kind of testimony that had previously been rather marginal now attracted growing interest: this was testimony about an individual's conscious states, feelings, images and fantasies, reported from within. Sometimes, older motives still adhered to such testimony – the hope that one might be relieved of a burden of guilt, for example. But more and more, this testimony, though often still tagged anachronistically as a 'confession', was valued for itself. It seemed to provide access to a newly fascinating human object, the unique personal identity of a human individual. This personal identity was entirely a this-worldly thing, not linked to immortality and to an otherworldly religious order as the concept of the individual soul had been. It was quite possible for individuals to think of themselves as having a secular personal identity as well as a spiritual soul, and for both to be treasured.

But the analytical type of introspection, characteristic of philosophical empiricism, was not an appropriate technique for exploring this personal inner world. It had been designed to answer general, philosophical questions, not to expose to view a secret private life. A new kind of self-observation was needed, one that remained much closer to the personal experience of reminiscence and reverie and was less dedicated to a rigidly intellectualized conception of truth. In the second half of the eighteenth century one does indeed find evidence of a new kind of self-report in the so-called literature of sensibility, some of it appearing in the guise of fiction,[31] but increasingly as non-fiction, especially as personal diary and autobiography. In this literature sentiments and feelings play a major role in the presentation of inner experience. It is difficult and unconvincing to maintain a posture of uninvolved objectivity towards one's own emotional life and consequently observers and reporters now come across as living in their experiences. Their aim has changed from self-dissection to self-presentation. A certain distancing of the self as observer from the self as observed is still crucial, but this is not modelled on a quasi-scientific subject–object split where the object is the source of analysable data. In this new form of self-observation, the self is preserved as both subject and object, perhaps as present self regarding past self or as an ironically linked duo.

The publication of the first part of Jean Jacques Rousseau's autobiography in France in 1782 marked a kind of watershed in the deployment of memory for purposes of self-presentation. Rousseau titled his autobiography *Confessions*,[32] a provocative choice at the time because the confessions he offered dispensed with the traditional institutionalized forms of the Church. Rousseau well knew that in a Catholic country the choice of *that* title for an autobiography was bound to draw attention to the contrast between his style of confessing and that of St Augustine, whose work had been exemplary for many centuries.[33] Both authors had drawn selectively on their personal memories in order to assemble a kind of life history but the considerations that governed their selection could not have been more different. Augustine, a Neoplatonist, had arranged his reminiscences around the theme of his conversion to Christianity, his progression from sinner to devout believer. His masterful construction of a self-narrative and his explicit recognition of the problems of autobiographical memory were unequalled and had remained historically unique. But it was clear that his autobiography had a didactic function: the presentation of an example of successful conversion that might be helpful to others embarking on the same path. Memory, to Augustine, opened up a path to God in a way that ultimately remained mysterious.

Rousseau's autobiography lacked the profound religious sensibility of Augustine, though it was still concerned with questions of morality. There was nothing exemplary about Rousseau's collection of reminiscences, at least not in any institutionally sanctioned sense. At most, these memories had exemplary value for mankind at large, but the principle of their selection was derived from the need to present the unique quality of the individual life. What made the individual life interesting, moreover, was not its path to salvation nor its worldly achievements, but the emotional quality of its experiences.

In this respect Rousseau's *Confessions* were not very different from many literary productions of the time. In Germany, the turn towards secularized emotional self-observation was especially strong, finding expression in the literature of 'storm and stress' exemplified by J. W. Goethe's *The sorrows of young Werther* (1774). By the close of the century, the valorization of the inner emotional life was being intensively cultivated by the literature of Romanticism.

But this was not simply a literary phenomenon, a shift in aesthetic taste. In the personal diaries of the late eighteenth century, including those not intended for publication, there is a noticeable concern with the affective aspects of life, stripped of the religious context in which they would have been embedded at an earlier time.[34] Feelings have become worth reflecting on simply as part of an individual life history. But this reflection is seldom characterized by cool analysis; its aim is usually the adequate representation of a lived experience. These tendencies are found in exaggerated form in the *journal intime* that became popular in France during the first half of the nineteenth century.[35] In the diaries of this period there are many 'confessions', but these are not public confessions in an institutionalized setting. They are private confessions made only to oneself in the hope that their recorded sum will help the diarist make sense of his life history. For a later generation, this function of the intimate diary would be taken over by trained professionals.[36]

There were early signs that a space was gradually opening up for the intervention of a new class of experts in the interpretation of private emotional experience. An important development was the appearance of a new form for the organization of intimate memories. Older forms, governed by religious or aesthetic considerations, did not die out but were joined by a new form in which the public recording of an individual's private life became an end in itself. This form of self-presentation first reached considerable dimensions in Germany in the late eighteenth century. At that time there appeared a number of journals or magazines with titles referring to 'empirical psychology' or the equivalent German term, *Erfahrungsseelenkunde*.[37] Although these journals published some general articles, 70 per cent of the contributions to the most successful of them were devoted to individuals' reports on their private experiences. In the majority of cases, these experiences have a distinctly pathological tinge, a fact that is apparent to the authors.[38] Their report, based on memories of their inner experience, therefore constitutes a kind of psychological case-history related in the first person.

All these publications, whether they take the form of diaries, confessional autobiographies or first-person case-histories, are indicative of a new relationship of truth and memory. Although they often pay lip service to the classical Greek prescription 'know thyself', their understanding of what knowing oneself meant is vastly different. For the moderns, the task is no longer one of unravelling the normative precepts that govern all individual lives but one of knowing oneself *as an individual* with a unique history. In this task the marshalling of personal memories takes on central importance. Understanding individuality means knowing how one got to be that way, and this knowledge can only be obtained by mobilizing memory. However, the truth that memory is expected to reveal is not an intellectual but an emotional one.

The cultural ambience of Romanticism may have provided a nourishing environment for the growth of this orientation, but in many individual cases it is clear that the immediate impulse for retrospective self-examination came from the experience of personal problems that were no longer interpreted primarily as problems of religious faith but as psychological problems. The high incidence of psychopathology in the self-reported case-histories has already been noted, and this was true of confessional autobiographies and diaries as well. There is evidence that by the beginning of the nineteenth century there was a significant interest in exploring the truth behind experienced personal problems by turning to affectively charged reminiscences.

This interest at first seems to have arisen among members of the lay public, and the medical profession was actually rather slow in taking advantage of it. The authors of the early self-reported case-histories did not lay claim to professional expertise, and this contributed greatly to the ephemeral nature of the publications devoted to this kind of material. There was no professional organization to provide continuity for this enterprise, and there were no professional standards to prevent this kind of literature from becoming trivialized and merging with general popular literature. The very notion of a psychiatric profession did not exist in the year 1800 and it was not until the late nineteenth century that professionally organized psychiatric knowledge became a significant factor in the history of memory.[39]

Alienated memory

At the time Locke proposed his theory of the person it was already a matter of common knowledge that consciousness of self was subject to various disturbances. He recognized four: sleeping, dreaming, drunkenness and madness. In sleep we are not conscious of ourselves except in dreams, when peculiar things happen and are not necessarily remembered. Quite rightly, we are not held responsible for our dreams, and in dreamless sleep there are no actions to be held accountable for. Drunkenness and madness are more troublesome, and debates around questions of criminal responsibility in these states gradually became more vehement.

If, like Locke, one accepts the continuity of self-consciousness as the basis of personal identity, then any state in which this continuity is disrupted becomes a potentially troubling exception. Perhaps that is one of the reasons why, in the course of the very Lockean eighteenth century, a state then known as *somnambulism* attracted increasing attention. This term was used in a very wide sense to refer, not merely to walking in one's sleep, but more generally to a state in which individuals carried out actions and had experiences of which they had no memory in their ordinary lives. This might include 'automatic writing', speaking in strange voices and languages, as well as episodes of disorientation and much of what would later be described as hysterical fugue states or even cataleptic trance. All these were cases of what might be called *memory alienation*, situations in which individuals were cut off from significant areas of their own life that had become inaccessible to conscious recall. Dreams constituted another example of alienated memory, because their content might become wholly or partially unavailable after waking, while, conversely, things might be remembered in dreams that had long been forgotten in waking life.

Phenomena of alienated memory became troubling in the wake of the privatization of memory and a general process of secularization that affected all attempts at explaining human experience. Earlier on, severe cases of memory alienation would have been explained in terms of possession, where a spirit had taken over the life of the individual. But once belief in spirits declined or disappeared, this explanation was no longer available. At the same time, the privatization of memory, described in the previous section, endowed the phenomena of memory alienation with new qualities of threat and wonder. As the Lockean tie between personal identity and personal memory became a common article of faith, the phenomena of memory alienation were seen as a threat to personal identity but also as a source of puzzlement. However, attempts at explaining these phenomena naturalistically made little progress until late in the nineteenth century.

As I have emphasized before, conceptions of memory have always been linked to particular techniques and practices. Familiarity with writing provided the ultimate source for the abiding metaphor of memory as an inscription that experience left on the soul or the mind (chapter 2). The development of mnemonic techniques, especially those connected to the use of books and manuscripts, went hand in hand with later reflections on memory (chapter 3). What I have referred to as the privatization of memory in the previous section of this chapter showed a practical side in the keeping of diaries and the composition of introspective autobiographical reports. If one were to ask whether there was a social practice or technique with a particular link to the new ideas about memory that emerged in the late nineteenth century, one would have to say – hypnosis.

The switch to a naturalistic understanding of somnambulistic phenomena partly depended on the recognition that such phenomena could be induced artificially by means of what became known as hypnotism after the middle of the nineteenth century.[40] In its late eighteenth-century beginnings as 'mesmerism', hypnosis, and its associated theory of 'animal magnetism', had been rejected by the scientific establishment. Very gradually, it gained sufficient respectability to be added to the range of treatments advocated by at least a small group of medical practitioners. Medical help for problems of memory had been offered and sought for many centuries in the form of potions, salves, heat applied to the back of the head and so on. But what came to be known as psychological treatment was not medicalized until the nineteenth and twentieth centuries, and even then the attitude of the medical profession as a whole remained ambivalent at best. This area of practice was generally relegated to new specialties outside the mainstream of medical practice, neurology and later psychiatry. Some of those practising in these areas began to apply hypnosis quite regularly in a context of healing and scientific investigation.

Hypnosis was not part of ordinary life. Any memory phenomena observed in the context of hypnosis could be regarded as artefacts of a deliberate interference with normal mental functioning. In a sense, hypnotic memory phenomena were analogous to the artificial memory of the ancients, though, peculiarly, they were marked by odd feats of forgetting rather than by prodigious feats of memory. But the ancients knew that the effectiveness of artificial memory depended on its basis in natural memory;

no worthwhile art of memory could ever be completely artificial. Similarly, the practitioners of rational medicine who became intrigued by hypnotic phenomena in the late nineteenth century believed that these phenomena were part of the same natural world as other phenomena of human personality and memory. That was why hypnotic interventions could sometimes be medically effective, and, in a specifically modern turn, provide a potential source of insights about the natural functioning of human personality and memory.

Certain phenomena of alienated memory could now be made to appear at the behest of the medical expert. They no longer had the status of spontaneous natural events, but could be studied systematically in a more or less scientific manner. The entire range of strange and unusual manifestations and failures of memory was becoming medicalized. Any suggestion that these manifestations were of spiritual or supernatural significance was rejected in favour of widespread speculation about their natural causes. They were regarded as pathological conditions, departures from health, that required treatment by the means available to medical science.

Compared to the immediately preceding centuries, there was now a very noticeable increase in the amount, but also in the nature, of attention devoted to the topic of memory. The excesses of the art of memory were by now forgotten, and mnemonics had been relegated to its intellectually trivial niche. Increasingly, memory becomes a subject worthy of serious attention in its own right. But there is a peculiar quality to all this attention: More than ever before, memory is regarded as *problematic*. The invocation of memory takes place in a variety of contexts that all have in common a troubled relationship between present requirements and past experience.

This was a time of rapid and unprecedented social change in Western and Northern Europe. Rapid modernization, manifesting itself in the breakdown of traditional moral expectations, increased social and geographical mobility, individual isolation and anomie, confusion around gender roles and the uncertainties of a fast-changing political and economic landscape, led to a new set of concerns centring on individual memory. What was now becoming increasingly troublesome was the individual's relationship to his or her own past.[41] Profound disruptions in the continuity of life could transform individual memory into a site of problems marked by a sense of being carried along by forces over which one had no conscious control.

The consequences of urbanization, industrialization, migration and changed gender roles produced discontinuities in the lives of many individuals that upset the smooth integration of past and present. One symptom of this dislocation is the sympathetic hearing granted to neo-Romantic voices trying to recapture a happier past.[42] As this reaction co-existed with a continuing rejection of the past required by new life forms and new technologies, the overall effect was one of diffuse ambivalence and uncertainty.

Under these circumstances, forgetting, the dark shadow of memory, might assume a significance it had never previously enjoyed. There had never really been an art of forgetting, only an art of memory. Now there arose, not an art, but a science of forgetting that had its own scientific experts and practitioners. Their studies tended 'to show how the continuous or harmonious relation of present and past could be organized as a scientific/medical problem'.[43]

Biology and the science of forgetting

The social transformations that had made the relationship of past and present problematic also seemed to provide the potential means for alleviating the situation. This was because modernization had provided the basis for the establishment of institutionalized science whose steady progress was revolutionizing medicine. There was every hope that the scientific treatment of people's physical problems could be extended to their mental problems, including problems of memory. That hope led to the emergence of something new – a science of memory. Previously, discourse about memory had taken place largely in a philosophical context or in the context of the 'art of memory', and to a minor extent also in the context of pre-scientific medicine. But from the late nineteenth century, the solution to problems of individual memory is expected to come from science, especially scientific medicine.

During the last two decades of the nineteenth century there emerged a new public discourse on memory that promised to rescue the topic from its philosophical entanglements and establish it firmly as an object of science.

> Issues of memory and personal identity were henceforth to be discussed in the terms of and explored by the techniques of medical science. That meant agreement on the use of memory disturbances to throw light on the regular functioning of memory. Particularly in late nineteenth century France, the preoccupation with 'maladies of memory' owed its persistence to a more general interest in clarifying what a 'normal' relationship of past and present might be.[44]

Scientific medicine relied on the more fundamental science of biology for its credentials. A scientific approach to disease was made possible by rapidly advancing knowledge about the normal functioning of the human body as a biological organism. Therefore, it seemed that a truly scientific approach to problems of memory would require that memory be treated as, fundamentally, a biological phenomenon.

That was exactly the position adopted by Théodule Ribot (1839–1916), a French writer of books on recent developments in psychology that combined a wide popular appeal with some original contribution to the topics in question.[45] One of these books was specifically devoted to memory and immediately translated into English.[46] Right at the beginning of his monograph Ribot proclaimed the principle on which his exposition would be based, namely, 'that memory is, *per se*, a biological fact – by accident, a psychological fact'.[47] Consciousness plays but a small and merely symptomatic role in the extended operations of an essentially unconscious organic process. This means that virtually the entire traditional discourse on memory is rendered obsolete – by treating memory as essentially a feature of the mind, it had wrongly substituted an untypical part for the whole. It was time to leave this legacy behind and turn to modern science for illumination on the nature of memory.

In fact, Ribot was not the inventor but merely a very effective popularizer of the notion that memory was essentially biological. In the late nineteenth century, the term 'organic memory' was frequently used in connection with a family of theories sharing the conviction that memory was an affair of the body in some very profound sense. Conscious aspects of memory were considered secondary, mere effects of what was *essentially* a biological phenomenon. There had certainly been a discourse on the material basis of mind in the eighteenth century,[48] but, unlike later conceptions of organic memory, these earlier speculations did not make memory the focus of their speculations. Moreover, the theorists of organic memory were able to rely on the findings and the prestige of established biological sciences, a resource that had grown enormously and taken forms that could hardly have been imagined a century earlier.

The opening shot in the campaign to transfer the subject of memory from the domain of philosophy, and its then sub-field of psychology, to the terrain of biology can be dated with exceptional precision. On 30 May 1870, Ewald Hering, a physiologist of renown, addressed the Imperial Academy of Sciences in Vienna on a topic which he provocatively titled 'Memory as a general function of organized matter'.[49] This lecture, frequently cited for several decades, expressed a view of memory that came to be quite widely shared in this period, though not everyone accepted all the details of its argument. Hering had no interest in the pathology of memory, but he lent a voice of scientific authority to the proposal that there were significant analogies between what is traditionally called 'memory' and phenomena that everyone recognized as purely biological. Those phenomena included the growth of muscle tissue as a result of exercise, the involuntary recall of sensations, and the inheritance of acquired characteristics in the form of instincts. All these, according to Hering, can be regarded as manifestations 'of one and the same faculty of organized matter, viz., memory, or the faculty of reproduction'.[50] Ordinarily, memory was considered to be a feature of mental life, but Hering's redefinition claimed it for biology.

Although Hering's lecture represented the most succinct and authoritative statement of the basic doctrine of 'organic memory', similar views were being developed around the same time quite independently by several British authors. These included the psychiatrist Henry Maudsley, the popular intellectual Samuel Butler, and the eminent medical theorist Thomas Laycock.[51] The linking of memory and heredity, and the implied annexation of the terrain of memory by biology, was certainly not the brainchild of a single individual; it constituted the characteristic turn taken by memory discourse in the social and scientific context that prevailed in north-western Europe in the latter part of the nineteenth century.[52]

Notions of 'organic memory' provided the conceptual frame for the development of a science of pathological forgetting in the late nineteenth century. A specialized branch of this science concentrated on localizing various memory functions in specific areas of the brain. I will return to this branch in chapter 8. However, many theorists of organic memory held to an ideal of scientific explanation that did not depend on the pinning down of psychological functions to specific locations in physical space. Their idea of imposing scientific order on a confusing collection of phenomena depended rather on arranging the phenomena in a hypothetical developmental sequence. Thus Ribot claimed that language impairment as a result of brain damage (aphasia) followed a regular sequence from rational to emotional language and finally gestures. Within rational language, memory for names was affected first, then substantives, followed by adjectives. This represented the inverse of an evolutionary sequence: 'The evolution of language takes place, as we would naturally infer, in an inverse order to that of its dissolution in aphasia.'[53]

The mode of explanation that seemed to bring order to the phenomena of aphasia was applied with rather greater success to the phenomena of *amnesia*, or pathological impairment of memory. Medical observations of memory loss after brain injury had been recorded in antiquity and had played some role in strengthening the case for the brain, rather than the heart, as the seat of the soul. But amnesia as such was not an object of profound interest until the modern period. The term seems to have entered systematic nosology in the second half of the eighteenth century, but the topic attracted little scientific attention until a century later.[54] By then, the aetiology of amnesia had broadened to include, not only physical injury to the brain, but also 'moral' shock, that is, causes that would soon be identified as psychological. The scope of the category of amnesia was also extended to include 'periodic' amnesia, a condition later referred to as multiple, or alternating, personality. By the time that Ribot wrote about 'the diseases of memory' amnesia provided the centrepiece.

A science of forgetting should have laws, and Ribot duly formulated the 'law of regression or reversion' that governed the loss of memories in amnesia:

> The progressive destruction of memory follows a logical order – a law. *It advances progressively from the unstable to the stable* [italics in the original]. It begins with the most recent recollections, which ... represent organization in its feeblest form. It ends with the sensorial, instinctive

memory, which become a permanent and integral part of the organism, represents organization in its most highly developed stage.[55]

This regularity constituted one more instance of 'a more general law in biology', namely, 'that structures last formed are the first to degenerate', dissolution acting in a contrary direction to evolution. All this provided further confirmation of the fundamental claim that 'memory is a biological fact'.[56]

Ribot was able to point to similar observations on the part of Hughlings Jackson, the eminent British neurologist, who had done clinical work on aphasia but had developed his interpretative framework under the influence of his mentor, Thomas Laycock, as well as such philosophers of evolution as George Henry Lewes and especially Herbert Spencer.[57] A tendency to see links between memory and biological inheritance became noticeable during the third quarter of the nineteenth century.[58] Both memory and inheritance were regarded as subject not only to progressive evolution, but also to deterioration and dissolution. Because these processes followed the same sequence in reverse order, it seemed to some that the study of pathological dissolution could throw light on normal development.

Memory as injury

The new prominence of amnesia studies in the late nineteenth century was a major example of a process of 'medicalization' that led to the annexation of significant aspects of human experience by medical science. In earlier times, there had been simply a large area of common experience that was known as 'forgetting'. But later a part of that area was sharply distinguished from the rest as pathological forgetting, a kind of illness that could be understood only in medical terms. As this was happening, the professionalization of medical specialties was making great strides, and the privilege of making authoritative pronouncements on memory and normality quickly devolved upon a group of experts, individuals who had received accreditation at a recognized medical institution. Lay people could listen in on this discourse of experts (and quite a few did), but their contributions would lack professional authority.

Though the concept of amnesia played a central role in this development, the process of medicalization was quite pervasive and also affected other memory phenomena. As an example, let us take a brief look at the experience that came to be known as *déjà vu*. This refers to the feeling that everything happening now has happened before, that one has been in the same place with the same people on some previous occasion, doing and saying the same things. But, typically, this previous occasion cannot be identified and it is quite impossible that it actually occurred. In the past, this phenomenon was sometimes taken to indicate that we have memories of previous lives, previous incarnations. In the nineteenth century it was described in novels, Charles Dickens and Walter Scott offering particularly clear examples.[59]

By the end of the century, this kind of experience had been appropriated by medical psychology. Conceptually, the phenomenon was taken out of the realm of the metaphysical or personal and given a general psychological categorization. It was now classified as a *paramnesia*, one among other memory experiences whose content does not correspond to anything that actually happened in the past. That made it a 'delusion' of memory and established a link to rare but serious disturbances in which persons believe that everything happening to them has happened before. A phenomenon, usually so fleeting that it had not even had a name, now became the target of endless medical and psychological speculation as well as empirical inquiry.[60]

The medicalization of memory phenomena was not limited to matters of surface classification. Medical categories also operated at a deeper level, involving the way in which people were taught to understand upsetting change in their personal lives. The concept of *trauma* provides by far the most important example of this more general effect. Originally, this concept had referred to a *bodily* injury or wound. The crucial late nineteenth-century development was the metaphorical extension of the concept to take in phenomena that were regarded as *psychological* injuries or wounds.[61] Medical authority on physical trauma was unquestioned, but now that authority was potentially extended to any case of inflicted individual human suffering that left behind a wounded person.

Individuals who would now be described as psychologically injured had been all too familiar in the course of human history and had been regularly depicted in many kinds of literature. But those accounts had been framed within the moral category of victimhood, accounts that could evoke compassion, a wish for justice or revenge, religious feelings, but not a desire for a medical examination. The novel concept of psychological trauma established a different way of looking at human victims: their injury was medical/ psychological. However, rather than replacing the old concept of moral injury, the new and the old concept existed side by side. Depending on circumstances, psychological injury could be confused with moral injury or substitute for moral injury.

In the latter part of the nineteenth century, railway accidents, associated with the hurried spread of new technology, were not infrequently the cause of such conditions. As a result of these accidents there would sometimes be persons whose medical condition – depression, fear, obsessive rumination, paralysis and other motor and sensory disturbances – transformed them into victims of culpable negligence who were entitled to compensation. In some of these cases medical examination could find no evidence of physical trauma. Perhaps the physical injury was simply undetectable by the then available medical technology, a molecular disarray within the brain or the spinal cord, as the original concept of 'traumatic neurosis' hypothesized. But perhaps there was no physical trauma, only its psychological analogue. After all, living through a serious accident would be a pretty upsetting event, and it was not difficult to believe that, in susceptible individuals, such a 'mental trauma' could interfere with the normal operation of the mind in a manner not unlike some of the effects of certain brain traumas.[62]

But living through a railway accident is only one among any number of highly disturbing experiences that a person might have to go through. It was common knowledge that such experiences were often followed by unpleasant and debilitating after-effects, at least for a while. If this age-old observation was to be interpreted in terms of the medical concept of 'trauma', these after-effects would come to be understood as 'symptoms'.

Suffering from the after-effects of a mental shock would no longer be acceptable as part of the ups and downs of ordinary life; it would now be a kind of illness. A new kind of medical specialist would become a source of privileged knowledge about that sort of illness. This knowledge would be constructed on the model of the existing natural sciences: it would be a knowledge of causes and effects, objective conditions and their observable consequences. Application of the concept of 'psychic trauma' transformed what were often uniquely contextualized and ambiguous circumstances into clearly identifiable, causally effective events that bore the responsibility for subsequent suffering.

The link between psychological trauma and memory was not there from the start. It was accepted that people would often be confused about the circumstances under which they had suffered a traumatic shock – an accident might be recalled inadequately or not at all. But at first there was no sense of a fundamental link between trauma and memory, no systematic emphasis on the theoretical importance of traumatic experience for understanding human memory. Two factors prepared the way for this development. First, there was the *delayed* appearance of some of the apparent after-effects of a traumatic event; second, there was the growing suspicion that many of these after-effects were the result not of any physical damage, but of a traumatic *experience*, a mental trauma. The notion of delayed mental effects would suggest a role for memory in the development of post-traumatic symptoms.

Delayed abnormal effects on memory were already known from increasingly popular and increasingly respectable demonstrations of hypnotic phenomena. Under the influence of a post-hypnotic suggestion individuals would carry out actions without remembering that they had been instructed to do so under hypnosis. Questioned as to their reasons for their action, they would usually make up some plausible excuse. Here there was undoubtedly memory – the suggested action was carried out as previously instructed – and yet there was no memory of the instruction itself. Under hypnosis individuals might also speak of things or engage in behaviour that they could not remember after returning to a waking state.

Claims for the medical effectiveness of hypnosis tended to focus on the treatment of a diverse range of symptoms, particularly paralyses and bizarre sensory disturbances, that shared the attribute 'hysterical'. The disease of which these symptoms were supposed to be the expression was traditionally viewed as a disease of women, linked to their anatomy or physical constitution. However, in the latter part of the nineteenth century some prominent French alienists were ready to extend the diagnosis of hysteria to men. That reinforced a tendency to regard hysteria as essentially a disease of the mind rather than the body, although a 'hysterical constitution' might still provide the necessary precondition for the development of the illness.[63] The crucial precipitating factor, however, must be sought in the life experiences of the patient.

An analogy between certain effects of hypnosis and of trauma was suggested by the influential French neurologist, Jean-Martin Charcot (1825–1893), who demonstrated the artificial production of hysterical symptoms by means of post-hypnotic suggestion. The human subjects of his experiments developed abnormalities of vision and of movement, but they had no memory of having been 'talked into' displaying these symptoms by the hypnotist. Subsequently, they could be 'cured' of their symptoms by being once again hypnotized. Similarly, the hysterical symptoms that some individuals had developed after they had experienced subsequently forgotten real-life traumatic situations could sometimes be removed or ameliorated by means of hypnosis. Charcot therefore proposed an analogy between the shock of a real-life trauma and a 'traumatic suggestion' under hypnosis. In both cases, he speculated, a part of the mind becomes separated from the rest and continues a subterranean existence as a 'fixed idea' that can have delayed effects without being conscious.[64]

Charcot was a great showman, whose dramatic (staged) clinical demonstrations were witnessed, not only by medical specialists, but also by invited members of a public that was becoming highly receptive to the notions of unconscious mental processes being advanced in several quarters.[65] From Charcot's clinic the word spread that sufferers from what were commonly called hysterical symptoms had often lived through highly disturbing situations that they had subsequently forgotten. Although forgotten, these traumatic memories manifested themselves in neurotic symptoms whose cure depended on reawakening the memories under hypnosis. Charcot's influential example encouraged others among the new breed of mind doctors to take up the search for the hidden memories that were causing so much distress to their patients.

Among Charcot's audience there were two young admirers whose commitment to this search – and to the theoretical explanation of its successes and failures – led to results of considerable historical significance. One of them was Sigmund Freud, who began by following in the footsteps of the master but went on to develop a far more complex system of concepts and practices, known as psychoanalysis, that will be discussed in chapter 7. The other was Pierre Janet (1859–1947), a philosopher by training, who took up medical studies at the age of thirty and became an authority on psychopathology. He published a series of pioneering case-studies that helped to disseminate the notion of subconscious traumatic memory. For example, in an early case known as 'Marie' he attributed the patient's monthly convulsive and delirious episodes to an apparently forgotten episode in which she had stopped her first menstruation by taking a cold bath.[66] Janet's early theorizing was essentially a more generalized and more psychologically sensitive development of some of Charcot's clinical interpretations. Psychological dissociation occurred when memories of vehemently unpleasant emotional experiences, not easily integrated with the bulk of a person's conscious associations, became inaccessible to voluntary recall yet lived on subconsciously to find an outlet in various debilitating symptoms.[67] In contrast to a long theological tradition that had emphasized the *unity* of the soul, Janet, and others of his period, presented an image of the human personality as fragile and subject to *splitting* or dissociating when put under strain. Memory might then also take on plural forms that did not communicate with one another.[68]

Freud's concept of *repression* (of which more later) and Janet's concept of psychological dissociation shared the distinction of being members of a historically new class of concepts relating to human memory: they were essentially *psychopathological* concepts, derived from the aberrations, not the ordinary or the ideal manifestations, of memory. Unlike previous notions about memory, they were deeply rooted in pathology and the medical gaze that was required for identifying this pathology.[69]

Another kind of victim

By the end of the nineteenth century the medicalization of disruptions in the ordinary relationship of past to present experience was well advanced. That can be linked to a deep and growing conviction, a 'depth knowledge', as Ian Hacking calls it,[70] that there are crucial facts about memory potentially available to us through the adoption of the methods of natural science and scientific medicine. As a consequence, moral issues that had previously been the preserve of doctrines about the human soul could be confronted objectively and impersonally. Scientific investigation of memory could take the place of theological or philosophical disputations, and scientific or medical experts on memory could take the place of ancient religious and moral authorities.

The modern aspiration to an amoral, scientific knowledge about memory is historically exceptional. Folk theories of memory usually evoke a moral context as a matter of course.[71] In written discourse the role of memory in moral *action*, not suffering, had long been recognized. Aristotle stressed that a background of experience – based on generalized memories – was necessary for sound moral judgment.[72] In medieval times, memory, along with intellect and foresight, was considered to be a part of prudence, enabling knowledge of good and bad actions.[73] Memory training, practised by means of the art of memory, could serve not only rhetorical, but also ethical purposes. A good memory would help in making morally wise choices and judgments. The medieval emphasis on memory training, discussed in chapter 3, was based on similar beliefs in the moral efficacy of a good memory.[74]

More individualistic, post-medieval, conceptions had retained a place for memory in the moral order. In John Locke's influential philosophy, consciousness of self, extended into the past, functioned as a criterion for being recognized as a person, not only by oneself but also by others. There was a link between remembering past actions as one's own and accountability for one's actions. Individuals could be held responsible, could be blamed, for what they had done in the past, because remembered consciousness of self constituted them as the same individuals then and now.

Whereas traditional sources had treated memory primarily as a resource of moral *agency*, in the medical context of modern discussions memory appears primarily as a source of suffering. However, that created an opening for re-establishing a link between memory and the moral order. What had been thrown out through the front door by adopting a morally neutral scientific stance re-entered through the back door opened by the medicalization of victimhood. Envisioning memory as a source of illness turned out to be a peculiarly modern way of introducing moral considerations into memory discourse in spite of all aspirations to scientific moral neutrality.

The concept of traumatic memory established not only a new category of sufferers (those who suffered from their reminiscences, as Freud put it), but also a new category of *victims*. The morally neutral language of scientific medicine might describe traumatic memories as pertaining to 'violently unpleasant' or 'seriously disturbing' experiences, but the question of who was to blame for those experiences could not always be evaded. In the traditional view that linked memory to moral agency a large category of memories owed their disturbing quality to the fact that they were *shameful*. People remembered and tried not to remember wrongful actions, or even intentions, for which they could be blamed. But the metaphor of psychic trauma constituted an important class of experiences as injuries inflicted by an outside agency. If there was any question of responsibility, then the suffering entailed by the memory of such experiences called for blaming others, not self-blame. Many cases of psychological trauma might simply be due to natural or accidental causes, but in other cases the sufferer was surely a victim who had endured not only psychological, but also moral injury. However, whether they had indeed been wronged depended on the confirmation of a medico-psychological diagnosis that could be supplied only by appropriately qualified experts. The scientific judgment of those experts would now have inescapable moral implications.

Once memory disturbance was conceptualized as a medically certifiable injury its forensic potential was quickly discovered. Psychic injuries might be the result of culpable actions or omissions by parties against whom civil claims could be entertained. Railway accidents had provided the first major occasion for displaying the forensic implications of the concept of psychic trauma. If the existence of such a condition as a result of the accident could be medically confirmed, the victim's claim for compensation from the railway company would be greatly strengthened.

In a legal context the diagnosis of psychic trauma would be relevant to the question of whether an injured person was to be categorized as a victim entitled to restitution. For an accident victim, that created an incentive to prolong the after-effects of the initial shock. As long as the symptoms persisted compensation could be claimed. If that kind of motivation lay behind the long-term effects of psychic trauma then its victims could hardly be said to be suffering from their memories – what they suffered from was an excessively generous social arrangement that entitled them to a life of idleness as long as their medical condition remained in place. In the Weimar period such arguments were indeed put forward by the bulk of the psychiatric profession in Germany, where a relatively generous insurance law had been in place since 1884.[75] The political intervention of these mental-health professionals played a significant role in the tightening of insurance law in 1926.

As this example illustrates, the recognition of psychic trauma as providing grounds for restitution claims established a category of victimhood that, like other categories of victimhood, had the potential to become politicized. Compensation payments to accident victims are a matter of social policy, and one's advocacy of one policy or another would depend on whether one believed such compensation was good or bad for the victims. Some professionals might have believed it to be bad, but the victims themselves probably had a different view. If they ever made themselves heard the politicization of the whole issue would become that much sharper. However, the political clout of accident victims is clearly limited. Survivors of armed conflict claiming compensatory pensions were a political force of a different order.[76] But once individual claims for restitution become part of a political cause championing the rights of victims it becomes increasingly difficult to keep medico-scientific expertise outside the political arena. That became apparent much later in the twentieth century, a development I will return to in chapter 7.

Notes

1. See chapter 2.
2. Plato, *Theaetetus*, 149a.
3. Plato, *Meno*, 81e, also *Phaedo*, 72e.
4. Sorabji, *Aristotle on memory*.
5. Opinions differ on the plausibility of Plato's account in the *Meno*. Some accept Plato's interpretation, others are unconvinced and see Socrates' leading questions as having put ideas in the boy's head that were not there before. Most contemporary psychologists are likely to find themselves in the latter group. I certainly do. However, that is beside the point here. The issue is not the empirical validity of Plato's interpretation but the nature of the conceptual distinctions that his account was meant to illustrate.
6. Yates, *Art of memory*; J. D. Spence, *The memory palace of Matteo Ricci* (New York: Viking Penguin, 1984).
7. The theatre was based on 'the idea of a unified cosmos, in which all levels of reality correspond ... the conviction, moreover, that it is possible to construct memory images that are not random and arbitrary, but magically effective because they are capable of representing the hidden connections between things'. L. Bolzoni, 'The play of images: The art of memory from its origins to the seventeenth century', in P. Corsi (ed.), *The enchanted loom: Chapters in the history of neuroscience* (New York: Oxford University Press, 1991), pp. 16–61 (p. 23).
8. For illustrations of this and the following generalizations, see Bolzoni, *Gallery of memory*.
9. The pioneering figure in this development was a French Protestant generally known as Peter Ramus (1515–72). He attempted to assimilate rhetoric to the logic of inquiry. For purposes of exposition it would be useful to construct diagrams showing the logic of one's argument, and such diagrams might also have a subsidiary mnemonic function. For a comprehensive account, see W. J. Ong, *Ramus: Method and the decay of dialogue* (Cambridge, MA: Harvard University Press, 1958).
10. This apt phrase is Yates's in *Art of memory*.
11. As mentioned in chapter 3, one of the casualties of this campaign was any form of the art of memory that extolled the use of imagery.
12. For an account of these developments see P. Rossi, *Logic and the art of memory: The quest for a universal language* (Chicago: University of Chicago Press, 2000).
13. For much detail on this, see Bolzoni, *Gallery of memory*.
14. Descartes, *The philosophical writings*, vol. I, p. 69.
15. T. J. Reiss, 'Denying the body? Memory and the dilemmas of history in Descartes', *Journal of the History of Ideas* 57 (1996), 587–607 (p. 601).
16. Fentress and Wickham, *Social memory*, chapter 1.
17. This is best illustrated in the Cartesian conflict between the somatically sourced passions and the rational soul that is capable of subjecting them to a moral order. R. Descartes, 'The passions of the soul', in E. S. Haldane and G. R. T. Ross (eds.), *The philosophical works of Descartes* (Cambridge: Cambridge University Press, 1931), vol. I, pp. 331–427. (Written in 1645/6.)
18. Queen Christina of Sweden and Princess Elisabeth of Bohemia.
19. These connections have been explored in the work of Alois Hahn. See his 'Identität und Selbstthematisierung', in A. Hahn and V. Kapp (eds.), *Selbstthematisierung und Selbstzeugnis: Bekenntnis und Geständnis* (Frankfurt: Suhrkamp, 1987), pp. 9–24; and his 'Beichte und Biographie', in M. Sonntag (ed.), *Von der Machbarkeit des Psychischen* (Pfaffenweiler: Centaurus, 1990), pp. 56–76.
20. See chapter 2, section headed 'Inscription: writing as memory'; and chapter 3, section headed 'Monastic memory'.

21. G. Poulet, *Studies in human time* (New York: Harper, 1959), p. 39.
22. See chapter 9, section headed 'The inner senses'.
23. S. Toulmin, 'Self-knowledge and knowledge of the "self"', in T. Mischel (ed.), *The self: Psychological and philosophical issues* (Oxford: Blackwell, 1977), pp. 291–317.
24. C. Taylor, *Sources of the self: The making of the modern identity* (Cambridge, MA: Harvard University Press, 1989), chapter 9.
25. Locke, *Essay*, p. 449. (The chapter containing this passage was added in 1694.)
26. C. Wolff, *Psychologia empirica*, in *Gesammelte Werke* (Hildesheim: Olms, 1968; originally published 1732), vol. V.
27. The prototype for this kind of mental analysis is to be found in David Hume, not in Locke, as often repeated in histories of psychology. For Locke, the concept of 'association of ideas' was an afterthought added at the end of the final edition of his magnum opus, and it was meant to explain irrational ideas, not the entire structure of mental life. 'Association of ideas' was an exceedingly vague notion that took its specific meaning from the discursive context in which it occurred. In its early days it was equally compatible with Francis Hutcheson's moral sense theory and David Hartley's speculative neurophysiology (see chapter 2). Reference to a universal mechanism, underlying all cognition, though anticipated by Hume, did not represent its generally accepted meaning until the early nineteenth century. James Mill's *Analysis of the phenomena of the human mind* (1829) is exemplary in this respect.
28. Locke, *Essay*, chapter 27, section 26.
29. I have discussed the historical importance of this development in K. Danziger, 'The historical formation of selves', in R. D. Ashmore and L. Jussim (eds.), *Self and identity: Fundamental issues* (New York: Oxford University Press, 1997), pp. 137–59.
30. Ian Hacking comments: 'In Locke's *Essay* memory defined what it is to be a person. Locke wanted to be as unplatonic as could be. He elevated memory into the bright light of what every good man knows and needs no tutor to recall. The moves made with memory in the *Essay* are different in kind from Plato's moves, but notice how the pawn of memory remains the same, and has an equally central status for philosophy.' Ian Hacking, 'Memory sciences, memory politics', in P. Antze and M. Lambek (eds.), *Tense past: Cultural essays in trauma and memory* (New York: Routledge, 1996), pp. 67–87 (p. 81).
31. For example in the work of Laurence Sterne (1713–68).
32. J.-J. Rousseau, *The confessions of Jean-Jacques Rousseau*, trans. J. M. Cohen (Harmondsworth: Penguin Books, 1953).
33. Augustine, *Confessions*. For a comprehensive modern treatment of Augustinian themes relevant to the topic of memory, see B. Stock, *Augustine the reader: Meditation, self-knowledge, and the ethics of interpretation* (Cambridge, MA: Harvard University Press, 1996).
34. P. Boerner, *Tagebuch* (Stuttgart: Metzler, 1979).
35. Some notable practitioners of this form were Stendhal, Maine de Biran, Benjamin Constant and Alfred de Vigny.
36. V. Kapp, 'Von der Autobiographie zum Tagebuch: Rousseau–Constant', in Hahn and Kapp, *Selbstthematisierung*.
37. The most successful of these publications was the *Magazin für Erfahrungsseelenkunde*, edited by K. P. Moritz, whose first number appeared in 1783. There were at least four others, and between them they put out a total of twenty-seven volumes, the last appearing in 1807. For a description of this literature see G. Eckardt, 'Psychologie um 1800', in O. Breidbach and D. v. Engelhardt (eds.), *Hegel und die Lebenswissenschaften* (Berlin: Verlag für Wissenschaft und Bildung, 2000), pp. 157–74.

38. G. Eckardt, 'Anspruch und Wirklichkeit der Erfahrungsseelenkunde, dargestellt an Hand periodisch erscheinender Publikationen um 1800', in O. Breidbach and P. Ziche (eds.), *Naturwissenschaften um 1800* (Weimar: H. Böhlaus Nachf., 2001), pp. 179–202. See also H. Förstl, M. Angermeyer and R. Howard, 'Karl Philipp Moritz' Journal of Empirical Psychology (1783–1793): an analysis of 124 case reports', *Psychological Medicine* 21 (1991), 299–304.

39. Some mid-nineteenth-century German representatives of what has been referred to as 'Romantic psychiatry' (see O. M. Marx, 'German Romantic psychiatry', *History of Psychiatry* 1 (1990), 351–81 for a bibliography) were in sympathy with the trends that had appeared in the earlier lay literature. Thus K. W. Ideler not only emphasized the importance of emotional factors in the genesis of mental illness, but also suggested that they be traced back to early childhood. Somewhat later H. W. Neumann understood the individual's life history in terms of a balance of self-destruction and reconstruction, forgetting being an important aspect of the former and memory a vital component of the latter. (See K. W. Ideler, *Grundriss der Seelenheilkunde* (Berlin: Enslin, 1835); H. W. Neumann, *Lehrbuch der Psychiatrie* (Erlangen: Enke, 1859). But these were individual voices, increasingly out of tune with the somatic orientation of the nascent psychiatric profession.

40. There is an immense literature on the history of hypnotism and mesmerism. For a comprehensive bibliography of the earlier literature, see A. Crabtree, *Animal magnetism, early hypnotism and psychical research, 1766–1925: An annotated bibliography* (New York: Kraus, 1988). A more recent general history is A. Gauld, *A history of hypnotism* (New York: Cambridge University Press, 1992). The study by J.-R. Laurence and P. Campbell, *Hypnosis, will, and memory: A psycho-legal history* (New York: Guilford Press, 1988), is particularly relevant in the context of this section.

41. R. Terdiman, *Present past: Modernity and the memory crisis* (Ithaca, NY: Cornell University Press, 1993).

42. Terdiman, *Present past*.

43. M. S. Roth, 'Remembering forgetting: Maladies de la mémoire in nineteenth century France', *Representations* 26 (1989), 49–68 (p. 63).

44. Roth, 'Remembering forgetting'; and by the same author: 'The time of nostalgia: Medicine, history and normality in nineteenth century France', *Time & Society* 1 (1992), 271–86; as well as: 'Trauma, representation and historical consciousness', *Common Knowledge* 7 (1998), 99–111.

45. On Ribot, see S. Nicolas and D. J. Murray, 'Théodule Ribot (1839–1916), founder of French psychology: A biographical introduction', *History of Psychology* 2 (1999), 277–301.

46. T. Ribot, *Diseases of memory: An essay in the positive psychology*, in D. N. Robinson (ed.), *Significant contributions to the history of psychology 1750–1920*, Series C (Washington, DC: University Publications of America, 1977), vol. I. Originally published in French in 1881 and in English translation in 1882, Ribot's book went through twenty-nine editions or printings and was also translated into German, Russian and Spanish. Clearly, it addressed a topic that had recently stimulated widespread interest. Other psychological topics to which Ribot devoted books were attention, affects, animal intelligence, creative imagination and 'diseases' of the will and personality.

47. Ribot, *Diseases*, p. 10.

48. For example, the writings of La Mettrie and Bonnet in France and Unzer in Germany.

49. In E. Hering, *On memory and the specific energies of the nervous system*, 3rd edn (Chicago: Open Court, 1902). Hering's lecture was published in the same year it was delivered (1870) and first translated into English in 1880.

50. Hering, *On memory*, p. 7. The Open Court edition mistranslates Hering's word *Äusserung*, i.e. 'manifestation', as 'results'.

51. H. Maudsley, *The physiology and pathology of mind* (London: Macmillan, 1867). S. Butler, *Unconscious memory* (London: Jonathan Cape, 1880). T. Laycock, *Mind and brain* (Edinburgh: Sutherland & Knox, 1860; reprinted New York: Arno Press, 1976). On later developments of the doctrine of organic memory, see D. L. Schacter, *Stranger behind the engram: Theories of memory and the psychology of science* (Hillsdale, NJ: Erlbaum, 1982).

52. For the cultural context of organic memory, see L. Otis, *Organic memory: History and the body in the late nineteenth and early twentieth centuries* (Lincoln: University of Nebraska Press, 1994).

53. Ribot, *Diseases*, p. 168.

54. Instances of mysterious forgetting and miraculous recovery of lost memories had, however, been of interest to early nineteenth-century literary Romanticism.

55. Ribot, *Diseases*, p. 121.

56. Ribot, *Diseases*, p. 127.

57. Laycock, *Mind and brain*; G. H. Lewes, *The physiology of common life* (London: Blackwood, 1859); J. H. Jackson, in J. Taylor (ed.), *Selected writings of Hughlings Jackson* (London: Staples, 1931). On the interrelated psychological theories of some of these figures, see K. Danziger, 'Mid-nineteenth century British psycho-physiology: A neglected chapter in the history of psychology', in W. R. Woodward and M. G. Ash (eds.), *The problematic science: Psychology in nineteenth century thought* (New York: Praeger, 1982), pp. 119–46.

58. It is important to note that this discourse owed much more to the inspiration of Lamarck than of Darwin. Belief in the inheritance of acquired characteristics was essential to it, natural selection was not.

59. On the history of *déjà vu*, see D. Draaisma, *Why life speeds up as you get older: How memory shapes our past* (Cambridge: Cambridge University Press, 2004).

60. On the late nineteenth-century medical debates regarding the classification of memory phenomena as 'symptoms', see G. E. Berrios, *The history of mental symptoms: Descriptive psychopathology since the nineteenth century* (Cambridge: Cambridge University Press, 1966); and more specifically, G. E. Berrios, 'Déjà vu in France during the nineteenth century: A conceptual history', *Comprehensive Psychiatry* 36 (1995), 123–29. For subsequent developments, see Draaisma, *Why life speeds up*, and A. S. Brown, 'A review of the déjà vu experience', *Psychological Bulletin* 129 (2003), 394–413.

61. The invention of a category of 'traumatic neuroses' marked a step in this direction, though initially this referred to a hypothetical disturbance within the nervous system: H. Oppenheim, *Die traumatischen Neurosen* (Berlin: Hirschwald, 1889). But as such disturbances were likely to have mental consequences, the next step – to psychic trauma – was not particularly difficult. The trajectory of Oppenheim's thinking is described in P. Lerner, 'From traumatic neurosis to male hysteria: The decline and fall of Hermann Oppenheim, 1889–1919', in M. S. Micale and P. Lerner (eds.), *Traumatic pasts: History, psychiatry and trauma in the modern age, 1870–1930* (New York: Cambridge University Press, 2001), pp. 140–71.

62. Much detail on the historically significant role of railway accidents in bringing together the forensic and the medical aspects of victimhood is presented in R. Harrington, 'The railway accident: Trains, trauma, and technological crises in nineteenth-century Britain', and in E. Caplan, 'Trains and trauma in the American Gilded Age', both in Micale and Lerner, *Traumatic pasts*, pp. 31–56 and 57–77; also W. Schivelbusch, *The railway journey: Trains and train travel in the nineteenth century* (Berkeley: University of California Press, 1986).

63. This is merely a hint at a complex development that led to a considerable secondary literature a century later. A useful introduction to the latter is provided in M. S. Micale, *Approaching hysteria: Disease and its interpretations* (Princeton, NJ: Princeton University Press, 1995).

64. For a more extensive treatment of Charcot's work on the 'traumatogenesis' of neurotic disorder, see M. S. Micale, 'Jean-Martin Charcot and *les névroses traumatiques*: From medicine to culture in French trauma theory of the late nineteenth century', in Micale and Lerner, *Traumatic pasts*, pp. 115–39. On the role of Charcot's demonstrations in the genesis of the notion of post-traumatic amnesia, see M. Borch-Jacobsen, 'How to predict the past: From trauma to repression', *History of Psychiatry* 11 (2000), 15–35.

65. For the medical background, the classic study by H. Ellenberger, *The discovery of the unconscious* (New York: Basic Books, 1970) retains much of its value. The more recent works of Michael S. Roth (see note 44) are an excellent source for the historical context with a focus on memory.

66. P. Janet, *L'automatisme psychologique: essai de psychologie expérimentale sur les formes inférieures de l'activité humaine* (Paris: Société Pierre Janet, 1973; originally published 1889).

67. After a long period of Freudian predominance there was a revival of interest in Janet and dissociation towards the end of the twentieth century: B. A. van der Kolk and O. van der Kolk, 'Pierre Janet and the breakdown of adaptation in psychological trauma', *American Journal of Psychiatry* 146 (1989), 1530–40.

68. The most dramatic illustration of this occurred in cases of split or multiple personalities that were beginning to be medically identified during this period. In these cases, the disassociation operated not merely between certain memories and a self that remained whole, but between distinct selves whose memories were not the same. For the historical significance of split personality, see I. Hacking, *Rewriting the soul* (Princeton, NJ: Princeton University Press, 1995).

69. Janet, however, always remained more exclusively preoccupied with pathological phenomena than Freud, who was inclined to look to this domain for explanations of the human condition in general. Perhaps this accounts for the latter's incomparably greater influence.

70. Hacking, *Rewriting*.

71. M. Bloch, 'Internal and external memory: Different ways of being in history', in Antze and Lambek, *Tense past*, pp. 215–33.

72. Aristotle, *Nichomachean ethics*, in J. Barnes (ed.), *The complete works of Aristotle* (Princeton, NJ: Princeton University Press, 1984), vol. II, pp. 1729–867.

73. Carruthers comments: 'We must remember that a trained and well-provided memory was regarded throughout this long period not as a primitive learning technique but as the essential foundation of prudence, *sapientia*, ethical judgment.' *Book of memory*, p. 176.

74. Both ancient art of memory and the modern therapeutics of memory seek to enhance the scope of voluntary recall, but modern methods are inordinately preoccupied with *obstacles* to effective remembering. Psychoanalysis was based on a perception of these obstacles as the primary target of intervention.

75. P. Lerner, *Hysterical men: War, psychiatry and the politics of trauma in Germany, 1890–1930* (Ithaca, NY: Cornell University Press, 2003); G. A. Eghigian, 'The German welfare state as a discourse of trauma', in Micale and Lerner, *Traumatic pasts*, 92–112; W. Schäffner, 'Event, series, trauma: The probabilistic revolution of the mind in the late nineteenth and early twentieth centuries', in Micale and Lerner, *Traumatic pasts*, pp. 81–91.

76. For the American case post-World War I, see C. Cox, 'Invisible wounds: The American Legion, shell-shocked veterans, and American society, 1919–1924', in Micale and Lerner, *Traumatic pasts*, pp. 280–305.

5   An experimental science of memory

Is memory a scientific category?

Several of the late nineteenth-century developments described in the last chapter attest to a growing belief that the way to unlock the mysteries of human memory was to subject them to the procedures of medical and natural science. Although the scientific context for modern memory discourse was by no means homogeneous, and 'science' could certainly mean different things at different times and in different places, there was a shared commitment to systematic observation and public reporting of empirical data, to sharp distinctions between fact and theory and to naturalistic, preferably materialistic, explanation. Not all of these commitments were important for all examples of memory science, and there were significant differences in their concrete instantiation, but there was sufficient commonality to distinguish this new type of memory discourse from its predecessors. Beyond all their differences, those who personified the scientific approach to memory relied on special skills of investigation available only to accredited members of certain professions who shared the conviction that there was a natural knowledge about memory waiting to be discovered by the procedures of science.[1]

Different versions of memory science looked for this knowledge in different places and by means of different practical procedures. One version, to be discussed in chapter 8, concentrated on the neuro-anatomical study of memory defects resulting from brain injury. Another version, already discussed in the last section of chapter 4, involved a psychopathologically orientated practice of exploring the disturbed relationship between past and present in individuals' personal lives. It was suggested that the attention devoted to this kind of problem should be viewed against a background of rapid social change that had disrupted traditional normative patterns.

But this was not the only kind of change that was accelerating at that time. Problems of memory also arose in a technological context. The unprecedented expansion in the technologies of external memory had given rise to a situation in which all aspects of social life were fast coming under the dominion of inscribed records. Not only was this true of commerce, public and private bureaucracies, the political process and jurisprudence, but hitherto private spheres were affected through the vast growth and greater effectiveness of medical, legal, educational and administrative records. As for individual memory, these records potentially relieved it of some of its ancient functions: it should not be necessary to remember texts verbatim when you shared a building with its reliable copy. But, as records expanded, and storage rooms became fuller, retrieval problems multiplied and placed new demands on memory. Technological solutions to these demands offered only limited help and often ended up imposing new demands on individual recall.[2] For the speedy and efficient location of recorded information the improvement of individual memory became a problem that merited growing interest.

Psychopathological memory science, given its fundamental preoccupation with intimately personal, autobiographical and clinical questions did not provide the tools for pursuing such an interest. In a technological context, memory as a constituent of individual personality was not the issue. What presented itself as problematic was the *efficiency* of memory as a function. Irrespective of whether it constituted the cement of individual identity, memory was also a tool for solving quite mundane tasks. How did it perform this function, and what conditions affected the efficiency of this performance? Would a different kind of memory science provide answers to such questions? At first, the answer was not obvious.

A new kind of psychology, based on the use of experimental evidence, emerged during the last two decades of the nineteenth century.[3] The historical roots of this development can be traced in several European countries, though soon the new science flourished best of all in the USA. However, during the earliest years of experimental psychology, the foundational role of certain German academic centres, especially the universities of Leipzig, Göttingen and Berlin, was very marked. Wilhelm Wundt (1832–1920), at Leipzig, was particularly effective in establishing a relatively large and productive laboratory, authoring key textbooks and training the largest contingent among the first generation of research students. Nevertheless, as far as the experimental investigation of memory is concerned, the great pioneer was not Wundt but a then very junior academic, Hermann Ebbinghaus (1850–1909), who was yet to have his own students and whose laboratory was simply his own study. Not only did Wundt miss the boat as far as the new psychology of memory was concerned, but had it been up to him, this development would have gone nowhere. Wundt, eighteen years older than Ebbinghaus, represented an older generation that did not regard memory as an appropriate object of scientific interest.

The first edition of Wundt's famous compendium, the *Principles of Physiological Psychology*,[4] did not mention memory at all in the body of its nearly 900 pages of text. Subsequent editions devote a few pages to the topic in passing. They occur in a chapter on 'mental endowments' ('complex intellectual functions' in the last two editions), where memory is lumped together with other topics that Wundt clearly considered peripheral, i.e. imagination and intelligence. Though Wundt's compendium of scientific psychology grew to three very large volumes in later editions, the subject of memory is never considered worthy of a chapter of its own.

In the first edition of this foundational text, the only explicit mention of memory as a psychological category is in the Introduction. There Wundt notes that ordinary language provides us with certain terms for classifying psychological events, e.g. feeling, understanding, sensibility and also memory, which, in pre-scientific psychology, are taken to identify distinct faculties or mental powers. Such ordinary-language psychological categories are dangerous for the project of a scientific psychology because they tend to confound description and explanation. Scientific psychology has to make a clear separation between categories of observed phenomena to be explained and theories that do the explaining. A reference to 'memory' explains nothing, but the phenomena popularly grouped under 'memory' constitute such a heterogeneous collection that the term is also useless for identifying a distinct category of phenomena to be explained. Elsewhere, Wundt expresses the view that memory is a surface product generated by more fundamental psychological processes: 'Memory and all processes of recollection are complex results ... analogous to a large number of other forms of mental work, such, for example, as reading, writing, counting, and using numbers for complex processes of calculation.'[5] So 'memory' is no more a core category of psychology than is 'reading' or 'counting'. Had Wundt's vision of experimental psychology prevailed, the topic of memory would not have become one of its major areas of research.

Wundt spoke in the name of a self-consciously scientific psychology that needed to distinguish itself sharply from the psychology of the streets. The elaboration of this boundary constituted one of the conditions for the emergence of a scientific psychology. Because everyone was a psychologist of sorts the science of psychology had to distinguish itself clearly from lay psychology. To a large extent, this was accomplished on procedural grounds, but conceptual differentiation also seemed to be important. The ill-defined and fluid categories of popular faculty psychology were regarded as unsuitable for providing the kind of explanatory account demanded by an exact science.

This did not mean that no memory experiments were ever conducted in Wundt's laboratory; it simply meant that their purpose was entirely subordinated to his overall project of investigating human consciousness. For

Wundt, memory could never become an object of investigation *per se*, though what he called 'reproductive' aspects of consciousness could. That often meant that experiments which would look like memory experiments to later generations of psychologists were identified in some other way, investigations on the span of consciousness, for example.[6] What is more, experiments designed to investigate the reproduction of conscious experience proved to be unsuitable for establishing an experimental science of memory. In Wundt's laboratory, experimental subjects would be asked to compare the pitch of a standard tone with that of comparison tones presented somewhat later.[7] The better they remembered the standard tone the more accurate their judgements would be. This was an exercise limited to investigating a temporal characteristic of consciousness: the decay over time of the effectiveness with which a simple sensory experience could be reproduced mentally. In order to flourish, however, an experimental science of memory had to make the switch from memory as conscious experience to memory as a kind of performance. That, however, resulted in a situation where the study of *memorizing* had to stand in for the study of *memory*.

The memorizing trap

Ebbinghaus's technique of testing memory for learned series of 'nonsense syllables' showed the way. Nonsense syllables consisted of pronounceable three-letter combinations that had no meaning in the language of the experimental subject.[8] Ebbinghaus prepared series of such syllables that varied in length and then made repeated attempts to memorize them. After some time he tried to recall the list and noted how many of the learned syllables he remembered. Conditions, such as the number of learning attempts or the interval between learning and testing, could be varied and related to the completeness of recall. Most important of all, remembering could be given a quantitative expression in terms of the number of syllables correctly recalled. This quantification of memory was accomplished by inventing an entirely artificial structure, a finite list of what were assumed to be perfectly homogeneous and unfamiliar items. Such items could be used as equivalent units for purposes of counting.[9] In fact, Ebbinghaus experimented with series of digits before he settled on syllables. Because the content of everyday or natural memory was not countable, it was unsuitable for the scientific investigation. Moreover, the meaningfulness of this content introduced far too many uncontrollable variations for the method of controlled experimentation to be applicable. The successful launch of an experimental science of memory depended on the invention of an investigative procedure based on a specially constructed situation that differed in crucial respects from the situations in which human memory ordinarily functioned. This was artificial memory in a new sense.

But the procedural innovation would have lacked plausibility without a concomitant *conceptual* reduction of the object that experimental science was supposed to investigate. I have already indicated that in Ebbinghaus's memory experiments it was not a question of investigating actual experiences of remembering but of demonstrating objective successes (and failures) in accomplishing a very specific kind of memory task. How could such demonstrations be seen as providing significant knowledge about memory in general? Ebbinghaus had apparently convinced himself that the phenomena of conscious memory were affected by two distinct processes, the first of which is *Erinnerung* (recollection or reminiscence), a process that is neither simple nor elementary and resists experimental investigation.[10] However, the second process, defined as *das blosse Behalten, das eigentliche Gedächtnis*[11] (mere retention, memory proper), is susceptible to precise scientific investigation, provided one does not focus on the conscious experience of memory, which is uncontrollably corrupted by reminiscence. Memory as such, pure retention, was not a matter of conscious experience, as it had been for Wundt. For Ebbinghaus, *Erinnerung* (self-conscious recollection or reminiscence) represented dross that must be removed to get to memory proper, defined as 'mere retention'. The latter was a purely functional notion with no necessary reference to consciousness, let alone self-consciousness.

Ebbinghaus saw retention as manifest in some overt accomplishment, an accomplishment, moreover, that was measurable, given certain kinds of materials and an objective standard of success. Unlike some later psychologists of memory, both Wundt and Ebbinghaus regarded memory as essentially reproductive, and in Wundt's case this meant the reproduction of a conscious experience, a qualitative conception. Investigation therefore proceeded by the comparison of experiences. But what did reproduction mean for Ebbinghaus? It meant the achievement of a match between an external input, a list of equivalent syllables, and an overt product of an individual's activity, the same list recalled. This match was a matter of degree, both memory input and memory output being quantified. Measurability was a crucial consideration for Ebbinghaus, but in a specific sense. It was not just a question of measuring the products of individual memory, but also of how those products *measured up* to an objective criterion of success.

Ebbinghaus had constructed the basic framework of what was to become the paradigmatic experimental situation for the psychological investigation of memory during the twentieth century. This construction depended on severely limiting the range of investigable memory phenomena in accordance with the criteria of measurability and what one might call experimentability. If memory was to yield to scientific investigation, it had to be defined in a way that allowed for the identification, experimental manipulation and objective measurement of relevant variables. This was not possible for the phenomena of *Erinnerung* and so they had to be set aside. These precepts reflected the paramount value that Ebbinghaus placed on certain aspects of the methods of the physical sciences, quantification and controlled experimentation in particular. Gustav Theodor Fechner, who had brought quantification to psychology in the form of psychophysics, was his hero.[12]

But there was another source of Ebbinghaus's practice, one that has been largely overlooked, namely his intuitive, pre-empirical understanding of the nature of memory. His belief that memory was essentially reducible to a reproductive function ('pure retention') has already been mentioned. But he also understood memory as depending on a kind of work, memorizing. This remains implicit in the published version of his classic monograph on memory but it is made explicit elsewhere. Near the beginning of his unpublished draft, he poses the question of retention in terms of the *Arbeit* (quantity of work) necessary to go from zero reproduction to perfect reproduction, and after his first investigation he reaches the conclusion that 'indeed the work which must be applied to a series of ideas ... is a real measure of the psychic process that it serves to produce'.[13] Later, in his general textbook, he returns to the topic and expresses his belief that 'reproduction and memory are related rather like work and energy'.[14]

The work invested in carrying out the task of rote reproduction could be measured in terms of the number of exposures of a list of syllables necessary for a criterion of perfect reproduction to be reached. Longer lists needed more exposures, more work, before all their items could be reproduced. After a lapse of time, forgetting would occur and some items could no longer be reproduced. For Ebbinghaus this was a signal to get back to work and make further attempts at learning the list. But now he needed fewer separate attempts to achieve perfect reproduction than he had the first time around, when the list was quite unfamiliar. So, although some forgetting had occurred, the effort put into the first learning of the list had not all been wasted. Some effect of all that work remained stored up in his head and made his subsequent work easier. Ebbinghaus thought of this stored-up effect of work done as a kind of latent energy that would reduce the amount of work required for a second completion of the task.

Ebbinghaus's methodology reflects this underlying conception of memory as a kind of work. Just as the stimulus material consists of a series of equivalent elements which allows a measuring of performance achieved, so the subject's activity, understood as work, is sub-divided into equivalent portions, known as repetitions or trials, whose number gives a measure of the work expended. In earlier versions of psychological experimentation, the main purpose of repeated trials was to increase the reliability of observations and allow for random errors. But now, the repetition of trials takes on a new significance, namely, as a measure of the effort expended by the experimental subject. Ebbinghaus thus studied the phenomena of memory by subsuming them under a model of far greater generality. The model is that of an energetic system which reaches varying levels of performance achieved, depending on the energy stored in it. This energy in turn depends on the amount of work invested in the system.[15]

With its emphasis on the work of memorization, Ebbinghaus's approach was soon seen as relevant in a pedagogical context. Research that treated memory as reproductive work done to meet set standards of accuracy had clear practical applications in school systems dedicated to promoting the learning of masses of information and testing their recall. In institutional settings that promoted an interest in improving the efficiency of objective memory performance, the conscious experience of reminiscence was indeed irrelevant. What was needed was knowledge cast in the form of empirical regularities linking techniques of learning and objective measures of recall. This was exactly what Ebbinghaus's functionalization of memory research provided. The investigations he launched constituted a model for establishing the kinds of empirical regularity that were in demand among potential consumers of psychological knowledge in the field of education.[16]

It was not unusual for the topic of memory to be addressed in a pedagogical context. Ebbinghaus was himself an ex-teacher with practical experience of memory work in schools.[17] By the early years of the twentieth century there was a flood of studies of memorizing and remembering in the context of what was called 'experimental pedagogics'. This field even had its own journal. A leading role in these developments was taken by Ernst Meumann, who had served as Wundt's assistant for six years but made a deliberate break with that tradition when he went into educational psychology.[18] He clearly recognized the need for a different kind of research practice, indicating that psychological processes like memory now had to be studied, not in terms of inner experience, but in relation to their 'intended or prescribed success'.[19] That meant they ought to be studied in terms of 'psychological economy', or how a criterion of success might be achieved with the least expenditure of time and effort. Meumann's post-Wundtian orientation is precisely reflected in the title of his major work, translated into English as *The psychology of learning: An experimental investigation of the economy and technique of memory*.[20] The kind of memory that was pedagogically interesting at this time was reproductive memory, and experimental psychology was to provide the empirical basis for rationalizing memory work.

The research practices most suited to the pursuit of such goals were essentially those pioneered by Ebbinghaus. They allowed for the comparison of different arrangements of memorizing tasks in terms of their effectiveness in enhancing reproductive performance. That promise of practical relevance outside the psychological laboratory provided an early, though short-lived, boost to the version of experimental memory research pioneered by Ebbinghaus. Experimental pedagogics became part of the new 'educational psychology' in America, where E. L. Thorndike shared Meumann's interest in establishing a quantitative psychology of school learning. Research on the efficiency of memorizing was part of that project.[21] Although educators increasingly lost interest in rote learning, the implicit promise that the experimental psychology of memory would help to increase the efficiency of school learning lingered for some time.[22]

However, in the long run the field survived, not because of any practical applications but because it developed a set of procedures that promised to yield scientific knowledge about memory in the form of quantitative 'laws' based on a manipulation of distinct factors under controlled conditions. These laws were believed to be generalizable from the artificial world of the psychological laboratory to the world outside.

In the development of these procedures Ebbinghaus's experimental studies were appreciated for their pioneering quality, but his techniques required some modification before they could form the basis for the development of a coherent research area. For a start, Ebbinghaus had experimented on himself, a practice he shared with other great nineteenth-century pioneers, such as Fechner and Helmholtz. Lacking resources, he had little choice, but with the establishment of psychological laboratories that were veritable research factories, the age of heroic self-experimentation had come to an end.

It was at one of these laboratories, at the University of Göttingen, that Ebbinghaus's methods were subjected to a process of standardization which converted them into a form that would serve experimental memory science for a century.[23] Most fundamentally, the roles of experimenter and experimental subject were separated. One person (or set of persons) would design the experiment, decide on the materials to be used, issue instructions, supervise the running of the experiment and also collect and evaluate the results. Another person (or set of persons) would agree to follow the instructions of the first person and do the actual work of memorizing. This not only lightened the load on all participants but also prepared the way for the use of so-called naïve subjects, that is, persons who were expected to be ignorant of the research area and the purposes of the experiment. With the subsequent migration of this type of research to North America the naïve subject was generally an undergraduate student, which meant that results from a relatively large number of subjects could be pooled and overall effects statistically separated from individual variations.[24] Moreover, the separation of experimenter and subject roles made it much easier to ignore the experiential side of remembering by simply not collecting such information from one's experimental subjects. That undoubtedly facilitated the perpetuation of mechanistic theories of memory.

In any case, such theories were congruent with the procedures of investigation. Casting the person whose memorizing was being studied in the role of an experimental subject also facilitated the increasing mechanization of investigative practices. Ebbinghaus had done his memorizing work by looking at syllables of his own construction written on strips of paper. Although he tried to monitor his actions to exclude undue variability he was still in control of what was going on. At Göttingen, however, the subject's pace of memorizing was controlled by a piece of hardware, the so-called memory drum, which rotated at a set speed and presented the material to be memorized item by item. This became standard practice in the experimental science of memory until the drum was generally replaced by a computer in the latter part of the twentieth century.

Mechanization of procedures went hand in hand with efforts to *standardize* the materials to be memorized. Ebbinghaus's principles for the construction of syllable series were transformed into much stricter rules in an attempt to ensure that no series was more memorable than any other. The construction of the lists was of course part of the experimenter's, never the subject's, role. As the investigators noted, this made it possible to conduct experiments with subjects who were ignorant of the purpose of the experiment. That ignorance became a taken-for-granted part of the experimental conditions when investigations on naïve subjects came to be the rule.

In general, the labours of the Göttingen group were designed to produce a somewhat less cumbersome version of the methods Ebbinghaus had invented and to transform them into a standard set of procedures that would produce comparable results in the hands of different investigators. It has been suggested that these efforts 'can be best understood as a series of attempts to bring the study of memory closer to the standards of experimental physiology ... a process of making the preparation (a person in this case) most possibly free to respond only to the syllables'.[25] This practical project gave expression to a pre-empirical conviction that memory depended on processes that were analogous to physical mechanisms and excluded anything resembling human agency or meaningful action. With the appropriate experimental restrictions the work of memorizing could be studied as robotic rather than human work.

However, these implications of the Göttingen project were realized only in the course of time and did not emerge in their most extreme form until after the entire experimental science of memory had effectively emigrated to America. In fact, the leader of the Göttingen group, G. E. Müller, tempered his strict regulation of experimental procedures with a more relaxed style of thinking about memory. Outside the confines of laboratory practice, he was quite prepared to consider the subjective aspects of memory experience, and his careful discussion of introspective methods was balanced and undogmatic. He also discussed the differences between the memory of everyday life and the memory of the laboratory with a sophistication that was not to be exceeded for the better part of a century. Everyday memories were usually vague and unclear, he pointed out, and varied greatly in the confidence a person had in them. Clear and distinct memories and memories one was prepared to affirm on oath were the exception, not the rule. Therefore the psychology of memory should not take perfect reproduction as the normal case and devote itself to explaining failures of perfectly accurate reproduction. On the contrary, it should take the imperfections of memory, including false memories, as the norm and try to understand how sometimes more reliable memories were constructed on such an unpromising foundation.[26]

These were bold thoughts that in many ways were well ahead of their time. Unfortunately, they bore little or no fruit. One reason for this was that Müller's earlier empirical work, the work on which his reputation was based, did not reflect the more insightful views of his later years. Thus his major theoretical contribution to the experimental science of memory was directed at explaining *interference* effects on the efficiency of reproduction, cases where memorizing one set of items makes it more difficult to recall another set of items. He theorized about *inhibitory* processes that operated among memory representations.[27] These suggestions were eagerly taken up by later generations of experimentalists in America, but they were hardly adequate to the kinds of issues raised in Müller's more mature writings, which never made it across the Atlantic.

The road not taken: Gestalt psychology

In the theoretical solutions he offered Müller was generally far more conservative than in the kinds of questions he was prepared to pose. Thus although he recognized the supreme importance of organization in explaining memory phenomena, he thought of organization associationistically in terms of 'complexes' formed by elements. That was not good enough for those of his German successors who formed the school of Gestalt psychology in the post-war years. Consider the following simple experiment, whose results had been known since 1912. Subjects learn a series of syllables so they can rattle off the whole series without hesitation. Then they are shown single syllables from the list and asked to supply the next one. Their performance declines dramatically. In the words of Wolfgang Köhler, a core member of the Gestalt school: 'When given alone, a syllable is obviously not the same thing as it is in the stream of the organized series.'[28]

For the Gestaltists, talk of elements combining to form organized complexes was missing the point, which was that cognitive elements had no intrinsic identity – their identity depended on their cognitive context. Every associationist working on the psychology of memory (and for a long time that meant almost everyone in the field) recognized the importance of organization. Even Ebbinghaus had used rhythmic patterns to memorize his syllables. But they saw this organization in terms of the formation of temporal or spatial bonds between elements that retained their identity from one organization to another. According to the Gestaltists, however, what is retained in memory consists of structured patterns and not of elements and the associative bonds between them.

This reorientation led to a somewhat different approach to the experimental study of memory. First of all, it affected the preferred materials used in this field. From the beginning, the preferred material had consisted of chopped-up verbal material, syllables or single words. Memory experiments inspired by Gestalt psychology, however, tended to employ non-verbal visual forms, usually line drawings without any very obvious meaning. With such materials, the primary importance of organized patterns could be demonstrated unambiguously. More profoundly, the Gestalt approach entailed a revised view of memory storage, of memory *traces*. The prevailing psychological view was that memory storage involved quantitative effects, such as the decay or inhibition of stored elements, but there would be no spontaneous qualitative change in the elements themselves. According to Gestalt psychology, however, memory traces consisted of organized patterns that had an intrinsic tendency to change in certain ways. Visual forms, for example, might be remembered as more symmetrical than they in fact were, or they might be reproduced as more closely resembling some meaningful object, a mountain perhaps, than was the case with the originally presented line drawing. In other words, memory traces were qualitatively fluid, though the Gestaltists also demonstrated that there were regularities in the direction of change.[29] This encouraged associationists to show that the direction of change in the memory trace could be influenced by experimental arrangements and instructions, factors that were under the control of experimenters.[30] From the start, the experimental science of memory had been dedicated to demonstrating the importance of experimentally manipulable factors in the memory process while turning a blind eye to other factors. That worked against the influence of Gestalt explanations of memory phenomena because these tended to emphasize spontaneous, autochthonous processes that could certainly be *demonstrated* but not precisely *controlled*.

Experimenting involves deliberate intervention in whatever one is studying. In psychological experiments that intervention includes *instructions* to the subject about what he/she is expected to do. Instructions in memory experiments had always told subjects to *memorize* some presented material so that later their memory could be tested. In this way the deliberate intervention of the experimenter had been transformed into purposive activity on the part of experimental subjects. What was being studied, therefore, were the effects of intentional memorizing under different conditions.[31]

It was assumed without question that this was equivalent to studying 'memory'. But was this assumption correct? Gestalt psychology denied it. Memorizing was only a part of memory, and not the most interesting part at that. Remembering depended on some sort of cognitive organization – a chaotic mind in which nothing was connected to anything else would be a mind without memory. But what was the source of that organization? In memory experiments the source was some intentional act, the decision to learn a list, to repeat a group of syllables rhythmically to oneself, to think of a similar-sounding word, and so on. But was all cognitive organization intentional? Obviously not, according to the Gestaltists. Our perception of the world is organized in terms of spatial dimensions, shapes and objects, but little of that is due to any intentional effort. Mostly, the organized nature of perception depends on spontaneously operating factors that Gestalt psychology thought it could identify. Similar factors operated within memory traces because the input that left these traces was already organized. In opting for lists of nonsense syllables as the paradigm case for investigating memory Ebbinghaus and those who followed in his footsteps had chosen material with poor intrinsic organization that could be remembered only by intentionally imposing some organization of one's own. In everyday life, on the other hand, memory depended less on that than on the organized way the world was perceived. Traditional memory experiments could therefore tell us little about memory outside the laboratory.[32]

One important implication of the Gestalt critique was that the relationship between memory and perception should be regarded as far closer than one would be led to believe by the kind of memory experiment that owed its origins to Ebbinghaus. Unfortunately, this implication was widely ignored, and for most of the twentieth century memory continued to be treated as a psychological function quite separate from perception. This separation extended to the organization of textbooks and academic courses as much as to scientific journals and research groups.

But the boundaries that separated the psychology of perception from the psychology of memory were only one manifestation of a more general problem that was inseparable from the division of labour on which experimental psychology depended. Because experiments were limited in the number of factors that could be investigated at one time, they necessarily focused on certain aspects of a task situation that was always extremely complex. This would often tempt experimenters to reify the aspect of human psychology they were targeting. Because their experiments picked out a certain aspect of a complicated reality it was easy to treat that aspect as a separate thing that could be understood in terms of its own inherent laws of operation. Yet in reality, it was always a whole person who participated in an experimental situation, whether the experiment was about 'memory', about 'perception' or about any other psychological abstraction.

In their time, the Gestalt psychologists were ahead of most other experimentalists in recognizing this kind of problem. To begin with, they emphasized the profound importance of *context* for memory processes. In their experimental work they sought to demonstrate the dependence of memory for a particular content on the relationship of that content to other contents that formed part of the same learning situation. It was not just a matter of looking at the effect of one part of a series (of syllables) on another, but of comparing the effects of different contents, for example syllables, digits and figures, on each other.[33] The difficulty of remembering some detail depended inversely on its distinctiveness; the more it stood out the better it was remembered. Ultimately, Gestalt psychology regarded such phenomena as examples of *field effects*: what experimenters think of as individual 'items' are in fact parts of fields of influence in which what happens in one part depends on what happens elsewhere.

The fields of influence that are relevant for effects on memory are not limited to what individuals take in from the world outside, but include personal attitudes, intentions, interests and so on. For example, one well-known experiment inspired by this approach showed that tasks that a person had left uncompleted were remembered better than tasks that they had completed.[34] Conventionally, a sharp distinction is made between a self or ego and the memories of things or events that the ego possesses. At its most extreme, this distinction rests on a Cartesian dualism between a material organism and its subjective, non-material memories. Gestalt psychology, however, softened this distinction by pointing out that, on the level of psychology, the ego to which memories belong is not a physical organism but an experienced entity that is ultimately part of the same conscious field as its memories. It is true that this field is divided into parts of experience attributed to the outside world and other parts attributed to the self, but they remain parts of the same field in which effects flow from one part to another. In terms of the Platonic distinction (discussed in chapter 2), between memories that are *possessions* of the person and those that become *part of* the person, the Gestalt psychologists were unique among experimentalists in allowing for the latter possibility. Until relatively recent times, the experimental science of memory limited itself to investigating the impersonal products of laboratory memorizing. Memories with personal significance were generally beyond the pale.[35]

In its origins Gestalt psychology had shared in this tradition, but as it attempted to systematize its position the need for its own ego psychology became obvious. In responding to this need, one of the Gestalt group, Kurt Koffka, borrowed a key concept from the British neurologist Henry Head, the concept of the *schema*.[36]

Head had introduced this concept in order to account for the disturbances of voluntary movement and body posture that occurred in some of the brain-injured casualties of World War I.[37] He concluded that normal bodily movement and orientation depended on a constantly changing record of the position of the body and its parts. A voluntary movement could be carried out effectively only against a background knowledge of the location and state of the somatic apparatus involved in that movement. To move off in a certain direction, for example, requires a known starting-point. But that starting-point is merely the end-point of some previous movement, and every new movement changes the baseline for the next movement. Directed action requires not only a goal, but also a record of present position, and this record is a memory of sorts. However, it is a memory that is not in storage but in constant revision. The knowledge of my arm's position is not constructed anew at each moment, nor does it depend on calling up a memory of where my arm was when I last thought about it. This knowledge depends on the history of my arm's movements, but the record of that history is not 'stored' as a succession of static images; it is a moving record that incorporates changes as they occur. That moving record constitutes a 'schema' in Head's sense, and Koffka thought that the concept was applicable to self-directed action in general.

The ego can be regarded as a schema that is built up over the years and comprises sub-schemas representing individual affects and interests. It interacts with trace systems formed as a result of interaction with the external world and determines the fate of these traces. That leads to a distinction between one kind of forgetting, where an item may be unrecoverable because it has lost its identity by being absorbed within a more effective cognitive organization, and another kind of forgetting, where an item is temporarily unavailable because, at that time, the ego schema is such that no communication with the relevant trace system can take place.

It should be fairly clear that the strong point of Gestalt psychology was its original emphasis on the role of spontaneous cognitive organization and reorganization in remembering. Once it attempted to account for the role of intention in recall its explanations not only became vague, they seemed to relapse into the ancient model of stored memory traces that had to be searched for to be recovered. There is little doubt that this failure was connected to its insistence that the concept of traces was indispensable for a psychology of memory.

Sir Frederic's insight: reproduction is reconstruction

The one prominent psychologist of the inter-war period who tried to do away with memory traces was Sir Frederic Bartlett, a talented British experimentalist in a country that had not been at the forefront of developments in the new science of experimental psychology.[38] He too regarded Head's concept of the schema as being crucial for an understanding of human memory – in fact, he undoubtedly preceded Koffka in this insight. But he employed the schema concept in the context of a somewhat different style of experimentation. Although the use of a variety of materials had been essential for the memory experiments of the Gestalt school, these materials had remained rather abstract. They may not have been quite as artificial as Ebbinghaus's celebrated nonsense syllables (though Gestaltists were not above using those, too), but they were certainly different from the kinds of materials on which human memory is most often exercised in everyday life. In particular, they lacked social content and narrative coherence. Everyday memory is not often called upon to recall a list of indifferent items, but it engages social images and narratives of social events all the time. Only if one had faith that there was knowledge about 'pure' individual memory waiting to be scientifically discovered could one believe in the value of the experimental data that psychologists were producing on the basis of the kinds of material with which they were working. Bartlett was far more radical than the Gestaltists in questioning this faith.

The very title of Bartlett's key publication, *Remembering: A study in experimental and social psychology*,[39] contains two highly significant pointers: First, this is not a study of 'memory' but of 'remembering', because for Bartlett the object of investigation is a human activity and not a separate reproductive capacity of the mind. Second, the study is not only experimental but also a part of *social* psychology. Both aspects represented a radical break with the conceptual and practical basis on which the experimental science of memory had operated. The most common investigative procedures of this science, based on Ebbinghaus's paradigmatic approach, had been such as to preclude questions about the actual *process* of remembering or about the fact that this was essentially a *social* process. Some of the Gestalt experiments were more process-orientated, but they never constituted mainstream memory science.[40]

Bartlett's experimental methods were very different from those that had been introduced by Ebbinghaus and perfected at Göttingen. First of all, he switched to the use of meaningful material, rejecting 'nonsense syllables' in favour not merely of isolated words, but entire prose passages or meaningful pictures. Empirical work had already shown that nonsense syllables failed to eliminate meaning from memory, because experimental subjects commonly imported meaning by finding meaningful associations for such 'nonsense' material. Thus even adherents of the traditional approach had sometimes switched from syllables to words. But testing for memory of isolated words was still investigating memory under highly artificial conditions. Bartlett did not believe that this was likely to provide significant insights into the factors at work during the ordinary operations of memory. Moreover, he rejected the common rationale that working with 'simple' stimuli, such as syllables and words, would enable one to discover scientific 'laws' that could later be extended to more complex material. The 'simplicity' of these laboratory materials was no more than an illusion, because their effect still depended on their interpretation by human individuals who remained as complex as ever. If one was ever to throw any light on what happens when people try to remember the sorts of material they are confronted with in ordinary life one ought to work with such material.

Bartlett therefore looked at memory for meaningful pictures and stories. But, unlike Ebbinghaus, he had no interest in the work of memorizing. He was not looking for quantitative relationships between the work invested and the excellence of recall. Memory was not to be measured on a unidimensional scale from total forgetting to perfect recall, and therefore there was no need for memory materials to be arranged in lists of homogeneous items. Memory was not simply the opposite of forgetting; it involved qualitative changes over time. On this point Bartlett agreed with the Gestaltists, and like them he made use of repeated reproductions of the same original material to study these qualitative changes. Unlike them, however, he considered socio-cultural factors to be of fundamental importance in accounting for these changes. His best-known item for studying memory was a story adapted from a translation of a native North American folk-tale. However, the people who read the story and tried to recall it later were not Amerindians but educated English men and women. To them this was a very strange story, both in content and in form. The parts of the story seemed disconnected and featured ghosts as well as an unfamiliar train of events. The intended meaning of this culturally transplanted narrative was unclear, though each bit made sense as one read through it.

Why choose such an odd medium to investigate remembering? The answer is, first of all, that Bartlett did not equate memory with mental reproduction, and regarded remembering rather as a kind of reconstruction. This meant that the experimental conditions had to provide ample opportunity for efforts at reconstruction to emerge. Being asked to recall a story that was strange and unfamiliar, but not senseless, would certainly do that. But to achieve that it would not have been necessary to look for materials outside one's own culture. Taking that step enabled Bartlett to demonstrate the culturally bound nature of mnemonic reconstruction, because one of the effects that would emerge would be the experimental subjects' tendency to minimize the cultural 'otherness' of the material.

The social aspect of remembering was also addressed in what Bartlett called the method of 'serial reproduction'. In everyday life remembering often involves more than one person. Several people may reconstruct a past event together, or versions of the event may get passed on from person to person. The standard investigative practices of psychologists did not, and still do not, address this aspect at all. Bartlett, however, made a start by using a chain of experimental subjects, such that the second subject in the chain would be asked to remember the version of the original material that the first subject had produced from memory, then the third subject would try to remember the second subject's version, and so on. Only the first person in the chain saw the original material, and attempts at reproduction always took place after some interval. (The method is similar to a popular party game.)[41] In the method of 'repeated reproduction' only one person was involved, and he or she was asked to repeat the original story at intervals of up to several years after the first effort at reproduction, which took place about 15 minutes after reading the original story.

What Bartlett was interested in were the *qualitative* changes in successive versions of the story, and, as might be expected, these were quite striking. The main story had been titled *The War of the Ghosts*, but, for the most part, any mention of ghosts dropped out very quickly. Human memory seems to be resistant to aspects that are culturally unassimilable. If they are not forgotten outright they are likely to be reconstructed so as to make them conform to cultural expectations. In their attempts at reproduction, these educated Britons came up with stories in which the parts fitted together more 'rationally' and coherently than in the original folk-tale. Unfamiliar details were transformed into more familiar ones, and the order of events was changed to make the motivation of the characters more comprehensible and appealing. On the whole, the activity of remembering tended to refashion previously received information so as to make it fit an established framework of understanding that had deep cultural roots. Bartlett thought all human cognitive activity involved an 'effort after meaning', and what was experienced as more or less meaningful depended to a large extent on culturally variable standards.

Repeated reproductions from a single individual showed similar tendencies of cultural assimilation and massive reconstruction. The latter included inventions and omissions, as well as accentuation of minor details, together with conventionalization and flattening of the verbal narrative.[42] There were interesting long-term effects that could have been demonstrated only by using Bartlett's methods. Generally, the first reproduction set the tone for subsequent ones, but there were also long-term changes that emerged gradually. The personal interests, attitudes and values of the remembering person were clearly relevant to their reconstruction of the original information. Accurate reproduction was very much the exception.[43]

Within the experimental science of memory Bartlett's methods and findings evoked a mixed response.[44] Although there was general agreement that this was a significant contribution, with which the science would have to come to terms, it was not easy to bridge the chasm that separated Bartlett's work and more traditional research based on the Ebbinghaus paradigm. Moreover, in the decades that followed the publication of Bartlett's monograph psychology as a whole became more narrowly scientistic, quantification (which was often pseudo-quantification) became an end in itself and theoretical interpretation that went beyond low level empirical generalization became suspect. This was not a disciplinary climate in which the potential of Bartlett's approach was likely to be recognized. His methods were regarded as sloppy, of course, and his findings were therefore regarded as unreliable. But attempts at probing the roots of that unreliability simply revealed the profound disagreements about the nature of human memory that separated Bartlett and his critics.

It was noted that Bartlett had never asked his experimental subjects to try to reproduce material *accurately*. When later investigators, in their experimental instructions, strongly emphasized the need to be as accurate as possible, the accuracy of reproductions did go up and the kinds of distortion reported by Bartlett became less marked.[45] Those who had always distrusted Bartlett's methods and results could now feel that Ebbinghaus and his progeny had been vindicated: memory 'really' was a matter of reproductive work, and not of reconstruction, as long as it was given the right instructions.[46] In fact, the issues raised by such attempts at experimental replication went right to the heart of some fundamental problems faced by an experimental science of memory.

The crucial role of experimental instructions, seldom addressed in experimental designs, is forced into the open. Whatever else they may be, memory experiments are social tasks in which a task-master issues instructions as to what is required from those whose memory is under investigation. It would be extraordinary if memory performance did not vary profoundly with the nature of the set task. The instructions defining success in the given task are surely among the vital conditions determining the outcome of memory experiments. In order to gather scientific data on human memory certain social situations have to be set up, and the data that become available will depend on those situations. Ignoring that simple fact can result only in inadequate interpretations of human memory performance. Yet that was precisely the ruling theoretical commitment within the experimental science of memory for much of its history. All kinds of factors were examined for their contribution to the experimental results, but, for the most part, investigators displayed an unbecoming modesty in airbrushing themselves out of the picture.

Their contribution, however, was all-important. Not only did they choose the carefully constructed materials to be recalled and decide on the variables worth investigating, they also made up the experimental instructions and thus defined the nature of the memory task that was to be studied. Inevitably, their own preconceptions about memory were reflected in these choices, decisions and constructions, for no experimenter ever entered an experimental situation without such preconceptions, rarely though they may have been articulated. In the case of the Bartlett replications this emerges particularly clearly. Does one or does one not ask one's experimental subjects to pay special attention to the accuracy of their reproductions? Unless one takes special care to maintain neutrality, that will depend on one's pre-theoretical understanding of the nature of memory. If one thinks of memory as essentially a copying machine, whose performance will be measured in terms of the accuracy of its reproductions, one will want to ensure that the machine is properly plugged in by issuing the appropriate instructions. If, however, one thinks of remembering as essentially a constructive activity, as Bartlett did, one would not wish to distort its performance by instructions emphasizing a particular mnemonic value.

There is little doubt that human individuals are capable of pretty accurate reproduction under certain conditions. The experimental method is uniquely suited to tease out these conditions. Unfortunately, it has often been used with the understanding that accurate reproduction constituted the only norm against which actual performance ought to be measured. Experiments designed on the Ebbinghaus paradigm tended to use simplistic measures of memory performance that reflected a simplistic view of memory. Scores were expressed in terms of number of presented items (syllables in a series, paired associates, figures, etc.) correctly reproduced, thus squeezing research questions into the format: more reproduction or less. Such experiments virtually precluded any hints of reconstructive memory finding their way into the experimental data.[47]

By the 1930s two very different conceptions of memory had emerged within the experimental science of memory. The one that counted the largest number of adherents followed Ebbinghaus in regarding memory as a copying device that functioned more or less well under different conditions. Good copying was construed as reproducing a large number of the items to be remembered, bad copying as leaving out many items. The recall of items that occurred in an experiment depended on an internal copy, a memory trace, established when an item was learned. The individual, itemized and fixed nature of these hypothetical internal copies was isomorphic with the memory materials typically employed in experiments following this paradigm. In the alternative conception of memory, representing a minority view, these materials had a purely artefactual status, to be rejected altogether, or to be used merely to highlight the differences between their structure and the operations of human memory. This alternative conception emphasized the unifying or organizing aspects of memory and its temporally flowing, ever-changing character.

Each of these viewpoints had its own specific problems. For the main-stream view, it was never easy to provide plausible accounts of integrative effects, and, for the most part, appropriate experimental arrangements made it unlikely that such effects would ever become observable. For the alternative view, the problematic cases were those where singular remembered items did stand out clearly and fixedly against a more fluid background, a certain sensation, a special word or phrase, a particular figure. Bartlett believed that imagery and 'appetite, instinct, interests and ideals' were crucial in making particular items stand out sharply, but this split between the schema itself and the personal factors making use of it spelled trouble for his theory. In opposition to the idea of distinct individual memory traces, the concept of the schema had originally been invoked to account for the way in which current and past action and experience are integrated in a seamless flow. But sometimes this flow seems to be interrupted, for instance when images of some distant past interrupt present activity. Is this a 'turning around on one's own schemata', as Bartlett suggested? If so, self and schema are separate, and schemata pertain only to objects. But this seems to turn schema theory on its head, because Head's concept had been introduced as a model for a (somatic) self capable of coherent intentional action. Bartlett left the problem hanging and turned to other areas of research.[48] But his work had at least indicated a general direction for an experimental science of memory to follow as an alternative to the cul-de-sac that the Ebbinghaus paradigm would prove to be. Unfortunately, many years of sterility were to pass before this and other alternatives began to be followed up.

The Dark Ages of memory research and its critics

At the beginning of World War II the experimental science of memory had entered its own Dark Ages, a period during which it almost disappeared. In Europe, ideological and military priorities put an end to work of any significance. In the USA it withered under the impact of behaviourism, for which the very word 'memory' carried suspicious mentalistic overtones. Its place was taken by something called 'verbal learning', a little sub-discipline[49] that had begun under the aegis of American functionalism and essentially continued using Ebbinghaus-type research practices in a severely restricted theoretical context. Memory was conceptualized as a stimulus-driven response, and theoretical issues centred on how materials from two memory tasks could interfere with each other. Much of the empirical work seemed to lack any theoretical inspiration whatsoever, and such theory as existed was built on associationistic presuppositions. A highly standardized form of investigative practice completed an epistemic circle in which certain metaphysical preconceptions functioned as a guide for constructing artificial situations that generated the kind of data that could be interpreted in terms of theories derived from the original preconceptions. A self-perpetuating system of interlocking theory and practice was the result. However, because of the impossibility of eliminating human agency, even under the most restrictive experimental conditions, specific predictions were often not confirmed. This, and the alienation from anything in common human experience, eventually seems to have had a demoralizing effect on some of the leaders of the field.[50]

By 1970 the sorry state of the experimental science of memory had become apparent to many within its own ranks. A scathing review of the field came to the radical conclusion that 'nothing much has changed over the past hundred years in the understanding of how people learn and remember things ... We have hundreds and thousands of little facts, we can make quantitative instead of qualitative statements, we can talk about all kinds of fine details in experimental data and characteristics of underlying processes – but the broad picture we have of human memory in 1970 does not differ from that in 1870'.[51] This was not a claim based on any historical evidence but an impression produced by a review virtually limited to (mostly recent) experimental studies conducted in North America. Within that narrow horizon such depressing conclusions seemed entirely justifiable. If nothing else, they served as an expression of a growing feeling within the field that things had to change.

During the next few years a number of respected experimentalists identified some of the main problems that would have to be faced. In a sort of *mea culpa*, J. J. Jenkins confessed to having been 'caught in a metatheoretical trap' of 'unexamined beliefs' that had limited research in the area.[52] The faulty presuppositions were identified as those of 'associationism', that is, assuming all mental structures to be chains of discrete units, regarding complex psychological phenomena as assemblies of simpler components, looking for explanations in terms of automatic mechanisms.[53] Associationism extended to beliefs about the structure of language that were implied by the way verbal materials were used in memory experiments. It was regarded as 'natural and obvious' that words were the fundamental units of language and that they were associatively linked in chains.

Jenkins's confession certainly throws some light on why so few researchers had bothered to employ narrative materials *à la* Bartlett, but had been quite content to stick to the 'paired associates' method that tested memory for associative links between single words. Despite its overwhelming concentration on *verbal* memory, the older experimental science of memory had been pursued in complete isolation from, and generally in complete ignorance of, the science of linguistics. The isolation of the field was so marked that even relevant experimental work on perception and thinking received little notice. As a result, many of the general points made by the Gestaltists, by Bartlett and even by Müller had to be painfully rediscovered decades later. It was only in the wake of the so-called cognitive revolution that a significant relaxation of these self-defeating boundaries could be observed.

In an influential article, one of the major figures in that revolution, Ulric Neisser, expressed his disappointment with the experimental science of memory in no uncertain terms. It had 'very little to show for a hundred years of effort', its empirical generalizations concerned banal practical facts that were known to 'every ten-year-old' and it had avoided studying the more interesting and socially significant memory phenomena.[54] The usual rationale for studying memory under artificial experimental conditions was based on the false assumption that memory was memory, wherever it manifested itself. If that were indeed the case, it would certainly make scientific sense to study it under conditions in which control and quantification were possible. But, Neisser observed, 'memory in general does not exist'. The way memory operates depends on context, on how people want to use their memory, on the tasks and resources in their social and physical environment, and so on. Before presuming to make generalizations about memory in general, psychologists should change direction and find out about the many different ways in which memory functions under a variety of circumstances.

By the time Neisser issued this appeal (1978), a number of psychologists had in fact begun to study memory under 'natural', i.e. non-laboratory, conditions, a trend that became known as the 'ecological' approach. In the years that followed, this approach flourished side by side with more traditional laboratory experimentation.[55] The latter did not disappear by any means, and two decades later the chapter on methods of memory research in a standard reference work was able to state: 'While acknowledging the importance of investigating natural memories, it is Ebbinghaus's experimental framework that remains the prototype for memory research.'[56] Vigorous defences of the traditional reliance on contextless experiments appeared from time to time.[57] Lists, whether of words, sentences or figures, continued to form the standard stimulus materials employed in laboratory experiments.

A different language

It had always been a hallmark of the Ebbinghaus tradition to gather empirical data on *forgetting*, on failures and errors in the recall or recognition of previously presented material, in the hope that this would throw light on what was not observed but assumed, namely memory. But this was possible only if one already had a general idea of how memory worked. Interpreting the failures of any complex system, even a motorcar engine, requires some schema of how that system is constituted. Without that, there would be an infinite number of interpretations from which to choose. One might change one's ideas in the course of time, but one would always have to have *some* framework within which to formulate one's hypotheses.

In the early days of the experimental science of memory the framework was often provided by associationism, the model of the mind as composed of a myriad of distinct cognitive units that had facilitating or inhibiting effects on each other. In experimental situations these units were usually regarded as copies of the units that comprised experimenters' lists. However, it was gradually recognized that remembering depended on the way in which experimental subjects reorganized stimulus materials rather than on what experimenters thought they had presented. One might say that this amounted to a rediscovery of the insight, common to the Gestaltists and to Bartlett, that memory was not a matter of reproduction or copying. In any case, the recognition that memory had to be studied as an active rather than a passive process led to changes in the design of memory experiments that provided more opportunities for active organizing processes to become manifest.

The overall framework for interpreting experimental data on the errors and failures of memory also changed. But it was not the ideas of Gestalt psychology, or of Bartlett, that shaped the new framework, but the metaphor of the computer (discussed at the end of chapter 2), and particularly the language of information processing linked to that metaphor. For much of late twentieth-century experimental work on memory, this language played a crucial constitutive role. It not only sanctioned inherited procedures based on the atomization of experience into 'items' or 'units', but also established a specific framework for understanding what was happening in memory experiments.

As indicated towards the end of chapter 2, the guiding metaphor encouraged the belief that human memory essentially depended on processes of symbol manipulation, quite separate from the sensory and motor activity of the human organism. Such a model necessarily comprised three stages: one in which sensory input was converted into symbolic form, or *encoded*, a second stage in which symbolic representations were *stored*, and a third stage in which they were *retrieved* from storage. If memory were perfect, the output after retrieval would mirror the input before encoding. But memory is full of imperfections, and it is these that are studied in memory experiments. Conditions during encoding and retrieval, as well as the effects of time and other influences on storage, all affect the ultimate fate of the messages that are to be remembered.

Standard memory experiments studied these conditions, but they were not designed to question the overall framework for formulating experimental purposes and conclusions. When experimental goals and results were described in terms of categories such as coding and retrieval, a certain ground plan for the constitution of memory had already been presupposed. That ground-plan could not be questioned while staying within the framework of descriptions and practices provided by those experiments. The experiments were designed to answer questions formulated within a particular conceptual framework. Both the procedural–practical aspects of the experiment and the meaning assigned to experimental findings assumed that the general outline of how memory works was already known; that only certain details remained to be filled in.

Although the dominant position of the information-processing model appears to have been maintained well into the final decade of the century,[58] dissident voices had always been present. This led to still-ongoing debates whose merits are more appropriately discussed in current reviews than in the historical overview presented here. I will merely note a few landmarks that point to continuities with broader historical themes.

Relatively early, some investigators were unhappy with the assumed separation of content and context in an information store and with the way memory experiments focused on failures in the reproduction of content rather than the productive adaptation of content to new contexts.[59] From this perspective, experimenting with, and theorizing about, discrete units of 'information' would not provide the basis for a general account of how the past affected the present in the lives of organisms. Past experience provided, not stored representations of specific units of previous input, but general constraints, frameworks or 'stage settings' for interpreting new experience, giving some scope for an accommodation to the novel features that each new situation necessarily presented.

Apart from its too radical departure from traditional theoretical commitments, this approach was also unsuitable for generating the myriad small-scale, one-shot studies that filled the pages of academic journals and built careers. By contrast, the information-processing approach provided a congenial theoretical language for a form of investigative practice, dubbed 'the functional autonomy of methods', that obliged investigators to limit themselves to a small array of traditional experimental techniques, all dedicated to the collection of quantitative data under highly circumscribed conditions.[60] Unfortunately, the precision of the results was often purchased at the cost of the generalizability of the conclusions. Information theory, language and symbolism, however, could be used to impart an appearance of generality through the ambiguity of the term 'information' and through the use of diagrams of 'information flow' that linked purely hypothetical categories identified by broad terms, such as 'central processor', 'response system', 'current sub-goal' and so on.

Some critics characterized such attempts at theorizing as 'fanciful nominalizations'.[61] They were now in the 1980s and noticed a 'lack of cumulative progress in the information processing tradition', leading to the suspicion that 'many of the assumptions of the information processing approach are either wrong or are not testable'.[62] Even the three-stage model of encoding, storage and retrieval might not be warranted. They attributed the failures of the information-processing approach to certain assumptions that had their origins in the computer metaphor. If one took that metaphor too seriously one ended up believing in a representation of experience by discrete traces, usually propositional in form in psychology experiments. Memory then involved the action of various processes on these traces, including 'decoding', 'search' and so on. But this separation of process and content was simply prescribed by the metaphor and then applied to the interpretation of one's data. The critics believed it to be the wrong prescription, mainly because of its complete bracketing off of the action component that is always present for humans but always absent for computers, which are pure symbol processors. To repair this fatal mistake the authors proposed recognizing the dependence of memory on specific skills and procedures, concepts of doing or action that combine content and process. The details of what such an alternative approach might entail were left rather sketchy. Their elaboration depended on other contributions that were slow to be recognized. The dominance of the information-processing approach had not yet run its course.

But by the final decade of the century, expressions of dissatisfaction with the prevailing orthodoxy tended to take on a more radical tone. The very notion that memory traces could be investigated by the methods of psychology was sometimes rejected. Those methods, it was claimed, were ultimately incapable of deciding between alternative explanations of memory phenomena in terms of coding, storage or retrieval processes. The conventional three-stage framework was based on the reification of what was merely a metaphor, and sanctioned an unconstrained multiplication of *ad hoc* hypotheses. To escape from this dead end, psychologists were advised to change the direction of their scientific attention from unobservable inner processing to the external context in which memory phenomena actually occurred.[63]

Variants of the call to look at memory in the world became more frequent during these years. The experimental psychology of memory had too long been dominated by the study of memorization – it was time to ask what memory was really for, what function memory played in human life.[64] Participants in typical memorization experiments were given tasks in which little or nothing was at stake for them, in which their own reaction was widely separated in time from the perceptual input and had no influence on the latter, for which only the verbal, not the bodily, aspect of their reaction was of relevance. Experimenters, for their part, did not address the fundamental question of how sensory, mnemic and motor functions converged to produce an adaptive response. By limiting their goal to accounting for experimental results in the context of memorization they were left with a greatly diminished explanandum, namely alterations in a precisely known input after it has spent some time in the cognitive machinery of the human subject. But such accounts lose their force in situations demanding continuous use of mnemic resources to structure a fluid input with promising or threatening implications for the subject.

By the end of the century, calls for innovation in the psychological study of memory had become noticeably focused on the twin issues of embodiment and situatedness. Memory serves action in the world. It cannot be understood only in terms of the manipulation of symbols in the head. In the end, it is closely implicated in bodily action in specific contexts. For this, it depends on aids that are often external. These are the basic parameters that an experimental study of memory cannot afford to ignore.[65]

Within the framework of a broad conceptual history, much of what needs to be said about the defining notions of the experimental psychological science of memory will necessarily be critical. However, this does not mean that the contributions of this field have been entirely trivial. A certain number of empirical generalizations have proved to be quite robust, though they are not part of the subject-matter of this book. What is more relevant here are some of the conceptual developments that link the modern science of memory with the past, often unintentionally. If one was asking questions about memory, even if one was asking them in a laboratory, one could not escape some questions that had been addressed before, though often in somewhat different terms. Most of these questions are very old, and though none of them originated with the experimental science of memory, they did end up forming part of its agenda. As a result, this science certainly left its mark on the conceptual history of memory, and this means that we shall have to return to it from time to time in the chapters that follow.

Among these questions there are four which seem to be of rather profound importance. The first of them, addressed in the following chapter, concerns 'memory kinds', the question of whether all memory is one or whether there are different sorts of memory. If there are, how should they be characterized, on what basis are they to be distinguished? This is an issue that is closely linked to the very idea of memory as such. Words like 'remember', 'recall', 'reminisce', 'recognize' and so on are used in many different contexts in everyday life. The Platonic notion that the various situations covered by this usage all imply the existence of a common essence that dwells within individuals stands at the very beginning of the memory concept and has accompanied it ever since. Inevitably, this has led to problems, because of the huge variety of situations in which this essential ingredient seems to become manifest. One way of dealing with this problem is to postulate the existence of not one, but several essential forms of memory, all, however, strictly confined to individuals. In chapter 6 the long history of these attempts to rescue the original Platonic insight is discussed, ending with their reverberations in the modern experimental psychology of memory.

Second, there is the question of memory and truth, some aspects of which are discussed in chapter 7. Is memory a faithful copying machine, does it perhaps hold secret truths, or does it lie? Versions of this question are very old, and the answers have been diverse. This issue is closely tied up with the personal aspect of memory. A striking feature of the experimental psychology of memory for most of its history was its overwhelming preference for studying memory in an utterly impersonal context. This, more than anything else, isolated it from everyday memory. When a part of the discipline broke with this tradition, its interest began to focus on personal memory, a topic on which others had preceded it. The incursion of experimentalists into this field constitutes a recent chapter in a history that stretches much further back.

Another set of questions concerns the 'place' of memory. By definition, memory has something to do with time, but does it also have a location in space? If so, in what sense? Opinions are not unanimous on this, and in recent years these have become very active issues, both conceptually and empirically. As indicated in chapter 8, the experimental science of memory has participated in this discourse, though often not as a senior partner.

Finally, there are questions relating to the conceptual place of memory, addressed in chapter 9. How is any kind of memory distinguished from other categories of cognition, such as perception and thinking? Is memory even to be considered an essentially 'inner' property of individuals, or is it a feature of how they relate to the world they live in? These are questions that resonate with some of the issues that have come up in the present chapter. It will be necessary to return to them.

Notes

1. Hacking, *Rewriting*.
2. An early solution was the multiplication of 'pigeonholes' on desks. But with forty pigeonholes you would need to devise a system of mnemonically effective labelling; in other words, you would still have a memory problem, though its nature would now be different. As records multiplied, pigeonholes became hopelessly inadequate in any case and filing systems had to be devised. Individuals with specialized memories, archivists and filing clerks reminiscent of the record-keepers of more ancient times, had to be trained. A good introduction to these problems is provided in Norman, *Things that make us smart*.
3. The story of this emergence has often been told, though with different emphases and from different perspectives. For many years the quasi-official intra-disciplinary account was to be found in E. G. Boring, *A history of experimental psychology*, 2nd edn (New York: Appleton-Century-Crofts, 1950; first edition 1929). Revisions of this account, including my own, appeared towards the end of the last century, e.g. K. Danziger, *Constructing the subject: Historical origins of psychological research* (New York: Cambridge University Press, 1990); and K. Danziger, 'Wilhelm Wundt and the emergence of experimental psychology', in R. C. Olby, G. N. Cantor, J. R. R. Christie and M. J. S. Hodge (eds.), *Companion to the history of modern science* (London: Routledge, 1990), pp. 396–409. For a more recent historical analysis, see M. G. Ash, 'Psychology', in T. M. Porter and D. Ross (eds.), *The Cambridge history of science: The modern social sciences* (Cambridge: Cambridge University Press, 2003), vol. VII, pp. 251–74.
4. W. Wundt, *Grundzüge der physiologischen Psychologie* (Leipzig: Engelmann, 1874).
5. W. Wundt, *Outlines of psychology* (Leipzig: Engelmann, 1907; first German edn 1896), pp. 281–2.
6. E. Scheerer, 'Wilhelm Wundt's psychology of memory', *Psychological Research* 42 (1980), 135–55. See also, S. K. Carpenter, 'Some neglected contributions of Wilhelm Wundt to the psychology of memory', *Psychological Reports* 97 (2005), 63–73.
7. H. K. Wolfe, 'Untersuchungen über das Tongedächtnis', *Philosophische Studien* 3 (1886), 534–71.
8. This description applies to subsequent American adaptations of Ebbinghaus's methods, not to the original. Working in German, Ebbinghaus also included some four-letter syllables. Moreover, 'nonsense syllables' was a somewhat literal translation of Ebbinghaus's term *sinnlose Silben*, whose intent might have been better rendered as 'meaningless syllables'. In any case, he usually referred to meaningless material rather than syllables, because the target of his research was always the *list* and not its syllabic components. For further background see R. R. Hoffman, W. Bringmann, M. Bamberg and R. Klein, 'Some historical observations on Ebbinghaus', in D. S. Gorfein and R. R. Hoffman (eds.), *Memory and learning: The Ebbinghaus centennial conference* (Hillsdale, NJ: Erlbaum, 1987) pp. 57–75.
9. K. Danziger, 'Hermann Ebbinghaus and the psychological experiment', in W. Traxel (ed.), *Ebbinghaus-Studien* 2 (Passau: Passavia Universitätsverlag, 1987), pp. 217–24.
10. In the published version of his celebrated monograph on memory Ebbinghaus gives few clues to the thinking that lay behind the procedures he adopted. But in an earlier, unpublished draft he is more explicit. See H. Ebbinghaus, *Urmanuskript über das Gedächtniss 1880* (Passau: Passavia Universitätsverlag, 1983).
11. Ebbinghaus, *Urmanuskript*, p. 70.
12. He dedicated his textbook on psychology to Fechner with the words: 'I owe everything to you.'

13. Ebbinghaus, *Urmanuskript*, p. 43 ('dass in der That die Arbeit, die auf eine Vorstellungsreihe verwandt wird … ein wirkliches Mass ist für den psychischen Vorgang, zu dessen Erzeugung sie dient').

14. H. Ebbinghaus, *Grundzüge der Psychologie* (Leipzig: Veit & Co., 1902), p. 608.

15. Ebbinghaus, *Grundzüge*, pp. 221–2. The elements of this model are also to be found in Fechner.

16. Danziger, *Constructing the subject*.

17. For example, F. Fauth, *Das Gedächtnis: Studie zu einer Pädagogik auf dem Standpunkt der heutigen Physiologie und Psychologie* [Memory: A pedagogical study on the basis of current physiology and psychology] (Gütersloh: Bertelsmann, 1888).

18. As might be expected, Wundt did not approve of this development. He was much concerned with preserving the academic purity of experimental psychology and avoiding its entanglement with practical issues of life outside the laboratory. His rejection of memory as a significant psychological category was an outcome of that concern. See K. Danziger, 'Sealing off the discipline: Wilhelm Wundt and the psychology of memory', in C. D. Green, M. Shore and T. Teo (eds.), *The transformation of psychology: Influences of nineteenth-century philosophy, technology, and natural science* (Washington, DC: American Psychological Association, 2001), pp. 45–62.

19. E. Meumann, *Abriss der experimentellen Pädagogik* (Leipzig: Teubner, 1912), p. 240.

20. E. Meumann, *The psychology of learning: An experimental investigation of the economy and technique of memory* (New York: Appleton, 1913).

21. E. L. Thorndike, *Educational psychology* (New York: Teachers College, Columbia University Press, 1913) vol. II.

22. Thus an authoritative text on experimental psychology of the 1930s still referred to laboratory memory tasks as 'lessons'. See R. S. Woodworth, *Experimental psychology* (New York: Henry Holt, 1938), chapter 9.

23. These procedures were introduced in G. E. Müller, and F. Schumann, 'Experimentelle Beiträge zur Untersuchung des Gedächtnisses', *Zeitschrift für Psychologie und Physiologie der Sinnesorgane* 6 (1894), 81–190 and 257–339.

24. I have discussed the far-reaching implications of this in *Constructing the subject*. According to a count by one of my students, 83 per cent of American experiments in this area were still relying on data from undergraduates in 1987 (J. Parker, unpublished).

25. E. J. Haupt, 'Origins of American psychology in the work of G. E. Müller: Classical psychophysics and serial learning', in R. W. Rieber and K. D. Salzinger (eds.), *Psychology: Theoretical-historical perspectives*, 2nd edn (Washington, DC: American Psychological Association, 1998), p. 52.

26. These ideas were put forward in an extended monograph, published in three parts between 1911 and 1917. G. E. Müller, 'Zur Analyse der Gedächtnistätigkeit und des Vorstellungsverlaufes', *Zeitschrift für Psychologie* Ergänzungsband 5 (1911); Ergänzungsband 8 (1913); Ergänzungsband 9 (1917).
    None of this material was ever translated into English. An English summary of the main points has been made available quite recently: D. J. Murray, and C. A. Bandomir, 'G. E. Müller (1911, 1913, 1917) on memory', *Psychologie et Histoire* 1 (2000), 208–32.

27. G. E. Müller and A. Pilzecker, 'Experimentelle Beiträge zur Lehre vom Gedächtnis', *Zeitschrift für Psychologie* Ergänzungsband 1 (1900).

28. W. Köhler, *Gestalt psychology* (New York: Liveright, 1929), p. 283. In the mid-1920s Müller and Köhler had engaged in debate on this issue.

29. The classic study demonstrating these effects was F. Wulf, 'Über die Veränderung von Vorstellungen (Gedächtnis und Gestalt)', *Psychologosche Forschung* 1 (1922),

333–73. Abridged English translation in W. D. Ellis (ed.), *A source book of Gestalt psychology* (London: Routledge & Kegan Paul, 1938), pp. 136–48.

30. The Gestalt impetus gave rise to a small research area on memory for form that was always eclipsed by the more usual paradigm of verbal memorizing. The earlier history of the area is reviewed in D. A. Riley, 'Memory for form', in L. Postman (ed.), *Psychology in the making* (New York: Knopf, 1962), pp. 402–65.

31. There was a famous experiment in which, when instructions to memorize were omitted, memory for presented material was very poor. K. Lewin, 'Das Problem der Willensmessung und das Grundgesetz der Assoziation', *Psychologische Forschung* 1 (1922), 191–302; 2 (1922), 65–140.

32. Köhler, *Gestalt psychology*, pp. 284–6.

33. H. von Restorff, 'Über die Wirking von Bereichsbildung im Spurenfeld', *Psychologische Forschung* 18 (1933), 299–342.

34. B. Zeigarnik, 'Über das Behalten von erledigten und unerledigten Handlungen', *Psychologische Forschung* 9 (1927), 1–85.

35. For the most part, the implications of Gestalt ego psychology were not followed up by the core members of the school, Wertheimer, Koffka and Köhler, but by individuals close to their point of view, especially Kurt Lewin and some of his students. This work went far beyond the experimental psychology of memory.

36. K. Koffka, *Principles of Gestalt psychology* (New York: Harcourt, Brace, 1935).

37. H. Head, *Studies in neurology* (London: Oxford University Press, 1920).

38. The historical relevance of Bartlett's teacher, James Ward, and the Lotzean views which the latter propagated, are briefly described in M. L. Northway, 'The concept of the "schema"', *British Journal of Psychology* 30 (1940), 316–25. For the intellectual context of Bartlett's work and the trajectory of his interests, the following is indispensable: A. Collins, 'The embodiment of reconciliation: Order and change in the work of Frederic Bartlett', *History of Psychology* 9 (2006), 290–312.

39. Originally published by Cambridge University Press in 1932 and republished in 1995. It is one of only two 'classics' in the experimental science of memory, the other being, of course, Ebbinghaus's original monograph.

40. With the notable exception of the experiments directed by Kurt Lewin they were also quite asocial in their orientation. The assumption that memory is essentially a private phenomenon is common to virtually all psychological investigations of memory and continued to determine the form of most memory experiments to the end of the century: 'A hallmark of the typical experimental approach is that subjects are essentially tested alone, attempting to recollect prior events by themselves.' H. L. Roediger III, E. T. Bergman and M. L. Meade, 'Repeated reproduction from memory', in A. Saito (ed.), *Bartlett, culture and cognition* (Guildford: Psychology Press, 2000), pp. 115–34 (p. 129).

41. It can also be used to study the psychology of rumour; see G. W. Allport and L. Postman, *The psychology of rumor* (New York: Henry Holt, 1947). However, in that case the method of transmission from person to person is oral, whereas Bartlett's subjects had to write out their efforts at recall.

42. In many secondary accounts these changes are described in terms of 'sharpening' and 'levelling'; however, these are terms specifically of Gestalt psychology.

43. Those who have had the clearest understanding of Bartlett's insistence on the cultural rootedness of remembering have regretted the limitation of his methods on the grounds that their social aspect was unidirectional and provided no opportunity for the interpersonal construction of memory accounts that is more typical of everyday memory. Conversation and discourse analysis are therefore regarded as being more in line with Bartlett's most profound theoretical commitments than his own methods. See D. Edwards and D. Middleton, 'Conversation and remembering: Bartlett revisited', *Applied Cognitive Psychology* 1 (1987), 77–92. These authors also make the interesting observation that many of Bartlett's insights seem to depend more on

the informal 'metacognitive dialogue' which he carried on with his experimental subjects than on the written results of the formal part of his experimental methods.

44. For an excellent account of the chequered history of Bartlett's reception within the experimental science of memory, see E. B. Johnston, 'The repeated reproduction of Bartlett's *Remembering*', *History of Psychology* 4 (2001), 341–66. The experimental aspects are reviewed in Roediger *et al.*, 'Repeated reproduction from memory', in Saito, *Bartlett, culture and cognition*.

45. The most influential attempt at revising Bartlett's studies along these lines was that of A. Gauld and G. M. Stephenson, 'Some experiments relating to Bartlett's theory of remembering', *British Journal of Psychology* 58 (1967), 39–49.

46. This was often expressed in the form of the unwarranted conclusion that Bartlett's results were not replicable. On their replicability, see E. T. Bergmann and H. L. Roediger III, 'Can Bartlett's repeated reproduction experiments be replicated?', *Memory and Cognition* 27 (1999), 937–47.

47. The crucial innovation was to explore 'memory' for items that had never been presented. But the real potential of this technique was not exploited until much later in the history of the experimental science of memory.

48. The conceptual problems of Bartlett's adaptation of schema theory seem to have contributed to its rejection by the next generation of British psychologists. See R. C. Oldfield and O. L. Zangwill, 'Head's concept of the schema and its application in contemporary British psychology III: Bartlett's theory of memory', *British Journal of Psychology* 33 (1943), 113–29. Many years later the term 'schema' was revived by some American psychologists to refer to fixed generic knowledge relevant to some domain, e.g. a narrated story. See W. F. Brewer and G. V. Nakamura, 'The nature and function of "schemas"', in R. S. Wyer Jr. and T. K. Srull (eds.), *Handbook of social cognition* (Hillsdale, NJ: Erlbaum, 1984), vol. I, pp. 119–60. This use of 'schema' stands in opposition to Head's version, which postulated ongoing revision of a schema in the course of activity leading to new situations. W. F. Brewer has noted Bartlett's inconsistent use of the concept and has attempted to work out a compromise solution in W. F. Brewer, 'Bartlett's concept of the schema and its impact on theories of knowledge representation in contemporary cognitive psychology', in Saito, *Bartlett, culture and cognition*, pp. 69–89. However, the reason for inconsistent uses of the schema concept seems to lie in the difference between regarding schemata as structures stored in individual brains or regarding them as 'organized settings' involving individual–environment relations. See D. F. Middleton and C. Crook, 'Bartlett and socially ordered consciousness: A discursive perspective. Comments on Rosa', *Culture & Psychology* 2 (1996), 379–96; and D. Middleton and S. D. Brown, *The social psychology of experience: Studies in remembering and forgetting* (London: Sage, 2005).

49. In his reminiscences the major representative of this research area observes that 'verbal learning research was not an interest of many psychologists ... about 1960 there were relatively few investigators working systematically in verbal learning'. B. J. Underwood, *Studies in learning and memory: Selected papers* (New York: Praeger, 1982), pp. 2, 3. The decline of the area, relative to other areas of experimental psychology, is suggested by a comparison of two editions of a widely used and highly regarded textbook. The 1938 edition of Woodworth's *Experimental psychology* opens (after an 'Introduction') with three chapters about memory and retention and contains two other chapters with related content; in the 1954 edition, R. S. Woodworth and H. Schlosberg, *Experimental psychology*, rev. edn (New York: Holt, Rinehart & Winston, 1954), there is a single chapter on memory, which has slipped to the back of the book (chapter 23 of 26) and is followed by updated versions of the two older chapters containing some related content.

50. At the end of his career, Benton Underwood, whose name had become synonymous with the verbal learning approach, came to the sad, but commendably honest

conclusion that 'an associationistic approach to serial learning has not been productive', serial learning being 'the task that Ebbinghaus bequeathed us'. Moreover, 'our attempt to build a theoretical bridge from the laboratory to real life was unsuccessful'. Underwood, *Studies in learning and memory*, pp. 9 and 279.

51. E. Tulving and S. A. Madigan, 'Memory and verbal learning', *Annual Review of Psychology* 21 (1970), 437–84 (pp. 476–7).

52. J. J. Jenkins, 'Remember that old theory of memory? Well forget it', *American Psychologist* 29 (1974), 785–95.

53. The author declared 'this view is so pervasive in American psychology that it is almost coextensive with being an experimentalist. Indeed I think many of us confuse the dicta of associationism with the grounds of empirical science itself.' Jenkins, 'Remember that old theory', p. 786.

54. U. Neisser, 'Memory: What are the important questions?', in U. Neisser (ed.), *Memory observed: Memory in natural contexts* (San Francisco: W. H. Freeman, 1982; original lecture 1978), pp. 3–19. In a much-cited book of this period Neisser had already expressed the view that 'nonsense-syllable learning is probably the archetype of psychological irrelevance'. U. Neisser, *Cognition and reality* (San Francisco: W. H. Freeman, 1976), p. 49.

55. See, for example, U. Neisser and E. Winograd (eds.), *Remembering reconsidered: Ecological and traditional approaches to the study of memory* (Cambridge: Cambridge University Press, 1988); L. W. Poon, D. C. Rubin and B. A. Wilson (eds.), *Everyday cognition in adulthood and late life* (Cambridge: Cambridge University Press, 1989); and J. E. Harris and P. E. Morris (eds.), *Everyday memory, actions and absent-mindedness* (London: Academic Press, 1984). The stage-setting chapter of the last volume suggests that one reason 'why psychologists are increasingly showing a willingness to move out of the laboratory is economic. In the last few years, research funds have become tighter, and demands for accountability have become stronger. In such a climate, it is much harder to justify research on human memory that appears to say nothing about memory as it impinges on everyday life.' A. D. Baddeley and A. Wilkins, 'Taking memory out of the laboratory', in Harris and Morris, *Everyday memory*, pp. 1–17 (p. 3).

56. R. S. Lockhart, 'Methods of memory research', in E. Tulving and F. I. M. Craik (eds.), *The Oxford handbook of memory* (Oxford: Oxford University Press, 2000), p. 46.

57. See for example, D. G. Mook, 'The myth of external validity', in Poon *et al.*, *Everyday cognition*, pp. 25–43; and M. R. Banaji and R. G. Crowder, 'The bankruptcy of everyday memory', *American Psychologist* 44 (1989), 1185–93.

58. During this period a collection of contributions by various authorities in the field referred in its preface to 'the information-processing approach, a theoretical perspective that has dominated the study of memory during much of the past several decades'. E. L. Bjork and R. A. Bjork (eds.), *Memory* (New York: Academic Press, 1996), p. xx. In this context 'the study of memory' is understood as limited to experimentalists within the discipline of psychology.

59. J. D. Bransford, J. J. Franks, N. S. McCarrell and K. E. Nitsch, 'Toward unexplaining memory', in R. Shaw and J. Bransford (eds.), *Perceiving, acting and knowing* (Hillsdale, NJ: Erlbaum, 1977), pp. 431–66. There is some historical continuity between the approach adopted by these authors and the work of Bartlett and Gestalt psychology.

60. The term was coined by Tulving and Madigan (in 'Memory and verbal learning'), who had linked it to the sterility of the field as long ago as 1970. As I see it, the syndrome manifests itself in research that is held together entirely by a specific technique of investigation, studying only phenomena whose existence is entirely dependent on the use of this technique, and always framing questions in terms dictated by the limitations of this technique.

61. P. A. Kolers and H. L. Roediger III, 'Procedures of mind', *Journal of Verbal Learning and Verbal Behavior* 23 (1984), 425–49 (p. 427).

62. Tulving and Madigan, 'Memory and verbal learning', p. 443.

63. For the expression of these views, see M. J. Watkins, 'Mediationism and the obfuscation of memory'.

64. A. M. Glenberg, 'What memory is for', *Behavioral and Brain Sciences* 20 (1997), 1–55.

65. I return to this issue in the last section of this book. A clear and concise end-of-century summary of the relevant developments can be found in Pfeifer and Scheier, *Understanding intelligence*. For overviews of prominent research topics in the experimental investigation of memory during the latter part of the twentieth century, see H. L. Roediger III, 'The future of cognitive psychology?', and G. Snodgrass, 'The memory trainers', both in R. L. Solso (ed.), *Mind and brain sciences in the twenty-first century* (Cambridge, MA: MIT Press, 1997), pp. 175–98, and 199–233; and also P. E. Morris and M. M. Gruneberg, 'The major aspects of memory', in P. E. Morris and M. M. Gruneberg (eds.), *Theoretical aspects of memory*, 2nd edn (London: Routledge, 1994), pp. 29–49.

6   Memory kinds

A coat of many colours

The language of everyday life has many ways of referring to the activity of memory. Not only do we speak of *remembering* an appointment, we also *recollect* what was said at yesterday's meeting, *reminisce* about that vacation in the Alps, *recognize* the face of a friend not seen for many months, *memorize* the text of a favourite poem, are *reminded of* a scene in a film and so on. Moreover, each of these memory words can be used in several different senses, as a glance at any good dictionary will show.[1]

What this seems to tell us about 'memory' is that it is essentially an abstraction, a convenient but rather loose way of referring to a large array of activities that are all felt to have something in common. What that something might be is not so easily said. Is it that they all refer to the past? Aristotle thought so. But what about remembering tomorrow's appointment? I may have forgotten making the appointment, but still remember that tomorrow there is this appointment. Philosophers have not found it easy to pinpoint the essence of memory – St Augustine frankly threw up his hands and proclaimed it a mystery.

Attempts at solving the mystery have generally followed one of two paths. One path is that of scepticism: if we cannot pin down the essence of memory, no matter how hard we look, this probably means that there is no such essence, that 'memory' and its associated words are just that, words. The reality to which these words refer comprises a multiplicity of activities, which may not have anything very significant in common. Behind the abstraction of 'memory' there lurks neither a single fundamental power nor a small assembly of such powers. Memory is a feature of all or most human activity, and it is a mistake to treat it as a separate entity or as a collection of separate entities that can be precisely identified.

As a rule, the sceptical view did not arise spontaneously but as a reaction against the difficulties encountered along the second path of solving the mystery of memory. This path follows a time-honoured and usually appropriate precept: when confronted by a baffling problem, try to break it down into more manageable pieces. So those who have followed this path, especially in recent times, have divided memory up into different *kinds* of memory. We may not be able to say much about memory in general, at least not much that is particularly enlightening, but we can be much more specific about the various ways in which memory manifests itself, how they differ from one another and how each of them functions. In proceeding thus, it is always assumed or claimed that the memory kinds one has distinguished are not simply inventions made for one's own convenience but that they correspond to *natural* kinds, that is to say, divisions in the real world and not just in one's own imagination.

In contemporary memory research the topic of memory kinds has been hot for at least a generation. A great deal of experimental work assumes that there must be different kinds of memory, but there is widespread disagreement as to the proper distinctions between these kinds. Those who are most insistent on the importance of such distinctions usually refer to them as differences between memory 'systems' that each have a separate location in the brain. This certainly underlines the claim that the memory kinds one has constructed correspond to fundamental divisions in the real world, that one has succeeded in 'carving nature at its joints', as the well-known butcher's shop analogy has it. Unfortunately, there is no consensus on the nature and number of such 'systems' or on how they are best defined. This has resulted in some fundamental scepticism regarding the whole notion of separate memory systems.

Historical studies might have some relevance to this issue. If it were to turn out that awareness of different kinds of memory stretched very far back, this would support the suggestion that such differences had a basis in the human constitution. Unfortunately, there are no simple answers to questions regarding the antiquity of speculations about memory kinds. One can indeed make a case for great antiquity. For one thing, most languages have more than one term to refer to memory phenomena, and some ancient texts discuss the different references of these terms. But in most cases there is a crucial difference between these discussions and the modern preoccupation with kinds of memory. With few exceptions, the modern discourse frames the problem as existing *within* the overall category of memory, whereas pre-modern discourse is much more concerned with distinctions *between* memory and other human capabilities. As we will soon see, the extension of what is included under 'memory' has expanded greatly in relatively recent times, with the result that topics once assigned to other domains are now routinely regarded as problems of memory. This fundamental historical discontinuity should not be overlooked.

In this volume questions pertaining to the place of memory among a network of human capabilities are specifically addressed in chapter 9. In the present chapter the discussion of pre-modern examples of distinctions between memory kinds will therefore be brief and limited to the one case that can be outlined without too much reference to memory's relationship to other human capabilities. This case comes down to the distinction between a memory that involves a recapturing of some kind of sensory experience and a memory that does not.

Sensory memory and memory of the intellect

Ancient Greek was no exception to the generalization that most languages contain more than one term to refer to memory phenomena. Two of its terms were of particular significance in discussions on the nature of memory, *mneme* and *anamnesis*. The account of the theories of Plato and Aristotle presented in chapter 2 was entirely based on their remarks occasioned by the first of these terms. What they had to say about *anamnesis* was postponed because it raises issues that have little bearing on the topic of metaphor, which was the focus of that chapter. One of those issues is that of memory kinds.

Both Plato and Aristotle distinguished clearly between two groups of memory phenomena identified respectively by *mneme* and *anamnesis*, but they did so in very different ways. For Plato, the distinction was one between mundane, everyday memory phenomena and the less obvious phenomena of innate knowledge, which Plato, who believed in the transmigration of souls, attributed to a kind of unconscious memory that outlasted generations of individuals. The Platonic doctrine of *anamnesis* may appear to be highly esoteric, but it has been of considerable historical importance, reappearing in various guises right up to relatively recent times. However, the issues it raises are less pertinent for the question of memory kinds than they are for questions about the relationship between memory and knowledge, and memory and truth. Further discussion of this doctrine and its historical progeny must therefore be left to chapter 7, which is concerned with these questions.

Aristotle's version of the distinction between *mneme* and *anamnesis*, however, provides a good starting-point for any historical review of memory kinds. He would have nothing to do with Platonic speculations regarding former lives, and restricted himself to mundane memory phenomena in living individuals. The diversity of these phenomena, he seems to have felt, called for their discussion under two headings, namely memory itself and recollection – the usual translation of *anamnesis*. The Aristotelian text specifically devoted to memory is divided into two distinct sections, one concerned with memory, and the other with recollection. Right at the start Aristotle refers to an empirically observed dissociation between the two: 'the persons who possess a retentive memory are not identical with those who excel in power of recollection'.[2] Whereas what he discusses under 'memory' is essentially a passive process of registration, he treats recollection as an active, deliberate activity of the person. Memory is something that animals also have; it involves the retention of sensory images, as described in chapter 2. Recollection, however, seems to be a distinctly human activity that is subject to training.[3] Better recollection can be taught and learned; it is a skill for practical employment by trained individuals, not a pathway to universal truths, as it had been for Plato.

Instead of the Platonic concern with hidden inborn knowledge, we get a rather technical account of practical methods of recall.[4] Aristotle is not much exercised about the epistemological significance of recollection – what interests him is the actual *process* of recall and its practical utility. In pursuit of these interests he seems to have taken some hints from early mnemonic practices, as we saw in chapter 3.

Taking off from Aristotle's distinction between the images of sensory memory and the rationally guided activity of recollection, the later literature generally mentions two kinds of memory, sensory and intellectual. The first involved the retention of sensory images; the second referred to the ability to remember and call up general principles. Animals were credited with sensory memory, but intellectual memory was a human quality. Moral action depended on the ability to retain and recall general principles, and therefore this kind of memory had ethical significance.

To some extent the distinction between sensory and intellectual memory overlaps later distinctions between remembering and knowing. We *remember* things we have seen and heard, but we *know* the Golden Rule or the principle of multiplication. But we must be careful not to read our own distinctions into those of a time that was marked by preoccupations that were very different from ours. For example, personal experience often plays the role of a major criterion in modern distinctions among memory kinds. Do I recall something I remember experiencing or something I simply know without remembering how I learned about it?

But is the ancient notion of a memory based on the primary senses the same as a memory based on personal experience? In so far as one cannot have a personal experience without an involvement of the senses there is some overlap, but it is evident that there is a profound difference of emphasis. In the modern case the emphasis is on the *personal* nature of the experience, the fact that the experience forms part of my unique biography, whereas the ancient distinction involves no explicit reference to a *self* at all. We can easily read an implicit reference into the text, but would people have done so who lived many centuries before the modern concept of the self emerged?[5] It seems unlikely.

The medieval distinction between sensory and intellectual memory puts the emphasis somewhere else entirely, on the distinction between a spiritual soul that includes an intellect and a body of which the senses are a part. This distinction was deeply embedded in a pervasive doctrinal framework that provided the intellectual and institutional context for any discussion of memory kinds. To mention only one specific example, Christian doctrines regarding the immortality of the soul had relevant implications. Did dead souls remember their past lives, and could they form new memories in heaven or hell? If the formation of memories depended on the bodily senses, and their retention on parts of the brain, both of which were mortal, then immortality would seem to involve the complete loss of the function of memory. The blessed would be a bunch of amnesics.[6] The division of memory into a bodily based sensory memory, and an intellectual memory that shared the intellect's immortality must have had its attractions from this point of view.

But any such division raises problems of its own. How should one conceive of the relationship between sensory and intellectual memory? The Church placed tremendous reliance on the display of sensory images to deliver its message. How could that be explained and defended? This was a problem, especially for Christian philosophers, such as Thomas Aquinas, who were confronted by texts that had originated in a very different cultural environment. For example, Avicenna, an eleventh-century Persian Muslim author, highly regarded for his development of Aristotelian philosophy, had sharply separated sense and intellect, and claimed that in considering abstractions the intellect did not need to rely on a storehouse of images. This position was acceptable within a religious outlook that strongly prohibited concrete imagery, but it surely demanded revision in the face of religious practices that depended utterly on the use of such images. It comes as no surprise to find Aquinas directly contradicting Avicenna and reaffirming that intellectual memory, though certainly different from sensory memory, would not be able to function without it.[7]

Distinctions between different kinds of memory were influenced by concurrent metaphysical assumptions, unquestioned dogmas of the time and powerful institutional interests. The criteria we use for making distinctions between memory kinds are quite different from those that were important in ancient and medieval times, and so the products of those distinctions are quite different. For example, the constant presence of an experienced personal self, fundamental to the late twentieth-century category of episodic memory (discussed later in this chapter), plays no role whatsoever in the earlier distinctions between memory kinds. Nor would the postulation of a distinct emotional memory have made much sense to medieval theorists, because it was generally taken for granted that all sensory experience was affective in character, not simply a matter of 'information'. Even 'intellectual' memory was not purely cognitive in character, for its major content was formed by affectively toned moral and religious precepts.

Enter phrenology

Debates regarding the nature and relationship of sensory and intellectual memory continued over a long stretch of time. Its echoes can be found even in post-medieval Cartesian philosophy which, as mentioned in chapter 2, distinguished pure intellect from memory with a somatic basis. But in these seventeenth-century texts we already find a modern tendency to leave pure intellect to the theologians and to concentrate on memory of a more mundane kind. However, with certain exceptions, memory was not a major object of inquiry during this period, and it is only at the very end of the eighteenth century that one can clearly discern some new directions that were to play a significant role in the transition to historically recent discourse on memory kinds.

Franz Joseph Gall (1758–1828), an Austrian neuroanatomist who gained considerable notoriety as the father of *phrenology*,[8] is an important figure in the history of memory because his sensational and always controversial claims were partly based on two principles that were to play a major role in later inquiries into the nature of memory. One principle involves the conviction that psychological functions, including different kinds of memory, have a sharply defined spatial localization in the brain. This aspect of his long-term influence will be discussed in chapter 8. The second principle, consistently followed by Gall, was that the classification of psychological functions, again including different kinds of memory, must be based on activities of everyday life rather than on the abstract human faculties that were the legacy of a long philosophical and theological tradition.

On the basis of these principles Gall generated a list of some twenty-seven basic human 'functions', each associated with a specific region of the brain.[9] This included three distinct kinds of memory: memory of things and facts, memory for people and verbal memory (related to words and names). If one juxtaposes this list with the ancient distinction between sensory and intellectual memory, the turn towards everyday life is immediately apparent. The memory kinds on Gall's list are not faculties defined by inherent Aristotelian powers of the soul – they are more like different *domains* within which the activity we call 'remembering' takes place.[10] In terms of the ancient distinction all of Gall's memory kinds look like instances of sensory rather than intellectual memory. In fact, the memory of the pure intellect without somatic basis has disappeared. All memory has its seat in the body, and is preoccupied with this-worldly content.

Gall's fatal mistake was to suppose that differences in the size of brain regions could be detected by manual exploration of the outside of the skull. Equally problematic was the claim that inter-individual differences in the gross size of brain regions correlated with corresponding differences in the development of specific psychological functions. Not only were his attempts at assigning these functions to specific cerebral locations a disaster, but his understanding of somatically based functions was indebted to an older vitalistic biology that was about to be abandoned by mainstream science.[11]

Nevertheless, Gall's systematic use of evidence from individual differences marked an interesting departure from tradition. Although Aristotle had remarked on the fact that some people were better at retaining memory images and others at recalling them, this line of argument had not been developed in subsequent discourse on memory kinds. Instead, interest focused on the general features of these kinds that were to be found in all human individuals. Gall's reliance on individual differences as a way of grounding the distinctions between mental faculties was new.[12]

Perhaps the best way to sum up Gall's contribution is to say that his reach exceeded his grasp. In certain ways he was a man ahead of his time. He attempted a radical application of principles that were not to become widely accepted until much later. But his practical application of these principles was in any case doomed to failure because of the grossly inadequate technology at his disposal and the misleading conclusions he drew from the biology of his time.

Phylogenesis and individual memory

For a while, the discrediting of phrenology dampened enthusiasm for linking memory to biology, but in the long run, speculation about that link was hard to resist. As I indicated in chapter 4 (the section on biology and the science of forgetting), a new wave of theorizing about 'memory as a biological fact' did become quite significant in the latter part of the nineteenth century. In the meantime, evolutionary perspectives had revolutionized biology, so that the new biology of memory was quite different from anything Gall had contemplated.

The new discourse on the biological foundations of memory made much use of an analogy between memory and heredity, regarding both as layered structures extended in time, so that later layers would be superimposed on earlier layers. Memory and heredity differed in their time-frame, the span of an individual life in the one case and the span of biological evolution in the other, but they shared a common structure. This conflation of memory and heredity turned memory into a layered structure whose strata had been laid down at different times and therefore differed in their relationship to the present. The relative age of memories now served as a significant distinguishing mark, older memories being more stable, more fixed, more organized than later memories.

Works on the pathology of memory, particularly those of Hughlings Jackson and Théodule Ribot referred to in chapter 4, established the notion that memories formed during different periods differed in kind. More recently acquired memories were more fragile, more susceptible to disruption and injury. The dimension of time began to assume a hitherto inconceivable importance for the differentiation of memories. Moreover, time was thought of as reversible. It moved forward in evolution, but it could also move backward in dissolution. By interpreting memory phenomena in terms of these time-bound processes, some sort of order could be imposed on the hitherto puzzling phenomena of pathological memory.

The notion that earlier traces enjoyed some sort of priority over later traces assumed a close correspondence between biological evolution and individual development. Heredity was due to the traces left behind by the life of previous generations, while individual memory depended on the traces of past experience in the life of the individual. The life experiences of previous generations became solidified in the form of instinctive reactions laid down in the phylogenetically older parts of the brain. These reactions were conducive to the survival of the organism and the species.

Newborn individuals were spared a great deal of painful learning, which they probably would not survive, because they arrived already equipped with the useful memory of their ancestors in the form of instincts. They knew that certain stimuli – those that supported its life – were worth going for and hanging on to, while other stimuli spelled danger and must be avoided. Most useful of all, the newborn already knew that pleasurable sensations were associated with the good things of life, while pain was associated with bad things.[13] At some point its ancestors had had to learn those things at enormous cost, but thanks to phylogenetic memory later generations could benefit from that. This precious inheritance had to be well protected because it was the basis of all later learning on the part of the individual and an insurance policy for later generations. It formed the first and most stable level of memory, the foundation on which the life of the individual was built.

Once one had taken the conflation of memory and heredity to this point, it was not too hard to swallow the next claim, namely, that the ontogenetic development of individuals recapitulated the phylogenetic development of their biological ancestors.[14] Partly based on misinterpretations of embryological observations, this idea was later extended to the post-natal life of children, which was seen as a *recapitulation* of stages in the historical development of human culture, for example the hunting stage.[15] Such ideas implied the operation of an unconscious ancestral memory in the growing child that would propel it in the direction of particular interests and activities in turn.

Of more general and lasting significance than these speculations, however, was the broad implication that earlier memories were foundational for the life of the individual in a way that later memories were not. This was perfectly clear in the case of inherited ancestral memories that were supposedly responsible for the basic instinctive reactions that protected individuals from harm and propelled them towards the things that were good for them and for the survival of their species. But it was easy to extend this perspective to the memories acquired during the lifetime of the individual. Surely the earliest memories, the ones that established basic expectations about life and laid the foundations of habits of coping with life's commonest situations, would be the most important ones. Early on, the plasticity of the individual organism would be at its height, later it would progressively decrease, and what was learned later would have to be superimposed on what was already well established. Clinical studies, as we have seen, taught that later acquisitions were less stable, more vulnerable, than earlier ones. It seemed natural to conclude that, in general, childhood memory, infantile memory, was a particularly important kind of memory that might have a shaping effect on the rest of the individual's life.

This emphasis on early memory came to be particularly associated with the name of Sigmund Freud, but he had merely expressed more sharply what many of his audience were prepared to believe in any case. But Freud had not only been particularly explicit about the importance of memories of childhood, he had also been more analytical. In particular, he had been struck by two evident paradoxes of childhood memory. First, although childhood memories are presumed to be important, almost all of them are regularly forgotten, a phenomenon known as childhood amnesia. Second, although these memories are believed to be rather significant, they very often turn out to be wrong or distorted. These puzzles ultimately led Freud to abandon some of the doctrines of 'organic memory', which he had shared with most biologists of his generation,[16] and to develop theories of memory that were of an entirely different stamp. I will take up the issues posed by these theories in chapter 7.

Philosophers make distinctions

Although Freud's determined though incomplete struggle against the pervasive influence of organic memory took a unique direction, he was not unique in sensing the limitations of a purely biological approach. By the closing years of the nineteenth century, a few critical voices were pointing out that the enthusiasm for biological memory was leading people to forget that memory had crucial and irreducible *psychological* aspects.

William James (1842–1910), a philosopher who was also the doyen of American psychology, was one voice that commanded particular respect. In his magisterial textbook he had certainly given the neurophysiology and pathology of memory its due, but he also indicated that a core aspect of memory had not received sufficient consideration in that literature. Where memory had been analysed in terms of the principles of heredity and biological evolution, it had come to be seen as essentially an affair of reproduction and repetition. That perception did not originate with organic memory but it was certainly strengthened by it. Yet, as James pointed out, this characterization of human memory missed two of its essential features: the fact that a thing remembered must be 'thought as *in the past*', and even more important, that 'it must be dated in *my* past' (italics in original).[17] Organic memory had relegated consciousness to the status of an epiphenomenon, an incidental by-product of biological mechanisms, and consequently had hardly taken notice of the conscious aspects of memory, let alone explained them. This applied particularly to the intimate link between memory and the sense of a personal past. Yet the dependence of memory on biologically evolved cerebral structures and processes could no longer be doubted. A certain duality was therefore noticeable in the way James (and some of his cohorts) treated memory: in some of its aspects it seemed to be of an essentially biological kind, but in its most distinctive features it remained irreducibly psychological.

The challenge of this duality was directly confronted by the French philosopher Henri Bergson (1859–1941), whose influence, direct and indirect, on subsequent discussions of memory kinds was considerable. Bergson ended up proclaiming a profound philosophical dualism between a spiritual world and the world of science and practical affairs, but his analysis of memory does not start that way, nor does it necessarily lead to that conclusion. To begin with, Bergson presents an easily recognizable distinction between two ways in which the past survives in the human individual. Well acquainted with the experimental psychology literature of his time, Bergson takes the learning of a 'lesson' as his example. To say that I remember a lesson can have two quite different meanings. It can mean that I have learned its content after several trials and am now able to repeat it without error. But it can also mean that I remember the occasions on which I applied myself to the lesson. In that case, 'each reading stands out in my mind as a definite event in my history'.[18] In this usage, a memory is a representation of an event in my life, according to Bergson, whereas in the first usage remembering the lesson is much like exercising a certain habit.

A habit and the recall of an event in one's life are quite different and imply 'a difference in kind between two sorts of recollection'. Exercising a habit involves no conscious reference to either the past or the self, whereas recalling an occasion when I was learning something involves not only placing that occasion in the past, but specifically in *my* past. Once a lesson is mastered it becomes impersonal; I just go ahead and repeat it without thinking of it as something that is part of my life in particular. Anyone else might have learned this material. But this is not the case for my memory of the times when I was still trying to achieve mastery. Those memories will always remain part of my personal life, and they will be different from anyone else's personal memories. Bergson therefore distinguished between what he called *habit-memory*, which he considered to be an affair of the body, dependent on biological mechanisms, and memory of one's own past, which involved an irreducible spiritual element. This second kind of memory was 'memory *par excellence*', it *represented* the past to us, whereas habit-memory simply *acted* the past and hardly deserved the name of memory. What the men of science had been studying in recent years was mostly habit-memory; their attempts to treat all memory as habit-memory were futile.

Bergson went off in the opposite direction to develop a philosophy of 'pure' memory. Even when we remembered scenes from our own lives (rather than exercised mere habits), he maintained, our personal experience was contaminated by a tendency to chop up our memories into distinct spatialized images strung together like separate pearls on a string. At a deeper level, however, there was the occasional experience of *pure duration*, a sense of temporal continuity unaffected by the spatial organization derived from the experience of our physical bodies. The spiritualistic intent of Bergson's philosophy tended to divert attention from the initial steps in his argument. These involved distinctions between memory kinds that had their own merits without being linked to his philosophical conclusions by any logical necessity. At another time psychologists might have found these distinctions quite useful, but in the early twentieth century they focused on cutting their ties with philosophy and philosophers and asserting their new scientific persona. Bergson's writings, with their pronounced spiritualistic slant, were not the kind of source to which the new generation of psychologists would look for inspiration.

Much the same could be said of other twentieth-century philosophical forays into the field of memory.[19] But turning one's back on philosophy was not accomplished without cost, because within psychology recognition of the importance of distinctions among memory kinds was delayed until the latter part of the century. For most of this period that whole topic was simply left to the philosophers to quibble over. The philosophers did quibble, but they also introduced a new dimension into the discourse around memory kinds. That was a result of their growing interest in the analysis of language usage and the way it is related to the analysis of concepts. Previous proposals for distinctions between memory kinds had always been made on the basis of philosophical realism: such distinctions were held to reflect differences among distinct processes or capacities that existed out there in the real world. But suppose we start at the other end and look at the different ways in which people use terms like memory or remember. This nominalist turn may not lead us directly to the discovery of how the world outside language is carved up, but it should at least help us to overcome the common confusion between the divisions that exist in nature, independently of human thought and action, and the divisions we make for ourselves in our interaction with the world.

In the 1920s the philosopher C. D. Broad began to examine the different senses in which the word 'memory' is used. One of these corresponds to the usage characteristic of the proponents of 'organic memory' (by then in decline), that is, describing as 'memory' the tendency of living organisms to repeat learned movements when suitably stimulated. Broad regarded this as a misuse of the term and felt that 'retentiveness' would be more appropriate. A second usage also referred to learned skills, but with the added understanding that there was voluntary activation involved. In the third case, the motor skill that was 'remembered' was one that involved the parrot-like repetition of verbal signs without understanding their symbolic meaning. Fourth, we speak of remembering when a person calls up an image of something experienced in the past. Here the question for Broad was whether the image was accompanied by a feeling of familiarity and led to memory judgments. If not, it was not really a case of remembering but of retention, as were all the other cases considered so far.[20]

Broad's analysis was really directed against the rampant claims of behaviourism, the new American psychological gospel that had recently found unexpected support from a respected European source, the British philosopher Bertrand Russell.[21] Broad wanted to rescue mental phenomena from behaviourist reduction to bodily activity, and therefore made a sharp distinction between those phenomena of memory that were indeed reducible to bodily activity and those that were not. All the uses of 'remember' considered so far applied only to habit-memory based on retention. But these cases, according to Broad, did not really deserve the name 'memory'; they were 'modes of *behaviour*, not modes of *cognition*'.[22]

There were two kinds of remembering that were irreducibly cognitive in character. One was 'perceptual memory', essentially the memory of events that the remembering person had experienced. The other kind of cognitive memory was a matter of remembering propositions, or, strictly, a certain type of proposition. Perceptual memory might involve propositions, too, but these always referred to past events. This was quite different from memory for propositions about matters that had no temporal reference, propositions that were timeless, such as the propositions of geometry. Both kinds of cognitive memory were of course to be distinguished from habit-memory. Psychologists who were studying memory via the medium of nonsense syllables were merely studying habit-memory, not cognitive memory in either form. Few, if any, psychologists took any notice, and it was not until their discipline experienced its own 'cognitive revolution', almost half a century later, that their thoughts turned to distinctions between memory kinds that had something in common with those suggested by Broad.

In the meantime, philosophers who paid attention to language usage continued to remark on the different ways in which the verb 'to remember' was commonly employed. In a very widely read book, Gilbert Ryle, whose motives were very different from those of Broad, pointed to two senses of 'remember' that ought to be clearly distinguished.[23] In one sense we say that a person remembers if she has learned something and not forgotten it. What she has learned could range from the proof of a theorem to riding a bicycle – if she has not forgotten it, she remembers it. In this use we could often, though not always, substitute 'know' for 'remember'. In the other use of 'remember' the person is recalling some episode of his or her own past.

So far, Ryle's distinction is reminiscent of earlier distinctions. But instead of a mere juxtaposition of two memory kinds, he proceeds to explore their interrelationship. Remembering in the sense of knowing is a dispositional concept, whereas recollecting is an 'occurrent', usually a current performance. This means that recollecting entails knowing, whereas knowing does not entail recollecting. I cannot recall something I do not know, but I know many things without recalling them. The distinction between memory kinds should not be made only in terms of differences in their content but also in terms of their logical status. It was a suggestion that does not seem to have reached those attempting to identify memory kinds empirically because by the time it was made in the mid-twentieth century, the philosophical and the scientific discourse on memory had each gone their separate ways.

Amnesics speak

Let us now return to the medico-scientific discourse where we left it before our philosophical interlude. It seemed as if, by the end of the nineteenth century, there was a strong tide sweeping the unstable vessel of memory towards the safe shores of scientific biology. The idea of strata being laid down by evolution over time had provided a new scheme for distinguishing different forms of memory and for analysing 'diseases' of memory. However, by the early years of the twentieth century the glory days of 'organic memory' were over. A new genetics, distinguishing sharply between phenotype and genotype, had undermined the Lamarckian underpinnings – principally a belief in the inheritance of acquired characteristics – of organic memory. Those who held on to doctrines that resembled those of organic memory were effectively marginalized.[24]

Nevertheless, the prominence that the topic of amnesia had achieved in the era of organic memory survived the passing of that era. The pervasive modern worry about disruptions of memory, as well as the continuity provided by now well-established clinical and professional institutions, played a role in establishing amnesia as an object of perennial interest. In fact, there is a line of psychiatric and neuropsychological discourse on this topic that stretches to the present day.

During the first part of the twentieth century, however, medical discourse on amnesia was affected by a reaction against the enthusiastic scientific positivism that had been associated with theories of organic memory. This reaction was not limited to philosophers like Henri Bergson and his followers, though it was much more visible in continental Europe than in the Anglo-Saxon world. The early years of the new century also marked a high point in the embrace of introspectionism by European experimental psychology,[25] while continental psychiatry was discovering the inner world of psychopathological states.

In an early, much-cited case-study Edouard Claparède described a woman suffering from Korsakoff syndrome who showed a fascinating disparity between her intact memory for knowledge she had acquired years ago and her striking inability to remember recent events.[26] While she could do mental calculations or name European capital cities correctly she did not recognize the nurse who had looked after her for six months or remember the date despite being told repeatedly. After Claparède pricked her hand with a pin she forgot the event almost immediately, but when he reached for her hand again she quickly withdrew it, not knowing why. The clinician's conclusion was that there were 'two sorts of mental connections: those established mutually between representations, and those established between representations and the me, the personality'. In this patient only the capacity to form the second type of connection had been lost. Not being able to relate recent events to her sense of self, she was unable to recall them voluntarily or recognize their repetition, though some trace of those events seemed to remain.

Claparède's conclusion was echoed by others who had made analogous observations on Korsakoff patients. Katzaroff decided that a feeling of familiarity would become attached to particular sensations because they had been associated 'with the very feeling of our ego'.[27] That was the specific memory function that was lost in these patients. Later, MacCurdy tried another little experiment with these cases.[28] He told the patient his name, which was promptly forgotten, but then presented him with a list of names and asked him to guess which one of them might be the forgotten name. Surprisingly, the guess was usually correct, so memory in some form seemed to exist. However, these patients could never give a reason for their guess, and lacked any personal recollection of being told this name. As in Claparède's original observation, memory for matters that formed part of one's personal life experience seemed to be separate from memory in the form of unconscious associations. A certain neuropathological condition could selectively destroy the one form of memory and not the other.

Gradually, a consensus developed that what was lost in Korsakoff patients was not so much the content of memories as their temporal and personal contextualization. The impairment specifically affected the integration of memories into an experience of self structured in time. By 1959 these and other lines of evidence had encouraged some authors to make a sharp distinction between two forms of memory which they called *memoria* and *remembrances*.[29] Memoria consist of acquired knowledge without any autobiographical reference, for example the multiplication table, vocabularies, telephone numbers, but also learned historical dates and events, scientific facts and so on. Habits and skills represent another sub-class of memoria. Remembrances, on the other hand, are accompanied by the experience of an autobiographic index, a location in the personal time structure of the rememberer. Knowing that President Kennedy was assassinated in 1963 would represent an item of memoria, but recalling the circumstances under which one heard the news of this event would be an instance of remembrance.

Contrary to what one might have expected, this distinction did not receive much recognition at the time. It was rooted in a largely European clinical tradition for which the experience of the rememberer, the evocation of his or her sense of self, the awareness of a personal history, provided the crucial criterion for distinguishing between memory kinds. American experimental memory research was not ready for such forays into 'subjectivism', and clinical work on aphasia was about to enter a new phase that was essentially driven by technology.

Two years before Reiff and Scheerer's monograph, there appeared the first of a series of clinical reports stretching over many years that described the case of an individual, known by his initials H. M., who has been described as 'probably the most famous neurological case in the literature'.[30] This young man suffered from amnesia, not because he had developed Korsakoff syndrome as a result of alcoholism, but because significant parts of his brain had been surgically removed in an attempt to alleviate his frequent epileptic seizures.[31] After the operation he had permanently lost the capacity to acquire new everyday memories, though he retained memories of his childhood and knowledge of language, facts, social skills and so on, acquired long before. Post-operatively he no longer recognized the hospital or its clinical staff, never learned the locations of places and objects he encountered, and generally forgot events once they had left his immediate awareness. This was a severe *anterograde* amnesia, in contrast to a less severe retrograde amnesia for events from his pre-operative life.

This distinction, first proposed in the latter part of the nineteenth century, now acquired a new emphasis. It represented one example of a return to objective temporal criteria for distinguishing between memory kinds. Such criteria had flourished in the days of organic memory and its models of reversible evolution, but had been overshadowed in the meantime by criteria that depended on personalized time. Now they were back in. H. M.'s amnesia was defined within a framework of four time periods: immediate memory, a matter of seconds, which was intact; severe anterograde amnesia involving recently experienced events; retrograde amnesia whose severity depended on temporal distance from the operation (the further back in time the better the memory); and remote memory, which was normal. In contrast to the earlier explorations with Korsakoff patients, these temporal divisions were not linked to the autobiographical experience of a personal history, but to the time by the clock, the calendar and the objective events of a case-history.

The case of H. M. became a showpiece for the technological advances that had been made, and continued to be made, since the earlier studies of memory loss in humans as a result of cerebral lesions. These advances proceeded in two directions. Most obviously they concerned precision in neuroanatomy which allowed for sharper definition of cerebral injury, whether accidental or surgically inflicted. But psychological assessment had also come a long way since the rough and ready experiments of a Claparède or a MacCurdy. H. M. was subjected to an extraordinary number and variety of tests and procedures for many years after his operation in an attempt to pinpoint exactly what aspects of psychological performance had been affected and to what degree.[32] No doubt his was an extreme case, but it did usher in a period dedicated to the fine-grained analysis of memory functions and their exact cerebral localization. The issues raised by such a programme will be discussed in chapter 8.

Memory systems in experimental psychology

Recognition of different forms of memory by philosophers and clinicians had no impact on the experimental psychology of memory until late in the twentieth century. Only then did dissatisfaction with the sterility of this field, discussed in the previous chapter, raise the possibility that memory might not all be of one kind, and that experimentalists might have been confused about what kind of memory they were investigating. Some members of this scientific community now suspected that the reason for the poor historical record of their field should be sought in a kind of blindness that had beset their fellow investigators when they considered what they were actually doing in their experiments.[33] Their standard procedures involved requests for the recognition or the recall of words that had previously been presented in word lists, often paired with another word. The words (or pairs of words) were referred to as *items*, and experiments were designed to answer questions about the conditions that affected the varying memorability of 'items'. That kind of question made sense only if it was assumed that items retained their psychological identity in different situations and at different times, that valid generalizations about memory for word units could be made irrespective of the social and personal context in which the word occurred.

Items were what experimenters saw in the experimental situations they constructed. But what experimental subjects remembered was the experimental situation they had been in. When asked whether a particular word had been seen during a previous experimental session they had to remember the session of which that word's presentation had been a part. That session was an event in their ongoing lives; it was not an item on a list. The memory *task* that the subjects faced involved some sort of autobiographical recall, a point that experimenters had generally failed to notice.

The reasons for that are hardly mysterious. In North America the experimental psychology of memory had grown out of the 'verbal learning' sub-field of the broad domain of 'learning', an area in which behaviouristic attitudes were rooted more deeply and persisted much longer than in any other area of psychological research. Experimental research papers on the psychology of human memory demonstrate that taboos against acknow-ledging the conscious experience of experimental subjects were still in operation quite late in the twentieth century. As outlined in chapter 5, the most common practices of experimental memory research still followed precepts that had been laid down by Ebbinghaus. Though nonsense syllable lists had been replaced by word lists, the empirical yield of the experiments still consisted of performance measures, and excluded subjective aspects of memory. Weighty traditions, both practical and ideological, made it very difficult for memory researchers to accept the crucial importance of the rememberer's viewpoint.

But there are always people on whom tradition sits more lightly than on their colleagues. Often they are people with deviant backgrounds. In the field of experimental memory research a refugee Estonian, Endel Tulving, made a point of contradicting some of the unquestioned norms that had guided the field: 'recollective experience should be the ultimate object of interest, the central aspect of remembering that is to be explained and understood. The what, how, and why of those aspects of the mind that we think of as remembering, in the final analysis, applies to the mental stuff on which the expression "I remember" is predicated.'[34]

In traditional memory experiments, using words in pairs and lists or sin-gly, a distinction therefore ought to be made between *word* and *word event*. A word is a component of language whose meaning is linked to that of other words and whose usage is governed by syntactic rules. A word event, however, is the particular experience of a word by a certain individual on a unique occasion. What the experimental psychology of memory had gen-erally been dealing with was the recall (or recognition) of word events. However, its queries and experimental hypotheses were hardly ever directed at the exploration of these events as events in the experience of an individual. Tulving proposed the term *episodic memory* to identify the kind of memory that was addressed when experimental subjects were required to remember words encountered in previous experimental sessions. This was very dif-ferent from being asked questions whose answers depended on remembering the meaning of words or categorical relationships among words. That sort of task tapped another kind of memory, *semantic memory*.

Episodic memory refers to matters that the individual has witnessed; its units are events that have a certain localization in personal time and space. Semantic memory is impersonal and timeless. It refers to a fund of information for which the context of acquisition is irrelevant. The two forms of memory are mobilized by different kinds of memory task. In one case the person is asked whether something previously occurred in their experience – was a particular word, sentence or object part of an earlier experimental session, for instance. In the other case they are asked questions whose answers depend on their correct knowledge of definitions, impersonal facts, categorical relationships and so on.

Even when the distinction was introduced it was recognized that the term 'semantic memory' was a poor choice. What was intended was a reference to knowledge of a world that exists independently of the knower. It is true that words play a large role in that kind of knowledge, but there is much more involved than the meaning of words, which the term 'semantic memory' seems to imply. That term was an unfortunate legacy from earlier work on language processing with the help of digital computers.[35] Quite apart from the inappropriate use of 'semantic', the use of 'memory' in this context was in itself questionable, essentially relying on a metaphorical equivalence of human and computer memory. It would have made for greater clarity had experimental psychologists opted for a distinction in terms of memory and knowledge, instead of episodic and semantic memory. In fact, they generally knew that that was what they meant, though somehow they felt stuck with the old term for historical reasons beyond their control.

Around the time that the episodic–semantic distinction was beginning to generate a considerable amount of experimental research, another kind of memory was also demanding a place in the sun. Amnesic patients, it was found, often showed serious impairment of both episodic and semantic memory, while performing well on tasks requiring retention of perceptual skills, such as reading mirror-reversed words.[36] The idea that a third kind of memory, *procedural memory*, should be added to the list of 'memory systems' was soon accepted, episodic and semantic memory being sometimes contrasted with the procedural variant as examples of *declarative memory*. Procedural memory would be involved in learned skills, such as swimming or cycling, where what is remembered is *how* to perform an action, not a verbal description of that action. If I talk about my swimming I rely not on procedural, but on declarative memory. I remember *that* I swam for half an hour yesterday, not how I did it. Unlike declarative memory, procedural memory is not verbally expressed in propositions *that* something is the case; it is a potential ability to carry out certain directed activities.[37] In due course, procedural memory fractionated into several components, including retention of learned general skills, habits and conditioned responses.

According to Tulving, each of these three types of memory is characterized by a particular kind of consciousness.[38] Procedural memory involves *anoetic* (non-knowing) consciousness, sensing external and internal stimulation. Semantic memory relies on *noetic* consciousness, employing internal representations of aspects of the world that are not perceptually present. In episodic memory individuals are aware of their personal existence in subjective time and experience a sense of the past. This is referred to as *autonoetic* consciousness. The three memory systems form a hierarchy, such that semantic memory is a sub-system of procedural memory and episodic memory a sub-system of semantic memory. The higher levels of the hierarchy are dependent on the lower levels. For example, memory for events in one's personal history presupposes some world knowledge, but world knowledge is not dependent on personal memories. When it is further claimed that the higher each system is on this scale the later it appears phylogenetically[39] we seem to be right back in the days of organic memory. The yield from a century of psychological grappling with the problem of memory kinds might well be described as disappointing.

Criticism of the entire notion of distinct 'memory systems' was not long in coming. It was quickly noticed that such divisions had at best a descriptive or classificatory value, without being in any way explanatory.[40] However, to Tulving, the leading proponent of psychological memory systems, this was no bad thing. Science would not get far, he claimed with some justification, if it did not try to develop 'classificatory systems that are true by the standards of nature'.[41] So we are faced by the old problem of carving nature at its joints; memory systems are meant to be 'natural kinds', not mere heuristic devices. No doubt this was one of the reasons why the search for memory systems increasingly turned to neurological data, hoping to see the divisions between these systems engraved on the brain in the form of physically distinguishable localities.

Not surprisingly, the possibility that differences between memory kinds might have a cultural and historical basis was ignored by most psychologically trained investigators. Relevant historical evidence was systematically overlooked while phylogenetic and neurophysiological speculations were pursued as a matter of course. Yet the ties, both practical and conceptual, that bound the psychological study of memory to a culture of literacy were extremely close. The 'verbal' material employed in the stimulus and the instructional elements of laboratory memory tasks was of the permanently recorded, i.e. literary, kind; it was not the verbalization encountered in spontaneous speech situations. Without the use of fixed, recorded materials neither the measurement of memory performance nor the standardization of experimental conditions would be possible. Conceptually, too, when psychologists use the term 'semantic memory' in the sense of world knowledge, this represents more than a historical accident. It reflects a bias to think of world knowledge in terms of an encyclopaedia, a written record of facts about the world in propositional form. This discounting of figurative knowledge and of the interpersonal construction of knowledge is as strikingly culture-bound as the emphasis on the experience of a unique personal autobiography, an internal diary, in the conceptualization of episodic memory. For most human groups memory was more likely to be organized in terms of natural and cultural cycles than in terms of a dimension of linear time that, for the most part, had not even been invented.[42]

But even within the culturally closed world of psychological research the empirical evidence for the separation of memory systems began to look increasingly shaky as the field proliferated. There was first of all the problem of defining and consistently applying the criteria that would make it possible to distinguish empirically between different kinds of memory. Typically, different versions of the idea of memory systems used different criteria for establishing distinctions between their systems.[43] Several of the criteria proposed by those most committed to the idea of memory systems were very seldom employed and all of them were shown to be ineffective, because the results of empirical studies were always open to alternative interpretations.[44]

There is an insuperable obstacle to the empirical verification of the existence of distinct memory systems: there are no 'pure' memory tasks. None of the performance tests employed in the experimental study of memory tap only a single memory system; in all cases several systems must be involved. So-called semantic memory, which is really world knowledge, can hardly be excluded from any task administered in a psychological laboratory with the use of verbal instruction, a point that is allowed for in the theoretical embeddedness of episodic in semantic memory. But in that case, how does one use laboratory tasks to demonstrate the separation of systems? Traditionally, the dissociation of performance on different tasks was used to provide empirical confirmation of the existence of separate memory systems. But in the closing years of the century it became increasingly obvious that that was not a viable strategy.[45] At its worst, this procedure ended in the circularity of using a particular task to define a certain kind of memory and then 'explaining' performance on that task in terms of the postulated memory system. There was little constraint on the number of postulated memory systems and less regard for the principle of scientific parsimony.

The lesson was taken that distinctions among memory systems were *conceptual* and classificatory, not causal and explanatory. An essentially heuristic function was claimed for them. But in practice they were never treated as mere heuristics, for, as their empirical foundation in experimental psychology crumbled, attempts at finding them a place in the brain intensified. The temptation to reify memory kinds once again proved irresistible. By the end of the century research on memory systems had virtually fused with research on brain localization,[46] a topic that will be taken up in chapter 8. But first a brief look at what has become by far the most widespread distinction among memory kinds, that between so-called short-term and long term-memory.

The memory that is short

A content analysis of six introductory psychology textbooks of the 1990s came up with a number of concepts that were common to all of them. When these were compared to the results of other similar analyses of psychology texts a total of fifty-eight common 'core concepts' remained. Apart from 'memory' itself, the only memory concepts among these fifty-eight were long-term and short-term memory.[47] Whatever else modern psychology may have been teaching its students, it was certainly transmitting the distinction between these two kinds of memory. Indeed, the long-term–short-term terminology entered everyday language.

Yet the history of this distinction is quite a recent one. In fact, among all the distinctions between memory kinds it bears the stamp of modernity like no other. There is no indication that anyone attached the slightest significance to short-term memory before the late nineteenth century, and it was not until the second half of the twentieth century that the *concept* of short-term memory began its ascent to the status of a core concept of psychology.

Interest in short-term memory has been intimately linked to practical concerns at every stage of its brief history. In the late nineteenth century this interest grew out of concerns about the differential performance of school pupils that resulted from the enforcement of universal school attendance. These concerns sparked attempts at assessing the mental capacities of children, so that they could be directed into appropriate educational channels, attempts that eventually resulted in the construction of so-called intelligence tests. One of the ways of assessing a child's mental capacity that suggested itself to educationists was by recording the number of digits or letters that a child could repeat correctly after hearing a list of such items. It was soon observed that those children at two London schools who did better school work tended to remember more digits or letters than the weaker pupils, and also that older children performed better than younger children.[48] This seemed to indicate a link to general mental ability, and tests of 'digit span' were indeed incorporated into intelligence test batteries.[49]

There was as yet no sense that these procedures were tapping 'memory', conceived of as a special sub-department of the mind. They were seen as providing information about a general feature of the mind, its 'span'. Where the mind as an object of psychology was equated with consciousness the mental span was regarded as the span of consciousness. This was the case in psychology's first major laboratory, that of Wilhelm Wundt in Leipzig. Together with the notion of 'focus of attention', the concept of the span of consciousness (*Bewusstseinsumfang*) was in fact a cornerstone of Wundt's theoretical system. The idea was that a limited number of elements, presented simultaneously or sequentially, could be consciously attended to at one time and therefore integrated into a complex whole, a *Gesamt-vorstellung*. Wundt used this kind of analysis, not only to interpret laboratory data involving judgments of identity applied to sequential auditory stimuli, but also to explain the production and comprehension of speech.[50] What he did not do was to describe such processes as instances of 'memory'. As indicated in chapter 5, he did not regard memory as a category that would be helpful in building a science of psychology. A brief temporal span was a basic feature of human consciousness that made many of its achievements possible; assigning this feature to a distinct part of the mind called memory he would have regarded as a step back in the direction of faculty psychology.

As in so many other respects, the views of the 'father' of experimental psychology proved to be historically out of step. In America, experimental investigations of mental span were regarded as studies of 'memory' from the beginning, and by 1898 a reviewer was able to point to many such studies.[51] William James had introduced the term 'primary memory' in 1890 to refer to what, in Wundt's terms, would have been regarded as the temporal span of consciousness. Quite soon, however, this early interest fell victim to the reaction against anything reminiscent of a psychology of consciousness. Behaviourism's increasing sway over American psychology during the first part of the twentieth century relegated memory studies to the backwaters of experimental psychology. The revival of interest in the memory span was due to developments outside the discipline, and once again these developments were of a distinctly practical character.

This time, however, it was not the practice of education that was at issue but the practice of war. Compared to previous armed conflicts, World War II involved a much intensified use of complex machines whose effective employment depended on a close integration of the machine and its human operator. The navigation of aircraft, the targeting of anti-aircraft guns, the use of various types of signals equipment and so on all required appropriate human reactions during brief periods of time. Typically, the machine would generate a stream of signals that the operator had to interpret correctly and respond to. Correct interpretation often depended on simultaneous consideration of a sequence of signals emitted over a brief period of time. That could make considerable demands on the resources of the human operator and mistakes could be fatal. When psychologists were mobilized to apply their expertise to military situations this was one of the problems that engaged their attention. The end of the war did not end their interest, however. Particularly in the United States, the ensuing Cold War ensured a continuing flow of funds to psychological research with military applications, but some of the military technology had also been transferred to peacetime employment, together with its human problems. Air traffic control and civilian telephony, for example, were the sites of continuing interest in the limitations of human operators faced with evanescent signals that had to be kept in mind long enough to respond appropriately. Certain laboratories, ultimately funded for 'applied' research, therefore maintained active programmes of investigation in this area.[52] Much of this work was not designed to lead to immediate practical application, but helped the emergence of a vigorous new sub-field of experimental psychology.

In due course, this sub-field acquired its own identifying label: it was held to be working on 'short-term memory', thus adding a new member to the expanding family of memory kinds. The label underwent some changes over the years. In Britain the term 'immediate memory' was used at first, and in the US there was an attempt to bring back the term 'primary memory' in honour of William James.[53] By 1970 almost everyone was using 'short-term' memory, probably under the burgeoning influence of computer metaphors.[54] However, this too did not last very long, as experimental studies provided increasing evidence of strong mutual interaction and considerable similarity between so-called short-term and long-term memory. Soon the whole idea of a separate short-term memory system was being questioned.[55] However, another name-change helped to calm the controversy. By the 1980s the term *working memory* was being more and more widely adopted as an alternative to short-term memory.[56] This term certainly came closer to an essential quality of the kind of memory studied in these investigations: the fact that this memory was being constantly updated and revised in the course of a person's engagement with a set task.

What this area of research had inherited from its wartime progenitors was an experimental paradigm in which individuals were required to perform as well as possible under conditions that taxed their powers of concentration. In the military studies the taxing conditions were often provided by excessive noise or exposure to simultaneous bombardment by several rapidly changing and sometimes ambiguous stimuli. In subsequent experimental studies distracting conditions would be simulated in various ways, by listening to two sources of speech simultaneously, for example, or by mentally rehearsing a string of digits while trying to solve other cognitive tasks. Always, there was pressure of time: the task could not be postponed till conditions improved, nor was there time to consult manuals or colleagues, or even for quiet reflection while one considered alternatives. This imposed limitation of time, together with the presence of distracting conditions, defined the kinds of issues that these studies were designed to address. One was the issue of human capacity to handle cognitive tasks that required quick solutions. In Baddeley's words, 'the concept of limited capacity lies at the heart of empirical research on short-term and working memory'.[57] In due course, much psychological research on language comprehension became focused on issues of capacity limitations when working with printed textual materials.[58]

But when capacity limitations had been duly accounted for, another major issue, that of selectivity, became ever more urgent. Task performance under conditions of temporal constraint will very likely depend on an individual's ability to make an effective selection among competing possibilities. Whereas limitations on capacity might be explained in terms of limited short-term memory *storage*, this was clearly the wrong model for explaining selectivity. Explanations of working memory must therefore account for the presence of an *active* component in addition to limitations on short-term storage. In what had become the standard model towards the end of the century, this theoretical task was accomplished by invoking a 'central executive', an 'attentional controller', that performed this function. Allan Baddeley, its candid inventor, referred to it as 'a pool of residual ignorance', a 'homunculus' that would eventually be made redundant by further experimental research.[59]

In view of modern psychology's consistent record of avoiding conceptual problems by hoping they would turn out to be empirical problems, it may be advisable to regard such expectations with a certain measure of scepticism. From a historical perspective, however, a curious circularity is not without interest. Wundt, it may be recalled, had distinguished between a limited 'span' of consciousness – which was after all a capacity function – and attentional focus, which he explained in terms of the process of 'apperception', an expression of 'psychic causality'. His (and others') reference to properties of consciousness was duly submerged by the behaviouristic tide that engulfed twentieth-century psychology, and his relatively agentic explanation of attention was soon repudiated as 'too metaphysical', even by his own students.[60] In spite of the consequent historical amnesia, a dual explanation of mental task performance in terms of a passive capacity function and an active selective function recurs a century later. That makes the differences in the understanding of these dual factors particularly interesting.

Apperception, a key term of mentalistic psychology, is replaced by a 'central executive', signalling a change of metaphor to the realm of bureaucratic control. At the same time, the span of consciousness becomes short-term memory storage, a metaphor relying on familiarity with digital computers. Mentalistic explanations have obviously gone the way of the dodo and been replaced by models based on metaphors drawn from social administration and information technology. In employing those sorts of models the sub-field of working memory was doing no more than following pervasive trends that characterized cognitive psychology in general during the latter part of the twentieth century.[61]

One of the consequences of these trends was the annexation by the field of memory of phenomena that had not previously been regarded as exemplifying 'memory' in any significant sense. Some cognitive psychologists did not feel entirely comfortable with this development. Ulric Neisser, speaking of the mechanisms of working memory, was moved to comment: 'it stretches a point to call such mechanisms "memories". They fit the formal definition, but what most people mean by "memory" is quite different. It is disconcerting that contemporary textbooks of memory devote a quarter or a third of their pages to "memories" that last less than a minute. Shouldn't memory have something to do with the past?'[62]

There were, however, quite specific historical reasons for this development. After becoming involved in problems of human–machine interaction some psychologists became quite enchanted with models of communication engineering during the post-World War II period. That entailed a revival of interest in what used to be referred to as 'mental span'. There had been practical cooperation between psychologists and communication engineers when both were working on problems caused by noise that reduced the effectiveness of auditory communication. This common work required a common language in which the human operator was represented as one part of a communication system among others. The common language was that of 'information processing', developed by engineers like C. E. Shannon and W. Weaver. The psychologists of the time had by and large abandoned mentalism for a behaviouristic approach, and adopting the language of information processing raised no problems of incompatibility for them. In adopting the engineering language they also adopted engineering models, usually with considerable enthusiasm.[63] For Donald Broadbent, who played a key role in putting 'immediate' memory on the map, the model of the telephone system was an acknowledged source of inspiration.[64] In the US psychologists associated with Harvard's Psycho-Acoustics Laboratory similarly appreciated the possibilities of building a psychology of human cognition in the idiom of communication engineering.[65]

Of all the memory kinds ever identified, that of immediate or working memory has the shortest history. This is a memory whose features have been uniquely shaped by the human requirements of recent technology. It is a memory that has nothing to do with the past and very little to do with consciousness. Its semantic currency is that of channels, capacities, inputs and outputs, and its questions are dominated by the value of optimizing working performance. No wonder it has led to doubts about whether it should be considered a kind of 'memory' at all.

Yet, in so far as conceptions of human cognition are constructed within the discourse of information technology, effects lasting a few seconds may well be considered a form of 'memory'. A switch from the language of conscious experience to that of information processing involves a profound change in the conception of time. Mentalistic psychology works with subjective time, whereas the time of information technology is clock time. Subjective time is lumpy, uneven and qualitatively differentiated into such units as the present, the future, the recent past, the remote past and so on. Brief periods of clock time can be experienced as very long and vice versa. By contrast, clock time always passes at an even rate and is measured in identical units too small to be part of experienced time. The present in clock time is just a line between past and not yet past, and an event that occurred even a second or two in the past definitely belongs to the past and not the present. If such an event has effects now they must be due to some trace it left behind. It is not unreasonable to think of this as some sort of memory, especially if any link between memory and conscious experience has already been ruled out of court.

In subjective time, however, there is an experienced or lived present that is not a point, but includes much that would have to be assigned to the past or the future if measured by clock time. This insight was most famously expressed by William James, who distinguished 'primary' memory from 'memory proper'. Primary memory consisted of impressions that had never left consciousness and thus formed part of our awareness of the just-past. His account of the distinction provides a good illustration of how 'short-term memory' appears from the perspective of subjective time:

> An object which is recollected, in the proper sense of that term, is one which has been absent from consciousness altogether, and now revives anew. It is brought back, recalled, fished up, so to speak, from a reservoir in which, with countless other objects, it lay buried and lost from view. But an object of primary memory is not thus brought back; it never was lost; its date was never cut off in consciousness from that of the immediately present moment. In fact, it comes to us as belonging to the rearward portion of the present space of time, and not to the genuine past.[66]

Similar distinctions were not uncommon in the psychology of consciousness that flourished at the beginning of the twentieth century. G. F. Stout, a psychologist much respected in Britain, distinguished *primary retentiveness* from true memory. The former was a kind of sensory after-effect, the latter was ideational and depended on retrieval after a lapse of time.[67] Influenced by James, the phenomenologist Edmund Husserl recognized that present experience was not punctiform, but included a 'comet's tail' of just-past experience, a phenomenon to which he referred as the 'living present'.[68]

From the perspective of subjective time, storage metaphors are applicable only to 'memory proper', they are not applicable to the contents of 'primary memory' because those have never left the experienced present and hence have no need to be stored and recovered. Modern models of 'working memory' have to include memory stores because they are based strictly on clock time and therefore cannot consider any notion of an extended experienced present. The 'strict present', as James pointed out, is 'an altogether ideal abstraction', a product of 'philosophic reflection', not of experience.[69] This abstract present, it is worth noting, is a product of counting time in abstract units that no one has ever experienced.[70] The inclusion of short-term or working memory among genuine memory kinds depends on how seriously one takes the abstraction of a punctiform present measured by clock time. That will depend on one's culturally grounded biases. But there does seem to be an element of irony in the pursuit of an ideal of objectivity in psychology that rejects subjective experience in favour of abstractions that have no psychological reality at all.

By the closing years of the twentieth century the viability of the standard model of short-term memory was being seriously questioned. A great deal of evidence had accumulated that capacity limitations largely depended on the circumstances under which recall was required, particularly on the cues to which experimental subjects were given access. In any case, capacity varied with the kind of material an individual had to remember. There was certainly no single short-term memory store but a multiplicity. As a result of these empirically based insights, the true status of the concept of short-term memory became more and more evident. It was essentially a label for identifying a domain of psychological research whose members were loosely linked by certain similarities of experimental procedure. Attempts to integrate this domain by means of theoretical models might have had a certain heuristic function, but had not led to the identification of a particular kind of memory that was in itself sharply distinct from any other kind. There were now calls for the abandonment of the whole idea of short-term memory storage of experimentally presented 'items' and the adoption of alternative models for explaining the relevant empirical data in terms of the means available for coping with particular memory tasks.[71]

Notes

1. A more extensive discussion of the many meanings of 'remembering' is to be found in L. Munsat, *The concept of memory* (New York: Random House, 1967); and in E. S. Casey, *Remembering: A phenomenological study* (Bloomington: Indiana University Press, 1987).
2. Aristotle, *On memory*, 449b, 6.
3. Aristotle, *On memory*, 453a, 9.
4. There is some disagreement about whether Aristotle's distinction between memory and recollection is essentially a distinction among memory kinds. See J. Adams, 'Aristotle on memory and the self', in M. C. Nussbaum and A. Oksenberg Rorty (eds.), *Essays on Aristotle's* De anima (Oxford: Clarendon Press, 1992), pp. 297–312.
5. Danziger, 'Historical formation of selves'.
6. This seems to have been partially true of the souls consigned to Dante's *Inferno*, who suffered from anterograde but not retrograde amnesia: they could form no new memories but were forever stuck in the memories of their sinful past.
7. T. Aquinas, *Summa Theologica*, vol. I, Q. 78, Art. 4 and Q. 79, Art. 6 (New York: Benzinger Bros., 1947). See also Carruthers, *Book of memory*, chapter 3.
8. Although Gall was certainly responsible for the fundamental errors on which phrenology was based, its eventual relegation to the status of a pseudo-science had more to do with the activities of Johann Spurzheim, Gall's assistant, who was less cautious in his conclusions and less careful in his methods than the senior partner. The two disagreed and separated in 1813. See S. Zola-Morgan, 'Localization of brain function: The legacy of Franz Joseph Gall (1758–1828)', *Annual Review of Neuroscience* 18 (1995), 359–83.

9. The original list of twenty-seven underwent some changes subsequently, especially at the hands of Gall's followers.

10. Gall has cast a long shadow on the more recent history of conceptualizing psychological functions, such as memory. His project affected not only questions relating to the differentiation and identification of psychological functions, but also their physical localization in the brain. I will therefore return to different aspects of his ideas in chapter 8, and in the third section of chapter 9 ('Faculty psychology and its demise').

11. For further explication see T.L. Hoff, 'Gall's psychophysiological concept of function: The rise and decline of "internal essence"', *Brain and Cognition* 20 (1992), 378–98.

12. The statistical treatment of individual differences, pioneered by Francis Galton, was a later development. But before that could happen the evidentiary potential of individual differences had to be recognized. Gall certainly played a role in that.

13. The most influential propagator of the concept of phylogenetic memory was the philosopher Herbert Spencer, whose entirely speculative biological psychology was based on a then widespread belief in the inheritance of acquired characteristics. See H. Spencer, *The principles of psychology*, 2nd edn (London: Longman, Brown, Green, Longmans, 1880).

14. This idea was first popularized in the form of Ernst Haeckel's *biogenetic law*, put forward in German in the 1860s and published in English translation, in E. Haeckel, *The evolution of man: A popular exposition of the principal points of human ontogeny and phylogeny* (New York: International Science Library, 1874). Haeckel was no journalistic hack but a scientifically productive biologist. Note how at this time a speculation by an established scientist could immediately claim the status of a 'law' of nature.

15. The notion that the development of the individual recapitulated the development of the 'race', step by step, did not long survive the extreme version presented by G. Stanley Hall at the beginning of the twentieth century. See G.S. Hall, *Adolescence: Its psychology and its relations to physiology, anthropology, sociology, sex, crime, religion and education* (New York: Appleton, 1904).

16. Freud began as a typical biologist of his time and never completely shed those early influences, a situation that was thoroughly documented by F.J. Sulloway in his *Freud: Biologist of the mind* (New York: Basic Books, 1979). However, as reviewers of this work pointed out, there is also another Freud who struck out in directions that were unrelated to, and sometimes incompatible with, this legacy.

17. James, *Principles*, vol. I, p. 650.

18. H. Bergson, *Matter and memory* (New York: Zone Books, 1908/1991) p. 79.

19. In the earlier part of the twentieth century a distinction between remembering as an intellectual exercise and recollecting as an affect-laden personal experience was not uncommon among Central European authors, prominent examples being Otto Weininger, Ludwig Klages and Karl Jaspers. A review of this literature, as well as a relatively late variant of the genre, is to be found in A. Wellek, *Ganzheitspsychologie und Strukturtheorie* (Bern: Francke, 1955). Bergson was only one among a variety of influences that can be detected in the work of these authors. But at the turn of the twenty-first century there was an unexpected revival of interest in Bergson's philosophy and its relevance for a new psychology of memory. That development goes beyond the temporal framework of this book, but see Middleton and Brown, *Social psychology of experience* for relevant material.

20. C.D. Broad, *The mind and its place in nature* (London: Routledge & Kegan Paul, 1925).

21. B. Russell, *The analysis of mind* (New York: Humanities Press, 1921).

22. Broad, *Mind and its place*, p. 270.

23. G. Ryle, *The concept of mind* (London: Hutchison, 1949), p. 272ff.

24. The most important figures among this second generation of organic memory theorists were E. Rignano, *Biological memory* (New York: Harcourt Brace, 1926), and R. Semon. The latter, an inveterate inventor of neologisms, received some belated recognition from a few experimental psychologists; see Schacter, *Stranger behind the engram*.

25. K. Danziger, 'The history of introspection reconsidered', *Journal of the History of the Behavioral Sciences* 16 (1980), 240–62.

26. E. Claparède, 'Recognition and me-ness', in D. Rapaport (ed.), *Organization and pathology of thought* (New York: Columbia University Press, 1951; French original published 1911), pp. 58–75.

27. D. Katzaroff, 'Contribution à l'étude de la recognition', *Archive de Psychologie* 11 (1911), 2–78.

28. J.T. MacCurdy, *Common principles in psychology and physiology* (Cambridge, MA: Harvard University Press, 1928)

29. R. Reiff and M. Scheerer, *Memory and hypnotic age regression* (New York: International Universities Press, 1959).

30. W.B. Scoville and B. Milner, 'Loss of recent memory after bilateral hippocampal lesions', *Journal of Neurology, Neurosurgery and Psychiatry* 20 (1957), 11–12. The quotation appears in H. Eichenbaum and N.J. Cohen, *From conditioning to conscious recollection* (New York: Oxford University Press, 2001), p. 44.

31. The operation was carried out in 1953. At that time radical neurosurgical intervention was much in favour, the most notorious examples being supplied by the practice of prefrontal lobotomy.

32. B. Milner, S. Corkin and H.L. Teuber, 'Further analysis of the hippocampal amnesic syndrome: 14-year follow-up study of H.M.', *Neuropsychologia* 6 (1968), 215–34; S. Corkin, 'Lasting consequences of bilateral medial temporal lobectomy: Clinical course and experimental findings in H.M.', *Seminars in Neurology* 4 (1984), 249–59; S. Corkin *et al.*, 'H.M.'s medial temporal lobe lesion: Findings from magnetic resonance imaging', *The Journal of Neuroscience* 17 (1997), 3964–79.

33. E. Tulving, 'Episodic and semantic memory', in E. Tulving and W. Donaldson (eds.), *Organization of memory* (New York: Academic Press, 1972), pp. 382–403; E. Tulving, *Elements of episodic memory* (New York: Oxford University Press, 1983).

34. Tulving, *Elements of episodic memory*, pp. 184–5.

35. M. Minsky (ed.), *Semantic information processing* (Cambridge, MA: MIT Press, 1968).

36. N.J. Cohen, 'Preserved learning capacity in amnesia: Evidence of multiple memory systems', in N. Butters and L.R. Squire (eds.), *The neuropsychology of memory* (New York: Guilford Press, 1984), pp. 83–103.

37. L.R. Squire, *Memory and brain* (New York: Oxford University Press, 1987).

38. E. Tulving, 'How many memory systems are there?', *American Psychologist* 40 (1985), 385–98. For a later and more elaborate version of this approach, see M.A. Wheeler, D.T. Stuss and E. Tulving, 'Toward a theory of episodic memory: The frontal lobes and autonoetic consciousness', *Psychological Bulletin* 121 (1997), 331–54.

39. Sherry and Schacter, 'Evolution of multiple memory systems'.

40. G. McKoon, R. Ratcliff and G.S. Dell, 'A critical evaluation of the semantic-episodic distinction', *Journal of Experimental Psychology: Learning, Memory, and Cognition* 12 (1986), 295–306. Another division among memory kinds that became popular around this time, but that seemed to have a purely descriptive function from the beginning, was that between *explicit* and *implicit* memory. The former refers to memory as a conscious and intentional act, the latter to demonstrable effects of past training that do not show these attributes. See D.L. Schacter, 'Implicit memory:

history and current status', *Journal of Experimental Psychology: Learning, Memory, Cognition* 13 (1987), 501–18.

41. E. Tulving, 'What kind of a hypothesis is the distinction between episodic and semantic memory?', *Journal of Experimental Psychology: Learning, Memory, and Cognition* 12 (1986), 307–11 (p. 309).

42. For the evidence against the temporal organization of episodic memory, see W. J. Friedman, 'Memory for the time of past events', *Psychological Bulletin* 113 (1993), 44–66. On the privatization of time, see D. S. Landes, *Revolution in time: Clocks and the making of the modern world* (Cambridge, MA: Harvard University Press, 1983). The dubious cross-cultural validity of psychological concepts of memory kinds has been noted in Fentress and Wickham, *Social memory*.

43. D. L. Schacter and E. Tulving (eds.), *Memory systems of 1994* (Cambridge, MA: MIT Press, 1994). Potentially, one could use memory tasks, memory experiences or hypothetical memory processes as a basis for distinguishing between memory kinds. But because the ways of sub-dividing each of these are unlimited, and because firm intercorrelations proved elusive, the results were always rather arbitrary and led to what was accurately described as a 'persistent debasement of existing terminology': J. M. Gardner and R. I. Java, 'Recognising and remembering', in A. F. Collins, S. E. Gathercole, M. A Conway and P. E. Morris (eds.), *Theories of memory* (Hillsdale, NJ: Erlbaum, 1993), pp. 163–88 (p. 184).

44. H. L. Roediger III, R. L. Buckner, and K. B. McDermott, 'Components of processing', in J. K. Foster and M. Jelicic (eds.), *Memory: systems, process, or function?* (New York: Oxford University Press, 1999), pp. 31–65.

45. See the contributions to Foster and Jelicic, *Systems, process or function*; also the discussion of problems of task dissociation in T. J. Palmieri and M. A. Flanery, 'Memory systems and perceptual categorization', in B. H. Ross (ed.), *The psychology of learning and motivation: Advances in research and theory* (New York: Academic Press, 2002), vol. XLI, pp. 141–89.

46. For examples of this development, see J. R. Hanley and A. W. Young, 'The cognitive neuropsychology of memory', in Morris and Gruneberg, *Theoretical aspects of memory*, pp. 238–72; E. Tulving and M. Lepage, 'Where in the brain is awareness of one's past?', in D. L. Schacter and E. Scarry (eds.), *Memory, brain and belief* (Cambridge, MA: Harvard University Press, 2000), pp. 208–28; E. T. Rolls, 'Memory systems in the brain', *Annual Review of Psychology* 51 (2000), 599–630; E. Tulving, 'Episodic memory: From mind to brain', *Annual Review of Psychology* 53 (2003), 1–25.

47. S. L. Nairn, J. H. Ellard, C. T. Scialfa and C. D. Miller, 'At the core of introductory psychology: A content analysis', *Canadian Psychology* 44 (2003), 93–9.

48. J. Jacobs, 'Experiments on prehension', *Mind* 12 (1887), 75–9. The founder of eugenics immediately seized on this procedure to demonstrate that the mental span of 'idiots' was very low; see F. Galton, 'Supplementary notes on "prehension" in idiots', *Mind* 12 (1887), 79–82.

49. Oliver Wendell Holmes likened tests of mental span to 'a very simple mental dynamometer'. Cited in W. H. Burnham, 'Memory, historically and experimentally considered IV', *American Journal of Psychology* 2 (1888/9), 568–622 (p. 608).

50. Wundt's use of the 'span of consciousness' concept in the context of the psychology of language is to be found in the first volume of his *Völkerpsychologie* (Leipzig: Engelmann, 1900). For a comprehensive English-language account of those of Wundt's theories that are relevant to memory, see E. Scheerer, 'Wilhelm Wundt's psychology of memory', *Psychological Research* 42 (1980), 135–55.

51. F. Kennedy, 'On the experimental investigation of memory', *Psychological Review* 5 (1898), 477–99. See also D. J. Murray, 'Research on human memory in the nineteenth century', *Canadian Journal of Psychology* 30 (1976), 201–20.

52. Key centres were the Bell Telephone Laboratories in the US and the Applied Psychology Unit in Cambridge, UK.

53. D. E. Broadbent, *Perception and communication* (London: Pergamon Press, 1958); N. C. Waugh and D. A. Norman, 'Primary memory', *Psychological Review* 72 (1965), 89–104.

54. An influential model that demonstrated this influence and proposed separate short-term and long-term memory *stores* was presented in Atkinson and Shiffrin, 'Human memory: A proposed system and its control processes'.

55. A key publication was F. I. M. Craik and R. S. Lockhart, 'Levels of processing: A framework for memory research', *Journal of Verbal Learning and Verbal Behavior* 11 (1972), 671–84.

56. The new term was introduced by Alan Baddeley in the UK. For an overview, see A. Baddeley, 'The concept of working memory', in S. E. Gathercole (ed.), *Models of short-term memory* (Hove: Psychology Press, 1996), pp. 1–27.

57. Baddeley, 'Concept of working memory', p. 2.

58. An influential earlier example of this trend was W. Kintsch and T. A. van Dijk, 'Toward a model of text comprehension and production', *Psychological Review* 85 (1978), 363–94.

59. Baddeley, 'Concept of working memory', p. 12.

60. K. Danziger, 'The positivist repudiation of Wundt', *Journal of the History of the Behavioral Sciences* 15 (1979), 205–30. The unacknowledged parallels between Wundt's model and some trends in latter-day cognitive psychology were pointed out in A. Blumenthal, 'A reappraisal of Wilhelm Wundt', *American Psychologist* 30 (1975), 1081–8; and in T. H. Leahy, 'Something old, something new: Attention in Wundt and modern cognitive psychology', *Journal of the History of the Behavioral Sciences* 15 (1979), 242–52.

61. Some classics of the period exemplifying these trends were: G. A. Miller, E. Gallanter and K. Pribram, *Plans and the structure of behavior* (New York: Holt, Rinehart & Winston, 1960); H. A. Simon, *The sciences of the artificial* (Cambridge, MA: MIT Press, 1969); A. Newell and H. A. Simon, *Human problem solving* (Englewood Cliffs, NJ: Prentice-Hall, 1972); M. Minsky, *The society of mind* (New York: Simon & Schuster, 1985).

62. Neisser, 'Memory: What are the important questions?', p. 7.

63. The ideal of an experimental science manipulating entirely asocial objects had a profound appeal. Describing the emergence of short-term memory as a focal scientific object, Alan Collins writes: 'It [short-term memory] represented a circumscribed "component" that could be described in terms of information theory and which, through its relation to physical devices and quantitative measurement, appeared an appropriate object for an experimental psychology. At least a part of memory was now defined and delineated in such a way that it seemed divorced from social contexts, and this allowed the experiment to be deployed, apparently unproblematically, as the method of investigation, while at the same time these laboratory-based studies promised some practical utility.' A. Collins, 'The psychology of memory', in G. C. Bunn, A. D. Lovie and G. D. Richards (eds.), *Psychology in Britain: Historical essays and personal reflections* (Leicester: BPS Books, 2001), pp. 150–68 (p. 166).

64. D. Cohen, *Psychologists on psychology* (London: Routledge, 1977). In an autobiographical account Broadbent mentions his close working relationship with Colin Cherry, Professor of Telecommunications at Imperial College, 'leading activist in the early days of information theory [whose] students were often doing work that might just as well have been done in a psychological laboratory'. For a number of years Broadbent examined more doctorates in electrical engineering than in psychology. D. E. Broadbent, in G. Lindzey (ed.), *A history of psychology in autobiography* (San Francisco: W. H. Freeman, 1980), vol. VII, p. 59.

65. P. N. Edwards, *The closed world*, chapter 7. The importance of the sense of *hearing* for at least the earlier phase of research on problems of short-term memory cannot be overestimated. From Aristotle's ideas about memory images, through centuries of mnemonic advice on the use of vivid imagery, to twentieth-century work on perceptual fields, the sense of *vision* had been the major source of exemplars for discourse on memory and cognition. The practical problems that gave rise to systematic experimentation on short-term memory, however, were specifically problems of audition, and auditory stimuli continued to predominate even when the questions became more theoretical. Different sensory paradigms tended to favour different theoretical models, even though each model claimed general validity. The reification of these models then confirmed the separation of memory kinds. Later on, with the advent of models of 'working memory', vision once more had a role (in the form of a hypothetical 'visual sketch pad'), though the early history of the field may well have had a foundational effect.

66. James, *Principles*, vol. I, pp. 646–7.

67. G. F. Stout, *Analytic psychology*, 2nd edn (London: Swann Sonnenschein, 1902).

68. E. Husserl, *The philosophy of internal time consciousness*, trans. J. S. Churchill (Bloomington: Indiana University Press, 1964); the original lectures were delivered in1904/5.

69. James, *Principles*, vol. I, p. 608.

70. At its simplest level the unit organization of conscious time can be appreciated in rhythms and melodies. Gestalt psychology had discussed the issue in that context (Koffka, *Principles of Gestalt psychology*, pp. 431ff.), but although the psychology of short-term memory was founded on problems of audition it was hardly interested in the sense of hearing as a source of musical understanding. Had aesthetic interests rather than technological rationality played a predominant role in its development, a very different psychology of short-term memory might have emerged.

71. J. S. Nairne, 'Short-term/working memory', in E. L Bjork and R. A. Bjork (eds.), *Memory* (New York: Academic Press, 1996), pp. 101–26; J. S. Nairne, 'Remembering over the short-term: The case against the standard models', *Annual Review of Psychology* 53 (2002), 53–81.

7 Truth in memory

So far from being inherently linked, questions of testimony and questions of memory arose in different institutional and discursive contexts. In the context of judicial institutions and jurisprudence the value of testimony was seen to depend on the trustworthiness of witnesses as persons who were defined by their social relations. The trustworthiness of persons involved in legal proceedings depended on factors that were public and social, such as self-interest, age, gender, relationship to other persons involved in the proceedings and, not least, social standing. Memory remained a largely taken-for-granted aspect of legally implicated persons. The reliability of testimony was tested in recognized court procedures, but until relatively modern times this remained an overt, public matter that did not involve much questioning of what was going on inside people's minds. There might be passing remarks about the unreliability or the special trustworthiness of this or that individual's memory, but there was no systematic attempt to address the issue in this context.

The ancient discourse on memory arose mainly in the context of dialectical argument (see chapter 2) and in the context of rhetoric (see chapter 3). Only in the former case was it linked to questions of truth; and then not necessarily truth in the sense of factual accuracy.[1] Rhetoric was a matter of persuasion, not of truth. In striking contrast to this situation, an important thread in the twentieth-century history of memory involves issues of testimony. Memory became saddled with politically tinged questions of trustworthiness that evoked problems which had long been regarded as the concern of lawyers. How did this come about?

At the end of chapter 4 I pointed to the forensic potential inherent in the medicalization of alienated memory that had gained widespread attention by the end of the nineteenth century. Parts of the present chapter are concerned with some twentieth-century developments that played a role in actualizing this potential. But the simultaneous development of a specifically psychological, as distinct from a medical/biological, approach tended to complicate the accepted relationship of truth and memory. Psychoanalysis and empirical psychology both contributed to this complication in so far as both – in very different ways – supported constructivist concepts of memory. A memory that constructs will not be a friend of the literal truth.

Psychology claimed and greatly expanded the territory stretching between lying and reproducing the literal truth. However, this territory was not always neglected. In many older theories the boundary between memory and imagination was not as sharply drawn as it came to be in more recent times. That point needs to be made before moving on to twentieth-century developments.

Imagination and memory

The words 'invention' and 'inventory' have the same Latin root. Yet today their very different meanings involve an opposition between that which is constructed or created anew and that which has assumed a stable form suitable for listing and storing. Imagination and memory often seemed to be at opposite ends of the conceptual universe of experimental psychology, as we saw in chapter 5.

This opposition is a relatively modern development. In the ancient world reproduction and construction were productively allied. For the Roman lawyer or orator the art of memory was valued less as an aid to verbatim reproduction than as an aid to finding the right forms for influencing a live audience while addressing them (see chapter 3). Memory served invention. In monastic life memory was extolled as the resource that enabled one to incorporate sacred models into the various tasks of one's daily life. The medieval concept of *memoria* was much broader than more recent concepts of 'memory'.[2]

According to the Aristotelian tradition that long dominated European discussions regarding the nature of memory there was a close connection between the categories of memory and imagination. If we turn back to Aristotle's account of the formation of memories, outlined in chapter 2, we find that imagery plays a necessary role. In fact, the dependence of memory on the ability to form, retain and recall images is so strong that one might begin to wonder why a separate category of memory is needed at all. Perhaps this question also occurred to Aristotle, causing him to introduce a very specific criterion by which memory images are to be distinguished from other sorts of images: 'The object of memory is the past. All memory, therefore, implies a time elapsed; consequently only those animals which perceive time remember, and the organ whereby they perceive time is also that whereby they remember.'[3] So although memory and imagination have much in common, they are not to be confused with each other, because only memory images carry a sense of time elapsed, a reference to a past which once existed. One can have all kinds of images, but unless they are felt to show what was in the past, they are not memory images.[4]

Note that Aristotle (and those who followed in his footsteps over the centuries) did not make *retention* the distinguishing characteristic of what was called 'memory'. That was a much later idea. In the Aristotelian tradition memory certainly involved retention, but so did other parts of the soul, imagination especially. The power of imagination manifested itself not only in the formation of images from sensory experience, but also in the combination of several images into a new composite image. We should therefore distinguish 'sensitive' or 'sentient' imagination from 'calculative' or 'deliberative' imagination[5] that produces a unity out of many images. But for that to happen the sensory images must have been retained or stored. This capacity was usually assigned to imagination, supposedly located in the front of the head, rather than memory, supposedly in the back. In addition to the ability to form images in the absence of sensory input, there was also the ability to evaluate and judge the things presented to us by our senses or by our imagination. This ability, commonly attributed to a *vis aestimateva*, a power of judgement, was provided with its own store of past judgements by some writers.

The modern break with this structuring of psychological categories becomes very evident in the eighteenth-century philosophy of *empiricism* that shattered the old association between memory and imagination. For this philosophy the opposition between imagination and memory was in fact a basic requirement. Let us take the version of empiricism represented by the philosophy of David Hume as an example because, for a while, the implicit, taken-for-granted preconceptions of many scientifically orientated psychologists came to resemble the Humean type of empiricism more closely than any other philosophy.

Empiricists believe that the contents of our minds are essentially reflections of the experiences to which we have been exposed. Originally, these experiences are given to us by our primary senses, but we can also recall them later in the form of *copies* of the original. That is what is called memory. Hume thought we would be able to distinguish between the original and the copy because the copy would be weaker and less vivid than the original.

If this were all there was to the story, empiricism would not have seemed all that plausible, because one would have had to accept that the human mind was a purely receptive, passive organ. How, then, to account for all the evidence of spontaneity, creativity and autonomous activity in human affairs while yet preserving the primacy of sensory perception? Hume's answer was to stay with the copy theory of memory and to add imagination as a further complicating factor. In addition to sensory perception and memory, we also have imagination, which jumbles up and adds to the impressions formed by the senses. As a result, we end up with some mental contents that were never part of our original perception.

What we get here is a radical sundering of the traditionally blurred relationship between memory and imagination. Hume did not invent the separation, he radicalized it. Among the seventeenth-century members of London's Royal Society, for instance, there had already been an understanding that true knowledge of the natural world would depend on separating 'fancies' from the observational records of reliable witnesses.[6] This was only the beginning of a trend that would run full course in the nineteenth century, with the social construction of the 'two worlds' of the sciences and the arts, one valuing accurate records, the other imagination.

Hume was well aware that the separation of memory and imagination played a crucial role in his theory of the human mind. Perhaps he also realized that his evidence for this separation was a bit shaky, because he first introduces it with the words ' 'tis evident at first sight', but later returns to it and admits that sometimes imaginary ideas may be so strong and vivid as to be mistaken for memories.[7] For empiricist theories of memory this has indeed been the problem that won't go away. Often, Hume's criteria were replaced by others, for instance a feeling of familiarity or of pastness, to mark a memory as distinct from a product of the imagination.[8]

This was indeed a slender thread on which to hang empiricism's sharp distinction between those of our ideas that were true, veridical, trustworthy, and those that were false, imaginary, untrustworthy. But in a period that urgently needed to divest itself of the superstitions of the past in order to clear the ground for observation-based science, the need for a sharp distinction between fact and fiction was widely felt, no matter how weak the grounds for an absolute separation.

Ever after, memory and imagination went their separate ways, their subsequent histories quite divergent. At first, imagination was the clear winner in this separation. Memory was reduced to a kind of shadow of perception, a copying machine whose products were often too faint to be useful. But imagination, being the source of all invention, would come to be worshipped as a kind of goddess of artistic creation or else condemned as the origin of mistaken beliefs. Either way, imagination was credited with a power and significance that was not accorded to mere memory. In eighteenth-century philosophies of the mind memory was not very important, but imagination played a crucial role for Humeans and their idealist opponents alike. Hume, an extreme sceptic, made imagination responsible for all the philosophical fictions that have led people astray over the centuries, including even such commonly accepted notions as the idea of a self or the idea of causality.[9] But Immanuel Kant (1724–1804), offering a widely influential alternative to the Humean philosophy, attributed just as much importance to imagination, regarding it as necessary for transforming elementary sensations into the perceived world of meaningful objects.[10]

Imagination was highly esteemed by Romanticism in the arts, providing a psychological foundation for the qualities of individual originality and creativity that were now so highly valued.[11] Memory was valued in the highly privatized form of personal reminiscence that was discussed in chapter 4 (section headed 'The privatization of memory'). Romantics believed that this form of memory was capable of yielding truths of a personal, moral, or aesthetic kind. A deep split separated this notion of truth from the discourse of scientific empiricism, whose authority was growing throughout the nineteenth century. For the empiricists, Romanticism dealt in subjective beliefs and imaginings whose truth could never be established by looking inwards. The truthfulness of memory could be established only by means of an objective standard, an unambiguous record of the facts. So the sharp distinction between memory and imagination led to a split within the category of memory itself. On the one hand, there was memory for objective facts, increasingly encouraged by nineteenth-century educational systems and supported by the newer mnemonics (see chapter 3). On the other hand, there was the personal recollection of subjective experience, the foundation for some of the most significant trends in High Romantic, and later popular, art.

For the experimental science of memory allegiance to scientific empiricism was foundational from the start. As we saw in chapter 5, Ebbinghaus's construction of a viable technique for a scientifically respectable study of memory was closely linked to his separation of the essentials of memory from personal reminiscence. For virtually a century, when academic psychologists investigated or discussed what they referred to as 'memory' they meant the kind of memory whose measure was the accuracy of reproducing units of impersonal information.[12] A special sub-field of 'autobiographical memory' did emerge rather late in the history of the discipline but was far from constituting its core in the closing years of the twentieth century.[13] However, the reductive empiricism of the Ebbinghaus tradition was not the only way of applying a scientific perspective to problems of memory. In chapter 5 I discussed Bartlett's constructionist approach, in which the boundaries between memory and imagination became quite indistinct. But many years before Bartlett's intervention two other areas of scientific practice had indicated that what lay between memory and imagination was not so much a line as a vast space. One of these areas developed as a result of the annexation of hypnotism by the scientific medicine of the late nineteenth century (see chapter 4). Among the phenomena that were now accepted as scientifically demonstrable was the ability of hypnotists to alter the memories of their hypnotized subjects. After receiving the appropriate suggestions these subjects would claim to 'remember' things that were after all only imaginings. Yet they were not lying – there was no apparent intention to deceive; instead, they had been made to deceive themselves. On a strictly Humean view self-deception is very difficult to explain. If memories are ultimately reproductions of sensory experiences how can I believe in memories of experiences I never had? An answer that appealed to those who followed the example of Charcot was to relegate such phenomena to the realm of pathology, to attribute false memories to a weakness in the nervous system of highly suggestible individuals. If that were the case, there would be no frightening implications for the mental processes of normal people.

Others, notably those affiliated with the so-called Nancy school, considered the suggestions of the hypnotist to be only a particularly powerful example of a phenomenon that was part of all social life. Suggestion emanating from other people, particularly people in positions of authority, frequently affected our beliefs and attitudes, and in some cases even our memories. Sometimes it was not necessary to resort to hypnotism to induce people to accept mere imaginings as memories of things they had actually experienced. This was particularly likely to happen where children were exposed to the suggestions of adults, women to the suggestions of men, and generally when there was a significant difference in power and status between the source of the suggestion and its target.

A science of testimony

Medical discourse on the possible effects of hypnosis and suggestion always had forensic implications that fed a growing anxiety about the reliability of witness testimony in legal proceedings. In law courts the issue of trustworthiness cannot be evaded. What witnesses say they remember often establishes the truth of the matter. But sometimes witnesses' memories contradict each other or are in conflict with other evidence. Traditionally, such failures were most often attributed to intentional lying or to the unreliability of certain classes of persons as witnesses. A developing sensitivity to mental pathology, however, gave more salience to the possibility of 'honest' self-deception.

Legal institutions had developed to deal with the ancient recognition that while memory may not always be a reliable guide to truth, there is truth in memory. Special procedures and conditions had been established to ensure the veracity of what was recalled: formal courts, taking oaths, being subjected to ordeals, swearing on a holy book, cross-examination, juries and so on. Very frequently the testimony of certain people was privileged: adults versus children, men versus women, noblemen versus peasants, gentlemen versus labourers, and increasingly, experts versus lay people. By the beginning of the twentieth century the prestige of science provided grounds for claiming a more prominent role for psychological experts on the value of testimony. In France and Germany there was talk of a 'science of testimony'[14] based on new skills and knowledge relevant to the credibility of witnesses. A major effect of the new science would be an undermining of the trust that courts placed in the confidently asserted memories of witnesses. But psychological experts would offer to mediate the transformation of private memories into public testimonies. In practice, the contributions of these experts were very largely concerned with the memories of women and children, categories of persons whose testimony had been traditionally more likely to be distrusted.

Alfred Binet (1857–1911) in France and William Stern (1871–1938) in Germany were the two most prominent figures in laying the foundations for a science of testimony.[15] Significantly, both men were also pioneers in the development of intelligence testing, Stern being the inventor of an index he called an intelligence quotient or IQ, and Binet being responsible for the first successful assembly of tests in a 'battery'. Their work provides outstanding early examples of an expanding effort to subject the lives of human individuals to the discipline of scientific analysis and control.[16] From then on, discourse on the relationship between memory and imagination was increasingly conducted in the terms that had been chosen by modern scientific psychology.

A key element in the theoretical language of late nineteenth-century French medical psychology was an entirely modern concept of *suggestion*. This term quickly became ubiquitous whenever it became necessary to acknowledge the fact that mental processes, including memory, were not entirely individual achievements but often involved a social interaction with other human agents. 'Suggestion' was made responsible for a vast range of interpersonal phenomena, from the political behaviour of crowds to the responses of patients to their treatment in neurological clinics, to the behaviour of children in psychological experiments.[17] Originally a description of an interpersonal phenomenon, 'suggestion' was quickly transformed into the very different concept of 'suggestibility', a fixed property of individual persons and classes of persons, especially children, women and hysterics. Suggestibility was in principle measurable, and many practical instantiations of this measurability were proposed over the years. But the fundamental inspiration of these projects was always derived from the ideal of sorting and calculating human conduct to which I have already referred.

In Alfred Binet's pioneering experimental studies of children's memory the concept of suggestion occupied centre stage.[18] Error-free reproduction functions as an implicit default setting for the operations of memory. Faulty reproductions are demonstrably related to the interventions of the adult experimenter. Unlike Ebbinghaus, a more influential experimenter in the long run (see chapter 5), Binet was less interested in forgetting, or *amnesia*, than in *hypermnesia* or *paramnesia*, 'remembering' things that were never there in the first place, or distorting the original experience when recalling it. This interest relates to old questions about the relationship of memory and imagination, but these are now addressed within a new framework. The concept of imagination has lost much of its former respectability, and suggestion must do some of its work. Even when memory distortions are not traceable to the interventions of the experimenter Binet attributes them to another kind of suggestion. This time they are *autosuggestions*, functioning like specific instructions that individual subjects issue to themselves. The advantage of this formulation for a would-be scientific analysis is that, in principle, it allows for a causal analysis of specific conditions producing distortions of memory. As it turned out, this aspect of Binet's project did not flourish, largely because the auto-suggestive instructions of the self to itself were not suitable candidates for practical measurement and calculation. Mechanistic models of memory distortion, developed later in the twentieth century, could do this job much better.

In the meantime, the pseudo-scientific discourse of suggestibility supervened on the older philosophic reflections regarding the relationship of memory and imagination. In a curious way, the new emphasis on the powers of suggestion preserved the innocence of memory, implying memory's inherent veridicality when not exposed to the blandishments of suggestion. The boundary between 'true' memory and suggestive influence was often drawn as sharply as the radical empiricist boundary between memory and imagination. What the evocation of 'suggestion' often accomplished was the outward projection of the inherently constructive aspects of human memory.

Talk of suggestion did, however, introduce a new, social, dimension into discussions of memory as a vehicle of truth or falsehood. Memory's weakness for confabulation was no longer to be explained in terms of the single soul's capacities but was to be laid at the door of the individual's social dependencies. Yet those dependencies were typically conceived in negative terms. Suggestibility made individual memory vulnerable to corruption and error, especially the memory of immature, female and congenitally weak individuals. Only in a therapeutic context was a potentially positive role conceded to suggestion, mainly in helping patients to forget upsetting experiences. But even in this case the concept of suggestion served to maintain the strict division between the memory inside and the tampering influences located outside. Hypnotism always remained the paradigm case of suggestion. For the recognition of the profoundly social nature of normal human memory, the doctrine of suggestion remained a major obstacle throughout the twentieth century.

Whereas Binet's work was inspired by the promise of experimental techniques, Stern's approach to child study was more representative of a trend towards systematic naturalistic observation that had been sparked by the application of evolutionary perspectives to child development.[19] Unlike most of his predecessors, however, Stern did not perceive the young child primarily as a biological organism but as a participant in the social life of the family. His wife, Clara Stern, meticulously recorded and analysed interactions with their three children, and they both paid particular attention to the problematic of truthfulness in children's talk. This was not an idiosyncratic interest of theirs: in the early years of the twentieth century there was a flurry of German-language publications on the reliability of children's testimony.[20] That children were not good witnesses was a fact of life that had been widely accepted in legal proceedings. For the new psychological expertise this was a challenge. If the reasons for children's 'bad memory' could be laid bare, a rewarding field of practical application would open up for the new science. William Stern was not only a child psychologist; he was also a pioneering figure in the establishment and early institutionalization of an entirely new field – the 'psychology of testimony' (*Psychologie der Aussage*).[21] As a psychological problem, the unreliability of children's testimony presented itself in the form of children's apparent failures to make distinctions between reality and fantasy that were important to adults. Like others, the Sterns had observed these failures. However, they recognized that the blurring of the distinction between reality and fantasy was a *failure* only from the point of view of the adult. In the lives of young children there is as yet no sharp separation between serious business and playfulness, so that confabulation and truth-telling are often intermingled: 'when seriousness and play are still not separated in the life of the child, truth and lying cannot be separated either'.[22] This introduces a new, developmental, perspective into the conceived relationship between memory and imagination. The elevation of strictly reproductive recall to a normative position that devalued imaginative construction could now be seen as a gradual developmental *achievement*, the result of parental and other educational influences.[23] The Sterns recognized that the path to this achievement was complicated and that it varied between individuals. Between scrupulously accurate reporting and intentional deception there was 'a wide middle ground of pseudo-lies' that characterized much of the communication of young children. A child might have a cognitive understanding of the difference between pretence and reality, yet be insensitive to the normative force of this difference, especially when this meant avoiding blame and earning adult approval.

After its promising start the psychology of testimony, especially children's testimony, languished for many years. In the mid-twentieth century the growth of new developments in psychology as a discipline depended on their North American appeal, and the psychology of testimony did not make a successful Atlantic crossing.[24] The most obvious reason for this is the difference between the Anglo-Saxon and continental European systems of jurisprudence. In establishing the reliability of witnesses the procedures of the Anglo-Saxon system relied heavily on an adversarial system with cross-examination by contending lawyers, as well as on the judgement of lay juries. The continental European system assigned a more pervasive role to judges and examining magistrates, who were sometimes quite ready to accept the assistance of expert advice. This contrasted with the situation in countries where traditional court procedures were felt to be quite adequate for assessing the reliability of witnesses.[25] Indeed, the 'psychology of testimony' of the early twentieth century was essentially a French and

German enterprise that encountered fierce resistance from the US legal profession.[26] This situation hardly changed until the century's last quarter, when the relationship between memory and imagination acquired an intense political significance that reopened the issue of witness reliability under altogether different auspices. Those developments will be examined in the last section of this chapter.

Psychoanalysis as an art of memory

For much of the twentieth century the major intellectual influence on conceptualizations of personal memory emanated from psychoanalysis, a movement with its own distinct patterns of professional practice, theoretical tenets, rules of accreditation and institutional forms. Although the historical roots of psychoanalysis lie in the late nineteenth-century medicalization of knowledge about memory that was described in chapter 4, and although there were periods when psychoanalysis played a significant role in twentieth-century psychiatry, psychoanalysis did not owe its importance to its medical credentials but to its broad cultural appeal. Its tenets, often distorted and bowdlerized, circulated widely in literary and media circles, among members of the so-called helping professions, among educators and among members of the general public.

The vast literature on psychoanalysis covers much subject-matter that is unrelated or merely tangential to the topic of memory and need not be considered here. Much of the literature that is more directly concerned with memory restricts itself to very specific empirical questions that have no bearing on the clarification of conceptual issues. But psychoanalysis has also been wide open to reinterpretation, and it is difficult to discern the original inspiration behind layers of screens erected by later commentators. This is due partly to the fluid nature of Freud's own conceptualizations, the lack of rigorous definitions and the changes in implicit definitions over time. But it must also be recognized that reinterpretations of Freud have not occurred in a geographically random manner but have reflected some significant cultural differences.[27] Psychoanalytic approaches to the topic of memory have been particularly controversial in regard to the relationship of truth and memory. They imply that the truths revealed by memory are not all of one kind, as empiricist metaphysics assumes, but that memory is the keeper of more than one kind of truth. If so, what might these other kinds of truth be? Answers to that question then lead to questions about the relationship between outer events and their inner preservation over time and about how memory is falsified, if not by intention or by decay.

The more immediate roots of the psychoanalytic approach to the problem of truth in memory can be traced to the late nineteenth-century use of hypnosis for the treatment of certain 'nervous illnesses' (see chapter 4).

Hypnosis seemed to produce a curious splitting of memory. What could be remembered under normal conditions was not all that could be remembered under special conditions. That complicated the supposed relationship between remembering and forgetting. The one could not simply be equated with the absence or loss of the other. A memory might exist and have effects without being accessible at will. Therefore, memory could sometimes carry a *hidden* truth.

Pierre Janet in Le Havre and Josef Breuer (1842–1925) in Vienna had been able to demonstrate a connection between hysterical symptoms and earlier painful experiences that had been 'forgotten' but were recoverable under hypnosis. In other words, hypnosis could not only create memories that remained causally effective (via post-hypnotic suggestions), though inaccessible, it could also do the opposite: annul the inaccessibility of certain active memories formed at an earlier stage of life. It appeared that memories of this type, causally active though consciously inaccessible, were not merely an artefact of hypnosis, they were also to be found in the lives of persons suffering from some form of 'nervous' illness.

Individuals afflicted by memories of this kind harboured a hidden truth, a personal truth that explained their illness but that remained unrecognized by themselves and those around them. Neurologists, medical specialists charged with the diagnosis and possible cure of nervous illnesses, took up the task of drawing the pathogenic fangs of these hidden truths. How this was to be accomplished was not immediately clear. Breuer, assisted by his younger associate Sigmund Freud (1856–1939), employed hypnosis to call up painful inaccessible memories that would then have to be lived through again with full emotional intensity, a process labelled 'abreaction'.[28] This 'cathartic' method was more successful in capturing the popular imagination than in gaining widespread professional acceptance. Within a few years Freud had abandoned it and Breuer had turned to other interests. Pierre Janet wrestled with the problem of memory cures for a long time, beginning with an early inclination to advocate the virtues of forgetting. In due course he came to distinguish between the fixed repetition of an isolated memory episode and the integration of the previously inaccessible memory into a coherent autobiographical account.[29] Only the latter provided a genuine cure for the problems of the nervous patient.

With the shift of therapeutic emphasis from the cathartic abreaction of a walled-off memory to the construction of an autobiographical narration the topic of hidden memories acquired a much broader significance than it had had originally. In their attempts at interpreting the meaning of such memory phenomena neurologists had not been keen to leave the safe ground of biologically grounded medicine. Borrowing the term 'trauma' from the medical vocabulary of physical injury, neurological discourse had derived the term 'traumatic memory' to refer to the aftermath of injuries that were psychological rather than physical (see chapter 4). This analogy preserved the status of hidden memories as essentially a medical topic, referring to distinctly abnormal phenomena occurring only in the context of abnormal nervous states (hypnoid), biologically weakened constitutions or injurious life experiences. But if traumatic memories could be rendered harmless only by involving the patient's autobiography as a whole, then their significance clearly extended beyond conventional nineteenth-century medicine to much broader issues of human life and personality. The prevailing empiricist account of what used to be called the individual soul had identified the person with their cumulative experiences. A hidden traumatic memory would therefore signify a serious disruption of the personality, a fact of more than narrowly medical interest.

Such an implication was bound to arouse attention among people who were already troubled by problems of personal and social disruption linked to the rapid decay of traditional patterns of life. Could it be that hidden memories were active not only in the patients of neurologists, but in everyone? Hints to that effect were certainly to be found in the literature of the time, and some neurologists were already beginning to play with the conceptual implications of such a possibility. Among these, Breuer's former collaborator Sigmund Freud quickly occupied a leading, though never unchallenged, position. Because of the boldness with which he pursued the practical and theoretical consequences of his beliefs, and because of their wide appeal, Freud's contributions to the memory discourse of his time provided a focal point for debate throughout the twentieth century.

Freud was clearly impressed by the novel views on the affinity between memory and heredity that had been expressed by Ewald Hering, his senior in Viennese medicine, who had once offered him a job as an assistant. Those views cleared the way for the expanded meaning of 'memory' during the late nineteenth century (see chapter 6), and Freud was in broad company when he referred to Hering's 1870 lecture as 'a masterpiece'. It was hardly surprising that Freud shared some of the tenets of 'organic memory',[30] but there were other implications of Hering's speculations that were of more immediate significance for Freud's work. They seemed to 'allow psychology the right to assume the existence of unconscious mental activity'.[31] Freud understood that this 'right' could never be derived solely from the existence of inaccessible memories in hysterics, for there one was dealing with relatively unusual, psychologically abnormal phenomena whose relevance for psychology in general was disputable. But it was possible to use the limited knowledge of the neurologists as a starting point for bolder speculations that seemed to be licensed by a few selected authorities.

One way in which Freud established his position as more than a dedicated clinician was his readiness to apply his theories to phenomena and problems of everyday life. As he also had a talent for persuasive exposition he soon outdid any of his medical colleagues in recruiting a wide public to the view that insights gained in the neurologist's or psychiatrist's consulting room were relevant not only in the context of abnormal psychology, but in the lives of ordinary individuals.[32] At a very early stage in the emergence of what was to be called 'psychoanalysis' Freud turned to the explication of phenomena with which everyone was acquainted but that were widely shrugged off as being without serious intellectual interest. These were the phenomena of verbal humour, of dreams and of so-called parapraxes, slips of the tongue, slips of the pen, misreading, mislaying, bungled actions and inexplicable instances of forgetting.[33] In all these cases failures, distortions and implicit allusions of memory were involved. Freud's explanations of these phenomena helped to establish the plausibility of an interpretation of human memory that differed in some important respects from the received view.

For one thing, Freud was quite ready to upset the age-old image of memory as an archive, as a set of inscriptions engraved once and for all.[34] It was clear to him that memories were arranged in interconnected layers reaching back in time, so that no memory stood alone but formed part of a system of reminiscences in which the effect of later arrivals would depend on earlier deposits.[35] The interaction was reciprocal, so that later memories would also produce changes in earlier memories: 'Our childhood memories show us our earliest years not as they were but as they appeared at the later periods when the memories were aroused. In these periods of arousal, the childhood memories did not, as people are accustomed to say, *emerge*, they were *formed* at that time'.[36] The link between time and memory was an ancient one. Memory, as Aristotle had said, was of the past. But Freud's reflections seemed to introduce a new dimension into the relationship between memory and time. Memory was not only *of* time past, it also moved *with* time. The image of memory as a preservative, or as *only* a preservative, had to be given up. Living memory did not freeze time in the way that writing did, it accommodated itself to time and changed as time ran its course.

This insight received a potent expression in Freud's concept of *Nachträglichkeit* (deferred action, or simply deferral), a notion that appears early and not infrequently in his writings but whose meaning must be gathered from the context. Deferred action occurs whenever the trace of an earlier experience is modified by later events, especially the acquisition of a new cognitive context or biological maturation. The meaning of an earlier experience is changed when it can be interpreted within a framework of understanding that had not yet existed at the time of the earlier experience. It may also be changed when its memory is revived in an organism that has undergone changes in its level of sexual development. Thus childhood memories previously lacking any sexual connotation may become sexualized when they are revived in an individual in whom they now produce somatic reactions that did not occur before.[37] Retrospective change in the meaning of earlier memories also leads to change in the effect of these memories, the role that they play in the individual's self-understanding and in the formation of any neurotic symptoms. An early memory may seem relatively trivial to begin with, because it was not very meaningful to the small child, but may lead to great distress later when it is endowed with new meaning. For Freud memory was intrinsically temporal. It was not merely a container, a storage place for memory traces that did not change itself. Memory did not simply store a person's history, it *had* a history. For those trapped in the traditional understanding of memory as a static container, Freud's emphasis on the importance of early experience usually resulted in a profound misunderstanding that slanted his theories in the direction of a linear developmental determinism. In fact, the historical importance of his views on the effect of the past lies in their break with a conception of memory that had become an intellectual strait-jacket.

If Freud was right about the vulnerability of memory to time then the relationship of memory to truth was bound to be a troubled one. If memories were apt to change under the impact of subsequent understanding and experience, then few memories could be taken at face value, and certainly no memory that touched on sensitive areas of autobiography. Far from being reliable testimonies to the truth, personal memories had to be assumed to represent the truth in garbled, distorted and disguised forms. Yet Freud never seems to have lost his faith that somewhere beyond layers of distortion important truths were to be found, truths that held the key to the nervously ill person's suffering and the normal person's idiosyncrasies.

Uncovering the truth hidden by memory would require a special approach. Very early on Freud decided that hypnosis was not that approach. Hypnosis assigned a passive, somnambulant role to patients, which they either yielded to or rebelled against. In either case the path to the truth was blocked, because it was the patient's truth that was wanted, not the hypnotist's, or because no progress could be made in the face of rebellion. Only a collaborative relationship between two wide-awake partners could be expected to unravel the secrets of memory. The one would encourage the other to proceed from one memory fragment to another, gradually filling the gaps and correcting errors to recover a fully formed memory sequence.[38] A worthy goal, but it did not work in practice. Patients would piously promise their full collaboration, but very soon their silences, blockages, fidgeting, feigned fatigue and sly manoeuvres would make it obvious that they, or something in them, was resisting the whole process. Freud decided that the structure of interconnected memories was in fact being held in place by various intra-psychic 'defences' involving affective forces that resisted any uncovering of the truth. The only way forward seemed to be to confront these defences and to reveal them for what they were. Unravelling the skein of misleading memories therefore proceeded by an analysis of resistances, unmasking the defensive role of successive mnemic associations produced by the patient.

A new kind of therapeutic practice had been born, named *psychoanalysis* by Freud. Very soon other features of the new practice came to the fore, particularly *transference*, the tendency for hidden memories of early, affectively charged relationships to be expressed in feelings and conduct directed at the psychoanalyst. Action in the present, or 'acting out', substituted for remembering the past, implying a kind of memory that found expression in conduct rather than in conscious experience. Patients would typically resist any avowal of such tendencies, so that an analysis of the transference became a necessary component of the therapeutic process.

As he gained experience with the new procedures Freud began to amplify his practical suggestions for their use, partly through illustrative case-histories, partly through the development of an elaborate theoretical framework that provided a way of conceptualizing the course of psychoanalytic treatment. It turned out that others had begun to develop similar interests and to experiment with analogous procedures. Several of these now grouped themselves around Freud as their acknowledged intellectual leader, leading to the formation of the psychoanalytic movement and the institutionalization of psychoanalytic training, practice and doctrine.

Psychoanalysis has been characterized in various ways, as a sect, an intellectual or social movement, a pseudo-science, a force for cultural liberation and so on. But what gains it a place in the genealogy of memory is its resemblance to the arts of memory.[39] Here was another attempt at achieving a superior kind of knowledge by the application of techniques calculated to coax memory into performing feats that took it beyond its normal limitations. Psychoanalysis was sufficiently a product of its time to have explicit scientific pretensions. Like a science, it developed a technology designed to unlock some of the secrets of nature. But this technology had more in common with the technical framework of an art than with the precise methodological standards of a science. And the targets of its investigative practices resided not in the mute world over which the natural sciences sought control, but in the interpreted world of human intercommunication. Emerging and flourishing within a culture of autobiographical romanticism, it posited many of its knowledge objects as part of a private arena of inner psychological conflict.

But the burden of its cultural biases and its slightly ridiculous scientific pretensions do not provide valid grounds for denying the significance of psychoanalysis as, among other things, an art of memory. The therapeutic effectiveness of psychoanalysis is of course not the issue here, nor is the probative value of the mountains of evidence subsequently produced in confirmation or refutation of its specific theoretical propositions. It may be more illuminating to ask what psychoanalysis has contributed as art of memory than as therapy or science.

All arts of memory seek to improve on 'natural' memory in some way. The older arts offered assistance to a memory that was assumed to be willing but weak. Psychoanalysis, however, proceeded on the assumption that memory's most important failures were due not so much to its incapacity as to its unwillingness. To remedy this, what was needed was an art that would reduce this unwillingness and circumvent its effects. Such an art would have to break with the deeply ingrained prejudice that reproduction was the essence of memory. On the contrary, it would have to recognize the potency of forces that worked against reproduction and favoured forgetting. When these forces were active the products of memory were never copies, more or less complete, of some earlier input. Distortions would have taken place, so that the truth in memory became unrecognizable without the application of special techniques. Many of the most vivid memories of childhood were what psychoanalysts called *screen memories*, recollections whose true meaning was not to be found in their faithful reproduction of an actual event, but in their simultaneous expression of and defence against an unconscious fantasy.

In the tradition of the European Enlightenment all truths were considered to be reducible to unambiguous propositions about sensory experience or logical relationships. When memory was questioned about the truth it contained, those were the only kinds of truth to be considered. Post-Enlightenment mnemonics was designed to improve the mind's capacity for this kind of truth-telling. Psychoanalysis as an art of memory, however, was concerned with other kinds of truth. That fundamental reorientation was not without precedent. Freud's mentor and teacher, the neurologist Theodor Meynert (1833–92), had applied ideas derived from the anti-Enlightenment philosopher Arthur Schopenhauer (1788–1860) to the interaction of mind–brain systems. For Schopenhauer, human life is driven by an irrational force, the will, to which the intellect is forced to accommodate itself. One result of this conflict is the refusal to face unacceptable aspects of reality.[40]

The practice of psychoanalysis depended on the conviction that memory had two aspects, memory for feelings and memory for cognitive content. That was far from being a novel idea at the time. 'Emotional memory' had been a serious topic of contention in a period when it was common to make a fundamental distinction between two types of psychological phenomena, the intellectual and the affective.[41] In the latter part of the nineteenth century some writers, including T. Ribot,[42] reacted against what they perceived as a tendency to intellectualize memory, to talk of its contents in terms of 'ideas' that could be more or less clear and distinct, but that were in any case representational.[43] Ribot, on the contrary, believed that the memory of feeling states could also be preserved, and that such states could be re-experienced without being symbolically represented. For others, such as William James, what one remembered was the fact that one had had a particular feeling, not the feeling itself. Then, by an association of ideas, one could produce a new feeling that was similar to the old one.[44] Nevertheless, the concept of affective memory continued to have adherents.[45] Psychoanalytic theory and practice systematically distinguished between the affective and the intellectual aspects of memory. These aspects were not only treated as mutually irreducible but were regarded as frequently following a different course. In the case of any particular experience, the affective aspect might survive in conscious memory, whereas the cognitive component, the ideas and perceptions originally linked to the affect, might not. In that case the orphaned affect might convey a wordless kind of truth, one that could not be spoken or expressed in propositions, but that could in some sense be felt. The techniques of psychoanalysis were intended to make it speak, and, more particularly, to speak the truth. That was never easy, because affects whose original cognitive associations had become consciously inaccessible, had been 'repressed', often became attached to cognitions that disguised the true meaning of the affect.[46]

In other cases the affective component of a memory might have become repressed, while the cognitive component survived, at least in part. Such truncated memories concealed the significance they had for the one doing the remembering. The techniques of psychoanalysis were meant to expose that significance. Most often, however, they were applied to reveal how memory worked in previously unrecognized ways in a large group of phenomena that ranged from neurotic symptoms to parapraxes and symbolic productions. In all these cases, whatever the truth in memory, it was not the kind of truth contemplated by Enlightenment philosophy.

The emergence of psychoanalysis as a distinct body of doctrine and practice had been closely linked to the insight that the truth testified to by memory need not pertain to actual events and experiences, but to the desires and fears of the rememberer. When Freud first became involved in unravelling the reminiscences of hysterics he shared the common belief that a memory, however distorted, must pertain to something that had actually happened at some time in the past. Subsequently he concluded that this was not necessarily so, that the content of memories might seem real enough for the person concerned, but did not necessarily mirror an actual event. At this point he let go of any sharp distinction between memory and imagination, and replaced it with another: the distinction between memory and motive. What memory recalls depends on what a person wants or does not want to recall. Memory does not supply its own motivation; it is only a means for the expression of unconscious impulses.[47]

These impulses, however, are locked in more or less permanent conflict. Commonly, several, often incompatible desires are active at the same time and may all receive expression in a memory unconsciously distorted by fantasy. This emphasis on the ubiquity of psychic conflict was another distinguishing feature of Freud's vision of the human mind. Memory is not only at the service of unconscious impulses, it is at the service of *conflicting* impulses. A particular conscious construction, subjectively experienced as a memory, may simultaneously express an unconscious wish and a defence against the conscious avowal of that wish.

When people expressed their fantasies as memories they were objectively wrong, but it occurred to Freud that they 'must surely be right in some way'.[48] They were right in the sense that their fantasies were an expression of their desires and fears, and those were real enough. Moreover, the most important fantasies, desires and fears addressed in psychoanalytic practice were all unconscious. The hidden truth that psychoanalysis sought to uncover pertained to these. Of course, this is not the kind of reality attributed to facts and events in the outer world, but is 'objective' reality the only reality known to human experience? Feelings like hope and guilt, for which there may be little or no objective basis, can be as real to experience as the hardest of physical facts. Freud referred to this as *psychical reality*. The practice of psychoanalysis was addressed to psychical, not material, reality, and this made sense only on the assumption that subjective factors could be causally efficacious. What immediately made psychoanalysis controversial was its insistence that psychical reality was derived from biological instincts and was mostly unconscious. But in the long run, its most persistent critics were probably those who discounted subjectively generated psychological forces and believed that only 'objective' reality, in the form of brain processes or external stimuli, could have psychological effects.

As an art of memory, psychoanalysis was directed at revealing the hidden psychical reality of experiences that might consciously present themselves as memories. This it accomplished by clarifying the contribution of unconscious fantasies to these experiences. An original event, a *primal scene*, might stand at the beginning of a chain of reconstructions over time, but whether these subjective representations had any relationship to objective reality was not a concern of classical psychoanalysis, which concentrated on the relationship of reminiscence to unconscious fantasy. In pursuing this goal psychoanalysis introduced crucial elements of scepticism into the relationship of truth and memory: An experience that had the quality of a memory might not represent any objective truth at all, only a subjective truth in the form of an emotionally powerful, yet unconscious, fantasy.

Politics, truth and traumatic memory

Freud's ideas about the relative importance of external events and internal fantasies received a rude jolt during World War I. That catastrophe produced large numbers of soldiers who had broken down under the impact of undeniably horrible experiences and who were gradually recognized as psychological casualties rather than weaklings, malingerers or deserters. In line with the well-established trend towards the medicalization of human impairment, discussed in chapter 4, there was a strong movement to treat their collapse, not as a moral failure, but as a medical problem. The new diagnosis of 'war neurosis' gave expression to this trend.

Victims of the condition were often plagued for long periods by nightmares, by intrusive and highly disturbing memories, as well as by other symptoms previously associated with hysteria, including loss of speech, blindness, tremors and convulsions. Traumatic memory was implicated in cases of war neurosis because disabling symptoms persisted or appeared only after a significant lapse of time after the original traumatic experiences.

Exposure to violent shocks of external origin surely played a significant role in the aetiology of war neuroses; and that was reminiscent of the traumatic neuroses that had first been observed some years earlier in the wake of railway accidents and other disturbing events (see chapter 4). But psychoanalysis had moved away from paying much attention to externally inflicted traumatic experiences. How was it to deal with the traumatic neuroses of war?

Some of Freud's followers tried to interpret wartime breakdown without any fundamental change in the theoretical framework of psychoanalysis. However, Freud, as usual, did not feel bound by his previous pronouncements. Two years after the end of the war he published a fundamental revision of his views in a highly speculative little piece, provocatively titled *Beyond the Pleasure Principle*.[49] Much of that text is not directly relevant to the conceptualization of memory, but near the beginning Freud confronts the problem that traumatic memory poses for his theory. Under normal circumstances, memory works defensively, allowing relatively pleasant recollections into consciousness and keeping unpleasant aspects out, as far as possible. But in cases of traumatic war neurosis, extremely disturbing events are often experienced over and over again, usually in the nightmares that are a common symptom of that condition. The 'pleasure principle' that usually governs memory seems to have broken down. According to previous psychoanalytic expectations, the original experiences should have been repressed, to emerge only in disguised form in dreams.

Freud now postulates that memory can operate in two fundamentally different ways. I have described the first way in the previous section. The second way involves what Freud calls 'the compulsion to repeat'. This refers to an uncontrollable tendency to re-enact, to re-experience content stored in memory, no matter how disturbing that content may be. In the traumatic war neuroses we observe this in pure form. But Freud thinks the compulsion to repeat is always present, though under normal circumstances it is overlaid by defensive manoeuvres. For instance, in their feelings about their psychoanalyst analysands are compelled to repeat patterns they originally developed with their parents; this is 'transference', as already mentioned.

So it is not the compulsion to repeat that distinguishes the traumatic neuroses, but the failure of the defences that normally mitigate the effects of this compulsion. Under what conditions does such a failure occur? After the experience of the Great War, it seems to be clear that powerful traumata of external origin can result in rampant repetition compulsion and hence a breakdown in the psychological defences of everyday life. Another, more primitive, kind of defence takes over, the defence against 'the mental apparatus being flooded with large amounts of stimulus'.[50] In Freud's view, the repetitive return of the traumatic experience represents an attempt to 'master' that experience, to relive actively what was previously endured passively.

Though these speculations were too general to provide much direct help for dealing with the traumatic after-effects of war experience, they did seem to license the idea that memory might operate very differently under conditions of extreme trauma than under more normal conditions. The speculations of some psychoanalysts preserved the idea that different sorts of memory traces might be left behind by ordinary, adaptive experience and by the overwhelming experience of psychic trauma.[51]

None of these earlier attempts at conceptualizing traumatic memory of wartime experience seemed to be particularly troubled by the question of *truth* in the memories of afflicted soldiers. In effect, the medical personnel who originally assigned a case to the category of 'war neurosis' had already decided that question by making their diagnosis. When a soldier was not believed he was apt to be classified as a malingerer and not a medical casualty. Military bureaucracy required a clear distinction that favoured an either–or approach to the truthfulness of evidence based on individual memory. If one was dealing with a genuine casualty, the truth of what he had experienced automatically entitled him to medical care by the military, but if one was dealing with a hypochondriac, fantasist or malingerer there was no such entitlement. Subsequent theorizing was intended to explain the puzzle of genuine psychic trauma, not malingering, for which no further explanation was needed.[52]

The question of truth did arise obliquely in the context of the medical *treatment* of psychological casualties. In World War I, a few British psychiatrists achieved an alleviation of symptoms in some soldiers, who were encouraged to live through their traumatic experiences under hypnosis. But there was no unanimity on how this therapeutic success worked. One possibility was that the intervention of the therapist helped the patient to confront his overwhelming memories of fear and impotence in the face of unspeakable horror, to come to terms with these memories, to integrate them with his sense of self. This work of cognitive assimilation would require the construction of a narrative the patient could live with, not the recall of exactly what happened to him.

However, there was always another possibility. Therapeutic success could be ascribed to the emotional reliving of traumatic experiences, facilitated by hypnosis. This was to be expected if memories of these experiences produced neurotic symptoms only until they were 'abreacted' with full affective involvement. In post-war discussions of the issue, that was the position taken by William Brown, who claimed that recovery from the after-effects of trauma depended on an affective reproduction of the original experience. Others disagreed.[53] The issue lay dormant for many years, though W. Sargant, a prominent military psychiatrist of the World War II era, expressed the view that distortions of the truth, even fantasies, could sometimes be more effective in securing emotional release from the after-effects of trauma than a completely true memory.[54] But that view was not a matter of central concern, either to Sargant himself or to his colleagues. The question of truth in memory aroused little attention over a long period in the middle of the twentieth century. Moreover, the literature on traumatic memory remained marginal to the major preoccupations of the psychological disciplines at this time. Only during the last quarter of the century did the situation change, but then it did so very rapidly and massively. Many factors contributed to this change; some of them were internal to certain disciplinary sub-groups, but the more general effects could not have come about without the intervention of more powerful social forces. Before I return to the latter, I will briefly consider two of the more specific developments that are related to matters discussed earlier in this chapter.

In the clinical practice of psychoanalysis and its derivatives there was always an ambiguity about what exactly was being 'recovered'. The difficulty of separating memory and fantasy was well recognized. But Freud had held on to an archaeological, or more accurately a palaeontological metaphor, that left room for the digging up of bits and pieces of fossilized but true memory fragments. Perhaps the claimed link to natural science accounted for Freud's adherence to this model. In any case, it gradually lost its appeal among many of his later followers, who had no stake in this outdated analogy.

One of the results of this development was a gradual reassessment of the kind of truth that might be achieved in the course of psychoanalytic treatment. Physical analogies – digging up buried artefacts, or drying out flooded land and exposing it to view – were replaced by interest in the concept of narrative and its importance for understanding the therapeutic process. The truth that would be revealed in the course of psychoanalysis was a narrative truth, a coherent verbal construction that integrated what analysands had learned about themselves into a meaningful personal account. What they had learned about themselves depended, in part, on memories, but these were memories that would be the product of multiple reconstructions in the past, admixed with fantasies and the interpretative contributions of the therapist. Nobody could ever know what had *really* happened, nor did it really matter therapeutically. This would be the *historical truth*, as it might have been described by an impartial and uninvolved bystander, had there been one. But this hypothetical observer's account would be irrelevant in a therapeutic context where only subjective meaning counts, a meaning that would have to be expressed in the form of *narrative truth*.[55]

Quite independently of this development, the long-dormant science of testimony was reviving. Experimental studies of the reliability of eyewitness memory became more frequent, so that by the early 1980s there was a significant body of recent knowledge to refer to.[56] This development was presumably encouraged by a gradual tendency for North American judges to become more receptive to psychological expertise,[57] a change that was to be expected in light of the increased scientific respectability of psychology since the early years of the century. But on the other side of the divide, some experimental psychologists were now doing work of more obvious relevance to real-world problems. In the field of memory research, as I noted in chapter 5, there had been a call to pay more attention to natural contexts in the design of empirical studies. This legitimized a new generation of studies concerned with the reliability of memory for events witnessed under relatively realistic conditions.[58] Many, though not all, of these studies tended to demonstrate the vulnerability of human memory to relevant but misleading information supplied after the remembered event.[59]

I now turn to three readily identifiable historical developments that provided important social reference points for late twentieth-century conflicts about memory; these are, first, the large-scale effort to preserve the collective memory of the Nazi genocide of the Jews; second, the sequel to the Vietnam War that resulted in the conceptualization of post-traumatic stress as a medical syndrome; third, the spotlight directed at child sexual abuse during the final decades of the century. A very substantial literature exists on each of these topics and there can be no question here of doing anything more than point to them as particularly salient aspects of the cultural framework that gave late twentieth-century memory discourse its peculiar quality.

All three of these trends began to take shape in the decade beginning around 1970. There had been relatively limited interest in the Holocaust before then,[60] but by the end of the decade it seemed that the day was not far off when more commemorative and archival material would have been gathered on this subject than on any other subject in human history.[61] Survivors' recollections became more and more significant as they were woven into the fabric of collective memory.[62] Questions about the long-term effects of experiences in Nazi concentration and death camps had previously arisen in the context of compensation claims and the trial of war criminals; a new psychiatric category of 'concentration camp syndrome'[63] provided a medical basis for what were primarily moral and legal issues. In a continuation of the practice discussed in chapter 4, the medical label put the stamp of scientific fact on long-term suffering as a result of victimization.

But the recourse to medicalization in an altogether different historical context resulted in a new model of professional practice. As I pointed out in chapter 4, late nineteenth-century medical discourse on the pathology of memory was a discourse of accredited experts. In discussing their cases they distanced themselves from the humanity of their objects of scientific study. In quite a few instances, for example in connection with compensation claims by World War I war veterans (chapter 4), they actively opposed the interests of the victims. By contrast, the psychiatrists who worked with survivors of the Nazi genocide were morally on the side of the victims and applied their medical expertise in the service of that moral commitment.

A comparable form of professional involvement occurred in the context of helping American veterans of the Vietnam War with the psychological problems they encountered after their demobilization. Here was another group that could be said to be 'suffering from their reminiscences', though beyond that they had little in common with other such groups. For one thing, a significant section of them became politically active in taking their claims to a wider public; something that would have been unimaginable for the hysterical patients of 1900, and for which concentration camp survivors had little scope at first. In their political efforts at gaining recognition of their long-term suffering the veterans had the support of parts of the psychiatric profession and this ultimately resulted in a major political victory: the construction of a new diagnostic category of post-traumatic stress disorder (PTSD) and its inclusion in the standardized nosology of American psychiatry in 1980.[64] This codification of the psychic trauma concept made it possible to see post-combat disorder as but a specific example of a more generalized disorder that afflicted individuals who had been exposed to severe stress, such as the survivors of Nazi death camps.[65]

Initially, the situations that were thought to result in post-traumatic stress were typically ones that lay well outside the regular course of civilian life. However, around this time, cultural anxieties about the dangers of sexual abuse of children also began to be reflected in the professional literature on psychic trauma and its effect on memory. There were claims that such abuse was far more widespread than had been commonly supposed.[66] If these claims were true, even in part, then the concept of traumatic memory would acquire great significance for interpreting the experience of many individuals who had never been exposed to historically exceptional situations. Traumatic memory would become a tool not merely for understanding individual responses to situations in which the rules of ordinary civil life had been suspended, but for understanding responses to situations that were a not uncommon feature of civil life itself. That would not only increase the importance of the topic for the discipline of psychology, it would also realize a potential for politicization that had always been latent in discourse on traumatic memory.

Memories of abuse in childhood acquired a prominent political dimension when this topic became a significant issue for gender politics. The recovery of forgotten or repressed memories of childhood sexual abuse became a goal in which there was a convergence of personal and political benefit: personal because the confrontation with a buried past had healing properties, political because testifying to the pain and pervasiveness of sexual victimization would weaken the patriarchy.[67] But the convergence of the personal and the political applied also to other classes of victims. Memories of individual Holocaust survivors were crucially relevant to political issues of reparation and collective guilt. For organized Vietnam War veterans recognition of the claim that they were suffering from their memories became a significant political issue.

This explicit political dimension clearly distinguished the new wave of interest in the topic of traumatic memory from the earlier discourse on psychic trauma discussed in chapter 4. Not that certain moral–political implications could ever be avoided in a topic of this nature, but in the latter part of the twentieth century the social pressures to which the field was exposed assumed a far more directly political form.[68]

What had been politically inaudible in the early literature was the voice of the victim. As I indicated in chapter 4, the nineteenth-century medicalization of psychic injury had been based on a model of objectivity, borrowed from the natural sciences, in which the object of investigation is mute. Being the victim of psychic trauma meant belonging to a category established by medical science; it did not mean having a human identity with a social voice of one's own. Certainly, individual victims had an influence on their therapists, an influence that was generally unacknowledged and always underestimated.[69] But the voice of the victim had no professional authority, and, unlike the professional voice, had no ready means of participating in a public discourse.

That changed decisively in the trauma discourse of the late twentieth century. Although accredited experts remained indispensable, a significant number of them now interpreted their role as formulators and facilitators of victims' claims. There was a powerful alliance of professionals and victims, whether the victims were Holocaust survivors, Vietnam War veterans or abused women and children. As a result, the voice of the victim was no longer confined to therapeutic situations but could be heard in public fora that ranged from mass media to law courts and professional conclaves.[70] However, this was not without consequence for defining the issues that became salient for late twentieth-century memory discourse.

By far the most important of these issues was the question of truth in memory. What kind of truth, if any, did memory preserve? The social claims of the most prominent types of victim depended on the truthfulness of their testimony. But society already had institutions to adjudicate rights and wrongs on the basis of testimony; in other words, legal institutions. Their involvement tends to be taken for granted in highly litigious societies, and hence the deeper implications of their influence are seldom recognized. However, from a broader historical perspective, one feature of late twentieth-century memory discourse is striking: significant sections of this discourse appear to be fuelled by the forensic aspects of memory.

In legal institutions victims could launch claims for restitution by various means, punishment of perpetrators and material compensation being the most important. The adjudication of such claims depended on a decision about contested versions of the truth. Either the claimants' suffering is due to the agency being sued, or it is not. The proof is supplied, wholly or in large part, by the victim's memory. If the trauma were physical there would be physical traces to confirm its occurrence. Psychic trauma also leaves traces, but they are psychological. They were memory traces that held the truth on which the claims were based. It was only a matter of making them speak their truth; something that could be achieved through the interpretation of an expert or through the voice of victims in whom memory had assumed a communicable form. A successful restitution claim depended on memory's capacity to reflect the truth.

But the appeal to memory as a guarantor of veridical truth was not limited to the institutional level. In an age in which 'both individual and group identities are increasingly based on historical instances of victimization'[71] the memory of survivors of those events acquires a special foundational quality. For the survivors of wars and genocides this memory was only too accessible, and questions about its veracity, though sometimes troubling, were never fatal, because of an abundance of recorded historical evidence. It was different for survivors of childhood sexual abuse, where the crucial memory had not been accessible but had been 'recovered' in the course of therapeutic intervention. In many cases there was little or no independent evidence to back up the truth conveyed by these memories. Yet their veracity was fiercely defended by victims and therapists alike.

Doubts about the veracity of that memory were easily seen as threats to the identities that had been built upon them. In a post-modern twist of the venerable Lockean tradition that made personal memory the foundation of personal identity (see chapter 4), individuals could now acquire new identities by recovering key memories they did not know they had. Those key memories – of sexual abuse in childhood – were capable of transforming them from persons adrift amid a sea of troubles, into heroic survivors and exemplary members of redemptory groups. During the last two decades of the century, recovered memory therapy was widely seen as promising, not unlike religious conversion, to bring intelligible order into the lives of people who had failed to understand the source of their misery.[72]

Specific memories could provide foundational truths for individual lives only in so far as they had been preserved as a faithful record of certain defining events in the past. They had to constitute a hidden, though permanent and unaltered, residue that could be brought back to life with the assistance of a self-help group or an expert who functioned as midwife of memory, rather like a Socrates of the therapeutic age.[73]

The conception of memory promoted by the therapeutic practices of memory recovery converged rather well with the kind of memory relied on by legal and administrative institutions. In both contexts memory was required to act as a vehicle for preserving the truth of what had actually happened. To play that role, memory had to be seen as a stable repository of uncorrupted content. This kind of memory functioned as a guardian of some definitive, though not easily accessible truth; it only needed appropriate help to yield up this truth.

There was no need to create this conception of memory anew, because it resonated with the ancient inclination to understand internal memory through an analogy with inscriptions in external memory.[74] Notions of human memory as a kind of surface for receiving deep traces representing past experience had never died out. If anything, they had achieved a wider currency in modern times because they fitted in so well with the proliferation of recording technology. In this conceptualization the inscription captured by memory is essentially a copy or re-representation of some definitive version. For founding a legal or political claim based on truth revealed by memory there is really no alternative to this model of memory. To serve as the rock on which a new identity may be founded, autobiographical memory must be shorn of its indeterminacy and become 'a "text" that is incontrovertibly knowable and claimable'.[75]

Any hint that memory does not record and preserve a definitive record of events but actively constructs and reconstructs its offerings weakens its value as a guarantor of truth in both a public and a private context. Yet strong hints to that effect – even virtual certainties – were emerging, not only from the revived experimental study of testimony, but also from the cumulative results of studying reproductive memory under controlled conditions.[76] The experimental psychology of testimony largely confirmed that ordinary memory was not a source of reliable evidence. One could dismiss this work as irrelevant for the situations encountered by real-life victims of psychological trauma, but that would imply that memory operated differently under drastically different conditions. The case for the scientific plausibility of veridical traumatic memory seemed to require the postulate of a special memory system that was profoundly different from ordinary memory and operated only under conditions of psychological trauma. For most experimentalists, however, the phenomena regarded as special features of traumatic memory could all be explained in terms of the same processes that were thought to underlie memory in the psychological laboratory and in everyday life.[77]

Are there indeed two entirely different systems covered by the term 'memory', one a system for reconstructing the past to suit the present, the other a recording system that preserves the true past? In the closing years of the twentieth century this idea was given form in a theoretical model that had links to the experimental and neuropsychological literature of the day.[78] In this model memory is sharply divided into narrative and traumatic memory with contrasting properties. Narrative memory is the cognitive-representational kind familiar from daily life and psychology experiments. It is subject to cognitive reconstruction, and therefore unreliable, but it also permits voluntary recall. Traumatic memory, as conceived here, has affinities with the older notion of emotional memory in that recall depends on the revival of affect. As the originally experienced affect requires special conditions for its revival, the memory of the trauma is ordinarily unavailable to consciousness. Neuropsychologically, this memory is preserved in a non-representational way that has more in common with the retention of motor skills or conditioned reflexes than the retention of verbal knowledge. Before therapeutic intervention, the content of traumatic memory remains outside the influence of cognitive reconstruction – it has been etched on the body and retains its timeless accuracy.

It is not at all clear that a dualistic model delivers the kind of truth-preserving memory that is desirable for forensic and political purposes or for personal redemption through memory recovery. Those functions are really served only by narrative accounts of what really happened, and any non-representational traces would still have to be translated into such accounts to convey the truth about events in the past. That translation could not proceed without interpreting the *meaning* of somatic conditions which, being non-representational, cannot speak of anything in the past. Interpretation, however, would be no less a reconstructive activity than narrative memory itself.

Though proposals for a special kind of traumatic memory had been offered before, they were now made in the context of an embarrassing split among psychologists. Those clinicians whose practice was framed by a discourse of victims and survivors held fast to the notion that a memory of trauma could deliver veridical representations, though that memory may have been unavailable to voluntary recall for many years. However, many researchers in the tradition of experimental psychology and some clinicians considered that the overwhelming weight of empirical evidence cast doubt on the plausibility of this view. Popular beliefs, widespread even among psychologists, tended to support the idea of memory as a permanent storehouse and thus tended to favour the first group.[79] Some clinicians complained that this polarization of opinions undermined the credibility of their work.[80] Others took on the role of peacemaker.[81]

In fact, many of the participants in these debates implicitly shared some fundamental assumptions about human memory.[82] The formulation and significance of the issues under debate depended on these implicit assumptions, and that in turn determined how empirical questions were formulated and which empirical questions were regarded as relevant.

There was, first of all, the assumption that memory is essentially a transaction between a single individual and an objective reality outside the individual. Traditional memory experiments reflected this assumption – individuals are exposed to an objective stimulus and their memory for that stimulus is tested later. Studies of traumatic memory recovery assumed the same model, except that the nature of the original stimulus had to be inferred. But only some special real-life situations fit this model: remembering texts, especially for examinations, does. What the model leaves out is the common role of other people, and of cultural categories of understanding, both in constructing the original experience and its recall. With the recognition of this factor the whole idea of some definitive version of a truth to be reproduced becomes deeply problematical[83] and empirical studies designed to discover the conditions that favour or deflect this process lose much of their point.

A second shared assumption that helped to keep the debate going was the reification of memory. There was a tendency to treat memory as a separate object that could be clearly distinguished from other psychological objects, such as fantasy, imagination, the self and so on. Undoubtedly, it is necessary to make these distinctions for purposes of discussion and practical investigation. But to forget that the categories created by these differentiations are ultimately artefacts of human effort, and to speak of them as though they were distinct objects, each with a definitive set of intrinsic properties, amounts to reification. Unfortunately, empirical questions addressed to the real world but framed in terms of reified categories are apt to leave the significant issues unresolved.[84]

When memory becomes reified it is easily substituted for the person who does the remembering. It then plays a metonymic role, where political and ideological conflicts involving people take the form of debates about memory.[85] This was not uncommon in the closing years of the twentieth century, with the result that 'memory' became an *arena* in which battles were fought out that went far beyond psychological issues. These were battles of gender politics, battles about forensic practice, battles about the reality of collective anxieties and delusions, battles of special interest groups, battles about the limits of science, battles about the sources of individual unhappiness, battles about the control of history, to name a few. Inevitably, the psychological professions were drawn into these battles.[86]

There is some danger of this resulting in the weakening of perspectives on memory that are specifically psychological. The distinction between 'true' and 'false' memories is not a psychological distinction. Psychology, as I showed earlier in this chapter, found its terrain in the vast gap that separates truth-telling from lying. In a psychological context the distinction between 'recovered' and 'false' memory of trauma (or of anything else for that matter) is indeed artificial, but it may be crucial in other contexts, where everything hinges on a sharp division between what is considered true and what false.[87] It is not obvious that the psychological conceptualization of memory has profited from the importance accorded to non-psychological criteria in the 'memory wars' of the late twentieth century.

Notes

1. Platonism, as we saw in chapter 4, was interested in another kind of truth.
2. Carruthers, *Book of memory*, chapter 3, repeatedly emphasizes this point.
3. Aristotle, *On memory*, 449b, 450b.
4. The modern reader wants to ask, what past: my own personal past or the pastness of what the image depicts? But Aristotle never puts this question, because he is not bothered by the post-Cartesian subject–object distinction and the even more recent preoccupation with the psychology of the 'self'. Those developments created a framework within which the modern category of 'episodic memory' could be constructed (see chapters 5 and 6).
5. Thomas Hobbes (1588–1679) had problems with the Royal Society and its empirical methods (see S. Shapin and S. Schaffer, *Leviathan and the air pump: Hobbes, Boyle*

and the experimental life (Princeton, NJ: Princeton University Press, 1985). He held that memory and imagination were both nothing more than decaying sense and equated them: 'This decaying sense, when we would express the thing itself, we call Imagination, as I said before: But when we would express the decay, and signify that the same is fading, and old and past, it is called Memory. So that Imagination and Memory, are but one thing which for divers considerations hath divers names'. T. Hobbes, *Leviathan* (New York: Dutton, 1950; originally published 1651), p. 11. Hume was much more understanding of the importance of preserving the purity of reports based on sensory evidence for the practical conduct of science.

6. Hume, *Treatise*, Book I, parts 1.3 and 3.5; also appendix, p. 628.

7. For discussions, see Russell, *Analysis of mind*; and Malcolm, *Memory and mind*.

8. On the role of imagination in Hume, see the chapters by D. F. Norton, J. Biro and R. J. Fogelin in D. F. Norton (ed.), *The Cambridge companion to Hume* (Cambridge: Cambridge University Press, 1993).

9. I. Kant, *Critique of pure reason*, trans. N. K. Smith (New York: St Martin's Press, 1929; originally published 1787), A124–5. Also I. Kant, *Anthropology from a pragmatic point of view*, trans. M. J. McGregor (The Hague: Martinus Nijhoff, 1974; originally published 1797).

10. D. Gross, *Lost time: On remembering and forgetting in late modern culture* (Amherst, MA: University of Massachusetts Press, 2000).

11. Different translators render Aristotle's Greek terms in different ways. The general nature of the distinction is, however, quite clear.

12. The details were discussed in chapter 5.

13. The category of 'autobiographical memory' only began to gain academic currency in the 1980s. An early collection was D. C. Rubin (ed.), *Autobiographical memory* (Cambridge: Cambridge University Press, 1986). Five years later, the great bulk of the material for a historical review came from medical psychology: see B. M. Ross, *Remembering the personal past: Descriptions of autobiographical memory* (New York: Oxford University Press, 1991). For a historically sensitive review of problems in the area of personal memory, see Draaisma, *Why life speeds up*.

14. Matsuda, *Memory of the modern*, p. 103.

15. The German courts were more receptive to the new science than the French. Consequently, Stern was soon joined by other experts in a field that had its own journal and research institute. See S. L. Sporer, 'A brief history of the psychology of testimony', *Current Psychological Reviews* 2 (1982), 323–40.

16. This diagnosis derives from ideas of Michel Foucault applied to the case of psychology by Nicholas Rose in *The psychological complex* (London: Routledge, 1985), and in 'Calculable minds and manageable individuals', *History of the Human Sciences* 1 (1988), 179–200. However, both Binet and Stern were transitional figures in regard to the new calculating psychology, which they did not embrace with the unreserved enthusiasm of their successors. I refer to other aspects of Stern's work in chapter 9. For the historical background of Binet's work, see R. Foschi and E. Cicciola, 'Politics and naturalism in the 20th century psychology of Alfred Binet', *History of Psychology* 9 (2006), 267–89. On Stern, see J. T. Lamiell, 'William Stern: More than "the IQ guy"', in G. A. Kimble, C. A. Boneau and M. Wertheimer (eds.), *Portraits of pioneers in psychology* (Hillsdale, NJ: Erlbaum, 1996), vol. II, p. 73–85; also I. Staeuble, 'Psychologie im Dienste praktischer Kulturaufgaben – Zur Realisierung von William Sterns Programm 1903–1933', in A. Schorr and J.Wehner (eds.), *Psychologiegeschichte heute* (Göttingen: Hogrefe, 1990), pp. 164–73.

17. The astounding career of 'suggestion' as a pseudo-scientific explanatory term began in the 1860s with A. A. Liébeault's largely successful medical appropriation of hypnosis. In an attempt to demystify hypnotic effects he attributed them to 'suggestion', a perfectly natural phenomenon based on the transmission of ideas from one mind to another through speech. The later extension of 'suggestion' to the field of

social and political psychology is associated with the spectacular success of Gustave Le Bon's popular tract, *Psychologie des foules* (1895), translated as *The crowd: A study of the popular mind* (New York: Viking, 1960).

18. A. Binet, *La suggestibilité* (Paris: Schleicher, 1900).

19. Charles Darwin's sketch of observations on his own infant was an early stimulus: C. Darwin, 'A biographical sketch of an infant', *Mind* 2 (1877), 285–94. In Germany extensive pioneering studies had been published by Wilhelm Preyer in the 1880s. By the time Stern entered the field the recording of children's natural behaviour had become an international industry.

20. See the bibliography in C. Stern and W. Stern, *Recollection, testimony, and lying in early childhood*, trans. J. T. Lamiell (Washington, DC: American Psychological Association, 1999; German original, 1909).

21. Sporer, 'Psychology of testimony'; and E. Müller-Luckmann, 'William Stern und die Forensische Psychologie', in W. Deutsch (ed.), *Die verborgene Aktualität von William Stern* (Bern: Peter Lang, 1991), pp. 107–16.

22. Stern and Stern, *Recollection, testimony, and lying*, p. 35.

23. In his widely used text *Psychology of early childhood* (New York: Henry Holt, 1924; German original, 1914) Stern generalized as follows: 'The sharp demarcation between objective and subjective – of real and apparent – is, after all, of very gradual growth, and ... passes through all possible degrees of transition' (p. 251).

24. Early American reviews of this area were little more than reports of what was being done in Europe. G. M. Whipple, 'The observer as reporter: A survey of the "Psychology of testimony"', *Psychological Bulletin* 6 (1909), 153–70.

25. W. D. Loh, 'Psychological research: Past and present', *Michigan Law Review* 79 (1981), 659–707.

26. Hugo Münsterberg, who had been imported by William James to look after experimental psychology at Harvard, made a determined but notoriously unsuccessful attempt to persuade the American courts of the value of psychological expertise in assessing the reliability of witnesses: H. Münsterberg, *On the witness stand: Essays on psychology and crime* (New York: Clark Boardman, 1909/1949). The authoritative legal response arrived in the form of J. H. Wigmore, 'Professor Münsterberg and the psychology of evidence', *Illinois Law Review* 3 (1909), 399–445. Münsterberg's style may have been brash, but he was clear about the complications introduced by psychological considerations: 'It is so much easier everywhere to be satisfied with sharp demarcation lines and to listen only to yes or no; the man is sane or insane, and if he is sane, he speaks the truth or he lies. The psychologist would upset this satisfaction completely ... We are too easily inclined to confuse the idea of truth in a subjective and in an objective sense' (Münsterberg, *On the witness stand*, pp. 46–7). For insightful comment on the significance of Münsterberg's clash with the American legal tradition, see M. Hale Jr, *Human science and social order: Hugo Münsterberg and the origins of applied psychology* (Philadelphia: Temple University Press, 1980), pp. 120–1.

27. 'Memory has no origin or root in a past object or experience: there are no memories *from* childhood, only *of* childhood. The French and, very differently, the British interest is not recovering secondarily repressed memories but with the formation of memory itself.' J. Mitchell, 'Memory and psychoanalysis', in P. Fara and K. Patterson (eds.), *Memory: The Darwin College lectures* (Cambridge: Cambridge University Press, 1998), pp. 95–112 (p. 106).

28. J. Breuer, and S. Freud, *Studies on hysteria*, in J. Strachey (ed.), *The standard edition of the complete psychological works of Sigmund Freud* (London: Hogarth Press, 1962), vol. II.

29. On the complexities of Janet's views about the curative effects of remembering, see R. Leys, *Trauma: A genealogy* (Chicago: University of Chicago Press, 2000).

30. Sulloway, *Freud: Biologist of the mind*.

31. On Freud and Hering, see Strachey, *The standard edition of the complete psychological works of Sigmund Freud* (London Hogarth Press, 1962) vol. XIV, p. 205.

32. This is not to suggest any single-handed achievement by Freud in dissolving rigid boundaries between the normal and the abnormal that were already being corroded by many other factors.

33. S. Freud, *The interpretation of dreams*, in Strachey, *Standard edition*, vols. IV–V; *The psychopathology of everyday life*, in Strachey, *Standard edition*, vol. VI; *Jokes and their relation to the unconscious*, in Strachey, *Standard edition*, vol. VIII. The term 'parapraxis' had to be invented to render Freud's category of *Fehlleistung* under which he grouped phenomena whose common features had not previously been considered of great theoretical interest.

34. Quite late in life, Freud wrote a note on a recently marketed invention, the so-called mystic writing-pad (S. Freud, 'A note upon the "mystic writing-pad"', in Strachey, *Standard edition*, vol. XIX). This device combined features of pen-on-paper and chalk-on-blackboard; it allowed new inscriptions to be superimposed on previous ones, not by erasing the old inscriptions but by making them *invisible*. Explicitly, he described the device as a metaphor for perception (rather than memory), but he also appreciated its modelling of *layers* of inscriptions in memory. For the layers of interpretation that can be constructed around Freud's interest in this device, see D. F. Krell, *Of memory, reminiscence, and writing* (Bloomington: Indiana University Press, 1990).

35. In 1896 he italicized this claim: 'No hysterical symptom can arise from a real experience alone, but in every case the memory of earlier experiences awakened in association to it plays a part in causing the symptom.' Strachey, *Standard edition*, vol. III, p. 197.

36. Strachey, *Standard edition*, vol. III, p. 322.

37. Earlier on, Freud emphasized the developmental changes of puberty, but with his acceptance of the reality of infantile sexuality he often moved the effects of sexual development back in time. However, this did not require any change in the principle of *Nachträglichkeit*, which he continued to evoke. There is an excellent discussion of this principle in J. Laplanche and J.-B. Pontalis, *The language of psycho-analysis* (New York: Norton, 1973), pp. 111–14.

38. The point that psychoanalysts always had to reconstruct childhood 'scenes' from memory fragments is often overlooked, not least by Freud himself. See A. Esterson, 'Jeffrey Masson and Freud's seduction theory: A new fable based on old myths', *History of the Human Sciences* 11 (1998), 1–22; also J. G. Schimek, 'Fact and fantasy in the seduction theory: A historical review', *Journal of the American Psychoanalytic Association* 35 (1987), 937–65.

39. See Hutton, *History as an art of memory*.

40. When he came to write his *History of the psychoanalytic movement* Freud, explicitly referred to the 'parallel' between his concept of repression and 'an element of Schopenhauer's philosophy': Strachey, *Standard edition*, vol. XIV, p. 11. This topic is discussed at greater length in J. McGrath, *Freud's discovery of psychoanalysis: The politics of hysteria* (Ithaca, NY: Cornell University Press, 1986). McGrath also shows that, in spite of its popularity, the derivation of Freud's psychology from that of Herbart is a historical myth.

41. Alexander Bain, Wilhelm Wundt and Sigmund Freud are only three of the better-known authorities to make this distinction.

42. See chapter 6.

43. This stance is often traced to Descartes, but the empiricists of the eighteenth century were very effective in continuing the trend.

44. James, *Principles*, vol. II, p. 474.

45. E. Claparède, 'La question de la "mémoire" affective', *Archives de psychologie* 10 (1911), 361–77.

46. Note that the centrepiece of Freud's contribution to the history of memory is the notion of 'defence', *not* the concept of repression, which merely provides a vague description of one aspect of the operations of defence. What was always primary in classical psychoanalysis was function (i.e. defence), not mechanism. On Freud's usual vagueness concerning the relationship between consciousness and repression and the later mechanization of the concept of repression, see M.H. Erdelyi, 'Repression, reconstruction and defense: History and integration of the psychoanalytic and experimental frameworks', in J. Singer (ed.), *Repression and dissociation: Implications for personality theory, psychopathology, and health* (Chicago: University of Chicago Press, 1990), pp. 1–31.

47. Freud's thinking at this crucial juncture in the genesis of psychoanalysis is documented in his letters to his then colleague and confidant, Wilhelm Fliess. See S. Freud, *The complete letters of Sigmund Freud to Wilhelm Fliess*, ed. and trans. J.M. Masson (Cambridge, MA: Harvard University Press, 1985).

48. Strachey, *Standard edition*, vol. XVI, p. 368.

49. S. Freud, *Beyond the pleasure principle* (New York: Norton, 1920/1975).

50. Freud, *Beyond the pleasure principle*, p. 23. The idea of protection against flooding by excessive stimulation was not an on the spot invention. It had played an important role in Freud's unpublished pre-psychoanalytic (1895) attempt to construct a model of the psychic apparatus. See Strachey, *Standard edition*, vol. I.

51. For a valuable analysis of the relevant contributions of Sandor Ferenczi and Abram Kardiner and the psychiatric history of the trauma concept, see Leys, *Trauma*.

52. For the history of military psychiatry in the twentieth century, see B. Shephard, *A war of nerves: Soldiers and psychiatrists in the twentieth century* (Cambridge, MA: Harvard University Press, 2001).

53. W. Brown, 'The revival of emotional memories and its therapeutic value', *British Journal of Medical Psychology* 1 (1920), 16–33. (Brown's views were controversial and were published with contrary comments by C.S. Myers and W. McDougall.)

54. See the discussion in Leys, *Trauma*, pp. 202–3.

55. The distinction between narrative and historical truth was presented most incisively by Donald P. Spence in *Narrative truth and historical truth* (New York: Norton, 1982).

56. In the US, this field of psychological research hardly had an identity before the 1970s, but at the end of that decade two texts (one by a Canadian author) were available: E.F. Loftus, *Eyewitness testimony* (Cambridge, MA: Harvard University Press, 1979); and A.D. Yarmey, *The psychology of eyewitness testimony* (New York: Free Press, 1979). Five years later there was enough activity and interest in the field for an edited collection of contributions: G.L. Wells and E.F. Loftus (eds.), *Eyewitness testimony: Psychological perspectives* (New York: Cambridge University Press, 1984).

57. S.J. Ceci and M. Bruck, *Jeopardy in the courtroom: A scientific analysis of children's testimony* (Washington, DC: American Psychological Association, 1995), p. 64.

58. Wells and Loftus, *Eyewitness testimony*, p. 7.

59. E.F. Loftus and G.R. Loftus, 'On the permanence of stored information in the human brain', *American Psychologist* 35 (1980), 409–20.

60. P. Novick, *The holocaust in American life* (Boston: Houghton Mifflin, 1999)

61. G.M. Kren and L. Rappaport, *The holocaust and the crisis of human behavior* (New York: Holmes & Meier, 1980).

62. S. Friedlander, *When memory comes* (New York: Farrar, Straus, Giroux, 1979).

63. L. Eitinger, 'Pathology of the concentration camp syndrome', *Archives of General Psychiatry* 18 (1961), 371–9.

64. *Diagnostic and statistical manual of mental disorders*, 3rd edn (American Psychiatric Association, 1980). Some changes were made in subsequent versions but PTSD remained as a diagnostic entity.

65. For much more extensive analyses of this development than I am able to give here, see A. Young, *The harmony of illusions: Inventing post-traumatic stress disorder* (Princeton, NJ: Princeton University Press, 1995); and W. J. Scott, 'PTSD in DSM-III: A case in the politics of diagnosis and disease', *Social Problems* 37 (1990), 294–310.

66. These anxieties tended to focus on two caring relationships marked by strong sexual taboos – those of father and daughter and of day-care providers and their charges. For influential examples, see J. L. Herman, *Father–daughter incest* (Cambridge, MA: Harvard University Press, 1981); and D. Finkelhor, L. M. Williams and N. Burns, *Nursery crimes: Sexual abuse in day care* (Newbury Park, CA: Sage, 1988).

67. J. L. Herman, *Trauma and recovery* (New York: Basic Books, 1992).

68. In 1999 the United States Congress unanimously condemned a technical psychological article on the after-effects of child sexual abuse, published in a reputable academic journal, for being morally and scientifically objectionable. Things can hardly become more political than that. But this highly symbolic act merely marked a stage in the development of political pressures that had been building up for a number of years. On the historically specific socio-political context of knowledge about memory, see J. Hult, 'The re-emergence of memory recovery: Return of seduction theory and birth of survivorship', *History of the Human Sciences* 18 (2005), pp. 127–42.

69. The extent of that influence has been appreciated only in relatively recent times. Some now regard the entire history of psychiatry as a co-construction of psychiatrists and their patients; see M. Borch-Jacobsen, 'Making psychiatric history: Madness as *folie à plusieurs*', *History of the Human Sciences* 14 (2001), 19–38. A brilliant fictionalized account of this phenomenon during World War I is to be found in the novels constituting the *Regeneration* trilogy by Pat Barker (New York: Penguin Books, 1998).

70. 'No movement in criminal law has been more powerful in the last twenty years than the victims' rights movement, which has sought to enhance the place of the victim in the criminal process.' Paul Gewirtz, 1995, cited in A. Douglas and T. A. Vogler, *Witness and memory: The discourse of trauma* (New York: Routledge, 2003), p. 38. Eventually, the notion of victimhood, especially in the form of a psychiatric condition like PTSD, becomes so debased that it can be marshalled in the defence of torturers and murderers. For an illustrative South African case, see L. J. Nicholas and L. Coleridge, 'Expert witness testimony in the criminal trial of Eugene de Kock: A critique of the posttraumatic stress disorder (PTSD) defence', *South African Journal of Psychology* 30 (2000), 33–6.

71. Douglas and Vogler, *Witness and memory*, p. 12.

72. 'This wish for a clarifying truth is the wellspring of religious experiences and recovered memories alike. With recovered memories, the vividness and verisimilitude of the memory dispel nagging uncertainty over its origin or meaning. It feels transparent and externally imposed, liberating the sufferer from some oppressive internal experience. An element of projection may be involved in such memories, as dreaded or unwanted aspects of the self are externalized onto a past scene, relieving the individual of anxiety.' J. Haaken, *Pillar of salt: Gender, memory, and the perils of looking back* (New Brunswick, NJ: Rutgers University Press, 1998), p. 253–4. On the significant role of memory in stabilizing and justifying self-designated identity, see A. Megill, 'History, memory, identity', *History of the Human Sciences* 11 (1998), 37–62.

73. Several times in the course of this history I have mentioned that the conceptualization of memory has often been linked to particular techniques and practices directed at memory. 'Recovered memory' does not seem to be exceptional in this respect. In interviews, therapists indicated that special techniques to help clients remember had been used in 42 per cent of the cases under review. B. Andrews, 'Recovered

memories in therapy: Clinicians' beliefs and practices', in G.M. Davies and T. Dalgleish (eds.), *Recovered memories: Seeking the middle ground* (New York: Wiley, 2001), pp. 189–204.

74. See chapter 2.

75. Haaken, *Pillar of salt*, p. 110. For a more extended discussion of written texts as templates for the construction of life histories, see S. Engel, *Context is everything: The nature of memory* (New York: W.H. Freeman, 1999), chapter 5.

76. S.J. Ceci and M. Bruck, 'Jeopardy in the courtroom'; E.F. Loftus and M.R. Klinger, *The myth of repressed memory: False memories and allegations of sexual abuse* (New York: St Martin's Press, 1994).

77. For a comprehensive exposition, see R.J. McNally, *Remembering trauma* (Cambridge, MA: Harvard University Press, 2003).

78. B.A. van der Kolk, 'Trauma and memory', in B.A. van der Kolk, A.C. McFarlane and L. Weisaeth (eds.), *Traumatic stress: The effects of overwhelming experience on mind, body and society* (New York: Guilford Press, 1996), pp. 279–302.

79. The tenacity of these beliefs was illustrated by several studies, including Loftus and Loftus, 'On the permanence of stored information'; and M.D. Yapko, 'Suggestibility and repressed memories of abuse', *American Journal of Clinical Hypnosis* 36 (1994), 163–71.

80. C.A. Courtois, 'Delayed memories of child sexual abuse: Critique of the controversy and clinical guidelines', in M.A. Conway (ed.), *Recovered memories and false memories* (New York: Oxford University Press, 1997), pp. 206–29.

81. D.S. Lindsay, 'Depolarizing views on recovered memory experiences', in S.J. Lynn and K.M. McConkey (eds.), *Truth in memory* (New York: Guilford Press, 1998), pp. 481–94.

82. J. Prager, *Presenting the past: Psychoanalysis and the sociology of misremembering* (Cambridge, MA: Harvard University Press, 1998).

83. I return to this issue in the final section of this book.

84. In spite of the considerable volume of current research, there was little agreement on 'what science says' in late twentieth-century discussions of traumatic memory. See K. Pezdek and W.P. Banks (eds.), *The recovered memory/false memory debate* (New York: Academic Press, 1996). For examples of how 'fact-making on either side of the debate is a social enterprise', see C. Macmartin and A.D. Yarmey, 'Rhetoric and the recovered memory debate', *Canadian Psychology*, 40 (1999), 343–58.

85. S. Campbell, *Relational remembering: Rethinking the memory wars* (New York: Rowman & Littlefield, 2003).

86. One effect of this involvement was the rhetorical construction of different historical backgrounds for current debates: C. Howard and K. Tuffin, 'Repression in retrospect: Constructing history in the "memory debate"', *History of the Human Sciences* 15 (2002), 75–93. I have not been involved in these debates, and in the present chapter I have tried to avoid rhetorical excesses but, as Howard and Tuffin observe, 'every analysis is predicated on selection' (p. 91). In my own selection for this chapter I have highlighted those aspects that seemed to exhibit broader historical discontinuities and, occasionally, continuities.

87. L.S. Brown, 'On the construction of truth and falsity: Whose history?', in Pezdek and Banks, *Recovered memory debate*, pp. 341–53 (p. 346).

8   A place for memory

Where is memory?

Unlike some other capabilities of the human soul, memory has been assigned its own place in the body for a very long time. Aristotle believed it resided in the heart, but a medical tradition systematized by Galen located it in the brain. This tradition, which dominated European medical speculation for well over a thousand years, located the powers of the soul in the ventricles, conceptualized as chambers of the brain filled with fluid. Three such ventricles were commonly distinguished, located in the front, middle and back of the brain respectively. Memory was regularly allocated to the posterior ventricle. Whereas medieval Christian authorities tended to favour a location in a cavity of the brain, the Arabic–Aristotelian tradition allowed that memory's place might be in the brain tissue.

Physicians had cause to reflect on the powers of memory, not only because of the role it played in their own training and practice, but also because they were occasionally faced with cases of memory failure that seemed to be associated with disease or physical injury. In his *Natural History* Pliny the Elder, for example, mentions the case of a man struck by a stone who forgot how to read and write but nothing else, and another who fell from a high roof and forgot his mother, relatives and friends.[1] If one already thinks of memories as inscriptions it is easy to accept that these inscriptions are *locatable* in some specific part or parts of the body. That leads to questions about the identity of those parts. With that kind of question in mind, the association of memory loss and physical injury becomes interesting, because it suggests that different kinds of memory may be locatable in different body parts.

The Galenic medical tradition commonly distinguished the three faculties of *phantasia*, *cogitatio* and *memoria* and assigned them to the anterior, middle and posterior ventricles of the brain respectively. That provided a basis for classifying cases of mental failure that were thought to be the result of injury to the brain. If the injury affected the posterior ventricle this would show up as some kind of memory impairment, while other functions remained unaffected. If more than one ventricle were injured, more complex forms of impairment would result.[2] Physical means for improving the memory were widely recommended. Some of these had a general effect, such as baths, moderation in eating, drinking and sleeping and the avoidance of certain foods. But local applications of heat and ointments to the back of the head were considered particularly effective, because that area was close to the seat of memory in the posterior ventricle.[3]

However, medical considerations were far from being the most important determinants of medieval memory discourse. According to the theologians, there was also a kind of memory that survived the death of the body and was not physically localizable, being part of the immortal soul. In so far as other forms of memory were assigned a location in the brain, this was not done on the basis of any empirical evidence but of philosophical and theological considerations.[4] Thus, when philosopher-theologians decided to multiply the number of sub-divisions among faculties of the soul, the number of spatially distinct areas shown in diagrams of the head also increased. These were now usually referred to as 'cells', and there were often five of them.[5] To the post-Cartesian mind it is important to decide whether these were physically distinct or conceptually distinct areas, but at the time these areas were invented this distinction was blurred. In the same manuscript memory would sometimes be described in terms of mental recall and then, quite unproblematically, in terms of the fluids that filled the posterior ventricle.

Among the philosophical issues that were intensely debated in the late Middle Ages and Renaissance there was one that had considerable historical relevance for the question of localization. Aristotle had already wondered whether the soul was present in the body as a whole and in each of its parts. This led to the question of whether distinctions in the operations of the soul were to be traced to distinctions in the body. Some late medieval philosophers argued that because the soul, with all its different capacities, was present everywhere in the body, the reason for the soul's different activities must be sought in the structure and nature of the bodily organ associated with each operation. Thus the soul may have a potential for vision, but the way vision actually works depends on the way the eye works.[6]

Such a doctrine could provide encouragement for taking a closer look at the organs of the body, including the brain, with a view to elucidating their contribution to the operations of the soul. By the sixteenth century systematic anatomical studies, particularly those of Vesalius (1514–64) had begun to downgrade the status of the cavities of the brain in the operations of the soul. If memory had a bodily organ, the solid matter of the brain gradually became a more likely candidate. With greater certainty about gross brain anatomy, memory was localized in the cerebrum rather than the cerebellum or medulla oblongata. But a major seventeenth-century anatomist, Thomas Willis, would still see the cerebral medulla, rather than the cortex, as the most likely seat of memory.[7] The inner regions of the cerebrum, which Willis referred to indiscriminately as the corpus callosum, were an area in which the *animal spirits* were active. Their role in memory was a matter of some interest in the seventeenth century, as was noted in chapter 2.

By then, animal spirits were beginning to be thought of in purely somatic terms, a component of the physical body, but in their previous history they had straddled the modern mind–body divide. They were part of a legacy of various kinds of 'spirits' that inhabited both microcosm and macrocosm and had psychical as well as tangible qualities.[8] Animal spirits were fluid and volatile, in contrast to the more solid parts of the living body. They had long been involved in communication between various parts of the body and between the body and the cosmos. But in the seventeenth and eighteenth centuries they were incorporated into a physicalistic physiology that was based on a dualistic separation of soul and body. An early and influential example of this was provided by Descartes. As described in chapter 2, he imagined the seat of bodily memory by analogy with a woven cloth that has tiny gaps between the fibres. These gaps formed patterns by their distance from each other, their difference in size, their relative narrowness and so on. But this patterning was affected by the animal spirits arriving at the gaps from nerves and blood vessels supplying the brain. The flow of the spirits was in turn affected by events in the sensory organs and other parts of the body. Descartes therefore seems to imply that patterns of sensory stimulation are replicated by patterns in the part of the brain that is like woven cloth, and that this accounts for sensory memory. (Intellectual memory is quite another matter and depends on the soul, not the body.)

It has been suggested that the role played by the animal spirits in this kind of memory model was at variance with the traditional representation of memories as separately stored entities. Descartes seems to have had 'at least an inchoate understanding'[9] of what would much later be called 'superpositional storage', namely, that the achievements of memory may be due to patterns of activation with a wide spatial distribution in the brain without any need for distinct memory images, each stored in its particular spot. Differences between memories would then depend on differences in the pattern of potential activation rather than on differences in the localization of the memory trace. Different memories could be stored in the same spatial location.

Though it is unlikely that Descartes fully grasped the implications of his speculations regarding the physical basis of memory, his model does signal the issues that were to become salient in post-Cartesian discourse about the localization of memory in physical space. Were there really two kinds of memory, one dependent on physical processes localized in a specific part of the body, the other not physically localizable? And if there were two kinds, what was the relationship between the two? As for memory's physical localization, did one have to think of this in terms of geographically distinct areas for different memories and kinds of memories, or was there an alternative, as Descartes himself perhaps implied?

The means for providing definitive answers to these questions were not available and what ensued were several centuries of speculation. Empiricist mental philosophers, such as Locke and Hume,[10] had an apparently sensible way of reacting to this situation. Let us leave aside anatomy and what was then called the 'animal economy', they said, and concentrate on what the inner sense reveals about the human mind, including memory. In their discourse the question of physical localization is simply sidestepped. During the eighteenth century this was undoubtedly the dominant attitude, and the issue of localization did not trouble many minds. It was the advent of phrenology that marked a major turning-point.

Generic phrenology

Phrenology advocated cerebral localization with a vengeance. Its popular diagrams and models of the human head displayed neatly separated brain areas, each devoted to a specific psychological function. Contrary to some textbook accounts, many respected contemporaries took phrenology quite seriously.[11] It aroused fierce and widespread controversy precisely because it gave radical expression to relatively new beliefs that proved highly attractive in an industrializing age that increasingly looked to science rather than religion for answers to its problems. Although speculation about a somatic aspect of memory had existed for centuries, it was only in the nineteenth century that the localization of memory in the brain became an intensely debated issue that divided modernists and traditionalists. On one side were those looking for the material seat of mental powers, and given the prevailing understanding of science, that meant finding a distinct location in physical space. Only the brain offered itself as an appropriate site for such endeavours. On the other side were those who perceived this enterprise as a threat to the immortal soul, or at least to free will and morality. Their best-known representative was Pierre Flourens (1794–1867), whose experiments on pigeons indicated that loss of 'intelligence' in these animals was correlated with the *amount* of brain tissue destroyed, not its location. Using experiments on pigeons to refute localization in humans was a questionable scientific tactic even then, but using science to refute the scientific materialists seemed like a neat move to those who shared Flourens' concern about the implications of Gall's doctrines for free will, and therefore for the moral order.[12]

But Gall's was only the historically first version of phrenology. As such it was crude, and over the years became scientifically unsupportable. But just when it had ceased to be of any account in scientific circles it rose from the grave in a far more viable form. The name 'phrenology', however, had become a casualty of the earlier disputes and had been pre-empted by the charlatans who claimed to be in Gall's direct line of succession. One has to distinguish between Gall's specific instantiation of phrenology and 'phrenology' as a generic category whose supporters differed among themselves in certain respects but shared certain fundamental principles.[13]

Generic phrenology represents the conviction that all and every aspect of mental life has a specific location in the brain. Hence there are no mental activities that are not locatable somewhere in the space of the brain. This space is not homogeneous, but is divided up into distinct regions that can be clearly distinguished from one another by technical means. (It is the advances in these technical means that are mainly responsible for the differences between earlier and later versions of phrenology.) The differentiation of brain space is correlated with a differentiation of psychological functions.[14] In later versions of phrenology it was recognized that this correlation did not necessarily imply point-to-point correspondence, that one physical region might house several (related) psychological functions and that the location of a complex psychological function might be distributed over several brain regions. But the notion of distinct functions and regions was always maintained.

A further essential feature of the phrenological attitude is the insistence on the *fixity* of the distinctions among physical regions and psychological functions, a fixity that is forcefully conveyed by the diagrams of brains or brain parts that have been so characteristic of the phrenological orientation from the beginning. The lines, colours or shadings that separate the parts are of course artefacts contributed by the phrenologist, whether imposed on a nineteenth-century skull or a twentieth-century photographic reproduction. But the context in which these artefacts are presented conveys the impression that they mark divisions imposed by nature itself. Phrenological-type diagrams, moreover, have only spatial dimensions – the temporal dimension is absent. What are shown are divisions and distinctions that are *fixed in time*. In the phrenological world there is no room for the transformation of structures over time, no accommodation of a developmental perspective. Indeed, if it were admitted that fundamental features of the activity of both brain and mind were profoundly affected by development over time, it would destroy the stable platform for psychological analysis that phrenology seeks to present. That outcome would be likely to meet with resistance, because the belief in fixed brain localizations may well have served as a protection against the anxiety and discomfort produced by the fluidity of mental life and the unreliability of memory.[15]

A new phase in the history of localizationalism is conventionally marked as beginning with the announcement of a discovery in 1861. The Société d'Anthropologie of Paris had been discussing the then popular topic of a correlation between brain size and intelligence. Opinions were divided, largely along ideological lines, just as they had been during the debates about Gall's phrenology. There was a tendency for those who identified themselves with modernity and republicanism (against the autocratic order established by Napoleon III) to favour a correlation between the dimensions of the brain and those of the mind. Social conservatives, on the other hand, were reluctant to accept the materialistic claim that mind, even in its specifically human aspects, had a close tie to the brain.[16] In these debates, language had emerged as a sort of test case for the proposition that even the most characteristically human capabilities could be assigned a physical location in the brain. Paul Broca, a medical authority who had been a leading figure in the foundation of the Société, was firmly on the side of localization. In 1861 he announced that he had collected clinical evidence indicating that the loss of the ability to speak was correlated with lesions in a circumscribed area of the left frontal lobe of the brain, subsequently known as 'Broca's area'. He attributed the language defect to a specific memory loss, the memory of the movements involved in the enunciation of spoken words.

During the next half-century or so, the search for the brain localization of other psychological functions spread to numerous clinics and laboratories in Europe and then in America. Some of the most famous names in late nineteenth-century medicine built their reputations on such work. Locations were assigned to centres controlling movement, various sensory modalities and specific linguistic accomplishments. Memory was sub-divided and brain locations were found for 'visual word images', 'auditory word images' and other components. Diagrams showing the regions of the brain and their psychological functions proliferated.

The products of this clinical research resembled those of the older phrenology to a considerable extent, but there were some important differences. First of all, there had been a subtle shift in the relative weight of psychological and anatomical considerations when it came to identifying physically located psychological features. For the phrenology of Gall, psychological considerations had been paramount in drawing up a list of the primary faculties. These were then mapped onto the cranium and assigned brain locations only by inference.[17] The second wave of generic phrenology, benefiting from technical advances in dissecting techniques, relied heavily on the results of brain autopsies in pinpointing the areas whose injury could be held responsible for the clinically observed loss of specific psychological functions. Brain anatomy became the primary consideration in determining the distinctions between psychological functions.[18]

A further difference between the older and the newer phrenology was particularly significant for conceptions of memory: Gall, still in the thrall of faculty psychology, had always thought in terms of specific mental *powers* – the new localizationalists tended to think in terms of *storage*. This was particularly evident in their conceptions regarding the localization of language, which continued to be the paradigm case for the 'higher' psychological functions, including memory. Language centres were thought of as *depots* in which the elements of language, representations of individual words and phrases, were stored.[19] According to the most influential of the new phrenologists, Carl Wernicke, it was not complex psychological functions that were localized at specific brain sites but the memory traces of past sensations and movements.[20]

By the middle of the nineteenth century empiricist mental philosophy had been linked to the emerging physiology of reflex functioning, with the result that associations between sense impressions and movements assumed a key role in the development of psychological functions, even the most complex.[21] Memory was constituted by these associations, so that brain localization of memory meant assigning them their specific place within the cranium. That place was in the supposed 'association areas', often adjacent to the primary projection areas, whose activity was devoted to the primary senses or to areas directly involved in motor activity. The strict division between primary sensory or motor areas and 'association' areas represented a projection onto the cerebrum of the categorical division between sensation/ perception and memory that had become an article of faith for the psychological discourse of the time. That division had philosophical origins, but its use in the interpretation of anatomical and clinical data made it appear to be engraved in the very structure of the brain.

Since the days of Gall, the discovery of the cellular structure of the brain had also changed the nature of the physical medium in which memory was to be located. The fact that this medium was now thought of as granular, composed of physically distinct units, neuronal cells, encouraged an analogous decomposition of memory into distinct elements. But empiricist philosophy had long established a tradition of decomposing mental life into elements, and the convergence of this mental philosophy with cellular neurophysiology became a key feature of the second wave of phrenology. An (inaccurate) estimate by the prominent Viennese neurologist Theodor Meynert that there were six hundred million cells in the cerebral cortex was widely quoted to show that there was sufficient storage space for the traces of a multitude of distinct units of knowledge.

An aura of scientific authority developed around the elementaristic model of memory in the late nineteenth century and lasted beyond the middle of the twentieth century. Without this aura, the research tradition that elevated lists of syllables and separate words as the paradigm case of memory[22] would hardly have enjoyed much credibility.

The units that were supposedly localized at specific cortical sites varied. Some authorities thought of them less in terms of units of verbal knowledge than of units of personal experience. That interpretation received strong support in the 1930s from the widely reported observations of the Canadian neurologist Wilder Penfield, who applied direct electrical stimulation to the brains of conscious patients and elicited 'recollections' of supposedly forgotten experiences. However, these supposed recollections, although vivid, often had a dream-like quality and contained elements that could not have been memories. In so far as the reported experiences did have a mnemic quality it was often unclear whether these were actual memories or generic reconstructions from several memory fragments. Re-examination of this evidence in the years after enthusiasm for crude localizationism had passed indicated that the implications of Penfield's observations had been widely misinterpreted. Only a very small percentage of individuals on whom the procedure was tried reported the experiences on which the fame of these experiments was based. Even in these cases there is reason to suspect that what was reported as a memory depended essentially on current experience rather than on a trace stored unchanged for many years.[23] In any case, the Penfield studies never provided convincing support for any strict localization of memory, because sometimes the same experience would be elicited by stimulation of different areas, and stimulation of the same area at different times would elicit different experiences.

Loss of geographical certainties

By the time of Penfield's investigations the enterprise of pinning down distinct memory units at a specific place in the brain had long been in decline. It had been at its height in the closing years of the nineteenth century, but, like the earlier phrenological wave, it quickly encountered opposition. There were two reasons for this. First, there was the obvious gap between the available empirical evidence and the theoretical structure it was meant to validate. In the case of Gall that gap was huge, but the late nineteenth-century localizationalists had narrowed it to only a limited extent. Their procedures relied on a 'logic of deletion'[24] according to which psychological deficits, occurring after injury or removal of a specific cortical area, were supposed to indicate what that area contributed to normal psychological functioning. But in any complex system the logic of deletion only works in so far as one already has a good understanding of the principles underlying the functioning of the whole. (Observing the effects of removing one part of a car's engine only informs us about the function of that part if we already know the principles of the internal combustion engine.) Practitioners of the 'new phrenology' of the late nineteenth century interpreted their findings on the assumption that the normal mind, and therefore the brain, obeyed the principles formulated by empiricist philosophical psychology. As faith in that philosophical under-standing wilted, as happened in the early twentieth century, the empirical basis for the localization of memory began to appear increasingly problematical.[25]

But apart from the highly questionable interpretation of limited clinical evidence, the ideological implications of radical localizationalism bothered some critics. At the time of Flourens' critique of Gall's version of phrenology, there were religious overtones to the ideological conflict that were no longer audible later on. It was now often those who adhered to a more holistic philosophy with intellectual roots in Romanticism that engaged in debate with the more radical localizationalists. They defended the view that the brain acted as a whole and pointed to the often-observed recovery of psychological function, in spite of permanent injury to specific cortical locations, as evidence against rigid localizationalism.[26] They also drew attention to the fact that the relationship between the anatomical location of a brain injury and psychological effects was quite variable in different cases, indicating that such effects depended on the condition of the brain as a whole and indeed the entire organism. Such views gained in influence during the first half of the twentieth century, and gradually dimmed the earlier enthusiasm for exact cerebral localization.[27]

Changes in the discourse of localization were closely related to changes in the professional and institutional affiliation of those who contributed to this discourse.[28] This emerged quite clearly during World War I and its aftermath. The war had produced cerebral injuries on an unprecedented scale, and the diffuse psychological disturbances associated with these injuries were often difficult to reconcile with existing models of localization. The older models had been produced by a collaboration of surgeons and neurologists, but now there was increasing participation by psychiatrists and, gradually, psychologists. Even before psychologists were directly involved, psychological considerations had entered medical discourse. These considerations could make the psychology of the nineteenth-century localizationalists seem crude and inadequate.[29]

By the second quarter of the twentieth century, experimental psychology had acquired a firm institutional basis and professional organization, at least in North America. That created the possibility for a parallel discourse on the localization of memory in brain space that was largely independent of the medical version. The possibility was realized in a rather spectacular fashion by the work of Karl Lashley, a former co-worker of the founder of behaviourism, J. B. Watson. Lashley's work was hard to overlook, not only because of its rare execution of a systematic experimental research programme over a period of several decades, but also because it seemed to provide massive support for an holistic version of memory localization from an unexpected direction.

Early behaviourism shared certain fundamental presuppositions with the medical localizationalists of the late nineteenth century. Both doctrines assumed that the behaviour of humans and animals ultimately depended on the establishment and retention of sensori-motor links, associations between sensory impressions and movements. These associations, it was believed, were retained at specific locations in the brain. Whereas neurologists had mostly guessed at these locations by looking at the effects of unintended but localizable cerebral injuries, it was also possible to inflict such injuries in a planned and relatively precise manner – provided one used animals for one's experiments. Behaviourists had a high opinion of the informative value of animal behaviour studies, and Lashley was no exception. In brief, his experiments allowed him to observe the effects of cortical ablations, varying in size and location, on the retention of laboratory tasks by trained rats. The net result of virtually a lifetime's work along these lines was that most retention deficits in these animals could not be linked to specific cortical locations (other than primary sensory and motor areas), but depended on the *amount* of cortical tissue put out of action. In other words, memory could not be localized. Most parts of the rat's cerebral cortex showed 'equipotentiality' for learning and memory, and the cortex as a whole seemed to act as one integrated unit.[30]

The relevance of such findings for localization in the human brain was of course questionable, just as Flourens's data on pigeons had been a century earlier. Nevertheless, this work had a strong general impact, because its theoretical implications seriously undermined the model of learning and retention on which the interpretation of classical localization studies had depended. Lashley went on to suggest that his studies had made it impossible to assume that simple and isolated associations constituted the prototype of all memory. If, as he had shown, 'it is not possible to demonstrate the isolated localization of a memory trace anywhere within the nervous system', then it surely followed that 'every memory becomes part of a more or less extensive organization'.[31] In that case the psychological defects of 'amnesia', following localized brain injury, should not be regarded as defects of memory at all but as defects in other functions, including level of vigilance and ability to categorize sensory input. Here Lashley the behaviourist found himself in broad agreement with the holism of Kurt Goldstein.

More immediately important was the congruence of Lashley's work with the change from the original Watsonian behaviourism of the 1920s to the neo-behaviourism of the thirties and beyond. In the 'classical' behaviourism of Watson, a legacy of reductive biologism had been combined with an insistence on the value of scientific generalizations derived purely from behavioural data. This somewhat unstable combination had broken up by about 1930, to be replaced by various schools of neo-behaviourism that were as little concerned with physiological mechanisms as they were with mental states. The organism became a 'black box', with inputs and outputs that were related in lawful ways. It was the business of psychology to study these relationships and to leave the brain to the physiologists, just as the mind had already been left to the philosophers. Lashley's work was widely taken to support these sentiments and to establish the irrelevance of questions of cerebral localization for the legitimate work of the psychologist.[32]

In the decades around the middle of the twentieth century, the question of finding a place for memory in the brain became virtually a dead topic within psychology. There were exceptions among a small number of psychologists, especially those who worked in neurological or neurosurgical settings, where practical clinical exigencies kept concerns about brain localization alive. For medical professionals, classical localizationism still had certain attractions, though it had lost its former scientific respectability. Newer electrophysiological research strongly supported the suggestion that cerebral retention of memory traces did not involve pinpointed areas in brain space but widely distributed assemblies of neurons.[33] Moreover, different memory traces might be represented by different activity patterns in the *same* set of neurons, so that, as described in the following section, memory storage would be *superpositional*.

The problem was to come up with a new theoretical model that would do justice to the newer climate of opinion regarding cerebral localization. Karl Pribram's proposal of the hologram as a metaphor for memory storage aroused interest for a time.[34] Since the nineteenth century there had been suggestions that photographic images could be thought of as a kind of memory trace.[35] That would imply a point-to-point correspondence of trace and object, a notion that was no longer plausible in the twentieth century. But during the post-World War II period a second source of light with particular properties was combined with the regular photographic beam to produce an interference pattern that could be projected onto a film. The image of the photographed object was now captured by an interference pattern that was distributed over the entire exposed surface. This image could subsequently be reconstructed on the basis of pattern traces on only part of the recording surface. The image seemed to be present in all parts of the film, hence the term 'hologram', from the Greek *holos*, meaning whole.

At a time when the plausibility of point-to-point localization of memory traces had sunk to its lowest ebb, the first appearance of a model for *distributed* memory seemed hopeful. Ever since Lashley's work, it had seemed likely that memory traces were held in the brain in a distributed rather than a localized fashion, but no physical model had been available that might help one to imagine how distributed storage might work. Perhaps holography could provide such a model?

In spite of the best efforts of Pribram and his associates, these hopes were soon dashed. First of all, it was clear that the kind of hardware necessary to process information in a hologram-like way had never been encountered in the brain, or the sense organs for that matter. But even as a mere metaphor the hologram had its problems. At bottom it was yet another version of the ancient metaphor of inscription.[36] Its model of inscription relied on a much more advanced technology than wax tablets, but, to function as a model for memory, inscriptions must not only be stored, they must also be capable of being read. In fact, storage has always been the easy part – it is the reading of what has been stored that is more difficult to explain. Supposing the brain does hold holographic representations, how will the content they represent be recovered in the process of remembering? Is memory recovery possible without the kind offices of a homunculus who reads the inscriptions for us? It is not clear that holography is any better at getting rid of the little reader in the head than other storage models.

There were also more practical reasons for the comet-like path of the hologram as a model for memory. The model could never be made sufficiently specific to lead to a sustained program of nitty-gritty empirical research. Yet nitty-gritty empirical research fills scientific journals and advances scientific careers. Holographic explanations of memory phenomena tended to be *post hoc*; there were few, if any, specific testable predictions to be had. Thus, after the initial flush of enthusiasm, the excursion into holography tended to be dismissed as a dead end.

A note on networks

The idea of a memory whose place in the brain was widely dispersed did not die. In fact, that idea long antedated its peculiar instantiation in the form of holography. Shortly after the end of World War II, a well-known Canadian psychologist, Donald Hebb, had already speculated about the role of neural 'cell assemblies' in cognitive processes.[37] Reverberating electrical activity in these assemblies would lead to the formation of memory traces that would be distributed over several brain areas. But although the general idea of such neural networks had considerable appeal, it was not sufficiently specific to launch any significant programme of empirical research, certainly not in the field of memory.

It was only in the 1980s that that situation changed to a marked extent as a result of an impetus that came, not from neurophysiology, but from computer modelling. At that time, some earlier suggestions for constructing computer models of networks were revisited and instantiated quite precisely as models of learning and memory. There followed a flurry of interest in the computer modelling of cognitive processes on the basis of network principles, a trend which is still current, though it exists side-by-side with more traditional approaches. That very recent history falls outside the scope of this book, but a brief summary of some major features of network models of memory is appropriate. Networks consist of patterns of ongoing activity between a number of units that are connected to each other though spread out in space. These patterns can change as a result of input into the system plus features that have been built into the system.[38] This can be considered a model of learning. But patterns of activity in a network can also stabilize to form a kind of memory trace. The location of such a trace could not be pinpointed as though it were a place on a map. Neural networks extend over an area, conceivably a very large area, that they share with other networks. The memory trace is constituted by a certain pattern of activity in the network, and its location is therefore as broad as the network itself. Moreover, the same *distributed* network is capable of storing different traces in the form of different patterns of activity. Memory therefore operates on *superpositional* principles, different memories relying on the same neuronal substrate. But even this is too static an image, because talk of *a* neural network is already an idealization of what one might find in a real brain, where networks overlap in their components and have no fixed edges. Taking the neural network model seriously tends to destroy the conventional meaning of 'localization' when applied to the brain.

A most important aspect of network models is the lack of any separation between the 'processing' of incoming activity patterns and their storage. The same units, the same machinery one might say, will assimilate whatever input reaches the system into its own activity and in doing so will preserve a trace of what has happened in its changed activity. This is in stark contrast to traditional computer models in which processing and 'memory' are strictly separate and performed by different units. For psychology this means that the clear separation of memory from other cognitive functions, so strongly encouraged by traditional computer models, is not a feature of network models.

Another advantage of network models is that they are 'content addressable', which means that patterns they store can be reactivated by incoming patterns without the need to look for them in a list of separately stored addresses. This eliminates one of the least plausible aspects of traditional computer models of memory and also reduces reliance on a homunculus reader. Because of the interaction of all currently active networks, the 'recovery' of past experience is much more like a process of reconstruction than of 'retrieval' of a stored item.[39]

However, network models share with most other models of memory the difficulty of accounting for what, since Aristotle, has been considered a crucial aspect of memory: its explicit reference to the past. Accounting for the *retrieval* of something from the past is not the same thing as accounting for the sense of pastness that is an essential aspect of what has been called 'episodic memory' (chapter 6). Network models seem better at accounting for knowledge than at accounting for memory. Reconciling the properties of computational networks with the neuronal architecture of the brain was also problematic, though for that very reason hypothetical models had a potential heuristic value.[40] The explanatory value of such models, however, would seem to be limited to questions of inner architecture. For explaining the adaptive meaning of the network's output in a specific ecological context the human designer's interpretation would still be necessary, just as with more traditional computer models.

The decade of the brain

By the time network modelling had achieved a viable form it had to share the limelight with another approach that was in some ways its opposite. The eighties of the last century also saw an explosive increase in direct investigation of the brain and its role in psychological processes. In the area of memory this kind of work proceeded on two levels. At the microscopic level it elucidated mechanisms of trace formation in individual neurons and their synaptic connections. At the macroscopic level the work involved much larger, anatomically localized systems of neurons and the nervous pathways that linked them.[41]

Some of this work was associated with a resurgence of the localizationalist project[42] that resembled earlier versions of the project in certain respects. There was the same determination to pin down memory at specific sites in the brain and to distinguish different kinds of memory on the basis of differences between these locations. In so far as these efforts continued to be based on the study of persons with brain injuries, the dangers of generalizing from the injured brain to the intact brain were still present.[43] However, there was a new confidence that the mistakes of the earlier localizers could be avoided, not only because the dangers were now more clearly recognized, but more particularly because innovations in technique were now available that an earlier generation of localizers could hardly have dreamed of.

Some of these innovations concerned the assessment of psychological functions, which was now precise and quantitative, whereas in the previous century it had been impressionistic and untrustworthy. However, psychological testing technologies required the construction and administration of tasks that inevitably depended on more than one psychological function. The interpretation of performance data from such tasks requires great care and is unlikely to provide unambiguous support for any rigorous definition and separation of the psychological functions that are each to find their own place in the brain.[44] The selection of appropriate control tasks for pinpointing the targeted psychological function cannot avoid additional assumptions limiting the claims that can justifiably be made.

More impressive than the psychological innovations were the technical advances in neurophysiology and anatomy that now made it possible to observe the activity of the intact brain and to describe brain areas with greater accuracy. A remarkable combination of mathematical, physical and chemical techniques had made it possible to record ongoing changes in metabolic level at specific brain sites and to transform such records for subsequent visual display. Among the various techniques of *neuroimaging* positron emission tomography (PET) and functional magnetic resonance imaging (fMRI) have been particularly important for pursuing attempts at localizing memory,[45] though their use in that context represents only a tiny part of their use in medical research and diagnostics and in the overall project of the new science of neuropsychology.

As is usual in a technological civilization, the prospects of new techniques tend to be overestimated initially, and recognition of their more problematic aspects comes only gradually and meets with resistance. This is particularly to be expected when the techniques in question involve the investment of large amounts of capital, both financial and human, and when their products, whether in the form of hardware or of images, become so widely disseminated as to achieve the status of cultural icons. In the 1980s the promise of various technologies converged to push the study of the brain to the forefront of scientific, and ultimately public, attention. By 1990 the President of the United States, following a resolution of both Houses of Congress, had officially proclaimed the 1990s the 'Decade of the Brain'. During the most recent period, therefore, the problem of localizing memory in the brain merged with a broad and powerful movement, whose course and cultural ramifications will provide rich material for future historians. In the present context a few preliminary remarks must suffice.

For the project of placing memory in the brain, the laboratory artefacts produced by neuroimaging techniques proved to be a mixed blessing. These artefacts take the form of computer-generated visual images showing 'levels of activation' located in specific areas of brain space while the possessor of the brain is engaged in various tasks. Gazing at such images, one could easily feel that one was actually *seeing* cognitive work being performed at various places, as in a workshop or office. Localization of psychological functions seemed to be displayed in front of one's eyes. For the lay public, and even for some psychologists and clinicians, it was tempting to regard those colourful images as quite transparent, allowing them to watch the brain at work. But specialists in the field knew this to be an illusion, because an image of this kind does not constitute an unambiguous physiological datum, but a carefully constructed artefact.[46] Neuroimaging revealed a whole new set of phenomena, but the meaning ascribed to these phenomena depended on a long chain of assumptions without which the computer generated images could not be interpreted as reflecting localized brain activity in any unambiguous way. At each stage in the production of brain images – the initial measurement of individual brain activity, the combination of individual into group data and the preparation of images for presentation – investigators are faced with choices, and those choices have a decisive effect on the meaning conveyed by the images.[47]

Data from brain imaging studies do not provide support for simplistic views about brain localization for many reasons, only a few of which can be briefly mentioned here. Not infrequently, oversimplified interpretations of brain images are based on the same subtractive logic that characterized the earlier, technically more primitive phases of the localizationist project. This logic remains suspect when applied to a system in which the components are not independent and serially arranged, but form a recursive system of mutually interacting parts.[48] Beyond the sensory and motor areas, specific locations are likely to be involved in many functions, and any particular function is likely to involve many locations.[49] That insight led to the replacement of old-style localizationalism by a more systemic approach that focused on interactions among parts rather than on point-to-point localization of psychological functions. However, common techniques of neuroimaging can also accentuate, or even create, boundaries between regions.[50]

Even when there is good evidence for some correlation between well defined task performance and elevated activity in an identifiable cerebral system there remains the problem of interpreting such a correlation. To use such a correlation as a basis for anything more than a tentative hypothesis one would have to rely on the logical fallacy of affirming the consequent: only if we are already convinced that our procedures have indeed isolated a modular psychological function and a bounded brain region, both of which are generalizable across individuals, can correlation of the two be regarded as demonstrating a localization of function. Supposing such a demonstration to be successful, the localized pattern of brain activity would constitute only a necessary, not a sufficient condition for the performance of a particular human action. These actions, remembering among them, are always part of a human situation, a social, cultural setting, from which they derive their meaning. Certainly, they are necessarily *enabled* by brain activity, but they are neither identical with that activity nor mechanically caused by it; as human performances or achievements, they can exist only within human situations. Without a hippocampus you may not be able to remember where you parked your car, but it is you who remembers, not your hippocampus.[51]

Difficulties in establishing unambiguous and uncontested empirical findings became particularly evident beyond the domain of so-called 'working memory', that is, the retention over a brief time-span of information closely linked to sensory input.[52] What had emerged by the closing years of the century were interesting hints about linkages between memory and certain other psychological phenomena, such as emotion and spatial understanding.[53] Undoubtedly, functionally specialized neural systems exist and are not homogeneously distributed over the brain, but there has been a developing recognition of the limitations that need to be placed on the goals of localization studies if they are to be realistic.[54]

The temptation to ask the wrong questions and to overinterpret ambiguous data has come not only from the media, politicians, community groups, administrators, funding bodies and so on, but also from some of the implicit philosophical commitments that were often part of professional socialization. What would have the greatest appeal for all these sources would be an unambiguous story of neatly separated psychological attributes, each residing in its own clearly bounded place in the brain, and linked to each other in a strictly linear fashion. Although some authors came rather close to telling precisely this story, a developing sense of the subject-matter's complexity gradually made it more difficult to do so.[55]

There can be little doubt that the localizationist wave of the late twentieth century produced significant advances in the elucidation of brain physiology. Its benefits for memory discourse are more questionable, and among practitioners one can find enthusiasts, sceptics and everything in between. More generally, it has given prominence to the image of memory as a kind of office organization whose various departments can be visited in their respective locations. Messages pass between these departments, but the coordination of the whole organization remains somewhat mysterious. Does this office have a boss, a chief executive officer? If so, where does he or she sit? There is great scope for variety in the answers. Sometimes it sounds as though the executive's is simply one office among others. Sometimes there seems to be no executive at all. In other versions the executive is an 'I' that is itself not located anywhere but that treats the various departments as tools or means to pursue its ends.

It is too soon to tell whether this Babel of voices heralds a new turn in memory discourse or whether it will subside into a refurbished Cartesianism that neatly separates remembering persons from the mnemonic machinery in their heads.

Notes

1. Pliny (the elder), *Natural History*, Book 7, trans. H. Rackham (Cambridge, MA: Harvard University Press, 1942), vol. II, p. 565.
2. E. R. Harvey, *The inward wits: Psychological theory in the Middle Ages and the Renaissance* (London: Warburg Institute, 1975).
3. Bolzoni, *Gallery of memory*, p. 136.
4. A scholar's warning: 'Those writers, who interpret the medieval doctrine of the *virtues animae* as a doctrine of cerebral physiology or of cerebral ventricular physiology, project their modern bias into an epoch of which the *Zeitgeist* was dominated by the ecclesia.' G. W. Bruyn, 'The seat of the soul', in F. C. Rose and W. F. Bynum (eds.), *Historical aspects of the neurosciences* (New York: Raven Press, 1981), pp. 55–82.
5. 'One cannot, without further qualifications, equate the cellulae with the ventricles.' Bruyn, 'Seat of the soul', p. 74.
6. These philosophers belonged to the school of *nominalism* that tended to champion 'modernistic' causes. See K. Park, 'The organic soul', in Q. Skinner and E. Kessler (eds.), *The Cambridge history of Renaissance philosophy* (Cambridge: Cambridge University Press, 1988), pp. 464–84.
7. Willis made much use of comparative anatomy, using correlations between the typical behaviour of animal species and their brain anatomy to draw conclusions about the functions of different areas of the brain. R. G. Frank, 'Thomas Willis and his circle: Brain and mind in seventeenth-century medicine', in G. S. Rousseau (ed.), *The languages of the psyche: Mind and body in Enlightenment thought* (Berkeley: University of California Press, 1990), pp. 107–46.
8. Even today the word preserves this legacy, for spirits are sold in bottles to be drunk as liquids, but in their other incarnation they are quite immaterial. For the history of animal spirits, see chapter 2, note 79, and J. Sutton, *Philosophy and memory traces: Descartes to connectionism* (Cambridge: Cambridge University Press, 1998).
9. Sutton, *Philosophy and memory traces*, p. 60.
10. See the remarks on Hume in chapter 2 and on Locke in chapter 4.
11. For the historical background see R. M. Young, *Mind, brain and adaptation in the nineteenth century: Cerebral localization and its biological context from Gall to Ferrier* (Oxford: Clarendon Press, 1970; E. Clarke and L. S. Jacyna, *Nineteenth-century origins of neuroscientific concepts* (Berkeley: University of California Press, 1987); C. Pogliano, 'Between form and function: A new science of man', in Corsi,

The enchanted loom, pp. 144–203; and chapter 1 of R. Cooter, *The cultural meaning of popular science: Phrenology and the organization of consent in nineteenth-century Britain* (Cambridge: Cambridge University Press, 1984).

12. Flourens reads Gall to mean this: 'There is no such thing as unity ... there is no *me*; and if there be no *me*, there can be no soul. In the same way he abolishes the *free-will*.' P. Flourens, *Phrenology examined*, in D.N. Robinson (ed.), *Significant contributions to the history of psychology 1750–1920*, Series E (Washington, DC: University Publications of America, 1978), vol. II, p. 58. (The original monograph was published in 1842; the translation is from the second edition of 1845.)

13. Gall himself did not call his system phrenology but 'organology', the term 'phrenology' being an invention of his one-time pupil and collaborator, Spurzheim, whose version of the system diverged from Gall's after they parted company. Later phrenologists, such as George Combe and the Fowler brothers, were identified with yet other versions, so that 'phrenology' already functioned more as a generic term than as the label for a singular system of thought and practice.

14. The application of the term 'function' to aspects of mental life originates with phrenology. See K.M. Dallenbach, 'The history and derivation of the word "function" as a systematic term in psychology', *American Journal of Psychology* 26 (1915), 473–84. Modern discussions of the specificity of mental functions are usually formulated in terms of 'modularity', a topic that is addressed briefly in chapter 9, section headed 'Faculty psychology and its demise'.

15. Sutton, *Philosophy and memory traces*.

16. For a detailed account of the origins of the modern concept of *aphasia* see L.S. Jacyna, *Lost words: Narratives of language and the brain 1825–1926* (Princeton, NJ: Princeton University Press, 2000).

17. In fact, Gall's scientific critics took him to task on precisely this point. Gall had recognized that the association between anatomy and psychology could be demonstrated only in cases where the manifestation of the function was extreme. His followers sought to improve the ratio of observation to speculation by convincing themselves that the association was empirically detectable in every case. This exposed them to easy refutation.

18. This interesting reversal has been noted by Anne Harrington. See her chapter, 'Beyond phrenology: Localization theory in the modern era', in Corsi, *The enchanted loom*, pp. 207–39.

19. Jacyna, *Lost words*, p. 176.

20. C. Wernicke, *Der aphasische Symptomencomplex: Eine psychologische Studie auf anatomischer Grundlage* (Breslau: Cohn & Weigart, 1874). (The sub-title of this work encapsulates the changed order of priority between the psychological and the anatomical: 'A psychological study based on anatomy'.)

21. The marriage of empiricist mental philosophy and sensori-motor physiology was consummated in the writings of Alexander Bain (1818–1903) and Herbert Spencer (1820–1903). Young, *Mind, brain and adaptation*, provides an account of their formulations that is particularly relevant for the present context. For other historical figures in this development see Danziger, 'Mid-nineteenth-century British psycho-physiology'.

22. See chapter 5.

23. Loftus and Loftus, 'Permanence of stored information'.

24. The term was introduced in this context in Susan Leigh Star, *Regions of the mind: Brain research and the quest for scientific certainty* (Stanford, CA: Stanford University Press, 1989).

25. The young Sigmund Freud was an early critic of the new phrenology. S. Freud, *On aphasia: A critical study* (London: Imago, 1891/1953). He did not abandon the localization project altogether but questioned the conception of cortical space as composed of discrete loci, each serving a bounded memory unit. The thrust

of his own thinking was to attach far greater significance to the *temporal* localization of memories in individual development than on their supposedly fixed *spatial* location.

26. The geography of brain localization could also carry a political meaning. See P. J. Pauly, 'The political structure of the brain: Cerebral localization in Bismarckian Germany', *International Journal of Neuroscience* 21 (1983), 145–50.

27. Basing himself on the earlier work of Constantin von Monakow, Kurt Goldstein had become the best known representative of this approach by mid-century. See his *The organism* (Boston: Beacon Press, 1939/1963).

28. For a detailed account of these relationships see Star, *Regions of the mind*.

29. The work of Kurt Goldstein (note 27) provides a good example. In his case the influence of Gestalt psychology (see chapter 5, section headed 'The road not taken: Gestalt psychology') is marked. But physiological work, showing that the retention of *patterns* of stimulation could not be localized, was among the factors that had made the Gestalt idea plausible in the first place; see M. G. Ash, *Gestalt psychology in German culture 1890–1967: Holism and the quest for objectivity* (Cambridge: Cambridge University Press, 1995), pp. 96–7.

30. K. S. Lashley, *Brain mechanisms and intelligence: A quantitative study of injuries to the brain* (Chicago: University of Chicago Press, 1929).

31. K. S. Lashley, 'In search of the engram', *Society of Experimental Biology symposium no. 4* (Cambridge, MA: Harvard University Press, 1950) pp. 454–82 (p. 501 and p. 497).

32. In discussing Lashley's 1950 paper a well-known textbook, published in 1978, stated categorically that 'a quarter century later, most of the general points made by Lashley could well serve as the credo for the most modern psychobiological learning theory'. W. R. Uttal, *The psychobiology of mind* (New York: Wiley, 1978), p. 539.

33. The work of E. R. John proved to be particularly impressive, see E. R. John, 'Switchboard versus statistical theories of learning and memory', *Science* 177 (1972), 850–64.

34. K. H. Pribram, 'The neurophysiology of remembering', *Scientific American* 220 (1969), 73–86; see also K. H. Pribram, *Languages of the brain: Experimental paradoxes and principle in neuropsychology* (Englewood Cliffs, NJ: Prentice-Hall, 1971).

35. Draaisma, *Metaphors of memory*. This work also contains an excellent account of holograms and other more recent attempts at modelling memory.

36. See chapter 2.

37. D. O. Hebb, *The organization of behavior* (New York: Wiley, 1949). Hebb had based himself on earlier neurophysiological work that provided evidence for neuronal networks. Long before that, Gustav Theodor Fechner had suggested that memories were not stored in specific cellular locations but involved oscillatory activity in a neural system. However, Fechner's thoughts on memory were utterly incompatible with the metaphysical commitments of late nineteenth-century physiology. Consequently they were totally ignored, in spite of his fame as the originator of psychophysics. See E. Scheerer, 'The unknown Fechner', *Psychological Research* 49 (1987), 197–202; and G. T. Fechner, 'Some thoughts on the psychophysical representation of memories (1882)', *Psychological Research* 49 (1987), 209–12.

38. These features comprise such factors as the relative weight assigned to connections between units and rules which change these weights under certain conditions. Specific values of network features are of course of crucial importance for research in this area but are not relevant for the general assessment of this approach. An influential account during the early years of the connectionist turn was J. L. McClelland and D. Rumelhart (eds.), *Parallel distributed processing: Explorations in the microstructure of cognition* (Cambridge, MA: MIT Press, 1986), vol. I. See also W. Bechtel and A. Abrahamsen, *Connectionism and the mind* (Cambridge, MA: Blackwell, 1991).

39. J. L. McClelland, 'Constructive memory and memory distortions: A parallel-distributed processing approach', in Schacter, *Memory distortion*, pp. 69–90.

40. For an example of late twentieth-century application of network modelling to the brain architecture of memory, see J. L. McClelland, B. L. McNaughton and R. C. O'Reilly, 'Why there are complementary learning systems in the hippocampus and neocortex: Insights from the successes and failures of connectionist models of learning and memory', *Psychological Review* 102 (1995), 419–57.

41. The microscopic approach produced some impressive scientific achievements, not least in the area of neural plasticity. At the end of the century this was a rapidly developing area of research whose fundamental implications were just becoming more widely appreciated. Any attempt at including these potentially revolutionary developments in this book's essentially backward-looking historical account seems to me unwise and impractical. The time for this addition to the history of memory will come later. In the meantime, there are some very readable accounts by prominent contributors to these historically recent developments, especially the following: S. Rose, *The making of memory* (London: Bantam, 1993); J. LeDoux, *Synaptic self* (London: Penguin Books, 2002); and E. R. Kandel, *In search of memory: The emergence of a new science of mind* (New York: Norton, 2006).

42. Three major publications that represent this trend in ascending order of enthusiasm: T. Shallice, *From neuropsychology to mental structure* (Cambridge: Cambridge University Press, 1987); L. R. Squire, *Memory and brain*; N. J. Cohen and H. Eichenbaum, *Memory, amnesia, and the hippocampal system* (Cambridge, MA: MIT Press, 1993). Displaying commendable historical insight, some researchers found aspects of classical phrenology to be worthy of respect; see M. I. Posner and M. E. Raichle, *Images of mind* (New York: Scientific American Library, 1994).

43. These dangers involved issues already mentioned, such as the perils of a 'logic of deletion' or 'subtractive logic', the variability of localizations over individuals and over time, the recovery of functions after injury and so on.

44. This issue links up with the problems of identifying 'memory systems' mentioned at the end of chapter 6. For an extensive discussion of this link, see M. S. Weldon, 'The memory chop shop: Issues in the search for memory systems', in Foster and Jelicic, *Memory: systems, process, or function?*, pp. 162–204.

45. Any description of these techniques, or of the empirical work utilizing them, would go far beyond the scope and aims of this book. For a sample of work in this field at the end of the century, see L. R. Squire and D. L. Schacter (eds.), *Neuropsychology of memory*, 3rd edn (New York: Guilford Press, 2002). For reviews covering work relevant to the localization of memory, see chapters 53, 54 and 57 in M. S. Gazzaniga (ed.), *The new cognitive neurosciences* (Cambridge, MA: MIT Press, 1999). Descriptions, intended for non-specialist readers, of major areas of brain research at the end of the century are to be found in G. M. Edelman and J.-P. Changeux (eds.), *The brain* (London: Transaction, 2001).

46. Diverging interpretations of the meaning of functional brain imaging among clinicians and researchers raise quite profound questions about the nature and role of scientific representations. See A. Beaulieu, 'Images are not the (only) truth: Brain mapping, visual knowledge, and iconoclasm', *Science, Technology, & Human Values* 27 (2002), 53–86.

47. The chain of assumptions was set out in W. R. Uttal, *The new phrenology: The limits of localizing cognitive processes in the brain* (Cambridge, MA: MIT Press, 2001). For a more extensive study of the creation of brain images as 'conceptual objects', based on interviews with researchers, see J. Dumit, *Picturing personhood: Brain scans and biomedical identity* (Princeton, NJ: Princeton University Press, 2004).

48. J. J. Kim and M. G. Baxter, 'Multiple brain-memory systems: the whole does not equal the sum of its parts', *Trends in Neurosciences* 24 (2001), 324–30.

49. D. Gaffan, 'Against memory systems', in A. Parker, A. Derrington and C. Blakemore (eds.), *The physiology of cognitive processes* (New York: Oxford University Press, 2003), pp. 234–51. The prefrontal area of the cerebral cortex, very large in humans, can provide a kind of *reductio ad absurdum* for any simple-minded execution of the localization project. By 1995 the list of psychological tasks and functions allegedly relying on this area extended over seven pages. See J. Grafman, A. Partiot and C. Hollnagel, 'Fables of the prefrontal cortex', *Behavioral and Brain Sciences* 18 (1995), 349–58.

50. Dumit, *Picturing personhood*. In certain respects, the conceptual distance between Gall's phrenology and neuroimaging is not as great as might appear. Gall assumed that size of the brain region correlated with prominence of the function located in that region. Empirically, this could not be confirmed. But some modern authors have recognized that, as a hypothesis, this 'is not conceptually all that different from the idea that greater activity in a brain area corresponds to greater metabolism and thus blood flow, an assumption that underlies contemporary neuroimaging'. T. Zawidski and S. Bechtel, 'W. Gall's legacy revisited: Decomposition and localization in cognitive neuroscience', in C. E. Erneling and D. M. Johnson (eds.), *The mind as a scientific object: Between brain and culture* (New York: Oxford University Press, 2005), pp. 293–316 (p. 294).

51. Various aspects of this issue are fully discussed in M. R. Bennet and P. M. S. Hacker, *Philosophical foundations of neuroscience* (Oxford: Blackwell, 2003). See also J. Coulter, 'Neural Cartesianism: Comments on the epistemology of the cognitive sciences', in Johnson and Erneling, *Future of the cognitive revolution*, pp. 293–301 (pp.296–7).

52. As was indicated in chapter 6, the practice of referring to such retention as 'memory' is historically recent.

53. For examples see J. O'Keefe and L. Nadel, *The hippocampus as a cognitive map* (New York: Oxford University Press, 1978); Cohen and Eichenbaum, *Memory, amnesia, and the hippocampal system*; E. T. Rolls, 'Memory systems in the brain'; J. E. LeDoux, *The emotional brain* (New York: Simon & Schuster, 1996); A. R. Damasio, *Descartes' error: Emotion, reason and the human brain* (New York: Putnam, 1994); E. T. Rolls, *The brain and emotion* (Oxford: Oxford University Press, 1999).

54. S. M. Kosslyn, 'If neuroimaging is the answer, what is the question?', *Proceedings of the Royal Society of London* B, 354 (1999), 1283–94.

55. Useful leads to the disparity of views among experts can be found among the peer discussions of position papers in the journal *Behavioral and Brain Sciences*; for example, the discussion of the paper by M. J. Farah, 'Neuropsychological inference with an interactive brain: A critique of the "locality" assumption', *Behavioral and Brain Sciences* 17 (1994), 43–104. By the end of the century, the notion of topographically stable neurological inscriptions was beginning to be seriously challenged by a mounting wave of studies on *neural plasticity*: D. V. Buonomano and M. M. Merzenich, 'Cortical plasticity: From synapses to maps', *Annual Review of Neuroscience* 21 (1998), 149–86. But this marked only the first stages in a historical chapter that is unfolding in the twenty-first century and can only be hinted at in this book.

9 Memory in its place

Fuzzy boundaries

Memory is not something we can see, touch or smell. What we observe and experience directly are human activities, our own and those of others. As we acquired our first language we learned to apply the appropriate labels to various kinds of experiences and events. We learned what counted as being surprised, being disappointed, lying, showing-off and, of course, remembering. In other words, we learned the categories currently used to make sense of human experience and human interaction in our cultural milieu. Common psychological categories all exist in everyday usage before they become a target for any philosopher's thought or any scientist's experiments.

The world would surely be pretty close to William James's 'blooming buzzing confusion' without the sense-making categories that enable us to identify any phenomenon as belonging to a certain kind. But where do these categories come from? For the individual, there is no mystery, because he or she is born into an environment in which they already exist. How they came to be there is a more difficult question. There are two extreme possibilities: One is that these categories are accurate representations of the way the various characteristics of human nature divide up. What argues against this view is, first, that there are huge differences between human cultures in the categories they use to represent human characteristics, and second, that these representations are subject to profound historical changes. This suggests the other extreme possibility, namely, that the network of categories for giving meaning to human experience has no 'natural' basis at all in the universal constitution of human beings and depends only on temporary local conditions. Alternatively, it may turn out that, in spite of much variation, there are some constants in all these sets of categories that suggest a common basis. However, we can be sure of that only if we have some grasp of the extent of the variations that exist across cultures and across historical time. This latter project, of course, provides the purpose of this book.

A category, such as memory, occupies a certain place in a semantic network. It is never independent of other, related categories, and its boundaries are apt to shift in the course of time. These shifts cannot be ignored in an account of its history, because the meaning of memory very much depends on how it is thought to relate to other categories representing human characteristics. In the special tradition that forms the limited focus of this study, the meaning of 'memory' has been strongly affected by its supposed relationship to a small number of categories that significantly impinged on its semantic boundaries, particularly 'reason', 'imagination', 'affection' and 'perception'. Not all these neighbours were important at the same time.

Memory's relationship to 'reason' provides an early example of an actual boundary dispute. Among the physicians of the Greek and Roman world, there developed a lively controversy about the nature of medical knowledge. An earlier break with ancient and purely traditional healing practices had involved the belief that there were principles of health and disease that could be discovered by the proper application of human reason. This led to the proliferation of numerous theories and systems, each of which sought a rational basis for medical observations in terms of certain basic principles. But there was no agreement on these principles, and the rivalry among competing theories soon provoked a radical reaction. The school of medical empiricism denied the role of reason in medical knowledge and asserted that the wisdom of the good physician was simply based on experience.

But because lay people also have some experience of health and illness, it was necessary to explain the nature of the medical expert's superior experience rather more precisely. Summing up the empiricist position of earlier theorists, Galen, writing in the second century AD, offered a succinct definition: 'Experience is the observation and the memory of those things which one has seen to happen often and in a similar way.'[1] Unlike the layperson, the medical expert has frequently seen similar manifestations of illness and is able to recognize their similarity. He has also had many occasions to observe the outcome of specific treatments. His memory preserves not just singular occurrences, but the sum total of similar observed conjunctions. It is this power of memory that makes expert medical knowledge possible, not any additional faculty of reason.

In making such claims, the medical empiricists were drawing on a philosophical tradition whose major works have been lost and whose tenets have to be inferred from the polemical remarks of their opponents, Plato and Aristotle.[2] For the ancient empiricists memory of observed conjunctions provided an adequate basis for knowledge, even scientific knowledge. But this meant attributing to memory something more than the function of making representative copies of perceptions. It meant crediting memory with the power of aggregating similar impressions and generalizing from such aggregates. When deployed in this way, the category of memory resembled a faculty of inductive reasoning that might make it unnecessary to posit the existence of any separate reasoning faculty.

Making knowledge equivalent to the memory of 'things which one has seen to happen often and in a similar way' is certainly something an eighteenth-century empiricist like David Hume would have approved of. But Aristotle was to be found on the other side of this divide. He did allow that some animals were able to do pretty clever things simply on the basis of memory. But memory, which was not a specifically human attribute, could not provide an adequate explanation for the human arts and sciences. For this one needed to take into account the power of human reason. Memory on its own could give rise to experience, but between mere experience, mere practical know-how, and the arts and sciences there was a fundamental gap that could only be bridged by the exercise of something other than memory, namely reason. It was reason, not memory, that enabled us to achieve an understanding of the essential features characterizing the objects of experience, and without such an understanding there could be no science. So simply remembering what kind of diet or medicine leads to an improvement in health does not make one a genuine purveyor of the science of medicine. One should also be able to offer a rational explanation for such outcomes.

If one adopts an inscription model of memory, one faces a fundamental difficulty: a memory store that is simply a repository of individual inscriptions – memory images in Aristotle's account – will never produce anything but individual inscriptions when it yields its contents for inspection. But human memory is not like that. It is constantly going beyond the individual items entered into it to yield generalizations, condensations, even fabrications. Now one can account for this in one of two ways. One way is to credit memory itself with the ability to group together separate inscriptions on the basis of 'similarity' or some other principle and to register, not just individual inscriptions, but also sets of inscriptions. This was the choice of the empiricists. The other way is to recognize that any kind of inscription will have to be read to yield an outcome that makes sense. In other words, there has to be a reader. For Aristotle and those he influenced, the inscriptions of memory merely provided the raw material for true knowledge. They could be transformed into the latter by recollection, reading inscriptions in the light of reason. On this view, memory was reduced to a kind of servant of reason, and the brevity of Aristotle's explicit remarks on memory may be a reflection of the topic's rather lowly status.

But there is a further complication. The kind of reasoning that the medical empiricists extolled is not really typical of Aristotelian reason, which worked deductively, proceeding logically from first principles. Aristotle would have assigned the physicians' inductive generalizations from experience to another category, one that he called *deliberative imagination*, an activity that is necessary for the exercise of what Aristotle called 'practical reason'.[3] In his terms, it was practical and not theoretical (deductive) reason that the medical empiricists favoured. They, however, claimed that they were only exercising their memories.

Who was right? Surely the answer can only be both or neither. There are any number of ways in which one might categorize whatever it was that these ancient physicians were doing. They themselves preferred one way, the Aristotelians opted for another, and we might well think of a third or fourth alternative. At the time, there was disagreement because two different sets of categories were in use, and the extension of a category, such as 'memory', was not the same in both cases. What would be attributed to 'memory' by some would be put down as due to a kind of imagination by others. Apart from anything else, the reach of a particular category would vary with the place it occupied in a network of categories. In the Aristotelian scheme of things 'imagination' is a profoundly important category, whereas hard-core empiricists, such as Hume (see chapter 7), tend to distrust imagination and feel more comfortable with 'memory'.[4]

The inner senses

In his book on the soul, *De anima*, Aristotle had traced human knowledge to the activity of the primary senses, of which there were precisely five. Each sense was able to perform its function by virtue of a special 'power' or capacity, that of vision or hearing, for example. But he also stressed that five separate sensory powers would not be enough to give rise to human cognition. We do not experience the world in terms of separate sensations but in terms of complex unities and coherent knowledge. Therefore there had to be an agency, or agencies, that combined and integrated what was provided by the primary senses. There was, for example, the ability to form images in the absence of sensory input, the power of imagination, as well as the activity of evaluating and judging the things presented to us by our senses or by our imagination. Among later generations of Aristotle's readers this kind of analysis developed into the doctrine of the 'inner sense', 'common sense', or *sensus communis*.[5] The capacity to remember shared this part of the soul with other cognitive faculties, among which imagination and the ability to evaluate and judge (*vis aestimativa*) were especially widely recognized. In order to function, each cognitive faculty had to have its own storage facility – imagination had to be able to store previous images, judgement had to rely on past judgements and so on.

Aristotle not only dissected sensory experience into five distinct modalities (vision, hearing, smell, taste and touch) but ascribed to each modality a specific power that made its particular form of activity possible, the power of vision, the power of hearing and so on. Ordinary language still retains the traces of this theory: we can speak of someone having lost their power of hearing, for example. Clearly, the idea of sensory 'powers' had a long life. But there was also a strong inclination to apply an analogous analysis to non-sensory processes, such as imagination, judgement, intellect and, of course, memory. The analogy was underlined by grouping all these activities under the concept of an 'inner sense'. This turned out to be an open invitation for endless and ultimately sterile speculations about the nature of the ingredients of the inner sense and their interrelationship. Although the terms 'inner' or 'common' sense are singular, their exemplification always involved a plurality of activities, such as imagining, judging and remembering. Unavoidably, that raised questions about the defining qualities and boundaries of memory in relation to the other functions of the inner sense.

It is hardly surprising that among the large array of relevant Arabic, Latin and Hebrew texts there was much disagreement regarding the precise nature of the powers of the inner sense and their distinction from each other.[6] In the case of the primary senses the differences between the modalities are sharp and intuitively obvious. People are not likely to be confused about the difference between seeing and hearing. These are distinctions with a strong claim to being 'natural'. But in the case of the 'inner senses' we can draw similar distinctions only by imposing arbitrary boundaries. Shall we assign the retention of sensory images to the faculty of memory or the faculty of imagination? And how shall we draw the line that separates memory and intellect? We cannot even be sure about the basic components of the inner sense.

In contrast to the primary senses, distinctions among the inner senses have an arbitrary quality that allows great scope for the influence of specific cultural and linguistic factors. Exploring their role lies far beyond the scope of this book, but there is one factor that must be mentioned because of its particular historical significance. Somewhat anachronistically, this can be referred to as 'professional interest'. Memory was a topic of interest for two kinds of discourse, shaped by different interests, philosophical and medical. These were 'professional' interests in a sense, though the term now has sociological implications that would not be valid at an earlier time. There were certainly individuals whose contributions were limited by either medical or philosophical considerations, but many, particularly among the Arab and Jewish scholars who contributed to this literature, had combined a philosophical with a medical training. Perhaps because of this, they were not unaware of the difference between the physician's and the philosopher's way of distinguishing among the activities of the soul.

Writing in the early eleventh century, the Persian Muslim philosopher who is known in the West as Avicenna[7] was quite clear about this. He observed that, because physicians' concern with the powers of the soul is derived from cases where an observed defect is associated with an injury to a particular part of the body, distinctions among these powers will be made on the basis of their bodily location. What is usually not considered from this perspective is the possibility that more than one power may reside in the same location. In that case, the medical approach may treat two, or perhaps more, distinct powers as one. The philosopher, on the other hand, is concerned with capability rather than location and distinguishes among the powers of the soul on that basis. So the two approaches can lead to different classifications.

Avicenna distinguished between two sensory functions, both supposedly located in the anterior ventricle, one of them receptive in function, the other retentive. The latter preserves sensory images. However, it is not only neutral sensory qualities that are preserved, but also the individual's reaction to the sensation, its subjective meaning, as one might put it in modern terminology. The name 'memory' (*virtus memorialis* in the Latin translation) Avicenna reserves for another kind of retention located in the posterior ventricle. What are conserved there are judgments of the *vis extimativa*, a power that has no specific material location. Its judgements represent the highest level of abstraction, which are entirely non-material. An abstraction like 'length', for example, would still be handled by the retentive imagination, but abstractions like 'malevolence' or 'humanity' would fall into the province of *memorialis*. In this scheme memory proper occupies a rather exalted place, having only a remote and indirect connection with mundane experience.[8]

Among later generations of Aristotelians it seemed to be assumed that there was a fixed, finite number of inner senses, that there were clear distinctions between them and that each was characterized by a specific 'power' that explained its particular activity. In all these respects conceptions of inner sense were closely modelled on Aristotelian doctrine regarding the primary senses. But Aristotle's rather vague remarks about matters that were later referred to in terms of inner sense were replaced by more rigid schemes with hard and fast distinctions between the various 'powers' of the soul. Scholarly discourse was then trapped in endless debates about the nature and number of these powers, and, if the debaters had medical interests, in their somatic location. What became known as 'faculty psychology' emerged out of these debates. It showed great staying power and was still alive in the eighteenth century.

Faculty psychology and its demise

Thanks to its protected existence in the institutions of the Catholic Church, medieval thinking on memory, in the form of 'Thomistic psychology', lived on well into the twentieth century.[9] But by then it had long been bypassed by numerous developments that were more in tune with the beliefs and values characteristic of the societies that had emerged after the break-up of the medieval order. Among these developments was the emergence, in the first half of the eighteenth century, of a distinct sub-division of knowledge labelled 'psychology' and recognizable as fundamentally similar to what has been understood by that term in more recent times.[10] Occasional uses of the term prior to this had referred to knowledge of spiritual beings, a category that was not specifically human, but could include angels, etc. The psychology that emerged in the eighteenth-century Enlightenment, however, was concerned with the human mind as a part of the natural world and sought to base itself on empirical observation rather than the authority of tradition.[11]

Of course, tradition was not so easily sloughed off. Its effects were felt particularly in the continued influence of faculty psychology, the division of human potential into a finite list of distinct 'powers' of the soul, later the mind. There had, however, been a change in the most widely accepted list of basic faculties. By the second half of the eighteenth century the primary contenders for inclusion in this list had been reduced to three: volition, the faculty of mental representation and feeling. In the Middle Ages memory had always appeared on any list of the basic sub-divisions or powers of the mind; its absence in eighteenth-century faculty psychology suggests a downgrading of its importance. Other signs of this trend have been noted in chapters 3, 4 and 7 of this book. Presumably, this was a symptom of a cultural complex for which the promise of the future was more important than a past that was increasingly seen as a source of ignorance and superstition.

Not only was there less interest in memory, but the criteria for distinguishing among mental faculties had changed. Different variants of eighteenth-century faculty psychology relied on one or other of three implicit criteria for deciding on the nature and number of mental faculties.[12] The first of these criteria was not entirely new in that it assigned a different somatic basis to each faculty, a practice that had a certain analogy to an old medically inspired tradition. Increasingly, however, ancient texts were being replaced by contemporary empirical studies as a source of knowledge about the relevant somatic structures and functions. As neuroanatomy, and later neurophysiology, got off the ground as scientific disciplines they were able to supply information about the nervous system that sealed the fate of the old speculative schemes. The proposals that replaced them were usually no less speculative, but they did raise altogether new questions about the somatic aspect of mental faculties and introduced empirical criteria for answering those questions.

A second criterion for distinguishing among mental faculties relied on the testimony of consciousness, obtained by introspection. Each faculty was supposed to be detectable by its own specific experienced quality. So an act of will, for example, constituted a different sort of experience from an act of thought. The reliance on an inspection of consciousness that had been stripped of all religious motivation and moral content was decidedly new,[13] a telling expression of a sensibility that was modern rather than medieval. In the history of memory kinds it played an indirect role, because it was used to distinguish among the mental qualities associated with the three basic faculties of cognitive representation, affect and will. Distinctions among memory kinds sometimes duplicated this tripartite division. For example, at the beginning of the nineteenth century Maine de Biran distinguished between a 'representative' memory for meaningful ideas expressed in language, a 'sensitive' memory for feelings and a 'mechanical' memory for movements that he regarded as ultimately originating in the activity of the will.[14]

Third, mental faculties were distinguished in terms of the targets or objects at which they were directed. For example, a distinction might be made between a faculty for mentally representing things past, i.e. memory, and a faculty for representing future things, anticipation or expectation. Applied to memory, this criterion led to distinctions between memory for numbers, for persons, for words, for spatial relationships and so on. As noted in chapter 6, Franz Joseph Gall, the inventor of phrenology, used this criterion.

Consistently applied, the use of this criterion can lead to the disappearance of memory as a separate faculty. Memory would simply be a word applied to the repetitive and reproductive features that each *type* of object-directed activity would have to have. A good musical memory, for example, would be part of having a well-developed musical faculty; being able to remember words would be part of a faculty of language; an ability to remember the multiplication table would be part of any faculty of calculation, and so on. But memory in general would not be a separate faculty. An analogy with 'acuity', derived from J. A. Fodor,[15] may be helpful. There is visual acuity, auditory acuity, gustatory acuity, perhaps intellectual acuity, but these are simply parameters of vision, audition, taste and intelligence; recognizing this, no one has proposed a separate faculty of acuity. The same approach may well be appropriate for memory.

Fodor distinguished between traditional 'horizontal' faculties that are placed side by side, like perception, imagination and memory, or affection, will and intellect, and 'vertical' faculties that are 'domain specific' and independent in the performance of their functions.[16] Gall would then be the pioneer of vertical faculties. Unfortunately, the effect of this classification is to displace the problem of a 'natural' division among faculties onto the question of how to establish a natural division among domains.

Once the boundaries between faculties are defined in terms of the objects or content to which the faculties are applied, rather than in terms of the powers of the soul, the need for the whole concept of faculties will surely be questioned. A leading voice in this questioning was that of Johann Friedrich Herbart (1776–1841), who proclaimed the utter unsuitability of an analysis in terms of faculties for a psychology with scientific ambitions. Regarding memory, he pointed to the huge variety of mental contexts in which it seemed to function: not only memory for names, places and numbers, but also memory for concepts, judgements and conclusions, for thoughts and reflections, for wishes and decisions, for things done and things suffered. In each case the phenomena described as 'memory' depended on factors that faculty psychology tended to disregard but that were in fact crucial. Among these factors he noted, for example, an individual's intention to remember, the interest of the material to be remembered, the length of time during which the material to be recalled was present in consciousness, the person's frame of mind in the interval between awareness of an object and its later recall. These were the kinds of factors that a psychology modelling itself on physics would have to focus on, and when that was done it would be found that 'of so-called memory nothing will remain but an empty name'.[17]

Many of the phenomena that had long been explained in terms of the power of memory Herbart was able to account for in terms of the interaction of the contents of the mind. To do that, one had to assume that the dynamic activity that caused mental effects resided in the mind's contents, not in some separate source for various mental powers.[18] Mental contents (so-called ideas) had an inherent tendency to persist, though not necessarily consciously, and their reappearance in consciousness depended on their interaction with other contents, not on some extra faculty of 'memory'. In his first attempt to sum up the implications of this point of view Herbart made a rather far-reaching proposal: 'The conjecture arises that all this distinction of the so-called mental faculties has more to do with the products of mental activity than with the internal nature of the latter, whether this nature be sound or diseased.'[19] Until the closing years of the nineteenth century, this was the dominant view among those who favoured a more 'scientific' approach to psychological questions.

Memory, perception and the individual

Assigning memory its place on the conceptual map of the soul always involved two sets of boundaries. One set served to distinguish memory from the other components of the 'inner sense'. But these differentiations depended on a prior distinction between the inner sense as a whole and the five primary senses. This distinction, with its roots in the separation of a sensory order from a rational order, formed the cornerstone of the entire Aristotelian edifice of speculation about the nature of a soul that was capable not only of sensing the world, but also of understanding it.

Aristotle's own scheme assigned sensory memory images to the sensory order, as described in chapter 2, but rational procedures had to intervene for intentional recollection to occur. There was already a profound split between the inscription of sensory experience on the tablets of the soul and the subsequent recovery and 'reading' of this inscription. If anything, this split became even more pronounced in the medieval development of Aristotelian doctrines, since the division of the world into 'sensibles' and 'intelligibles' assumed crucial importance for an entire normative order. As described in the section on the 'inner senses', the formation of sensory memory images was separated from other manifestations of memory, assigned to a different faculty and given a different location in the head.

Post-medieval empiricist philosophy did not make as clean a break with the scholastic tradition as its proponents liked to believe. Although they gradually made the mental mechanism of an 'association of ideas' do much of the work of the old rational faculties, they never freed themselves entirely from the legacy of faculty psychology, a point not lost on some of their critics.[20] A strict separation of 'faculties' pervades the relevant work of Hume, and, as already noted, preserving memory from contamination with imagination was a matter of some importance.

Even more important was the separation of primary sensory experience, increasingly referred to as 'perception', from any elaboration contributed by the inner resources of the mind, especially 'imagination'. Privately experienced sensory perceptions formed the bedrock of all knowledge for empiricist philosophy; eyewitness reports of personally observed natural phenomena provided the foundation for a new empirical science. The evidence of the senses provided by individual observers was in principle unquestionable. If the reports of some observers turned out to be unreliable, this was because they had allowed their imagination to influence what they believed they saw. This was much less likely to happen with experienced observers who were persons of good educational and social background. In any case, philosophical empiricism had maintain the strictest distinction between one part of the mind that registered events in the world through the medium of the senses and any other parts that might influence this registration process. In practice, this distinction would often function as an ideal, a norm by which the excellence of any particular observation could be judged. The high-value epithet of 'objective' came to be applied to perceptions that were apparently free from the influence of the perceiver, while those affected from within were regarded as merely 'subjective'. This outlook provided the intellectual context in which sensory perception could be transformed into a 'pure' category whose mechanisms could be investigated without even a cursory glance at other psychological functions.

Sensory perception became the first major field of investigation for the new experimental psychology of the late nineteenth century. Memory received at best marginal recognition as a kind of by-product of perception that resulted in copies of what had been perceived being stored and reproduced later with varying degrees of accuracy. Quantitative relationships between the original and the copy were considered amenable to scientific investigation, but other aspects of memory were often regarded as inappropriate for scientific research.

There were nineteenth-century figures with significant scientific credentials who rejected this view of science and sought for alternatives. Some of them, notably Rudolph Hermann Lotze (1817–81) and Wilhelm Wundt (1832–1920), had some influence on the early development of a scientific psychology, but by the early twentieth century that influence hardly extended beyond one or two German universities.[21] Both men opposed the traces of faculty psychology that were still a feature of the empiricist philosophy and psychology of their day. Such categories as 'intelligence', 'sensation', 'emotion', and of course 'memory', were still being treated as separate departments of the mind that could causally affect each other's operations as though they each had a distinct power of their own. For Lotze, this model of psychological relationships was based on an analogy with the interaction of physical forces, and hence inappropriate. The unity of the mind must become the primary consideration: 'While we see a plurality of capabilities, unity of being is the fundamental attribute of the soul.'[22]

What we call memory, according to Lotze, is not a separate mechanism for storing copies of sensory impressions, but the capacity of the mind or soul as a whole to relate mental contents to each other according to their meaning. 'This fluctuating light of combining attention'[23] generates recognition of the similarity of present and past experience. But the experience of remembering involves not only a recall of the past, but a sense of a past in the present. Whether in recall or in current perception, Lotze emphasized the focusing, combining activity of the mind rather than its receptivity to external stimuli. From this point of view no hard and fast distinction between memory and perception is possible, because the 'combining attention' that organizes present perception is itself informed by past experiences that were once present. The facts that a theory of memory had to explain were experiential in nature – Lotze's perspective was far removed from any notion of memory as a kind of performance.

Although Lotze's ideas made an impression on some key figures during the transition from philosophical to laboratory psychology, for example William James, they played no part in that transition. That cannot be said of Wilhelm Wundt, whose pioneering role in establishing the first of these laboratories has sometimes earned him the title of 'father' of that discipline. However, his influence depended largely on certain features of his *practice*, not his more general ideas about the scientific status of psychology. In America, at any rate, those were largely ignored, for the most part not even translated into English, a level of recognition that fell below that accorded to Lotze.[24]

At the beginning of chapter 5 I mentioned that Wundt did not consider memory a promising topic for a scientific psychology. With regard to the distinction between memory and other psychological categories, however, a more general feature of Wundt's standpoint becomes relevant. Briefly,

Wundt championed what he called the 'actuality' of psychological processes. One should always keep in mind, he cautioned, that there is a gap between the psychological phenomena of human consciousness and the categories we impose on these phenomena for the sake of practical convenience. Sensations do not form a separate compartment of consciousness, sectioned off from other compartments, such as feelings or acts of volition. The empirical basis of psychology is 'immediate' experience, whose various qualities all occur together. But when this experience becomes a subject-matter for investigation, whether speculative or experimental, distinguishable parts of it are categorized and brought into theoretical or experimental relationship. Investigators should not confuse their own abstractions with the raw experience that forms the actual subject-matter of their investigations.[25] Although he did not explicitly refer to the relationship between perception and memory, Wundt's principle would obviously apply to this case. An essentially similar position was taken by William James in discussing what he called 'the psychologist's fallacy', that is, substituting the schema of the psychologist for that of the person whose psychology was supposedly being studied.[26]

During the earlier part of the twentieth century, the problem of the relationship between memory and the personality as a whole was a topic for psychoanalytically orientated discourse but hardly for academic psychology. One notable exception to this occurs in the work of William Stern (see chapter 7, section headed 'A science of testimony'), a prominent psychologist of his time, who remained almost without influence in America.[27] Stern distinguished between two ways in which past experiences can act across an interval of time to affect present experience. If an experience is relatively isolated from the ongoing life of the individual personality, if it is poorly integrated with personal goals, if it has little or no personal significance, then it may form a 'trace' that remains relatively cut off from the rest of the personality. Recovery of such memories would then depend largely on associations by contiguity, similarity and similar quasi-mechanical links among memory elements. But traditional empiricist theories were wrong to generalize from these cases to all recollection. Most of the operations of memory (outside the laboratory) occur in personally significant contexts constituted not by abstracted 'items', but by integrated experiences structured in terms of their meaning for the individual. What is remembered or forgotten under these conditions depends on the organization of the personality as a whole, not on specific links between memory elements. The organization of the personality as a whole, however, does not remain the same over time, and so memories change, too, in terms of their accessibility, their vividness, their prominence, their significance. Personally integrated memories are not static.

One might say that, for Stern, the deployment of a distinct category of memory would be limited to either a very high or a very low level of abstraction. At a very abstract level one could discuss 'mnemic' effects in general, that is, the effect of the past on the present in the life of individuals. At a level permitting little generalization, one could observe memory effects among elements of experience that had been isolated from the normal flow of an individual's life, perhaps in the course of a memory experiment designed to achieve precisely this end. But as far as the interrelationship between past and present in everyday life is concerned, that would be an integral part of the psychology of personality and would not be well served by a separate psychology of memory.

Stern held an extreme position with respect to his metaphysically tinged 'personology', but his rejection of the conception of memory as a walled-off category was not unique. For Bartlett (see chapter 5, section headed 'Sir Frederic's insight'), 'remembering is not a completely independent function', and 'in order to understand how and what we remember, we must set into relation to this how and what we perceive'.[28] Indeed, he introduces his studies of remembering through experiments in perception, and constantly refers back to what is perceived when attempting to understand what is remembered.[29] Gestalt psychology initially established its principles of mental organization in connection with the phenomena of spatial perception. Applying analogous principles to the temporal organization of stimuli, as in the hearing of melodies, was a natural extension. This case is already on the fuzzy border of perception and memory, and the step to longer time intervals, clearly involving memory, is easily taken. In Koffka's words, 'our memory of temporal sequences should be similar to that of spatial patterns, since in the traces time becomes spatialized'.[30] Leaving aside the validity of this claim, it serves to illustrate the theoretical integration of perceptual and memory phenomena that Gestalt psychology sought to bring about. Indeed, Koffka, like Bartlett and other psychologists of the time, is anxious to avoid what he refers to as the tendency for the word 'memory' to become reified and for memory phenomena to be studied in isolation from the rest of psychology.[31]

Even behaviourism, much more influential than either Bartlett or Gestalt psychology, was not conducive to any special 'psychology of memory', though partly for the silly reason that words like 'remembering', 'recollecting' and 'reminiscing' reeked of the psychology of consciousness. But it is also true that, in defining the subject-matter of psychology as the behaviour of organisms, behaviourism encouraged a study of the activity of the whole organism and discouraged any dissection of this activity in terms that were even vaguely suggestive of distinct mental faculties.[32]

The crucial exception to this general avoidance of a reified category of memory was none other than Hermann Ebbinghaus, the inventor of the nonsense syllable and pioneer of experimental memory research. He wanted, as already mentioned in chapter 5, to study what he referred to as *das eigentliche Gedächtnis*, usually translated as 'pure memory'. Out of this intention grew the bizarre notion that the appropriate material for the scientific study of memory would have to be devoid of meaning. By excluding meaning, an experimenter would be eliminating the unpredictable and uncontrollable influence of all those psychological processes that normally interact with memory.

As it turned out, the use of nonsense syllables did not get rid of meaning, because the subjects in these experiments stubbornly imposed meaning on them. Eventually, lists of nonsense syllables were replaced by lists of words and word pairs, but this did not shake the conceptual foundations of the Ebbinghaus project. Pure memory, divorced from the rest of human psychology, continued to be the imagined target of these experiments. Any relationship between memory and other psychological functions would have to take the form of causal influences between entities that were kept conceptually and empirically distinct. But on the whole, the 'experimental psychology of memory' was much less concerned with such influences than with a search for the 'principles', or even 'laws' that governed the operation of memory *per se*.

This orientation was not a product of purely theoretical concerns. With the conversion of fluid fields of intellectual study into modern scientific *disciplines* and sub-disciplines, institutional arrangements and norms of investigative practice came to play important roles in defining the place and limits of different areas of inquiry. Interests became vested in the boundaries between these areas, and careers often depended on their maintenance. In many cases, especially that of psychology, rapid disciplinary growth was accompanied by a proliferation of sub-disciplines and an increasing isolation of different areas of specialization from each other. The experimental psychology of memory was no exception to this trend. Inevitably, the gulf between the psychology of memory and the psychology of perception, emotion, motivation, etc. widened. Everyone was aware of this unintended outcome, but occasional attempts at bridging the gulf remained without effect on the overall trend.

There was always a niche within the broad church of twentieth-century psychology for the project of studying 'pure memory'. But what kept this project going and even enabled it to grow? (It was hardly the weight of its empirical or intellectual contribution, whose non-cumulative nature was noted by more than one practitioner.) For a time, the separation of memory from other psychological functions seemed to be legitimized by the widespread acceptance of the digital computer as an appropriate model for human cognition. The separation of memory from processing in the computer appeared to support an analogous separation in the operations of the human mind. But the isolation of memory experiments from other areas of the discipline antedated and post-dated the period of maximum enthusiasm for the computer analogy.

More lasting and more pervasive influences can be traced to the investigative practice that had become standard procedures for much of the field.

The appeal of these procedures was based on their guarantee of quantitative results and their promise of controlled experimental conditions, features that were often felt to guarantee their scientific value, no matter how trivial the content. These procedures also had the great advantage of lending themselves most readily to employment in small-scale studies of modest theoretical scope, easily packaged as journal articles or doctoral dissertations. The form of investigative practice that had come to define the field for most of the twentieth century had largely committed it to substituting the study of memorization for the study of memory (see chapter 5, sections headed 'The memorizing trap' and 'The Dark Ages of memory research'). This certainly made it easy to maintain the practical, institutional and theoretical separation between the psychology of memory and that of perception and other psychological functions.[33]

If memorization, with the apparent necessity of information storage, was the paradigm case for memory as such, then a psychology of adaptation in a perceived environment could very well do without it. This was the position of J. J. Gibson, who insisted on the distinction between the dependence of current adaptations on past experience and their dependence on the *storage* of past experience. The perceptual system does become attuned to invariants in the sensory environment, but this can be achieved without recourse to stored memories of that environment.[34] This distinction is a variant of a more general distinction, found in philosophical discussions of memory, between retention and storage.[35] A person's face, for example, may *retain* the effects of persistent past experiences of worry, but this does not mean that the experience is *stored* within his worried face as though it were old furniture stored in an attic. Storage implies retention, but retention implies storage only metaphorically.

Gibson himself had little interest in exploring how the effects of past experience might affect the present, if not through a mechanism of storage and retrieval. Nevertheless, there were isolated attempts at probing the implications of his position for the psychology of memory. In one noteworthy instance there was a proposal to replace the deeply ingrained storage metaphor with the metaphor of a stage setting.[36] Implicitly, this metaphor harks back to Gestalt conceptions of figure–ground relationships, and even further back to Wundt's distinction between *Blickfeld* and *Blickpunkt*. Explicitly, it was based on suggestions made by Bartlett and Gibson.

The way we take up any part of our sensory experience, the way we actually experience it, the meaning we give to it, is always affected by the rest of our experience, some of it current as background perception, some of it past as something retained from previous encounters with the world. Metaphorically, current background and past experience set the stage on which specific scenes are presented for our interpretation. When we saw other staged performances before, to continue the metaphor, this did not result in a split process of seeing and then storing what we saw in 'memory'.

Rather, it resulted in some alteration, some 'tuning', in our disposition to see things in a particular way when encountered in a certain kind of context. A young child at its first live performance may initially be disturbed by some of what is happening on stage (more likely before the advent of television), but it soon learns the appropriate set for understanding a theatrical performance. Even if it has no recallable memory of the contents of its previous theatre experience, it is likely to go into the next performance with a different attitude, one more attuned to the social expectations and demands of the situation. The child has learned to recategorize what it sees on the stage as 'only a play', and it has done so on the basis of certain stage-setting cues, some of them of course contained in parents' talk.

One can apply this kind of analysis to a large range of situations in which people instantaneously find their cognitive bearings without searching through their memory stores for the right items. The paradigm case for storing and systematically retrieving specific items encountered in the past is provided by scholastic knowledge. In this context, the retention and retrieval of abstracted information, usually communicated via printed text, is adaptive. But the skills of this kind of remembering, the historical evidence strongly suggests (chapter 3), were gradually acquired in a centuries-long process of interaction with devices of external memory whose improvement went hand in hand with the development of the skills appropriate to them. Traditional theories of memory as a storage facility separate from the rest of human experience were essentially a reflection by scholars on their own experience. Likening memory to writing was the foundation stone of this tradition. But the tradition lives on in theories designed to account specifically for the 'data' provided by situations in which experimenters carefully set the stage for a scholastic-type retrieval of text items.

Before concluding this section we should take at least a brief look at an astonishingly bold impulse for rethinking the relationship between memory and perception that came from an unexpected direction late in the twentieth century: immunology. The effectiveness of the body's immune system depends on its ability to 'recognize' potentially harmful antigens. But specific immunities also have to be acquired through exposure to the relevant antigens. Once acquired, the immunity lasts for a period of time. During this time, whether it is relatively long or short, the immune system seems to have a 'memory' that enables it to recognize a subsequent invasion by the specific antigen. The analogy to what is ordinarily meant by 'memory' and 'recognition' is easy to see, and Gerald Edelman, a Nobel Prize winner in immunology, has elaborated on it in some detail.[37]

To do this Edelman has to tread in the footsteps of Ewald Hering a century earlier and greatly expand the ordinary meaning of 'memory'. He includes under this term not only aspects of genetics, as Hering had already done, but also, of course, immune responses as well as perceptual learning.[38] It is the latter that is important in the present context. The analogy between perceptual learning and immune responses leads to an emphasis on a basic point that was too often forgotten in late twentieth-century models of memory: sensory experience arrives *unlabelled*. In this respect it is similar to an unknown antigen. What the body's adaptive system has to do is to find an appropriate label, that is, to categorize the input, and then retain the ability to repeat this act of identification. In any such process perception and memory do not constitute two separate systems but are aspects of the same adaptive response. What is retained is the potential for recognition, for categorization, and on the psychological level this manifests itself as a perceptual achievement.

How is this feat of recognition memory accomplished? Here there are essentially two alternative types of model. The first type works with *pre-packaged* input which is then stored and retrieved when required again. This is the type of model that is implied whenever input is structured by a computer programmer or an experimental psychologist. It is called an *instructional* model and distinguished from the second, *selectionist*, type, whose mechanism depends on the fact that individuals' categorization of environmental input has adaptive consequences for them. Better consequences lead to a selection of the corresponding cognitive pattern, increasing the likelihood that this pattern will be reinstated in future encounters. Such patterns, or 'maps', according to Edelman's 'neural Darwinism', depend on variable synaptic links in populations of cortical neurons that overlap and fluctuate, both within and between individuals.[39]

The distinction between instructional and selectionist models is useful, but it is by no means impossible that both types of learning occur in practice. Their relative preponderance, however, would be expected to change over the life span. In younger individuals, for whom much of the world is still 'unlabelled', selectionism is presumably the way forward, but later on, the packaging of incoming information may become all too rigid and predictable. Quite apart from this developmental effect, the fact that information arrives both in pre-structured and in fluid forms suggests that different mechanisms may be mobilized for coping with each of these aspects. What is surely misleading is the implication, built into many late twentieth-century theories and experimental practices, that the instructional model, involving the storing and retrieval of pre-packaged information, provides the indispensable key to a science of memory.

Is memory in the head?

The localization theories, discussed in chapter 8, were based upon the firm conviction that memory could be located in a physical place and that place was inside the head. You might even watch memory at work by following the fluctuations of brain metabolism from one brain location to another. If you lived a few centuries earlier you might have tried to encourage memory by warming the back of the head. In any case, the idea that memory had its own seat within the physical individual was deeply ingrained. But even when there was no physical reference, when the issue was one of situating memory among other mental faculties, perception, imagination and so on, it went without saying that memory was to be found in the individual mind. Whether it was looked for in material brains or non-material minds, memory was unquestionably an attribute of individuals.

Yet there were always voices that insisted on certain qualifications to this commonplace. Surprisingly, Plato stands at the beginning of this discourse too. I say surprisingly, because, as the originator of the seemingly indestructible inscription metaphor for memory, Plato could be expected to place memory firmly within the individual soul. However, my account of Plato's memory metaphors in chapter 2 was incomplete. I mentioned the metaphor of the aviary and the even more famous wax tablet metaphor, but there is a third metaphor that occurs in the context of Plato's thoughts about memory. This is the metaphor contained in Socrates' claim that he and his mother were practitioners of the same craft, midwifery.[40] When engaged in his famous technique of drawing fresh insights out of people by a carefully structured line of questioning he was, he implied, acting as a kind of midwife.

When I referred to this metaphor near the beginning of chapter 4, I emphasized the more traditional point that pregnancy has to precede successful midwifery, which points to Plato's notion that innate ideas constitute a kind of memory. However, the midwife metaphor can also be read in a way that points in an altogether different direction. A midwife is needed to help in the process of giving birth, a difficult feat for a human female to bring to a successful conclusion on her own. If we accept the analogy between giving birth and remembering, the midwife metaphor can also suggest that human help is an important, often indispensable, aspect of remembering. In many cases, successful remembering may actually be impossible without this help. The role of the 'midwife' in helping a person to remember introduces a crucial qualification for any claim that memory is purely an individual matter. Whereas reading impressions on wax or catching hold of birds, Plato's previous metaphors for remembering, are activities one can engage in on one's own, being delivered by a midwife is not. What this last metaphor does is to alert us to the fact that in many cases, those with the best outcomes, remembering is not something that takes place only inside one head but that is the product of the joint effort of two people.

As I mentioned in chapter 4, in the dialogue known as the *Meno*[41] Socrates tries to show that a relatively untutored boy has a hidden knowledge of rather sophisticated geometrical theorems. He does this by subjecting the boy to a methodical series of questions, as is his usual practice. However, he does not merely question the boy verbally, he draws a series of geometric diagrams in the sand and asks questions about *those*. This is the technique by which the boy is led, step by step, to the recovery of what Plato believes is a knowledge no one knew he had, least of all the boy himself. The guided inspection of externally displayed diagrams plays a crucial role in the process of recovering this hidden knowledge. Such diagrams are tools of remembering, just as a wax tablet could be. But they are different sorts of tools that function in different ways. The wax tablet plays a passive role; it merely holds what has already been formed and gives it back unchanged when consulted later. The diagrams drawn in the sand are part of a very different process, a process of *construction*. Not only is their own construction an important part of the memory recovery process, that whole process becomes one of step-by-step construction. Meno's slave is not completely ignorant at the start. He knows what a square is, he has some knowledge of arithmetic and the quantitative representation of areas. These are things he knows that he knows. But then the 'midwife' steps in and, by means of questions about constructions in the sand, gradually brings the boy to a recognition of knowledge that is new to him, though Plato would have us regard it as, in some sense, a memory.

If we accept Plato's claim, then what we have been presented with is a model of memory's operation that is entirely at variance with the inscription model. This would be a memory whose contents do not consist of pre-formed records of previous personal experience, records that can be consulted whenever the need arises. This memory is not accessible without the help of another person (or perhaps persons) acting in the role of 'midwife'. It is also a memory, according to Plato, of knowledge that concerns universal truths rather than the concrete impressions of individual sensory experience.

There is no necessary connection between all these features. On the one hand, Plato's dialogue presents an illustration of a particular *technique* of what is said to be remembering, a technique in which diagrams in the sand and a human interlocutor play a major role. On the other hand, Plato uses this display of pedagogical technique to bolster his claim for the existence of a universal knowledge that everyone has, though usually without being aware of it. These components of his exposition do not entail each other.[42] It is possible to be a Platonist on the question of innate ideas (which is what this curious kind of memory comes down to) without being a devotee of the Socratic method, either in theory or practice. It is also possible to decouple the valuable technique from the wrong conclusions it leads to in Plato's case.[43]

Historically, the former alternative has been far more prominent than the latter. The essence of what became known as Platonism always centred on *doctrines* regarding knowledge of universals rather than on the special *methods* that were required to achieve consciousness of this knowledge. After the advent of Christianity, the doctrines and the methods both became highly spiritualized, prayer taking the place of mathematical demonstration and representatives of the Church taking the place of Socrates.[44]

But although it was not highly theorized, a practical understanding survived with regard to the importance of external props for the work of memory. Nowhere is this more evident than in the practices associated with the use of written manuscripts discussed in chapter 3. Textual composition, page layouts and illustrations were designed to enhance the book's function as a mnemonic device. The medieval metaphor of 'the book of memory' did not merely imply an analogy between the memory inside the head and the memory externally preserved on the pages of a book, it referred also to a recognized symbiosis of book and reader.[45]

But books functioned as memory devices not only through the medium of text, but also through the medium of the pictorial images they contained. These images had mnemonic functions, and that also held for many artistic images that proliferated outside the pages of written manuscripts, in paintings, carvings and sculptures. As image making became more professionalized, a pedagogy of artistic apprenticeship developed and gave rise to its own literature. It is in that literature, rather than in philosophical writings, that we find a more profound appreciation of the interdependence of external and internal memory. In the late Middle Ages and the Renaissance, memory was highly valued by artists, for whom it functioned as a repository of standard images to be drawn upon in their work. But in their pedagogical reflections they drew not on a static storehouse metaphor, but on their practical experience of developing an artistic memory.

Leonardo da Vinci, for example, described how an apprentice should proceed in acquiring a fund of images for future use. He was to trace an exemplar on a glass pane, copy it and then judge the copy by superimposing it on the exemplar. That way he would be able to see exactly where the copy had fallen short so that he could try to come up with a better copy next time. In due course, his memory would be enriched by another valuable image that would guide future work. Leonardo also advocated the use of portable sketchpads that help the artist's memory in transferring images from the world outside to the studio or workshop.[46] This was the kind of context in which the interplay between internal and external memory was simply a condition of good practice that could not be overlooked. The solitary philosopher might continue to speculate about memory as an internal storehouse, but the practising artist was more interested in how memory made contact with the world, both in its formation during apprenticeship and in its operation during artistic production.

The fading of the European Renaissance, and the early modern period that followed, did not lead to any reversal in this state of affairs. Quite the contrary; an ever-sharpening division of intellectual labour ensured that any general discussion of the nature of memory remained firmly within the province of philosophy. But this soon led to an interesting division.

By the end of the seventeenth century, philosophy, at least in the most important centres, France and Britain, had been strongly influenced by

Cartesian dualism, already alluded to in chapter 2. The Cartesian split between the realm of the mind and that of the body legitimized a division between two kinds of discourse that might address the topic of memory: the discourse of mental philosophy, where memory would make an appearance as a mental phenomenon, and the discourse of (speculative) natural philosophy, where possible physical analogies of memory might be described. The writings of Locke and Hume would fall into the first category, those of Hooke, Hartley and Descartes himself into the second.[47]

In spite of all their differences, the two types of memory discourse grounded in Cartesian dualism did, however, share one profound conviction. For both camps there was not the slightest doubt that the *location* of memory was entirely *within* the mind, or within the body, as the case might be. There was a shared belief in the autonomous individual as the seat of memory, an expression of the fiercely individualistic stance that was to be the hallmark of Western philosophy for several centuries. Individuals were regarded as metaphysically distinct and sharply separated from the world they lived in. It was therefore taken for granted that memory was strictly an attribute of individual minds, or, in the physicalist version, of individual brains.

When modern psychology hived off from the broader field of philosophy, the intellectual rupture was far from complete. Some of the deepest commitments of eighteenth- and nineteenth-century philosophies were transferred to the new, would-be scientific psychology without question. One of these commitments was an individualism that manifested itself in two norms that were decisive for the direction that the new discipline was to take.

The first norm operated on the level of psychological *taxonomy*. What were the primary kinds of phenomena that those working in the new discipline were to describe and explain? The norm of individualism, inherited from the preceding philosophical psychology, decreed that psychological kinds should be attributes only of autonomous individuals, attributes that resided in individuals thought of as separated from the material, social and cultural world that surrounded them. That world might provide the occasion for the operation of the primary psychological attributes, but it did not define the intrinsic nature of those attributes. Attention, perception, sensation, and of course memory, are examples of categories bequeathed to modern psychology by its ancestry. All of them carry the connotation of phenomena located within individuals. To understand them we should look at what individuals do or experience. What is quite foreign to this way of thinking is the notion of primary units constituted by individuals in a particular world context.

A second norm of individualism insists that the *explanation* of psychological events should always be looked for within each separate individual. For a scientific psychology, this generally meant *causal* explanation, following the example of the physical sciences.[48] Accordingly, the new psychology warmly embraced such explanatory categories as ability, motivation and association that could be regarded as causal factors operating inside each individual's head. Similarly, in the field of memory, hypothetical explanatory processes were situated inside the minds or brains of individuals, as indeed the philosophical tradition demanded. No consideration was given to the possibility that an adequate explanation might have to abandon the metaphysical status accorded to the boundary between individuals and the social as well as material context for the manifestations of memory.

These biases, inherited from an individualistic philosophical psychology, were not loosened by psychology's transformation into a would-be scientific discipline. On the contrary, these biases were incorporated in the ground-plan for the institutional division of emerging social science disciplines. Much has been made of psychology's historical separation from philosophy, but in the long run, its subsequent separation from all other social science disciplines had equally profound effects. The new disciplinary organization of knowledge production worked through powerful institutional structures that increasingly controlled accreditation, training, approved communication, standards of work and so on.[49] A certain disciplinary ideology provided the inspiration for and the justification of these structures. In the case of psychology, the notion of a science of *individuals* was a central component of disciplinary ideology. The social dimension of human experience and conduct could be bracketed off in the form of discrete social 'factors' that were not the province of psychology, but of one or other social science.

The disciplinary division of knowledge production put its stamp on twentieth-century memory science. For the most part, sociological or historical investigation of 'collective memory' remained entirely separate from psychological investigations of memory in which the social and cultural background of experimental 'subjects' was systematically disregarded. Institutionalized experimental practice therefore reinforced deeply ingrained beliefs about memory having its location in the heads of individuals.

It is hardly necessary to emphasize that the disciplinary division of knowledge production in the social sciences is historically contingent and not mandated by the structure of reality in some ultimate, metaphysical sense.[50] It *is* mandated by a particular interpretation of reality that draws a sharp line between individuals and their environment. With that line firmly in place, the cultural being of individuals can be displaced by an asocial environment. But the material features of the environment are affected, too, in so far as they have the character of tools. For the use of tools, including the symbolic tools that are so important for the operations of memory, negates any sharp line of separation between encapsulated individual and environmental 'stimuli'.

In twentieth-century psychology of memory, recognition of individuals as cultural beings and tool users was very much the exception, achieving real momentum only towards the end of the period. After the development of vigilantly policed disciplinary boundaries, sociologists and anthropologists might occasionally concern themselves with the social dimension of human memory, but for most psychologists this was alien territory. The major exceptions were Bartlett in England, to whose work I will return shortly, and a small group of psychologists in the then Soviet Union. L. S. Vygotsky (1896–1934) and Alexander Luria (1901–77) were the key figures in a group that was active in the late 1920s and early 1930s, trying to develop a psychology that was not in thrall to the individualistic metaphysics that had defined the boundaries of psychology in the West.

In reference to memory, this project entailed a basic distinction between sensory after-effects, most vividly seen in so-called eidetic imagery, and the greater part of human remembering which relies on external artefacts – knots, sounds, wooden figures, diagrams, inscriptions, etc. – to do its work.[51] In the development of memory in children, this distinction can be clearly observed. Improvements in memory during childhood are generally due to children's acquisition of skills in the use of external mnemonic tools to which they are introduced in the course of their socialization and education.[52] These mnemonic tools are the product of millennia of social development: the invention of paper, of the alphabet, of a convenient system of numerals, of textual layout, of schematic diagrams and so on. In accomplishing current memory tasks, individuals have learned to rely on the achievements of previous generations. These provide them with the tools required for undertaking such tasks.[53]

Vygotsky and Luria's rejection of the metaphysics of individualism came at the wrong time and in the wrong place. With few resources, largely cut off from international contacts, their work facing a wall of ignorance and suspicion both at home and abroad, they were unable to develop their ideas beyond a preliminary sketch of the basics. Vygotsky, the theoretical powerhouse of the little group, died of tuberculosis before his fortieth year; Luria had many interests and did not publish his popular case-study of a so-called mnemonist until much later.[54] By then, his work, and more particularly that of Vygotsky, was slowly beginning to find a readership among some Western psychologists. In the field of memory, however, there was no detectable influence from that source.

As one might have expected, sociologists were less inclined than psychologists to place memory exclusively inside individual minds and brains. But most sociologists had other priorities. Maurice Halbwachs (1877–1945), the pioneer of sociological studies of memory, had made his core contribution by 1925, but it remained accessible only in the original French for well over half a century, when excerpts from it were finally translated into English as part of a 'Heritage of Sociology' series.[55] Much of Halbwachs's work was concerned with the cultivation of shared memories of groups, especially religious groups, families and social classes. He was interested in the dependence of this cultivation on rites and symbols, in the way memories served group interests and in the merging of memory and legend, a phenomenon also found on the level of individual memory. Indeed, Halb-wachs made a number of observations on individual memory that were explicitly or implicitly critical of academic psychological practices. He pointed out, for example, that any memory that relies on verbal labels and categories cannot be considered to be the product of an isolated individual mind: the frameworks used by individuals for organizing their memories have a social origin, and in adopting such frameworks, individuals take over the point of view of particular groups. He also stressed that acts of remembering usually take place in a social context: we remember things in the course of conversations or joint tasks, our memories have social effects, some of them intended, and we turn to other people for confirmation of our version of past events.[56]

Among psychologists, Frederic Bartlett was very much the exception in paying some attention to Halbwachs's observations. Though he rejected the latter's tendency to express himself in terms of a collective mind, he agreed that 'Social organization gives a persistent framework into which all detailed recall must fit, and it very powerfully influences both the manner and the matter of recall.'[57] Bartlett's early interests tended in the direction of what would later be referred to as 'cultural psychology', and he certainly made an effort to provide his experimental investigations of memory with a socio-cultural dimension. As already described in chapter 5, he deliberately employed material from another culture in studying remembering. The fact that this material was often remembered in a culturally more familiar form surely illustrated the dependence of individual memory on the cognitive structures favoured by a particular cultural background.

In his method of serial reproduction Bartlett went further and introduced a social factor into the experimental conditions under which remembering took place. Instead of studying the products of recall by a socially isolated indi-vidual – which was and remains the standard procedure in memory experiments – he analysed the changes that occurred when material was reproduced through a succession of individuals forming a chain. This was at least a first step towards decreasing the gap that separated the conditions under which recall occurred in psychological experiments from the condi-tions under which it often occurred in everyday life, when the recall of an event depended on contributions from several people.

However, this aspect of Bartlett's work fell on even stonier ground than his emphasis on the reconstructive nature of memory, previously discussed in chapter 5. Even when interest in Bartlett's work revived, a generation after its completion, the socio-cultural aspects, which had been so signifi-cant to Bartlett himself, were left aside. Only towards the end of the century were these aspects considered worthy of serious critical consideration, and then only by a distinct group of British researchers whose work remained unassimilable by the mainstream. This was no surprise, since, in their re-evaluation of Bartlett's work, they adopted the view that his efforts to respect the socio-cultural context of memory had not gone nearly far enough. True, his method of serial reproduction had at least added some sort of social component to the techniques of studying remembering, but the communication that this method added was one-sided – one person retold a story and another listened. That was still a long way from the kind of context in which remembering most often takes place in ordinary life, a discursive, conversational or argumentative context in which there is much interaction among the participants.[58]

Moreover, Bartlett's approach, according to these critics, still showed an inappropriate preoccupation with deviations from accurate reproduction, as though accurate reproduction retained its normative importance even when it had been shown to be a rare exception in practice. But psychology experiments, including Bartlett's, were not representative of most human situations that involved questions of memory. In all these experiments a definitive version of the truth was available in the form of the stimulus material, verbal or pictorial, that psychologists presented to their experimental subjects, whose accuracy of recall then became measurable. But in many ordinary life situations there were no records of what had really taken place in the past, and often the very notion of 'what had really taken place' was moot, because different witnesses each had their own interpretation of what had happened.

Yet people are undeniably interested in coming to some agreement about events in the past, and they do engage in talk to establish an acceptable version of events. However, this social construction of memory is seldom motivated by a disinterested search for the truth; more usually, the issue is one of *justifying* certain actions, beliefs, interpretations. Versions of past events presented in social contexts generally have a *rhetorical*, persuasive function.

A traditional memory theorist might well agree with these observations and still maintain that each person carried around within herself a private version of what she remembered, irrespective of how she doctored this version to make it publicly acceptable. Memory research would then be trying to get at the principles that governed the formation, storage and retrieval of these private memories. The rules for publicly presenting these inner memories would be a topic for a separate, more sociologically orientated, discipline.

But since we cannot look directly into a person's private cognitions, such a dualistic solution would require us to accept that traditional experimental situations are different from all other social situations in acting as a kind of mirror reflecting the universal course of private cognitions. Is this possible? It would be possible if we could abstract from the content and meaning of people's memory reports to get at 'pure' memory and the laws of its operation. That hope is the kernel of the Ebbinghaus legacy; a hope that lingered on long after its ingenious concretization in the nonsense syllable had been discredited. But according to the latter-day critics of psychological cognitivism, this hope is unjustified in any case, because memory is *intrinsically* social. Memory reports are not produced by feral children, but by human individuals whose cognitive processes have been shaped by language and social interaction. The content and meaning of those reports cannot be treated as extrinsic variables whose causal effect on some mnemic essence can be studied. There is no such essence. The important, the realistic, questions to ask about memory are questions about its operation in social contexts.[59]

It is too early to dissect the historical factors that led to the emergence of a viewpoint profoundly opposed to the prevailing cognitivism of the late twentieth century. It would also go beyond the framework of this book to make such an attempt. However, there is one factor that must be mentioned because it is so evident and because it is relevant to other late modern developments. I am referring to the permeability of disciplinary boundaries that was obviously a prerequisite for the development of an approach so much at variance with traditional disciplinary practices and preconceptions. Psychologists who developed conceptions of memory as a social, rather than an essentially individual, accomplishment were open to influences from various branches of the social sciences and humanities that had begun to take an interest in problems of memory. These included historians, who had switched from an exclusive reliance on documents to the use of oral history; folklorists, who had to take into account variability in the reproduction of a core content; sociologists, who had followed in the footsteps of Halbwachs and developed the idea of communities of memory; communication researchers, who had elaborated techniques of conversation analysis; and philosophers, who had mounted a withering critique of the indefensible assumptions on which the whole project of an individualized science of memory rested.[60]

Strictly enforced norms of disciplinary practice insulated most work on the psychology of memory from such influences. It remained axiomatic that theories of memory must be theories about what happened inside individual heads. The fact that evidence for or against such theories was obtainable only in social situations could easily be masked by a special language that employed terms such as 'data', 'experiment', 'stimulus series', 'response variability', etc. to shut out any social reference.

With these institutionalized norms in place, any relaxation of disciplinary isolation was possible in only one direction. The axiomatic location of memory inside individual heads was shared by psychology and medical science. Collaboration was therefore possible and became increasingly attractive with the popularization and consequent generous funding of brain research in the late twentieth century. As indicated at the end of chapter 5, significant questions about the psychology of memory were being reformulated as questions about the brain by the end of the century. The revival of the localizationalist project in the wake of technical advances in neural imaging, described in chapter 8, meant that questions about the brain were often posed so as to be answerable in terms of the physical layout of the machinery in the head.

Memory research was therefore being pulled in two widely divergent directions. On the one hand, cognitive neuroscience was burrowing ever deeper into brain architecture, and on the other, discourse analysis was engaging widening networks of collective remembering. These were two varieties of memory studies that were mutually irrelevant. As they were also widely unequal in their degree of institutional and financial support, there could be no doubt as to which of them was more successful in defining the major direction of *fin de siècle* trends. However, discursive psychology was not the only source of alternatives to the traditional placing of memory inside the cranium.

One source of alternatives developed under the shelter of the discipline of anthropology, a social science that had traditionally relied on fieldwork, rather than experimentation, for 'disciplining' its subject-matter. Moreover, its evolving conception of 'culture' had little in common with the way the term was often used in psychology. For those psychologists who regarded controlled experimentation as the scientific version of the philosopher's stone culture was just one more extraneous variable, to be controlled by the selection of 'culturally homogeneous' groups of experimental subjects. Anthropologists, however, had largely rejected the homogeneous and static conception of cultural phenomena implied by such procedures. On the whole, they were more likely to regard culture as an arena of socially significant enactments, ritual and everyday, that were often contested, changing and ambiguous. Their focus on social practice was not compatible with any neat separation between 'beliefs' carried around inside individual heads and 'social norms' located somewhere outside.[61]

This background made it possible to develop anthropological approaches to human cognition that were quite at variance with any 'Cartesian psychology' founded on a thick line of separation between individual minds and their environments. Empirical studies of 'situated' cognition showed, for example, how very profoundly arithmetic operations could vary, depending on the social and material setting – supermarket, school, open air market – in which they were carried out.[62] The lesson to be learned from studying cognition in the real world was that cognitive processes did not take place exclusively inside individual heads but were 'seamlessly distributed across persons, activity and setting'.[63] The appropriate unit of analysis for the scientific study of human cognition is therefore not the psychologist's 'experimental subject', but persons acting in settings.

There were some powerful demonstrations of the need 'to move the boundary of the unit of cognitive analysis out beyond the skin of the individual'.[64] In extensive studies of navigational tasks, on water and in the air, Edwin Hutchins showed how these tasks were not solved inside any individual's head, but by an organized cognitive system that was *distributed* over several individuals and the material with which they worked. Certainly, individuals made their contributions, but they did this in the form of activities whose scope and direction were entirely determined by their role in the organization of the distributed cognitive system. The parts of the system located outside the skin of any particular individual were not merely an arena in which the products of inside-the-head processes were displayed; on the contrary, what went on inside the head depended, in form and substance, on the resources and the demands of the socio-technological system in which individual cognition was embedded.

Memory often enters into the tasks studied in this context. When an aircraft makes a landing, for example, a set of correspondences between airspeed and wing configuration must not only be computed but also remembered at the appropriate times. Where does this remembering take place? Inside the pilot's head? No, is Hutchins's reply after several years of detailed, partly participant, observation. The pilot consults data stored by instruments, but he or she must learn to use these instruments and interpret the data appropriately. So effective remembering requires contributions from both the individual brain and the material artefacts with which it interacts. Moreover, in multi-piloted aircraft, the pilots may collaborate in sharing out different aspects of the task. So the question that has to be addressed, according to Hutchins, is not 'how does a pilot remember speeds?' but 'how does a cockpit remember its speeds?'.[65]

It was easier for social anthropologists to adopt this perspective than for psychologists. Nevertheless, that discipline's long love affair with the encapsulated Cartesian mind was slowly being threatened by two stubborn facts of life; we might call them words and things. 'Words' refers to the role, already alluded to, that discourse plays in the working of memory. But one did not need to adopt the radically dissident stance of discursive psychology to undermine the traditional view. A long-standing 'ecological' perspective, originating in J. J. Gibson's work on perception, provided a framework for drawing attention to the way that memory relied on 'things' located outside the skin. Books and filing cabinets are obvious examples, but before that there were knots, notches and drawings on all kinds of materials. Humans have provided themselves with mnemonically helpful things throughout their history because they have understood that such things could lighten the burden of remembering. But making things share this burden implies that, for humans, memory is *distributed* over people and things. However, things can only play their mnemonic role if people have learned how to use them appropriately. To use a filing cabinet effectively one has to learn some principles of filing. In other words, the external and the internal components of memory are interdependent. I alluded to this point in discussing the role of medieval manuscripts in chapter 3. The same point can be illustrated by analysing the historical development of the modern office, a process of coupling material advances in record-keeping with the new skills required to take advantage of these advances.[66] Any modern office is a place where memory is distributed over several individuals and over the material record-keeping devices to which these individuals are linked.

Because of its specialized design, it is easy to appreciate that a filing cabinet functions as an external memory. The mnemonic functions of many everyday objects are more likely to remain hidden, eclipsed by their other functions. But failure of the normal biological resources of memory often shifts more of the burden of remembering onto external objects, and then their latent mnemonic functions become more visible. One of the minor consequences of intensified specialization of geriatric care was the professional recognition that, for older persons with memory impairment, the quality of everyday functioning could be significantly enhanced by a structured environment of 'reminders' in the form of appropriately displayed objects.[67] But this would hardly be possible if the mnemonic use of common objects had not been a well-established, if unnoticed, practice long before there was any impairment.

These and other pointers to the externalization of memory in practical contexts did little to change traditions of memory discourse that had existed for centuries. What did shake those traditions, the novelty that could not be ignored, was the broad integration of computers into an ever-expanding list of everyday activities. This was a revolutionary change from earlier incarnations of the digital computer, when it had been an expensive machine, limited in application and unfamiliar to most. Its first technical accomplishments produced the kind of awe that humans have often shown in response to the products of their own ingenuity. In its early years, the computer shared some characteristics with an idol whose creators are oblivious of their own role in maintaining the idol's status.

All that changed with the computer's widespread integration, especially personal computers, into daily life. Whereas at an earlier stage the most pressing problems had been problems of electronic architecture, the practical effectiveness of computers was now seen to depend quite significantly on the interaction between them and their human users. This became a major area of research and led to some rethinking of the way computers were regarded in certain more recent theories of human cognition. More theorists abandoned the analogy between an isolated logic machine and a disembodied mind in favour of a non-Cartesian unit that bound together embodied actors, cognitive tools and environmental affordances. In any case, the rapidly established ubiquity of the internet, made possible by computer networks, had fatally damaged the appeal of the single computer as a credible model for human cognition.

During the last decade of the twentieth century, this change of perspective led to a widespread questioning of the received wisdom that placed memory firmly in the head. Although even a cursory discussion of these developments is not possible within the historical scope of this book, some of the areas in which they became noticeable should be mentioned briefly here. In the field of education, the large-scale introduction of computers led to a non-traditional understanding of the tight connection between learner and cognitive tool in the improvement of intelligent performance, including memory.[68] In the huge field of artificial intelligence research, the advent of situated robotics was particularly salient for demonstrating the potential of mechanisms that relied, not on preconfigured plans held in 'memory', but on current actor–environment dynamics.[69] This kind of development had its reverberations in psychology, the discipline with the strongest roots in the past, and led to a new emphasis on the dependence of individual capabilities on external aids, symbolic and otherwise.[70] Giving external memory its due, as a crucial element in human evolution, Merlin Donald coined the term 'exogram' to supplement the 'engrams' that had been the staple of twentieth-century psychological speculations about memory.[71]

From the foreshortened perspective afforded by the lapse of what is hardly a moment in historical time, it would appear that the closing years of the millennium were marked by a broad swell of opinion running counter to a tradition stretching back almost to the very beginnings of memory discourse in Europe. That tradition, whose various expressions have filled most of this book, consistently tried to account for the influence of the past on human individuals by speculating about entities or processes firmly located inside those individuals' heads. 'Memory' was the collective name of these hypothetical objects. That tradition is still strong, and it continues to dominate folk wisdom as well as the best-resourced research projects. But an alternative discourse is now discernible. As usual, the alternative is presented in many, sometimes incompatible variants, though they share a crucial break with tradition.[72] Time will tell whether this is indeed the beginning of a new phase, whether alternative discourses will continue to exist in isolation from each other or whether more viable hybrid forms will emerge.

The significance of the extraordinary technical developments, briefly discussed in chapter 8, is widely recognized. Concurrent changes in memory discourse are phenomena of a more subtle kind, but their long-term effects may be no less profound. Seen in the light of recent developments, both technological and discursive, the conversation about memory, which has been continuing on and off for more than two millennia, can seem to be just starting.

Notes

1. Galen, *Three treatises on the nature of science*, ed. and trans. R. Walzer and M. Frede (Indianapolis: Hackett, 1985), p. 27.
2. M. Frede, 'An empiricist view of knowledge: Memorism', in S. Everson (ed.), *Companions to ancient thought: Epistemology* (Cambridge: Cambridge University Press, 1990), pp. 225–50.
3. H. G. Apostle, *Aristotle's On the soul (De anima)*, 434a 10 (Grinnell, IA: Peripatetic Press, 1981). Deliberative imagination was referred to in chapter 7.

4. There is a deeper problem here, because Aristotle's *phantasia* is not exactly equivalent to our 'imagination', though we lack a better translation. See M. Schofield, 'Aristotle on the imagination', in M. C. Nussbaum and A. Oksenberg Rorty (eds.), *Essays on Aristotle's* De anima (Oxford: Clarendon Press, 1992), pp. 249–78. A history of the semantics of psychological and quasi-psychological terms is much needed but tangential to the goal of the present discussion.

5. There is little consistency in the use of these terms among different authors. Quite often, as in Thomas Aquinas, 'inner senses' is the superordinate category that includes 'common sense' as well as other capabilities. In that case common sense refers only to the capacity for collating information from different sensory modalities.

6. H. A. Wolfson, 'The internal senses in Latin, Arabic, and Hebrew philosophic texts', *Harvard Theological Review* 28 (1935), 69–133. In spite of its age this review remains a valuable guide to this literature.

7. Avicenna is the Latinized name of Husain ibn Abdullah ibn Ali ibn Sina.

8. In some places Avicenna makes a further distinction between memory and recollection, but he does not maintain this consistently.

9. A good example is T. V. Moore, *Cognitive psychology* (Chicago: Lippincott, 1939).

10. The advent of this new field was signalled by the appearance of a text by Christian Wolff, *Psychologia empirica*, in 1732. The term 'psychology' was quite slow in spreading from Germany to other countries. It did not begin to be adopted in Britain and the United States until the middle of the nineteenth century.

11. In practice, these precepts were not always strictly adhered to, but there was no doubt about their regulative role for the new field of study.

12. M. Dessoir, *Geschichte der neueren deutschen Psychologie*, 2nd edn (Berlin: Duncker, 1902), pp. 381–2.

13. The practice of 'introspection' had its historical origins in the inspection of one's conscience, not of a morally neutered consciousness.

14. M. F. P. G. Maine de Biran, *The influence of habit on the faculty of thinking* (Baltimore, MD: Williams & Wilkins, 1929; reprinted 1971; French original published 1803). This is an early work, written in the shadow of Condillac, by an author whose increasing emphasis on the importance of inner experience and the activity of the will helped to turn him into an icon of the French 'spiritualist' school of psychology. His understanding of 'mechanical' memory is limited to repetitive verbal expression and hardly constitutes an anticipation of late twentieth-century concepts of non-verbal 'procedural memory' for skills, as has sometimes been claimed.

15. J. A. Fodor, *The modularity of mind: An essay on faculty psychology* (Cambridge, MA: MIT Press, 1983).

16. Fodor, *Modularity*, pp. 17–23.

17. J. F. Herbart, *Psychologie als Wissenschaft*, in K. Kehrbach (ed.), *Joh. Fr. Herbart's sämtliche Werke* (Langensalza: Hermann Beyer, 1890; original published 1824), vol. V, p. 198.

18. For a modern account of the scientific possibilities of Herbart's approach see G.-J. A. Boudewijnse, D. J. Murray and C. A. Bandomir, 'Herbart's mathematical psychology', *History of Psychology* 2 (1999), 163–93.

19. J. F. Herbart, *A text-book in psychology*, in D. N. Robinson (ed.), *Significant contributions to the history of psychology 1750–1920*, Series A (Washington, DC: University Publications of America, 1816/1977), vol. VI.

20. In his elaborate critique of John Locke, the founder of philosophical empiricism, Gottfried Wilhelm Leibniz (1646–1716) addresses Locke's representative thus: 'I am surprised that you can constantly rest content with bare "powers" and "faculties", which you would apparently not accept from the scholastic philosophers.' G. W. Leibniz, *New essays on human understanding*, ed. and trans. P. Remnant and J. Bennett (Cambridge: Cambridge University Press, 1765/1981), p. 140.

21. Both men had had a medical training and had made contributions to physiology before making philosophy and psychology the main focus of their academic lives. Lotze had played an active role in the defeat of vitalism in physiology. Traces of his influence can be found in the work of William James, who had considerable respect for his views.

22. R. H. Lotze, *Microcosmos*, trans. E. Hamilton and E. E. C. Jones (Edinburgh: Clark, 1887), vol. I, p. 181.

23. Lotze, *Microcosmos*, p. 215.

24. There is quite a literature on the troubled relationship between Wundt and American psychology. The issues were set out by A. L. Blumenthal, in 'A reappraisal of Wilhelm Wundt', *American Psychologist* 30 (1975), 1081–8, and 'The founding father we never knew', *Contemporary Psychology* 24 (1979), 547–50. More recent references to the topic are found in several of the contributions to R. W. Rieber and D. K. Robinson (eds.), *Wilhelm Wundt in history: The making of a scientific psychology* (New York: Kluwer/Plenum, 2001).

25. I have discussed this aspect of Wundt's thought at somewhat greater length in K. Danziger, 'Wundt and the temptations of psychology', in Rieber and Robinson, *Wundt in history*, pp. 83ff.

26. James, *Principles*, vol. I, pp. 196ff.

27. The 'almost' of this statement is due to Stern's significant role in the intellectual development of Gordon Allport, a respected Harvard psychologist. See I. A. M. Nicholson, *Inventing personality: Gordon Allport and the science of selfhood* (Washington, DC: American Psychological Association, 2003). On the recent rediscovery of Stern's ideas, see J. T. Lamiell, *Beyond individual and group differences: Human individuality, scientific psychology, and William Stern's critical personalism* (Thousand Oaks, CA: Sage, 2003).

28. Bartlett, *Remembering*, pp. 13, 15.

29. The importance of Bartlett's insistence on the integration of memory and other psychological functions is discussed in Edwards and Middleton, 'Conversation and remembering: Bartlett revisited'.

30. Koffka, *Principles of Gestalt psychology*, p. 446

31. Koffka, *Principles of Gestalt psychology*, p. 424.

32. This point has been elaborated by W. R. Uttal in *The new phrenology* and other books.

33. Nevertheless, during the latter part of the century, many experimental psychologists did become concerned about the artificiality of separating memory from other psychological functions. For pointers to this literature, see J. P. Toth and R. R. Hunt, 'Not one versus many, but zero versus any: Structure and function in the context of the multiple memory systems debate', in Toth and Hunt, *Memory: System, process, or function?*, pp. 232–72 (especially pp. 242–5).

34. J. J. Gibson, *The senses considered as perceptual systems* (Boston: Houghton-Mifflin, 1966).

35. For example, Malcolm, *Memory and mind*.

36. Bransford *et al.*, 'Toward unexplaining memory'.

37. Edelman was preceded by another Nobel Prize winner in immunology, the Norwegian Niels Jerne. However, it is in Edelman's writings that one finds a sustained discussion of the psychological implications of the immunological metaphor.

38. G. M. Edelman, *Bright air, brilliant fire: On the matter of the mind* (New York: Basic Books, 1992), pp. 203ff. For Hering, see chapter 4, section headed 'Biology and the science of forgetting'.

39. This is a very condensed account. For an extended exposition consult Edelman, both *Bright air* and *The remembered present*. Critical applications of Edelman's ideas can be found in I. Rosenfield, *The invention of memory: A new view of the brain* (New

York: Basic Books, 1988); and in Y. Shapiro, 'The perceiving brain: Turing's machine or Darwin's machine? Whose brain?', *Theory & Psychology* 6 (1996), 195–228.

40. Plato, *Theaetetus*, 149a.

41. Plato, *Meno*.

42. It has been argued that there is an inconsistency between the method Socrates employs and the conclusion he draws from its application. See H. Caygill, 'Meno and the internet: Between memory and the archive', *History of the Human Sciences* 12 (1999), 1–11.

43. Some modern psychologists who emphasize the rhetorical dimension of human cognition have deployed Plato's *Meno* quite effectively. See for example, Edwards, *Discourse and cognition*, pp. 33–7.

44. On the topic of memory, the writings of St Augustine (354–430) represent the best, as well as the best known, example of this kind of Christianized Platonism.

45. This emerges very clearly in Carruthers, *Book of memory*.

46. M. Prado, 'Memory, imagination, figuration: Leonardo da Vinci and the painter's mind', in S. Küchler and W. Melion (eds.), *Images of memory: On remembering and representation* (Washington, DC: Smithsonian Institution Press, 1991), pp. 47–73.

47. An outline of the physical analogies was presented in chapter 2; some of Locke's contributions were alluded to in chapter 4, and different aspects of Hume's position were discussed earlier in the present chapter, as well as in chapters 2 and 7.

48. Wilhelm Wundt tried to insist that his new science should work with a category of *psychic causality* that was different from physical causality, but very few of his students took any notice of this. See K. Danziger, 'The positivist repudiation of Wundt'.

49. There is a considerable historical and sociological literature on the formation and structure of disciplines. A relevant sociological treatment of the topic is provided by A. Abbott, *Chaos of disciplines* (Chicago: Chicago University Press, 2000). Specific consequences of disciplinization for psychology, relevant to the present context, are discussed in C. F. Graumann, 'Eigenart, Disziplinierung und Eigensinn der Psychologie', in C. Funken (ed.), *Soziologischer Eigensinn: Zur Disziplinierung der Sozialwissenschaften* (Opladen: Leske & Budrich, 2000), pp. 177–90.

50. For an extensive discussion, see R. A. Wilson, *Boundaries of the mind: The individual in the fragile sciences* (Cambridge: Cambridge University Press, 2004).

51. L. Vygotsky and A. Luria, 'Tool and symbol in child development', in R. van der Veer and J. Valsiner (eds.), *The Vygotsky reader* (Oxford: Blackwell, 1994), pp. 99–174 (pp. 142ff.).

52. This process can be studied experimentally. See A. Luria, 'The problem of the cultural behaviour of the child', in van der Veer and Valsiner, *Vygotsky reader*.

53. Many of the examples used by these Russian investigators represent instances of what would much later come to be known as 'chunking' – the grouping together of items to be remembered in some category, often labelled. But whereas the attention of the later (Western) psychologists was concentrated on questions of *inner* capacity limitations in chunking, Vygotsky and Luria had focused on the frequent reliance of cognitive grouping on historically evolved and culturally grounded artefacts and the learned skills for their effective use.

54. A. Luria, *The mind of a mnemonist: A little book about a vast memory* (New York: Basic Books, 1968). (The issues raised by this book were not those addressed in the earlier work.)

55. M. Halbwachs, *Les cadres sociaux de la mémoire* (Paris: Presses Universitaires de France, 1952; original edition, 1925). The translated excerpts appeared as M. Halbwachs, *On collective memory*, ed. L. A. Coser (Chicago: University of Chicago Press, 1992). A posthumous work, developing some of the ideas in the earlier publication, was translated much earlier under social anthropological

auspices: M. Halbwachs, *The collective memory* (New York: Harper, 1950). This had little or no impact on psychology, but eventually there was a significant revival of interest in the topic, especially in Europe; for examples, see J. W. Pennebaker, D. Paez and B. Rimé (eds.), *Collective memory of political events: Social psychological perspectives* (Mahwah, NJ: Erlbaum, 1997), and more recently, Middleton and Brown, *Social psychology of experience*. Interesting work in this area was also done in America, but not by psychologists; see M. Schudson, 'Dynamics of distortion in collective memory', in Schacter, *Memory distortion*, pp. 346–64.

56. 'One is rather astonished when reading psychological treatises that deal with memory to find that people are considered there as isolated beings. These make it appear that to understand our mental operations, we need to stick to individuals and first of all, to divide all the bonds which attach individuals to the society of their fellows. Yet it is in society that individuals normally acquire their memories. It is also in society that they recall, recognize, and localize their memories ... There is no point in seeking where they are preserved in my brain or in some nook of my mind to which I alone have access: for they are recalled to me externally, and the groups of which I am a part at any given time give me the means to reconstruct them.' Halbwachs, *On collective memory*, p. 38.

57. Bartlett, *Remembering*, p. 296.

58. A rationale for this approach was provided by Middleton and Edwards, in 'Conversational remembering'.

59. For a more extensive exposition of this viewpoint, see D. Edwards and J. Potter, *Discursive psychology*. Wider implications are discussed in J. Potter, *Representing reality: Discourse, rhetoric, and social construction* (London: Sage, 1996); and Edwards, *Discourse and cognition*. See also Engel, *Context is everything*.

60. Edwards and Potter, *Discursive psychology*, pp. 2–6, provide a brief account of these influences with salient references. See also Fentress and Wickham, *Social memory*, for further discussion of this background.

61. For an influential appraisal of social memory from this point of view, see Connerton, *How societies remember*.

62. Some of this work is reported in B. Rogoff and J. Lave (eds.), *Everyday cognition: Its development in social context* (Cambridge: Cambridge University Press, 1991), and in the foundational text by J. Lave, *Cognition in practice* (Cambridge: Cambridge University Press, 1988).

63. Lave, *Cognition in practice*, p. 171. A somewhat analogous reorientation occurred in a minority of neuroscientists, who were troubled by the fact that 'controlled experiments on higher brain function in non-human primates traditionally consisted of an isolated monkey faced with a series of challenges in the form of inanimate objects ... [such experiments] asked only nonsocial questions about the animal's brain'. L. Brothers, *Friday's footprint: How society shapes the human mind* (New York: Oxford University Press, 1997), p. 67. Such concerns had led to experimental explorations of specific aspects of brain function in social contexts.

64. E. Hutchins, *Cognition in the wild* (Cambridge, MA: MIT Press, 1995), p. 287. Suggestions that pointed in this direction had been made many years earlier by the anthropologist Gregory Bateson. See G. Bateson, *Steps to an ecology of mind* (New York: Ballantine, 1972).

65. E. Hutchins, 'How does a cockpit remember its speeds?', *Cognitive Science* 19 (1995), 265–88.

66. Norman, *Things that make us smart*.

67. Cases of sufferers from dementia who show unexpected levels of functioning are particularly instructive in this regard: D. Edwards, C. Baum and N. Morrow-Howell, 'Home environments in inner-city elderly with dementia: Do they facilitate or inhibit function?', *Gerontologist* 34 (1994), p. 64, as discussed in A. Clark, *Natural-born*

cyborgs (New York: Oxford University Press, 2003), p. 140. The interdependence of memory and context has been emphasized by others working in this field: C. L. McEvoy, 'Memory improvement in context: Implications for the development of memory improvement theory', in D. J. Herrmann, H. Weingartner, A. Searleman and C. McEvoy (eds.), *Memory improvement: Implications for memory theory* (New York: Springer-Verlag, 1992), pp. 210–31; and R. T. Zacks and L. Hasher, 'Memory in life, lab, and clinic: Implications for memory theory', in Herrmann *et al.*, *Memory improvement*, pp. 232–48.

68. A good example is the work of Roy Pea. See R. D. Pea, 'Practices of distributed intelligence and designs for education', in G. Salomon (ed.), *Distributed cognitions: Psychological and educational considerations* (Cambridge: Cambridge University Press, 1993), pp. 47–87, and other publications by the same author.

69. The profound links of these developments to historical memory debates are explored in W. J. Clancy, *Situated cognition: On human knowledge and computer representations* (Cambridge: Cambridge University Press, 1997).

70. For a particularly effective exposition of this position, see A. Clark, *Being there: Putting brain, body, and world together again* (Cambridge, MA: MIT Press, 1997).

71. M. Donald, *Origins of the modern mind*, pp. 314ff.

72. For the disagreements among a few of the variants, see B. A. Nardi (ed.), *Context and consciousness: Activity theory and human–computer interaction* (Cambridge, MA: MIT Press, 1996).

Bibliography

Abbott, A. *Chaos of disciplines* (Chicago: Chicago University Press, 2000).

Adams, J. 'Aristotle on memory and the self', in M. C. Nussbaum and A. Oksenberg Rorty (eds.), *Essays on Aristotle's* De anima (Oxford: Clarendon Press, 1992), pp. 297–312.

Allport, G. W. and Postman, L. *The psychology of rumor* (New York: Henry Holt, 1947).

Andrews, B. 'Recovered memories in therapy: Clinicians' beliefs and practices', in G. M. Davies and T. Dalgleish (eds.), *Recovered memories: Seeking the middle ground* (New York: Wiley, 2001), pp. 189–204.

Apostle, H. G. *Aristotle's On the soul* (De anima) (Grinnell, IA: Peripatetic Press, 1981).

Aquinas, T. *Summa Theologica* (New York: Benzinger Bros., 1947).

Ariès, P. *The hour of our death* (New York: Alfred A. Knopf, 1981).

Aristotle. *The complete works of Aristotle* ed. J. Barnes (Princeton, NJ: Princeton University Press, 1984).

Ash, M. G. *Gestalt psychology in German culture 1890–1967: Holism and the quest for objectivity* (Cambridge: Cambridge University Press, 1995).

Ash, M. G. 'Psychology', in T. M. Porter and D. Ross (eds.), *The Cambridge history of science: The modern social sciences* (Cambridge: Cambridge University Press, 2003), vol. VII, pp. 251–74.

Atkinson, R. L. and Shiffrin, R. M. 'Human memory: A proposed system and its control processes', in K. W. Spence and J. T. Spence (eds.), *The psychology of learning and motivation: Advances in research and theory* (New York: Academic Press, 1968), vol. II, pp. 90–197.

Augustinus Aurelius (St Augustine of Hippo), *Confessions*, trans. H. Chadwick (Oxford: Oxford University Press, 1991).

Baars, B. J. *The cognitive revolution in psychology* (New York: Guilford Press, 1986).

Baddeley, A. 'The concept of working memory, in S. E. Gathercole (ed.), *Models of short-term memory* (Hove: Psychology Press, 1996), pp. 1–27.

Banaji, M. R. and Crowder, R. G. 'The bankruptcy of everyday memory', *American Psychologist* 44 (1989), 1185–93.

Barker, P. *Regeneration* (New York: Penguin Books, 1998).

Bartlett, F. C. *Remembering: A study in experimental and social psychology* (Cambridge: Cambridge University Press, 1932/1995).

Bateson, G. *Steps to an ecology of mind* (New York: Ballantine, 1972).

Beattie, J. *Dissertations moral and critical* (London: 1783; reprinted by Verlag Günter Holzboog, Bad Cannstatt, 1970).

Beaulieu, A. 'Images are not the (only) truth: Brain mapping, visual knowledge, and iconoclasm', *Science, Technology, & Human Values* 27 (2002), 53–86.

Bechtel, W. and Abrahamsen, A. *Connectionism and the mind* (Cambridge, MA: Blackwell, 1991).

Belleza, F. S. 'Mnemonic devices: Classification, characteristics, and criteria', *Review of Educational Research* 51 (1981), 247–75.

Bennet, M. R. and Hacker, P. M. S. *Philosophical foundations of neuroscience* (Oxford: Blackwell, 2003).

Bergmann, E. T. and Roediger III, H. L. 'Can Bartlett's repeated reproduction experiments be replicated?', *Memory and Cognition* 27 (1999), 937–47.

Bergson, H. *Matter and memory* (New York: Zone Books, 1908/1991).

Berrios, G. E. 'Déjà vu in France during the nineteenth century: A conceptual history', *Comprehensive Psychiatry* 36 (1995), 123–9.

    The history of mental symptoms: Descriptive psychopathology since the nineteenth century (Cambridge: Cambridge University Press, 1996).

Binet, A. *La suggestibilité* (Paris: Schleicher, 1900).

Bjork, E. L. and Bjork, R. A. (eds.), *Memory* (New York: Academic Press, 1996).

Bloch, M. 'Internal and external memory: Different ways of being in history', in P. Antze and M. Lambek (eds.), *Tense past: Cultural essays in trauma and memory* (New York: Routledge, 1996), pp. 215–33.

Blumenthal, A. 'A reappraisal of Wilhelm Wundt', *American Psychologist* 30 (1975), 1081–8.

    'The founding father we never knew', *Contemporary Psychology* 24 (1979), 547–50.

Boerner, P. *Tagebuch* (Stuttgart: Metzler, 1979).

Bolzoni, L. *The gallery of memory: Literary and iconographic models in the age of the printing press*, trans. J. Parzen (Toronto: University of Toronto Press, 2001).

    'The play of images: The art of memory from its origins to the seventeenth century', in P. Corsi (ed.), *The enchanted loom: Chapters in the history of neuroscience* (New York: Oxford University Press, 1991), pp. 16–61.

Borch-Jacobsen, M. 'How to predict the past: From trauma to repression', *History of Psychiatry* 11 (2000), 15–35.

    'Making psychiatric history: Madness as *folie à plusieurs*', *History of the Human Sciences* 14 (2001), 19–38.

Boring, E. G. *A history of experimental psychology*, 2nd edn (New York: Appleton-Century-Crofts, 1950; first published 1929).

Boudewijnse, G.-J. A., Murray, D. J. and Bandomir, C. A. 'Herbart's mathematical psychology', *History of Psychology* 2 (1999), 163–93.

Bransford, J. D., Franks, J. J., McCarrell, N. S. and Nitsch, K. E. 'Toward unexplaining memory', in R. Shaw and J. Bransford (eds.), *Perceiving, acting and knowing* (Hillsdale, NJ: Erlbaum, 1977), pp. 431–66.

Breuer, J. and Freud, S. *Studies on hysteria*, in J. Strachey (ed.), *The standard edition of the complete psychological works of Sigmund Freud* (London: Hogarth Press, 1962), vol. II.

Brewer, W. F. 'Bartlett's concept of the schema and its impact on theories of knowledge representation in contemporary cognitive psychology', in

A. Saito (ed.), *Bartlett, culture and cognition* (Guildford: Psychology Press, 2000), pp. 69–89.

Brewer, W. F. and Nakamura, G. V. 'The nature and function of 'schemas', in R. S. Wyer Jr. and T. K. Srull (eds.), *Handbook of social cognition* (Hillsdale, NJ: Erlbaum, 1984), vol. I, pp. 119–60.

Broad, C. D. *The mind and its place in nature* (London: Routledge & Kegan Paul, 1925).

Broadbent, D. E., in G. Lindzey (ed.), *A history of psychology in autobiography* (San Francisco: W. H. Freeman, 1980), vol. VII.

Perception and communication (London: Pergamon Press, 1958).

Brockmeier, J. 'Literacy as symbolic space', in J. W. Astington (ed.), *Minds in the making* (Oxford: Blackwell, 2000).

Literales Bewusstsein: Schriftlichkeit und das Verhältnis von Sprache und Kultur (Munich: Fink, 1997).

Brothers, L. *Friday's footprint: How society shapes the human mind* (New York: Oxford University Press, 1997).

Brown, A. S. 'A review of the déjà vu experience', *Psychological Bulletin* 129 (2003), 394–413.

Brown, W. 'The revival of emotional memories and its therapeutic value', *British Journal of Medical Psychology* 1 (1920) 16–33.

Bruyn, G. W. 'The seat of the soul', in F. C. Rose and W. F. Bynum (eds.), *Historical aspects of the neurosciences* (New York: Raven Press, 1981), pp. 55–82.

Buonomano, D. V. and Merzenich, M. M. 'Cortical plasticity: From synapses to maps', *Annual Review of Neuroscience* 21 (1998), 149–186.

Burke, S. '"Who speaks? Who writes?" Dialogue and authorship in the *Phaedrus*', *History of the Human Sciences* 10 (1997), 40–55.

Burnham, W. H. 'Memory, historically and experimentally considered IV', *American Journal of Psychology* 2 (1888/9), 568–622.

Butler, S. *Unconscious memory* (London: Jonathan Cape, 1880).

Campbell, S. *Relational remembering: Rethinking the memory wars* (New York: Rowman & Littlefield, 2003).

Caplan, E. 'Trains and trauma in the American Gilded Age', in M. S. Micale and P. Lerner (eds.), *Traumatic pasts: History, psychiatry and trauma in the modern age 1870–1930* (New York: Cambridge University Press, 2001) pp. 57–77.

Carello, C., Turvey, M. T., Kugler, P. N. and Shaw, R. E. 'Inadequacies of the computer metaphor', in M. S. Gazzaniga (ed.), *Handbook of cognitive neuroscience* (New York: Plenum, 1984), pp. 229–48.

Carpenter, S. K. 'Some neglected contributions of Wilhelm Wundt to the psychology of memory', *Psychological Reports* 97 (2005), 63–73.

Carruthers, M. *The book of memory: A study of memory in medieval culture* (New York: Cambridge University Press, 1990).

Carruthers, M. and Ziolkowsi, J. M. *The medieval craft of memory* (Philadelphia: University of Pennsylvania Press, 2002).

Casey, E. S. *Remembering: A phenomenological study* (Bloomington: Indiana University Press, 1987).

Caygill, H. 'Meno and the internet: Between memory and the archive', *History of the Human Sciences* 12 (1999), 1–11.

Ceci, S. J. and Bruck, M. *Jeopardy in the courtroom: A scientific analysis of children's testimony* (Washington, DC: American Psychological Association, 1995).

Changeux, J.-P. and Connes, A. *Conversations on mind, matter and mathematics* (Princeton, NJ: Princeton University Press, 1995).

Cicero, M. T. *De oratore*, in J. S. Watson (ed.), *Cicero on oratory and orators* (Carbondale, IL: Southern Illinois University Press, 1970).

Clanchy, M. T. *From memory to written record: England, 1066–1307* (Cambridge, MA: Harvard University Press, 1979).

Clancy, W. J. *Situated cognition: On human knowledge and computer representations* (Cambridge: Cambridge University Press, 1997).

Claparède, E. 'La question de la "mémoire" affective', *Archives de psychologie* 10 (1911), 361–77.

'Recognition and me-ness', in D. Rapaport (ed.), *Organization and pathology of thought* (New York: Columbia University Press, 1951), pp. 58–75.

Clark, A. *Being there: Putting brain, body, and world together again* (Cambridge, MA: MIT Press, 1997).

Natural-born cyborgs: Minds, technologies, and the future of human intelligence (New York: Oxford University Press, 2003).

Clarke, E. and Jacyna, L. S. *Nineteenth-century origins of neuroscientific concepts* (Berkeley: University of California Press, 1987).

Cohen, D. *Psychologists on psychology* (London: Routledge, 1977).

Cohen, N. J. 'Preserved learning capacity in amnesia: Evidence of multiple memory systems', in N. Butters and L. R. Squire (eds.), *The neuropsychology of memory* (New York: Guilford Press, 1984), pp. 83–103.

Cohen, N. J. and Eichenbaum, H. *Memory, amnesia, and the hippocampal system* (Cambridge, MA: MIT Press, 1993).

Collins, A. 'The embodiment of reconciliation: Order and change in the work of Frederic Bartlett', *History of Psychology* 9 (2006), 290–312.

'The psychology of memory', in G. C. Bunn, A. D. Lovie and G. D. Richards (eds.), *Psychology in Britain: historical essays and personal reflections* (Leicester: BPS Books, 2001), pp. 150–68.

Connerton, P. *How societies remember* (New York: Cambridge University Press, 1989).

Cooter, R. *The cultural meaning of popular science: Phrenology and the organization of consent in nineteenth-century Britain* (Cambridge: Cambridge University Press, 1984).

Corkin, S. 'Lasting consequences of bilateral medial temporal lobectomy: Clinical course and experimental findings in H. M.', *Seminars in Neurology* 4 (1984), 249–59.

Corkin, S., Amaral, D. G., González, R. G., Johnson, K. A. and Hyman, B. T. 'H. M.'s medial temporal lobe lesion: Findings from magnetic resonance imaging', *The Journal of Neuroscience* 17 (1997), 3964–79.

Cottingham, J., Stoothoff, R. and Murdoch, D. (trans.). *Descartes: The philosophical writings* (Cambridge: Cambridge University Press, 1985).

Coulter, J. 'Neural Cartesianism: Comments on the epistemology of the cognitive sciences', in D. M. Johnson and C. E. Erneling, *The future of the cognitive revolution* (New York: Oxford University Press, 1997) pp. 293–301.

Courtois, C. A. 'Delayed memories of child sexual abuse: Critique of the controversy and clinical guidelines', in M. A. Conway (ed.), *Recovered memories and false memories* (New York: Oxford University Press, 1997), pp. 206–29.

Cox, C. 'Invisible wounds: The American Legion, shell-shocked veterans, and American society, 1919–1924', in M. S. Micale and P. Lerner (eds.), *Traumatic pasts: History, psychiatry and trauma in the modern age, 1870–1930* (New York: Cambridge University Press, 2001), pp. 280–305.

Crabtree, A. *Animal magnetism, early hypnotism and psychical research, 1766–1925: An annotated bibliography* (New York: Kraus, 1988).

Craik, F. I. M. and Lockhart, R. S. 'Levels of processing: A framework for memory research', *Journal of Verbal Learning and Verbal Behavior* 11 (1972), 671–84.

Crowther-Heyck, H. 'George A. Miller, language, and the computer metaphor', *History of Psychology* 2 (1999), 37–64.

Dallenbach, K. M. 'The history and derivation of the word "function" as a systematic term in psychology', *American Journal of Psychology* 26 (1915), 473–84.

Damasio, A. R. *Descartes' error: Emotion, reason and the human brain* (New York: Putnam, 1994).

Danziger, K. *Constructing the subject: Historical origins of psychological research* (New York: Cambridge University Press, 1990)

'Generative metaphor and the history of psychological discourse', in D. E. Leary (ed.), *Metaphors in the history of psychology* (New York: Cambridge University Press, 1990), pp. 331–56.

'Hermann Ebbinghaus and the psychological experiment', in W. Traxel (ed.), *Ebbinghaus-Studien* 2 (Passau: Passavia Universitätsverlag, 1987), pp. 217–24.

'How old is psychology, particularly concepts of memory?', *History & Philosophy of Psychology* 4 (2002), 1–12.

'Mid-nineteenth-century British psycho-physiology: A neglected chapter in the history of psychology', in W. R. Woodward and M. G. Ash (eds.), *The problematic science: Psychology in nineteenth century thought* (New York: Praeger, 1982), pp. 119–46.

Naming the mind: How psychology found its language (London: Sage, 1997).

'Sealing off the discipline: Wilhelm Wundt and the psychology of memory', in C. D. Green, M. Shore and T. Teo (eds.), *The transformation of psychology: Influences of nineteenth-century philosophy, technology, and natural science* (Washington, DC: American Psychological Association, 2001), pp. 45–62.

'The historical formation of selves', in R. D. Ashmore and L. Jussim (eds.), *Self and identity: Fundamental Issues* (New York: Oxford University Press, 1997), pp. 137–59.

'The history of introspection reconsidered', *Journal of the History of the Behavioral Sciences* 16 (1980), 240–62.

'The positivist repudiation of Wundt', *Journal of the History of the Behavioral Sciences* 15 (1979), 205–30.

'Wilhelm Wundt and the emergence of experimental psychology', in R. C. Olby, G. N. Cantor, J. R. R. Christie and M. J. S. Hodge (eds.), *Companion to the history of modern science* (London: Routledge, 1990), pp. 396–409.

'Wundt and the temptations of psychology', in R. W. Rieber and D. K. Robinson, *Wilhelm Wundt in history* (New York: Kluwer/Plenum, 2001), pp. 69–94.

Darwin, C. 'A biographical sketch of an infant', *Mind* 2 (1877), 285–94.

D'Assigny, M. *The art of memory: A treatise useful for such as are to speak in publick* (London: Andrew Bell, 1697).

Descartes, R. *Descartes: The philosophical writings*, trans. J. Cottingham, R. Stoothoff and D. Murdoch (Cambridge: Cambridge University Press, 1985).

'The passions of the soul', in E. S. Haldane and G. R. T. Ross (eds.), *The philosophical works of Descartes* (Cambridge: Cambridge University Press, 1931), vol. I.

Dessoir, M. *Geschichte der neueren deutschen Psychologie*, 2nd edn (Berlin: Duncker, 1902).

Diagnostic and Statistical Manual of Mental Disorders, 3rd edn (American Psychiatric Association, 1980).

Dobbs, B. J. T. and Jacob, M. C. *Newton and the culture of Newtonianism* (Atlantic Highlands, NJ: Humanities Press, 1995).

Donald, M. *A mind so rare: The evolution of human consciousness* (New York: W. W. Norton, 2001).

Origins of the modern mind: Three stages in the evolution of culture and cognition (Cambridge, MA: Harvard University Press, 1991).

'The mind considered from a historical perspective: Human cognitive phylogenesis and the possibility of continuing cognitive evolution', in D. M. Johnson and C. E. Erneling (eds.), *The future of the cognitive revolution* (New York: Oxford University Press, 1997), pp. 355–65.

Douglas, A. and Vogler, T. A. *Witness and memory: The discourse of trauma* (New York: Routledge, 2003).

Draaisma, D. *Metaphors of memory: A history of ideas about the mind* (Cambridge: Cambridge University Press, 2000).

Why life speeds up as you get older: How memory shapes our past (Cambridge: Cambridge University Press, 2004).

Dumit, J. *Picturing personhood: Brain scans and biomedical identity* (Princeton, NJ: Princeton University Press, 2004).

Ebbinghaus, H. *Grundzüge der Psychologie* (Leipzig: Veit & Co., 1902).

Urmanuskript über das Gedächtniss 1880 (Passau: Passavia Universitätsverlag, 1983).

Eckardt, G. 'Anspruch und Wirklichkeit der Erfahrungsseelenkunde, dargestellt an Hand periodisch erscheinender Publikationen um 1800', in O. Breidbach and P. Ziche (eds.), *Naturwissenschaften um 1800* (Weimar: H. Böhlaus Nachf., 2001), pp. 179–202.

'Psychologie um 1800', in O. Breidbach and D. v. Engelhardt (eds.), *Hegel und die Lebenswissenschaften* (Berlin: Verlag für Wissenschaft und Bildung, 2000), pp. 157–74.

Eco, U. *The open work*, trans. A. Cangogni (Cambridge, MA: Harvard University Press, 1989).

Edelman, G. M. *Bright air, brilliant fire: On the matter of the mind* (New York: Basic Books, 1992).

The remembered present (New York: Basic Books, 1989).

Edelman, G. M. and Changeux, J.-P. (eds.) *The brain*. (London: Transaction, 2001).

Edwards, D. *Discourse and cognition*. (London: Sage, 1997).

Edwards, D., Baum, C. and Morrow-Howell, N. 'Home environments in inner-city elderly with dementia: Do they facilitate or inhibit function?', *Gerontologist* 34 (1997).

Edwards, D. and Middleton, D. 'Conversation and remembering: Bartlett revisited', *Applied Cognitive Psychology* 1 (1987), 77–92.

Edwards, D. and Potter, J. *Discursive psychology* (London: Sage, 1992).

Edwards, P. N. *The closed world: Computers and the politics of discourse in Cold War America* (Cambridge, MA: MIT Press, 1996).

Eghigian, G. A. 'The German welfare state as a discourse of trauma', in M. S. Micale and P. Lerner (eds.), *Traumatic pasts: History, psychiatry and trauma in the modern age, 1870–1930* (New York: Cambridge University Press, 2001), pp. 92–112.

Eichenbaum, H. and Cohen, N. J. *From conditioning to conscious recollection* (New York: Oxford University Press, 2001).

Eitinger, L. 'Pathology of the concentration camp syndrome', *Archives of General Psychiatry* 18 (1961), 371–79.

Ellenberger, H. *The discovery of the unconscious* (New York: Basic Books, 1970).

Engel, S. *Context is everything: The nature of memory* (New York: W.H. Freeman, 1999).

Erdelyi, M. H. 'Repression, reconstruction and defense: History and integration of the psychoanalytic and experimental frameworks', in J. Singer (ed.), *Repression and dissociation: Implications for personality theory, psychopathology, and health* (Chicago: University of Chicago Press, 1990), pp. 1–31.

Esterson, A. 'Jeffrey Masson and Freud's seduction theory: A new fable based on old myths', *History of the Human Sciences* 11 (1998), 1–22.

Farah, M. J. 'Neuropsychological inference with an interactive brain: A critique of the "locality" assumption', *Behavioral and Brain Sciences* 17 (1994), 43–104.

Fauth, F. *Das Gedächtnis: Studie zu einer Pädagogik auf dem Standpunkt der heutigen Physiologie und Psychologie* [Memory: A pedagogical study on the basis of current physiology and psychology]. (Gütersloh: Bertelsmann, 1888).

Fechner, G. T. 'Some thoughts on the psychophysical representation of memories (1882)', *Psychological Research* 49 (1987), 209–12.

Fentress, J. and Wickham, C. *Social memory* (Oxford: Blackwell, 1992).

Finkelhor, D., Williams, L. M. and Burns, N. *Nursery crimes: Sexual abuse in day care* (Newbury Park, CA: Sage, 1988).

Finnegan, R. *Literacy and orality: Studies in the technology of communication* (Oxford: Blackwell, 1988).

Flourens, P. *Phrenology examined*, in D. N. Robinson (ed.), *Significant contributions to the history of psychology 1750–1920*, Series E (Washington, DC: University Publications of America, 1842/1845/1978), vol. II.

Fodor, J. A. *The modularity of mind: An essay on faculty psychology* (Cambridge, MA: MIT Press, 1983).

Förstl, H., Angermeyer, M. and Howard, R. 'Karl Philipp Moritz' Journal of Empirical Psychology (1783–1793): An analysis of 124 case reports', *Psychological Medicine* 21 (1991), 299–304.

Foschi, R., and Cicciola, E. 'Politics and naturalism in the 20th century psychology of Alfred Binet', *History of Psychology* 9 (2006), 267–89.

Foucault, M. 'Nietzsche, genealogy, history', in D. F. Bouchard (ed.), *Language, counter-memory, practice: Selected essays and interviews by Michel Foucault* (Ithaca, NY: Cornell University Press, 1977), pp. 139–64.

The order of things (London: Tavistock, 1970).

Frank, R. G. 'Thomas Willis and his circle: Brain and mind in seventeenth-century medicine', in G. S. Rousseau (ed.), *The languages of the psyche: Mind and body in Enlightenment thought* (Berkeley: University of California Press, 1990), pp. 107–46.

Frede, M. 'An empiricist view of knowledge: Memorism', in S. Everson (ed.), *Companions to ancient thought: Epistemology* (Cambridge: Cambridge University Press, 1990), pp. 225–50.

Freud, S. *A general introduction to psychoanalysis* (New York: Washington Square Press, 1924/1952).

Beyond the pleasure principle (New York: Norton, 1920/1975).

On aphasia: A critical study (London: Imago, 1891/1953).

The complete letters of Sigmund Freud to Wilhelm Fliess, ed. and trans. J. M. Masson (Cambridge, MA: Harvard University Press, 1985).

Friedlander, S. *When memory comes* (New York: Farrar, Straus, Giroux, 1979).

Friedman, W. J. 'Memory for the time of past events', *Psychological Bulletin* 113 (1993), 44–66.

Gadamer, H.-G. *Truth and method* (London: Sheed and Ward, 1979).

Gaffan, D. 'Against memory systems', in A. Parker, A. Derrington and C. Blakemore (eds.), *The physiology of cognitive processes* (New York: Oxford University Press, 2003), pp. 234–51.

Galen. *Three Treatises on the Nature of Science*, ed. and trans. R. Walzer and M. Frede (Indianapolis: Hackett, 1985).

Galton, F. 'Supplementary notes on "prehension" in idiots', *Mind* 12 (1887), 79–82.

Gardner, H. *The mind's new science: A history of the cognitive revolution* (New York: Basic Books, 1985).

Gardner, J. M. and Java, R. I. 'Recognising and remembering', in A. F. Collins, S. E. Gathercole, M. A. Conway and P. E. Morris (eds.), *Theories of memory* (Hillsdale, NJ: Erlbaum, 1993), pp. 163–88.

Gauld, A. *A history of hypnotism* (New York: Cambridge University Press, 1992).

Gauld, A. and Stephenson, G. M. 'Some experiments relating to Bartlett's theory of remembering', *British Journal of Psychology* 58 (1967), 39–49.

Gazzaniga, M. S. (ed.), *The new cognitive neurosciences* (Cambridge, MA: MIT Press, 1999).

Gibson, J. J. *The senses considered as perceptual systems* (Boston: Houghton-Mifflin, 1966).

Gigerenzer, G. 'Discovery in cognitive psychology: New tools inspire new theories', *Science in Context* 5 (1992), 329–50.

'From tools to theories: A heuristic of discovery in cognitive psychology', *Psychological Review* 98 (1991), 254–67.

Gigerenzer, G. and Goldstein, G. 'Mind as computer: Birth of a metaphor', *Creativity Research Journal* 9 (1996), 131–44.

Glenberg, A. M. 'What memory is for', *Behavioral and Brain Sciences* 20 (1997), 1–55.

Goldstein, K. *The Organism* (Boston: Beacon Press, 1939/1963).

Gould, S. J. 'Not necessarily a wing', in *Bully for Brontosaurus: Reflections in natural history* (New York: W. W. Norton, 1992), pp. 139–51.

Grafman, J., Partiot, A. and Hollnagel, C. 'Fables of the prefrontal cortex', *Behavioral and Brain Sciences* 18 (1995), 349–58.

Graumann, C. F. 'Eigenart, Disziplinierung und Eigensinn der Psychologie', in C. Funken (ed.), *Soziologischer Eigensinn: Zur Disziplinierung der Sozialwissenschaften* (Opladen: Leske & Budrich, 2000), pp. 177–90.

Green, C. D. 'The thoroughly modern Aristotle: Was he really a functionalist?', *History of Psychology* 1 (1998), 8–20.

Green, D. H. 'Orality and reading: The state of research in medieval studies', *Speculum* 65 (1990), 267–80.

Grey, R. *Memoria technica or method of artificial memory applied to and exemplified in chronology, history, geography, astronomy, also, Jewish, Grecian, and Roman coins, weights, measures, etc.* (London: C. King, 1730).

Gross, D. *Lost time: On remembering and forgetting in late modern culture* (Amherst, MA: University of Massachusetts Press, 2000).

Grote, G. *Aristotle*, ed. A. Bain and G. C. Robertson (New York: Arno Press, 1973, 1880).

Gutting, G. 'Continental philosophy and the history of science', in R. C. Olby, G. N. Cantor, J. R. R. Christie and M. J. S. Hodge (eds.), *Companion to the history of modern science* (London: Routledge, 1990), pp. 127–47;

Haaken, J. *Pillar of salt: Gender, memory, and the perils of looking back* (New Brunswick, NJ: Rutgers University Press, 1998).

Hacking, I. 'Memory sciences, memory politics', in P. Antze and M. Lambek (eds.), *Tense past: Cultural essays in trauma and memory* (New York: Routledge, 1996), pp. 67–87.

  Rewriting the soul (Princeton, NJ: Princeton University Press, 1995).

  The social construction of what? (Cambridge, MA: Harvard University Press, 1999).

Haeckel, E. *The evolution of man: A popular exposition of the principal points of human ontogeny and phylogeny* (New York: International Science Library, 1874).

Hahn, A. 'Beichte und Biographie', in M. Sonntag (ed.), *Von der Machbarkeit des Psychischen* (Pfaffenweiler: Centaurus, 1990), pp. 56–76.

  'Identität und Selbstthematisierung', in A. Hahn and V. Kapp (eds.), *Selbstthematisierung und Selbstzeugnis: Bekenntnis und Geständnis* (Frankfurt: Suhrkamp, 1987), pp. 9–24.

Halbwachs, M. *Les cadres sociaux de la mémoire* (Paris: Presses Universitaires de France, 1925/1952).

  On collective memory, ed. L. A. Coser (Chicago: University of Chicago Press, 1992).

  The collective memory (New York: Harper, 1950).

Hale Jr, M. *Human science and social order: Hugo Münsterberg and the origins of applied psychology* (Philadelphia: Temple University Press, 1980).

Hall, G. S. *Adolescence: Its psychology and its relations to physiology, anthropology, sociology, sex, crime, religion and education* (New York: Appleton, 1904).

Hanley, J. R. and Young, A. W. 'The cognitive neuropsychology of memory', in P. E. Morris and M. M. Gruneberg (eds.), *Theoretical aspects of memory*, 2nd edn (London: Routledge, 1994), pp. 238–72.

Harrington, A. 'Beyond phrenology: Localization theory in the modern era', in P. Corsi (ed.), *The enchanted loom: Chapters in the history of neuroscience* (New York: Oxford University Press, 1991), pp. 207–39.

Harrington, R. 'The railway accident: Trains, trauma, and technological crises in nineteenth-century Britain', in M. S. Micale and P. Lerner (eds.), *Traumatic pasts: History, psychiatry and trauma in the modern age, 1870–1930* (New York: Cambridge University Press, 2001), pp. 31–56.

Harris, J. E. and Morris, P. E. (eds.), *Everyday memory, actions and absent-mindedness* (London: Academic Press, 1984).

Harris, W. V. *Ancient literacy* (Cambridge, MA: Harvard University Press, 1989).

Hartley, D. *Observations on man, his frame, his duty, and his expectations* (London: 1749; reprinted by Scholars' Facsimiles & Reprints, Gainsville, FL, 1966; and by Georg Olms Verlagsbuchhandlung, Hildesheim, 1967).

Harvey, E. R. *The inward wits: Psychological theory in the Middle Ages and the Renaissance* (London: Warburg Institute, 1975).

Haupt, E. J. 'Origins of American psychology in the work of G. E. Müller: Classical psychophysics and serial learning', in R. W. Rieber and K. D. Salzinger (eds.), *Psychology: Theoretical–historical perspectives*, 2nd edn (Washington, DC: American Psychological Association, 1998), pp. 17–72.

Havelock, E. A. *The muse learns to write: Reflections on orality and literacy from antiquity to the present* (New Haven: Yale University Press, 1986).

Head, H. *Studies in neurology* (London: Oxford University Press, 1920).

Hebb, D. O. *The organization of behavior* (New York: Wiley, 1949).

Herbart, J. F. *A text-book in psychology*, in D. N. Robinson (ed.), *Significant contributions to the history of psychology 1750–1920*, series A (Washington, DC: University Publications of America, 1816/1977), vol. VI.
    Psychologie als Wissenschaft, in K. Kehrbach (ed.), *Joh. Fr. Herbart's sämtliche Werke* (Langensalza: Hermann Beyer, 1824/1890), vol. V.

Hering, E. *On memory and the specific energies of the nervous system*, 3rd edition (Chicago: Open Court, 1902).

Herman, J. L. *Father–daughter incest* (Cambridge, MA: Harvard University Press, 1981).
    Trauma and recovery (New York: Basic Books, 1992).

Hermann, D. J. and Chaffin, R. (eds.), *Memory in historical perspective: The literature before Ebbinghaus* (New York: Springer-Verlag, 1988).

Hesiod. *Theogeny*, in R. M. Frazer (trans.), *The poems of Hesiod* (Norman: University of Oklahoma Press, 1983).

Hobbes, T. *Leviathan* (New York: Dutton, 1651/1950).

Hobsbawm, E. and Ranger, T. *The invention of tradition* (Cambridge: Cambridge University Press, 1983).

Hoff, T. L. 'Gall's psychophysiological concept of function: The rise and decline of "internal essence"', *Brain and Cognition* 20 (1992), 378–98.

Hoffman, R. R., Bringmann, W., Bamberg, M. and Klein, R. 'Some historical observations on Ebbinghaus', in D. S. Gorfein and R. R. Hoffman (eds.), *Memory and learning: The Ebbinghaus centennial conference* (Hillsdale, NJ: Erlbaum, 1987), pp. 57–75.

Howard, C. and Tuffin, K. 'Repression in retrospect: Constructing history in the "memory debate"', *History of the Human Sciences* 15 (2002), 75–93.

Hult, J. 'The re–emergence of memory recovery: Return of seduction theory and birth of survivorship', *History of the Human Sciences*, 18 (2005), 127–42.

Hume, D. *A treatise of human nature*, 2nd edn, ed. L. A. Selby-Bigge (Oxford: Clarendon Press, 1739/1978).
  An abstract of a treatise of human nature, 1740, ed. J. M. Keynes and P. Sraffa (Cambridge: Cambridge University Press, 1740/1938).

Humphrey, G. *Thinking* (London: Methuen, 1950).

Husserl, E. *The philosophy of internal time consciousness*, trans. J. S. Churchill (Bloomington: Indiana University Press, 1964) (original lectures delivered 1904/5).

Hutchins, E. *Cognition in the wild* (Cambridge, MA: MIT Press, 1995).
  'How does a cockpit remember its speeds?', *Cognitive Science* 19 (1995), 265–88.

Hutton, P. H. *History as an art of memory* (Hanover, VT: University Press of New England, 1993).

Ideler, K. W. *Grundriss der Seelenheilkunde* (Berlin: Enslin, 1835).

Illich, I. *In the vineyard of the text: A commentary on Hugh's* Didascalion (Chicago: Chicago University Press, 1993).

Illich, I. and Sanders, B. *The alphabetization of the popular mind* (San Francisco: North Point Press, 1988).

Jacobs, J. 'Experiments on prehension', *Mind* 12 (1887), 75–79.

Jacyna, L. S. *Lost words: Narratives of language and the brain 1825–1926* (Princeton, NJ: Princeton University Press, 2000).

James, W. *Principles of psychology* (New York: Holt, 1890).

Janet, P. *L'automatisme psychologique: essai de psychologie expérimentale sur les formes inférieures de l'activité humaine* (Paris: Société Pierre Janet, 1889/1973).

Jenkins, J. J. 'Remember that old theory of memory? Well forget it', *American Psychologist* 29 (1974), 785–95.

John, E. R. 'Switchboard versus statistical theories of learning and memory', *Science* 177 (1972), 850–64.

Johnson, D. M. *How history made the mind: The cultural origins of objective thinking* (Chicago: Open Court, 2003).

Johnson-Laird, P. N. *The computer and the mind* (Cambridge, MA: Harvard University Press, 1988).

Johnston, E. B. 'The repeated reproduction of Bartlett's *Remembering*', *History of Psychology* 4 (2001), 341–66.

Kandel, E. R. *In search of memory: The emergence of a new science of mind* (New York: Norton, 2006).

Kant, I. *Anthropology from a pragmatic point of view*, trans. M. J. McGregor (The Hague: Martinus Nijhoff, 1797/1974).

Critique of pure reason, trans. N. K. Smith (New York: St Martin's Press, 1787/1929).

Kapp, V. 'Von der Autobiographie zum Tagebuch: Rousseau–Constant', in A. Hahn and V. Kapp, *Selbstthematisierung und Selbstzeugnis* (Frankfurt: Suhrkamp, 1987), pp. 297–310.

Katzaroff, D. 'Contribution à l'étude de la recognition', *Archive de psychologie* 11 (1911), 2–78.

Kemp, S. and Fletcher, G. J. O. 'The medieval theory of the inner senses', *American Journal of Psychology* 106 (1993), 559–76.

Kennedy, F. 'On the experimental investigation of memory', *Psychological Review* 5 (1898), 477–99.

Kim, J. J. and Baxter, M. G. 'Multiple brain-memory systems: The whole does not equal the sum of its parts', *Trends in neurosciences* 24 (2001), 324–30.

Kintsch, W. and van Dijk, T. A. 'Toward a model of text comprehension and production', *Psychological Review* 85 (1978), 363–94.

Koffka, K. *Principles of Gestalt psychology* (New York: Harcourt, Brace, 1935).

Köhler, W. *Gestalt psychology* (New York: Liveright, 1929).

Kolers, P. A. and Roediger III, H. L. 'Procedures of mind', *Journal of Verbal Learning and Verbal Behavior* 23 (1984), 425–49.

Koriat, A. and Goldsmith, M. 'Memory metaphors and the real-life/laboratory controversy: Correspondence versus storehouse conceptions of memory', *Behavioral and Brain Sciences* 19 (1996), 167–228.

Kosslyn, S. M. 'If neuroimaging is the answer, what is the question?', *Proceedings of the Royal Society of London* B, 354 (1999), 1283–94.

Krell, D. F. *Of memory, reminiscence, and writing* (Bloomington: Indiana University Press, 1990).

Kren, G. M. and Rappaport, L. *The holocaust and the crisis of human behavior* (New York: Holmes & Meier, 1980).

Lamberton, R. 'Introduction', in S. Lombardo (trans.), *Hesiod: Works and days* and *Theogeny* (Indianapolis: Hackett, 1993).

Lamiell, J. T. *Beyond individual and group differences: Human individuality, scientific psychology, and William Stern's critical personalism* (Thousand Oaks, CA: Sage, 2003).

'William Stern: More than "the IQ guy"', in G. A. Kimble, C. A. Boneau and M. Wertheimer (eds.), *Portraits of pioneers in psychology* (Hillsdale, NJ: Erlbaum, 1996), vol. II, pp. 73–85.

Landes, D. S. *Revolution in time: Clocks and the making of the modern world* (Cambridge, MA: Harvard University Press, 1983).

Laplanche, J. and Pontalis, J.-B. *The language of psycho-analysis* (New York: Norton, 1973).

Lashley, K. S. *Brain mechanisms and intelligence: A quantitative study of injuries to the brain* (Chicago: University of Chicago Press, 1929).

'In search of the engram', *Society of Experimental Biology symposium no. 4* (Cambridge, MA: Harvard University Press, 1950) pp. 454–82.

Laurence, J.-R. and Campbell, P. *Hypnosis, will, and memory: A psycho-legal history* (New York: Guilford Press, 1988)

Lave, J. *Cognition in practice* (Cambridge: Cambridge University Press, 1988).

Laver, A. B. 'D'Assigny and the art of memory', *Journal of the History of the Behavioral Sciences* 9 (1973), 240–50.

    'Gregor Feinagle, mnemonist and educator', *Journal of the History of the Behavioral Sciences* 15 (1979), 18–28.

Lawson, Rev. 'Recommendatory character of Grey's *Memoria technica*' (Oxford: J. Vincent, 1841).

Laycock, T. *Mind and brain* (Edinburgh: Sutherland & Knox, 1860; reprinted New York: Arno Press, 1976).

Le Bon, G. *The crowd: A study of the popular mind* (New York: Viking, 1895/1960).

Le Goff, J. *History and memory* (New York: Columbia University Press, 1992).

Leahy, T. H. 'Something old, something new: Attention in Wundt and modern cognitive psychology', *Journal of the History of the Behavioral Sciences* 15 (1979), 242–52.

LeDoux, J. *Synaptic Self* (London: Penguin Books, 2002).

    The emotional brain (New York: Simon & Schuster, 1996).

Leibniz, G. W. *New essays on human understanding*, ed. and trans. P. Remnant and J. Bennett (Cambridge: Cambridge University Press, 1981).

Lentz, T. M. *Orality and literacy in Hellenic Greece* (Carbondale, IL.: Southern Illinois University Press, 1989).

Lerner, P. 'From traumatic neurosis to male hysteria: The decline and fall of Hermann Oppenheim, 1889–1919', in M. S. Micale and P. Lerner (eds.), *Traumatic pasts: History, psychiatry and trauma in the modern age, 1870–1930* (New York: Cambridge University Press, 2001), pp. 140–71.

    Hysterical men: War, psychiatry and the politics of trauma in Germany, 1890–1930 (Ithaca, NY: Cornell University Press, 2003).

Leudar, I. and Thomas, P. *Voices of reason, voices of insanity: Studies of verbal hallucinations* (London: Routledge, 2000).

Lewes, G. H. *The physiology of common life* (London: Blackwood, 1859).

Lewin, K. 'Das Problem der Willensmessung und das Grundgesetz der Assoziation', *Psychologische Forschung* 1 (1922), 191–302; 2 (1922), 65–140.

Leys, R. *Trauma: A genealogy* (Chicago: University of Chicago Press, 2000).

Lindsay, D. S. 'Depolarizing views on recovered memory experiences', in S. J. Lynn and K. M. McConkey (eds.), *Truth in memory* (New York: Guilford Press, 1998), pp. 481–94.

Locke, J. *An essay concerning human understanding* (New York: Dover, 1690/1959).

Lockhart, R. S. 'Methods of memory research', in E. Tulving and F. I. M. Craik (eds.), *The Oxford handbook of memory* (Oxford: Oxford University Press, 2000), pp. 45–57.

Loftus, E. F. *Eyewitness testimony* (Cambridge, MA: Harvard University Press, 1979).

    Memory: Surprising new insights into how we remember and why we forget (Reading, MA: Addison-Wesley, 1980).

Loftus, E. F. and Klinger, M. R. *The myth of repressed memory: False memories and allegations of sexual abuse* (New York: St Martin's Press, 1994).

Loftus, E. F. and Loftus, G. R. 'On the permanence of stored information in the human brain', *American Psychologist* 35 (1980), 409–20.

Loh, W. D. 'Psychological research: Past and present', *Michigan Law Review* 79 (1981), 659–707.

Lord, A. B. *The singer of tales* (Cambridge, MA: Harvard University Press, 1964). *The singer resumes the tale* (Ithaca, NY: Cornell University Press, 1995).

Lotze, R. H. *Microcosmos*, trans. E. Hamilton and E. E. C. Jones (Edinburgh: Clark, 1887).

Lowry, R. *The evolution of psychological theory: 1650 to the present* (Chicago: Aldine, 1971).

Luria, A. *The mind of a mnemonist: A little book about a vast memory* (New York: Basic Books, 1968).

McArthur, T. *Worlds of difference: Lexicography, learning and language from the clay tablet to the computer* (Cambridge: Cambridge University Press, 1986).

McClelland, J. L. 'Constructive memory and memory distortions: A parallel-distributed processing approach', in D. L. Schacter (ed.), *Memory distortion: How minds, brains and societies reconstruct the past* (Cambridge, MA: Harvard University Press, 1995), pp. 69–90.

McClelland, J. L., McNaughton, B. L. and O'Reilly, R. C. 'Why there are complementary learning systems in the hippocampus and neocortex: Insights from the successes and failures of connectionist models of learning and memory', *Psychological Review* 102 (1995), 419–57.

McClelland, J. L. and Rumelhart, D. (eds.), *Parallel distributed processing: Explorations in the microstructure of cognition* (Cambridge, MA: MIT Press, 1986).

MacCurdy, J. T. *Common principles in psychology and physiology* (Cambridge, MA: Harvard University Press, 1928).

McEvoy, C. L. 'Memory improvement in context: Implications for the development of memory improvement theory', in D. J. Herrmann, H. Weingartner, A. Searleman and C. McEvoy (eds.), *Memory improvement: Implications for memory theory* (New York: Springer-Verlag, 1992), pp. 210–31.

McGrath, J. *Freud's discovery of psychoanalysis: The politics of hysteria* (Ithaca, NY: Cornell University Press, 1986).

McKoon, G., Ratcliff, R. and Dell, G. S. 'A critical evaluation of the semantic–episodic distinction', *Journal of Experimental Psychology: Learning, Memory, and Cognition* 12 (1986), 295–306.

Macmartin, C. and Yarmey, A. D. 'Rhetoric and the recovered memory debate', *Canadian Psychology* 40 (1999), 343–58.

McNally, R. J. *Remembering trauma* (Cambridge, MA: Harvard University Press, 2003).

Maine de Biran, M. F. P. G. *The influence of habit on the faculty of thinking* (Baltimore, MD: Williams & Wilkins, 1803/1929).

Malcolm, N. *Memory and mind* (Ithaca, NY: Cornell University Press, 1977).

Markus, G. 'Why is there no hermeneutics of natural sciences? Some preliminary theses', *Science in Context* 1 (1987), 5–51.

Marx, O. M. 'German Romantic psychiatry', *History of Psychiatry* 1 (1990), 351–81.

Matsuda, M. K. *The memory of the modern* (New York: Oxford University Press, 1996).

Maudsley, H. *The physiology and pathology of mind* (London: Macmillan, 1867).

Megill, A. 'History, memory, identity', *History of the Human Sciences* 11 (1998), 37–62.

Meumann, E. *Abriss der experimentellen Pädagogik* (Leipzig: Teubner, 1912).

The psychology of learning: An experimental investigation of the economy and technique of memory (New York: Appleton, 1913).

Micale, M. S. *Approaching hysteria: Disease and its interpretations* (Princeton, NJ: Princeton University Press, 1995).

'Jean-Martin Charcot and *les névroses traumatiques*: From medicine to culture in French trauma theory of the late nineteenth century', in M. S. Micale and P. Lerner (eds.), *Traumatic pasts: History, psychiatry and trauma in the modern age, 1870–1930* (New York: Cambridge University Press, 2001), pp. 115–39.

Middleton, A. E. *All about mnemonics* (London: Simpkin, Marshall & Co., 1885).

Middleton, D. and Brown, S. D. *The social psychology of experience: Studies in remembering and forgetting* (London: Sage, 2005).

Middleton, D. and Edwards, D. 'Conversational remembering: a social psychological approach', in D. Middleton and D. Edwards (eds.), *Collective remembering* (London: Sage, 1990), pp. 23–45.

Middleton, D. F. and Crook, C. 'Bartlett and socially ordered consciousness: A discursive perspective. Comments on Rosa', *Culture & Psychology* 2 (1996), 379–96.

Mill, J. *Analysis of the phenomena of the human mind* (New York: Kelley, 1829/1967).

Miller, G. A., Gallanter, E. and Pribram, K. *Plans and the structure of behavior* (New York: Holt, Rinehart & Winston, 1960)

Milner, B., Corkin, S. and Teuber, H. L. 'Further analysis of the hippocampal amnesic syndrome: 14-year follow-up study of H. M.', *Neuropsychologia* 6 (1968), 215–34.

Minsky, M. *The society of mind* (New York: Simon & Schuster, 1985).

(ed.), *Semantic information processing* (Cambridge, MA: MIT Press, 1968).

Mitchell, J. 'Memory and psychoanalysis', in P. Fara and K. Patterson (eds.), *Memory: The Darwin College lectures* (Cambridge: Cambridge University Press, 1998), pp. 95–112.

Mook, D. G. 'The myth of external validity', in L. W. Poon, D. C. Rubin, and D. A. Wilson (eds.), *Everyday cognition in adulthood and late life* (Cambridge: Cambridge University Press, 1989), pp. 25–43;

Moore, T. V. *Cognitive psychology* (Chicago: Lippincott, 1939).

Morris, P. E. and Gruneberg, M. M. 'The major aspects of memory', in P. E. Morris and M. M. Gruneberg (eds.) *Theoretical aspects of memory*, 2nd edn (London: Routledge, 1994), pp. 29–49.

Müller, G. E. 'Zur Analyse der Gedächtnistätigkeit und des Vorstellungsverlaufes', *Zeitschrift für Psychologie* Ergänzungsband 5 (1911); Ergänzungsband 8 (1913); Ergänzungsband 9 (1917).

Müller, G. E. and Pilzecker, A. 'Experimentelle Beiträge zur Lehre vom Gedächtnis', *Zeitschrift für Psychologie* Ergänzungsband 1 (1900).

Müller, G. E. and Schumann, F. 'Experimentelle Beiträge zur Untersuchung des Gedächtnisses', *Zeitschrift für Psychologie und Physiologie der Sinnesorgane* 6 (1894), 81–190 and 257–339.

Müller-Luckmann, E. 'William Stern und die Forensische Psychologie', in W. Deutsch (ed.), *Die verborgene Aktualität von William Stern* (Bern: Peter Lang, 1991), 107–16.

Munsat, L. *The concept of memory* (New York: Random House, 1967).

Münsterberg, H. *On the witness stand: Essays on psychology and crime* (New York: Clark Boardman, 1909/1949).

Murray, D.J. 'Research on human memory in the nineteenth century', *Canadian Journal of Psychology* 30 (1976), 201–20.

Murray, D.J. and Bandomir, C.A. 'G. E. Müller (1911, 1913, 1917) on memory', *Psychologie et Histoire* 1 (2000), 208–32.

Nairn, S.L., Ellard, J.H., Scialfa, C.T. and Miller, C.D. 'At the core of introductory psychology: A content analysis', *Canadian Psychology* 44 (2003), 93–9.

Nairne, J.S. 'Remembering over the short-term: The case against the standard models', *Annual Review of Psychology* 53 (2002), 53–81.

'Short-term/working memory', in E. L and R.A. Bjork (eds.), *Memory* (New York: Academic Press, 1996), pp. 101–26.

Nardi, B.A. (ed.), *Context and consciousness: Activity theory and human–computer interaction* (Cambridge, MA: MIT Press, 1996).

Narsimhan, R. 'Literacy: Its characterization and implications', in D.R. Olson and N. Torrance (eds.), *Literacy and orality* (Cambridge: Cambridge University Press, 1991), pp. 177–97.

Neisser, U. *Cognition and Reality* (San Francisco: W. H. Freeman, 1976).

'Memory: What are the important questions?', in U. Neisser (ed.), *Memory observed: Memory in natural contexts* (San Francisco: W. H. Freeman, 1982), pp. 3–19.

Neisser, U. and Winograd, E. (eds.), *Remembering reconsidered: Ecological and traditional approaches to the study of memory* (Cambridge: Cambridge University Press, 1988).

Neumann, H.W. *Lehrbuch der Psychiatrie* (Erlangen: Enke, 1859).

Newell, A. and Simon, H.A. *Human problem solving* (Englewood Cliffs, NJ: Prentice-Hall, 1972).

Nicholas, L.J. and Coleridge, L. 'Expert witness testimony in the criminal trial of Eugene de Kock: A critique of the posttraumatic stress disorder (PTSD) defence', *South African Journal of Psychology* 30 (2000), 33–6.

Nicholson, I. A.M. *Inventing personality: Gordon Allport and the science of self-hood* (Washington, DC: American Psychological Association, 2003).

Nicolas, S. and Murray, D.J. 'Théodule Ribot (1839–1916), founder of French psychology: A biographical introduction', *History of Psychology* 2 (1999), 277–301.

Norman, D.A. *Things that make us smart: Defending human attributes in the age of the machine* (Reading, MA: Addison-Wesley, 1993).

Northway, M.L. 'The concept of the "schema"', *British Journal of Psychology* 30 (1940), 316–25.

Norton, D.F. (ed.), *The Cambridge companion to Hume* (Cambridge: Cambridge University Press, 1993).

Novick, P. *The holocaust in American life* (Boston: Houghton Mifflin, 1999).

O'Keefe, J. and Nadel, L. *The hippocampus as a cognitive map* (New York: Oxford University Press, 1978).

Oldfield, R.C. and Zangwill, O.L. 'Head's concept of the schema and its application in contemporary British psychology III: Bartlett's theory of memory', *British Journal of Psychology* 33 (1943), 113–29.

Olson, D. R. 'Literate mentalities', in D. R. Olson and N. Torrance (eds.), *Modes of thought: Explorations in culture and cognition* (Cambridge: Cambridge University Press, 1996), pp. 141–51.

The world on paper: The conceptual and cognitive implications of writing and reading (New York: Cambridge University Press, 1994).

Ong, W. J. *Ramus: Method and the decay of dialogue* (Cambridge, MA: Harvard University Press, 1958).

Oppenheim, H. *Die traumatischen Neurosen* (Berlin: Hirschwald, 1889).

Otis, L. *Organic memory: History and the body in the late nineteenth and early twentieth centuries* (Lincoln: University of Nebraska Press, 1994).

Palmieri, T. J. and Flanery, M. A. 'Memory systems and perceptual categorization', in B. H. Ross (ed.), *The psychology of learning and motivation: Advances in research and theory* (New York: Academic Press, 2002), vol. XLI, pp. 141–89.

Park, K. 'The organic soul', in Q. Skinner and E. Kessler (eds.), *The Cambridge history of Renaissance philosophy* (Cambridge: Cambridge University Press, 1988), pp. 464–84.

Pauly, P. J. 'The political structure of the brain: Cerebral localization in Bismarckian Germany', *International Journal of Neuroscience* 21 (1983), 145–50.

Pea, R. D. 'Practices of distributed intelligence and designs for education', in G. Salomon (ed.), *Distributed cognitions: Psychological and educational considerations* (Cambridge: Cambridge University Press, 1993), pp. 47–87.

Pennebaker, J. W., Paez, D. and Rimé, B. (eds.), *Collective memory of political events: Social psychological perspectives* (Mahwah, NJ: Erlbaum, 1997).

Pepper, S. C. *World hypotheses* (Berkeley: University of California Press, 1942).

Pezdek, K. and Banks, W. P. (eds.), *The recovered memory/false memory debate* (New York: Academic Press, 1996).

Pfeifer, R. and Scheier, C. *Understanding intelligence* (Cambridge, MA: MIT Press, 1999).

Plato. *The collected dialogues of Plato*, ed. E. Hamilton and H. Cairns (Princeton, NJ: Princeton University Press, 1963).

Pliny (the elder), *Natural History*, Book 7, trans. H. Rackham (Cambridge, MA: Harvard University Press, 1942), vol. II.

Pogliano, C. 'Between form and function: A new science of man', in P. Corsi (ed.), *The enchanted loom: Chapters in the history of neuroscience* (New York: Oxford University Press, 1991), pp. 144–203.

Poon, L. W., Rubin, D. C. and Wilson, B. A. (eds.), *Everyday cognition in adulthood and late life* (Cambridge: Cambridge University Press, 1989).

Posner, M. I. and Raichle, M. E. *Images of mind* (New York: Scientific American Library, 1994).

Potter, J. *Representing reality: Discourse, rhetoric, and social construction* (London: Sage, 1996).

Poulet, G. *Studies in human time* (New York: Harper, 1959).

Prado, M. 'Memory, imagination, figuration: Leonardo da Vinci and the painter's mind', in S. Küchler and W. Melion (eds.), *Images of memory: On remembering and representation* (Washington, DC: Smithsonian Institution Press, 1991), pp. 47–73.

Prager, J. *Presenting the past: Psychoanalysis and the sociology of misremembering* (Cambridge, MA: Harvard University Press, 1998).

Pribram, K. H. *Languages of the brain: Experimental paradoxes and principle in neuropsychology* (Englewood Cliffs, NJ: Prentice-Hall, 1971).

'The neurophysiology of remembering', *Scientific American* 220 (1969), 73–86.

Quintilian *Institutio oratoria*, trans. H. E. Butler (Cambridge, MA: Harvard University Press, 1922).

Reiff, R. and Scheerer, M. *Memory and hypnotic age regression* (New York: International Universities Press, 1959).

Reiss, T. J. 'Denying the body? Memory and the dilemmas of history in Descartes', *Journal of the History of Ideas* 57 (1996), 587–607.

Rhetorica ad Herennium, in H. Caplan (ed.), *Cicero in twenty-eight volumes* (Cambridge, MA: Harvard University Press, 1954; reprinted 1981), vol. I.

Ribot, T. *Diseases of memory: An essay in the positive psychology'*, in D. N. Robinson (ed.), *Significant contributions to the history of psychology 1750–1920*, series C (Washington, DC: University Publications of America, 1977), vol. I.

Richards, G. *Mental machinery: The origins and consequences of psychological ideas from 1600 to 1850* (London: Athlone Press, 1992).

Richter, M. '*Begriffsgeschichte* and the history of ideas', *Journal of the History of Ideas* 48 (1987), 247–63.

Ricoeur, P. *The rule of metaphor*, trans. R. Czerny (Toronto: University of Toronto Press, 1977).

Rieber, R. W. and Robinson, D. K. (eds.), *Wilhelm Wundt in history: The making of a scientific psychology* (New York: Kluwer/Plenum, 2001).

Rignano, E. *Biological memory* (New York: Harcourt Brace, 1926).

Riley, D. A. 'Memory for form', in L. Postman (ed.), *Psychology in the making* (New York: Knopf, 1962), pp. 402–65.

Roediger III, H. L. 'Memory metaphors in cognitive psychology', *Memory & Cognition* 8 (1980), 231–46.

'The future of cognitive psychology?', in R. L. Solso (ed.), *Mind and brain sciences in the twenty-first century* (Cambridge, MA.: MIT Press, 1997), pp. 175–198.

Roediger III, H. L., Bergman, E. T. and Meade, M. L. 'Repeated reproduction from memory', in A. Saito (ed.), *Bartlett, culture and cognition* (Guildford: Psychology Press, 2000), pp. 115–34.

Roediger III, H. L., Buckner, R. L. and McDermott, K. B. 'Components of processing', in J. K. Foster and M. Jelicic (eds.), *Memory: systems, process, or function?* (New York: Oxford University Press, 1999), pp. 31–65.

Rogoff, B. and Lave, J. (eds.), *Everyday cognition: Its development in social context* (Cambridge: Cambridge University Press, 1991).

Rolls, E. T. 'Memory systems in the brain', *Annual Review of Psychology* 51 (2000), 599–630.

The brain and emotion (Oxford: Oxford University Press, 1999).

Rose, N. 'Calculable minds and manageable individuals', *History of the Human Sciences* 1 (1988), 179–200.

Inventing our selves (Cambridge: Cambridge University Press, 1996).

The psychological complex (London: Routledge, 1985).

Rose, S. *The making of memory* (London: Bantam, 1993).

Rosenfield, I. *The invention of memory: A new view of the brain* (New York: Basic Books, 1988).

Ross, B. M. *Remembering the personal past: Descriptions of autobiographical memory* (New York: Oxford University Press, 1991).

Rossi, P. *Logic and the art of memory: The quest for a universal language* (Chicago: University of Chicago Press, 2000).

Roth, M. S. 'Remembering forgetting: Maladies de la mémoire in nineteenth century France', *Representations* 26 (1989), 49–68.

   'The time of nostalgia: Medicine, history and normality in nineteenth century France', *Time & Society* 1 (1992), 271–86.

   'Trauma, representation and historical consciousness', *Common Knowledge* 7 (1998), 99–111.

Rouse, M. A. and Rouse, R. H. *Authentic witnesses: Approaches to medieval texts and manuscripts* (Notre Dame, IN: University of Notre Dame Press, 1991).

Rousseau, G. S. 'Discourses of the nerve', in F. Amrine (ed.), *Literature and science as modes of expression* (Dordrecht: Kluwer, 1989), pp. 29–60.

Rousseau, J.-J. *The confessions of Jean-Jacques Rousseau*, trans. J. M. Cohen (Harmondsworth: Penguin Books, 1782/1953).

Rozeboom, W. W. 'The concept of "memory"', *Psychological Record* 15 (1965), 329–68.

Rubin, D. C. *Memory in oral traditions: The cognitive psychology of epic, ballads, and counting-out rhymes* (Oxford: Oxford University Press, 1995).

   (ed.), *Autobiographical memory* (Cambridge: Cambridge University Press, 1986).

Russell, B. *The analysis of mind* (New York: Humanities Press, 1921).

Ryle, G. *The concept of mind* (London: Hutchison, 1949).

Saenger, P. *Space between words: The origins of silent reading* (Stanford, CA: Stanford University Press, 1997).

St Augustine, *Confessions* (Oxford: Oxford University Press, 1991).

Schacter, D. L. 'Implicit memory: history and current status', *Journal of Experimental Psychology: Learning, Memory, Cognition* 13 (1987), 501–18.

   Stranger behind the engram: Theories of memory and the psychology of science (Hillsdale, NJ: Erlbaum, 1982).

Schacter, D. L. and Tulving, E. (eds.), *Memory systems of 1994* (Cambridge, MA: MIT Press, 1994).

Schäffner, W. 'Event, series, trauma: The probabilistic revolution of the mind in the late nineteenth and early twentieth centuries', in M. S. Micale and P. Lerner (eds.), *Traumatic pasts: History, psychiatry and trauma in the modern age, 1870–1970* (New York: Cambridge University Press, 2001), pp. 81–91.

Scheerer, E. 'The unknown Fechner', *Psychological Research* 49 (1987), 197–202.

   'Wilhelm Wundt's psychology of memory', *Psychological Research* 42 (1980), 135–55.

Schimek, J. G. 'Fact and fantasy in the seduction theory: A historical review', *Journal of the American Psychoanalytic Association* 35 (1987), 937–65.

Schivelbusch, W. *The railway journey: Trains and train travel in the nineteenth century* (Berkeley: University of California Press, 1986).

Schofield, M. 'Aristotle on the imagination', in M. C. Nussbaum and A. Oksenberg Rorty (eds.), *Essays on Aristotle's* De anima (Oxford: Clarendon Press, 1992), pp. 249–78.

Schönpflug, W. and Esser, K. B. 'Memory and *graeculi*: Metamemory and control in extended memory systems', in C. A. Weaver, S. Mannes and C. R. Fletcher (eds.), *Discourse comprehension: Essays in honor of Walter Kintsch* (Hillsdale, NJ: Erlbaum, 1995), pp. 245–55.

Schudson, M. 'Dynamics of distortion in collective memory', in D. L. Schacter (ed.), *Memory distortion: How minds, brains, and societies reconstruct the past* (Cambridge, MA: Harvard University Press, 1995), 346–64.

Scott, W. J. 'PTSD in DSM-III: A case in the politics of diagnosis and disease', *Social Problems* 37 (1990), 294–310.

Scoville, W. B. and Milner, B. 'Loss of recent memory after bilateral hippocampal lesions', *Journal of Neurology, Neurosurgery and Psychiatry* 20 (1957), 11–12.

Scribner, S. and Cole, M. *The psychology of literacy* (Cambridge, MA: Harvard University Press, 1981).

Shallice, T. *From neuropsychology to mental structure* (Cambridge: Cambridge University Press, 1987).

Shapin, S. and Schaffer, S. *Leviathan and the air pump: Hobbes, Boyle and the experimental life* (Princeton, NJ: Princeton University Press, 1985).

Shapiro, Y. 'The perceiving brain: Turing's machine or Darwin's machine? Whose brain?', *Theory & Psychology* 6 (1996), 195–228.

Shephard, B. *A war of nerves: Soldiers and psychiatrists in the twentieth century* (Cambridge, MA: Harvard University Press, 2001).

Sherry, D. F. and Schacter, D. L. 'The evolution of multiple memory systems', *Psychological Review* 94 (1987), 439–54.

Shotter, J. 'The social construction of remembering and forgetting', in D. Middleton and D. Edwards (eds.), *Collective remembering* (London: Sage, 1990), pp. 120–38.

Shurkin, J. *Engines of the mind: A history of the computer* (New York: Norton, 1984).

Simon, H. A. *The sciences of the artificial* (Cambridge, MA: MIT Press, 1969).

Singer, B. R. 'Robert Hooke on memory, association and time perception', *Notes and Records of the Royal Society of London* 31 (1976), 115–31.

Small, J. P. *Wax tablets of the mind: Cognitive studies of memory and literacy in classical antiquity* (London: Routledge, 1997).

Smith, R. 'Does the history of psychology have a subject?', *History of the Human Sciences* 1 (1988), 147–77.

'The big picture: Writing psychology into the history of the human sciences', *Journal of the History of the Behavioral Sciences* 34 (1998), 1–13.

Snodgrass, G. 'The memory trainers', in R. L. Solso (ed.), *Mind and brain sciences in the twenty-first century* (Cambridge, MA: MIT Press, 1997), pp. 199–233.

Sorabji, R. *Aristotle on memory* (Providence: Brown University Press, 1972).

Spence, D. P. *Narrative truth and historical truth* (New York: Norton, 1982).

Spence, J. D. *The memory palace of Matteo Ricci* (New York: Viking Penguin, 1984).

Spencer, H. *The principles of psychology*, 2nd edn (London: Longman, Brown, Green, Longmans, 1880).

Sporer, S. L. 'A brief history of the psychology of testimony', *Current Psychological Reviews* 2 (1982), 323–40.

Squire, L. R. *Memory and brain* (New York: Oxford University Press, 1987).

Squire, L. R. and Schacter, D. L. (eds.), *Neuropsychology of memory*, 3rd edn (New York: Guilford Press, 2002).

Staeuble, I. 'Psychologie im Dienste praktischer Kulturaufgaben – Zur Realisierung von William Sterns Programm 1903–1933', in A. Schorr and J. Wehner (eds.), *Psychologiegeschichte heute* (Göttingen: Hogrefe, 1990), pp. 164–73.

Stam, H. J. 'Retrieving the past for the future: Boundary maintenance in historical and theoretical psychology', in D. B. Hill and M. J. Kral (eds.), *About psychology: Essays at the crossroads of history, theory, and philosophy* (Albany, NY: State University of New York Press, 2003), pp. 147–63.

Star, S. L. *Regions of the mind: Brain research and the quest for scientific certainty* (Stanford, CA: Stanford University Press, 1989).

Stern, C. and Stern, W. *Recollection, testimony, and lying in early childhood*, trans. J. T. Lamiell (Washington, DC: American Psychological Association, 1909/1999).

Stern, W. *General psychology from the personalistic standpoint*, trans. H. D. Spoerl (New York: Macmillan, 1938).

Psychology of early childhood (New York: Henry Holt, 1914/1924).

Stock, B. *Augustine the reader: Meditation, self-knowledge, and the ethics of interpretation* (Cambridge, MA: Harvard University Press, 1996).

Stout, G. F. *Analytic psychology*, 2nd edn (London: Swann Sonnenschein, 1902).

Strachey, J. (ed.), *The standard edition of the complete psychological works of Sigmund Freud* (London: Hogarth Press, 1962).

Sullivan, L. E. 'Memory distortion and anamnesis: A view from the human sciences', in D. L. Schacter (ed.), *Memory distortion: How minds, brains and societies reconstruct the past* (Cambridge, MA: Harvard University Press, 1995), pp. 386–400.

Sulloway, F. J. *Freud: Biologist of the mind* (New York: Basic Books, 1979).

Sutton, J. *Philosophy and memory traces: Descartes to connectionism* (Cambridge: Cambridge University Press, 1998).

Taylor, C. *Sources of the self: The making of the modern identity* (Cambridge, MA: Harvard University Press, 1989).

Taylor, J. (ed.), *Selected writings of Hughlings Jackson* (London: Staples, 1931).

Terdiman, R. *Present past: Modernity and the memory crisis* (Ithaca, NY: Cornell University Press, 1993).

Thomas, R. *Literacy and orality in Ancient Greece* (Cambridge: Cambridge University Press, 1992).

Thorndike, E. L. *Educational psychology* (New York: Teachers College, Columbia University Press, 1913), vol. II.

Tomasello, M. *The cultural origins of human cognition* (Cambridge, MA: Harvard University Press, 1999).

Toth, J. P. and Hunt, R. R. 'Not one versus many, but zero versus any: Structure and function in the context of the multiple memory systems debate', in

J. P. Toth and R. R. Hunt, *Memory: System, process, or function?* (New York: Oxford University Press, 1999), pp. 232–72.

Toulmin, S. 'Self-knowledge and knowledge of the "self" ', in T. Mischel (ed.), *The self: Psychological and philosophical issues* (Oxford: Blackwell, 1977), pp. 291–317.

Tulving, E. *Elements of episodic memory* (New York: Oxford University Press, 1983).
    'Episodic and semantic memory', in E. Tulving and W. Donaldson (eds.), *Organization of memory* (New York: Academic Press, 1972), pp. 382–403.
    'Episodic memory: From mind to brain', *Annual Review of Psychology* 53 (2003), 1–25.
    'How many memory systems are there?', *American Psychologist* 40 (1985), 385–98.
    'What kind of a hypothesis is the distinction between episodic and semantic memory?', *Journal of Experimental Psychology: Learning, Memory, and Cognition* 12 (1986), 307–11.

Tulving, E. and Lepage, M. 'Where in the brain is awareness of one's past?', in D. L. Schacter and E. Scarry (eds.), *Memory, brain and belief* (Cambridge, MA: Harvard University Press, 2000), pp. 208–28.

Tulving, E. and Madigan, S. A. 'Memory and verbal learning', *Annual Review of Psychology* 21 (1970), 437–84.

Ueno, N. 'The reification of artifacts in ideological practice', *Mind, Culture, and Activity* 2 (1995), 230–39.

Underwood, B. J. *Studies in learning and memory: Selected papers* (New York: Praeger, 1982).

Uttal, W. R. *The new phrenology: The limits of localizing cognitive processes in the brain* (Cambridge, MA: MIT Press, 2001).
    The psychobiology of mind (New York: Wiley, 1978).

van der Kolk, B. A. 'Trauma and memory', in B. A. van der Kolk, A. C. McFarlane and L. Weisaeth (eds.), *Traumatic stress: The effects of overwhelming experience on mind, body and society* (New York: Guilford Press, 1996), pp. 279–302.

van der Kolk, B. A. and van der Kolk, O. 'Pierre Janet and the breakdown of adaptation in psychological trauma', *American Journal of Psychiatry* 146 (1989), 1530–40.

Vernant, J.-P. 'History and psychology', in F. I. Zeitlin (ed.), *Mortals and immortals: Collected essays* (Princeton, NJ: Princeton University Press, 1991).

von Restorff, H. 'Über die Wirkung von Bereichsbildung im Spurenfeld', *Psychologische Forschung* 18 (1933), 299–342.

Vygotsky, L. and Luria, A. 'Tool and symbol in child development', in R. van der Veer and J. Valsiner (eds.), *The Vygotsky reader* (Oxford: Blackwell, 1994), pp. 99–174.

Walker, D. P. *Music, spirit, and language in the Renaissance* (London: Variorum Reprints, 1985).

Waller, R. (ed.), *The posthumous works of Robert Hooke* (London: Smith & Walford, 1705).

Warnock, M. *Memory* (London: Faber & Faber, 1987).

Watkins, M. J. 'Mediationism and the obfuscation of memory', *American Psychologist* 45 (1990), 328–35.

Waugh, N. C. and Norman, D. A. 'Primary memory', *Psychological Review* 72 (1965), 89–104.

Weldon, M. S. 'The memory chop shop: Issues in the search for memory systems', in J. K. Foster and M. Jelicic (eds.), *Memory: systems, process, or function?* (New York: Oxford University Press, 1999), pp. 162–204.

Wellek, A. *Ganzheitspsychologie und Strukturtheorie* (Bern: Francke, 1955).

Wells, G. L. and Loftus, E. F. (eds.), *Eyewitness testimony: Psychological perspectives* (New York: Cambridge University Press, 1984).

Wernicke, C. *Der aphasische Symptomencomplex: Eine psychologische Studie auf anatomischer Grundlage* (Breslau: Cohn & Weigart, 1874).

Westbury, C. and Dennett, D. C. 'Mining the past to construct the future: Memory and belief as forms of knowledge', in D. L. Schacter and E. Scarry (eds.), *Memory, brain and belief* (Cambridge, MA: Harvard University Press, 2000), pp. 11–32.

Wheeler, M. A., Stuss, D. T. and Tulving, E. 'Toward a theory of episodic memory: The frontal lobes and autonoetic consciousness', *Psychological Bulletin* 121 (1997), 331–54.

Whipple, G. M. 'The observer as reporter: A survey of the "Psychology of testimony"', *Psychological Bulletin* 6 (1909), 153–70.

Wigmore, J. H. 'Professor Münsterberg and the psychology of evidence', *Illinois Law Review* 3 (1909), 399–445.

Willis, J. *The art of memory as it dependeth upon places and ideas* (London: Jones, 1621).

Wilson, R. A. *Boundaries of the mind: The individual in the fragile sciences* (Cambridge: Cambridge University Press, 2004).
  Cartesian psychology and physical minds: Individualism and the sciences of the mind (Cambridge: Cambridge University Press, 1995).

Wolfe, H. K. 'Untersuchungen über das Tongedächtnis', *Philosophische Studien* 3 (1886), 534–71.

Wolff, C. *Psychologia empirica*, in *Gesammelte Werke* (Hildesheim: Olms, 1732/ 1968), vol. V.

Wolfson, H. A. 'The internal senses in Latin, Arabic, and Hebrew philosophic texts', *Harvard Theological Review* 28 (1935), 69–133.

Woodworth, R. S. *Experimental psychology* (New York: Henry Holt, 1938).

Woodworth, R. S. and Schlosberg, H. *Experimental psychology*, rev. edn (New York: Holt, Rinehart & Winston, 1954).

Wulf, F. 'Über die Veränderung von Vorstellungen (Gedächtnis und Gestalt)', *Psychologische Forschung* 1 (1922), 333–73. (Abridged English translation in W. D. Ellis (ed.), *A source book of Gestalt psychology* (London: Routledge & Kegan Paul, 1938), pp. 136–48.)

Wundt, W. *Grundzüge der physiologischen Psychologie* (Leipzig: Engelmann, 1874).
  Outlines of psychology (Leipzig: Engelmann, 1896/1907).
  Völkerpsychologie (Leipzig: Engelmann, 1900), vol. I.

Yapko, M. D. 'Suggestibility and repressed memories of abuse', *American Journal of Clinical Hypnosis* 36 (1994), 163–71.

Yarmey, A. D. *The psychology of eyewitness testimony* (New York: Free Press, 1979).

Yates, F. A. *The art of memory* (Chicago: University of Chicago Press, 1966).

Young, A. *The harmony of illusions: Inventing post-traumatic stress disorder* (Princeton, NJ: Princeton University Press, 1995).

Young, M. N. *Bibliography of memory* (Philadelphia: Chilton, 1961).

Young, R. M. *Mind, brain and adaptation in the nineteenth century: Cerebral localization and its biological context from Gall to Ferrier* (Oxford: Clarendon Press, 1970).

Zacks, R. T. and Hasher, L. 'Memory in life, lab, and clinic: Implications for memory theory', in D. J. Herrmann, H. Weingartner, A. Searleman and C. McEvoy (eds.), *Memory improvement: Implications for memory theory* (New York: Springer-Verlag, 1992), pp. 232–48.

Zawidski, T. and Bechtel, S. W. 'Gall's legacy revisited: Decomposition and localization in cognitive neuroscience', in C. E. Erneling and D. M. Johnson (eds.), *The mind as a scientific object: Between brain and culture* (New York: Oxford University Press, 2005), pp. 293–316.

Zeigarnik, B. 'Über das Behalten von erledigten und unerledigten Handlungen', *Psychologische Forschung* 9 (1927), 1–85.

Zinn, G. A. 'Hugh of St Victor and the art of memory', *Viator* 5 (1974), 211–34.

Zola-Morgan, S. 'Localization of brain function: The legacy of Franz Joseph Gall (1758–1828)', *Annual Review of Neuroscience* 18 (1995), 359–83.

Index

abreaction, 198
adaptation, 3, 4, 5, 257
alphabet, 5, 81, 82, 86
amnesia, 111, 168–71, 173, 231
  childhood, 164
anamnesis, 67, 93, 158–9
animal spirits, 43, 224
aphasia, 111, 112
Aquinas, Thomas, 75, 82, 160
archives, 4, 84
Aristotle, 67–70, 189, 223, 234, 251
  on memory and recollection, 158–9
  on memory defects, 41
  on memory images, 35–6, 41, 50
  on reason and memory, 245–6
  on the common sense, 246–7
art of memory, 17, 59–60, 67
  medieval, 72, 75, 117
  psychoanalysis as, 202–3, 205
  Renaissance, 94–5, 97
artefacts, 7, 32, 37, 48, 84, 270
artificial memory, 66, 70, 75, 80, 107, 127
  origins of concept, 63
assessment, psychological, 171, 235
association
  mental, 46
associationism, 47, 68, 88, 143, 144, 145
attention, 253
Augustinus, Aurelius (St Augustine of Hippo),
  25, 104, 156
autobiographical memory, 104, 192
  and inscription, 212–13
autobiography, 103, 104, 105
  and psychotherapy, 198–9
Avicenna, 160, 247–8

Baddeley, Alan, 178–9
Bartlett, Frederic C., 137–41, 142, 255, 266–7
behaviourism, 9, 143, 167, 172, 177, 230–1, 255
Bergson, Henri, 165–6, 169
Binet, Alfred, 194–5
brain injury, 111, 222, 230, 231
brain localization, 222–38
Breuer, Josef, 198
Broad, Charlie D., 167

Broadbent, Donald, 180
Broca, Paul, 227
Brown, William, 207
Butler, Samuel, 111

Charcot, Jean-Martin, 115
Cicero, Marcus Tullius, 32, 63, 66, 71
Claparède, Edouard, 169
cognition, 31
  modular, 10
  organization of, 69–70, 134, 137
  private, 267–8
  situated, 269–70
collective memory, 20, 29, 209, 264
communication engineering, 180
computer
  and distributed cognition, 271–2
  metaphor, 25, 147, 173, 178
  modelling, 233–4
confession, 100

declarative memory, 173
deferral, 200–1
déjà vu, 112–13
Descartes, René, 43–4, 45, 84, 98–9, 224
diaries, 84, 100, 103, 104, 105
disciplines, 269
  isolation of, 11–12, 16–17, 20, 256, 268–9
discourse analysis, 269
dissociation, 116
distribution, of memory, 270–2
Donald, Merlin, 3, 272
dualism, 44, 46, 99, 136, 165
  see also philosophy, Cartesian

Ebbinghaus, Hermann, 125, 127–9, 131, 135,
  138, 142, 171, 255
Edelman, Gerald, 258–9
embodiment, 148
emotional memory, 161, 203
  in psychoanalysis, 203–4
encoding, 10, 39, 51, 53, 146
episodic memory, 173, 175, 234
equipotentiality, 231
exogram, 272